THE
FOREIGN POLICIES
OF EAST EUROPE

THE FOREIGN POLICIES OF EAST EUROPE

New Approaches

Edited by
Ronald H. Linden

PRAEGER SPECIAL STUDIES • PRAEGER SCIENTIFIC

Library of Congress Cataloging in Publication Data
Main entry under title:

The Foreign policies of East Europe.

   Includes bibliographical references.
   1. Europe, Eastern--Foreign relations. I. Linden,
Ronald Haly.
DJK44.F67   327'.09171'7   80-21064
ISBN 0-03-056136-1

Published in 1980 by Praeger Publishers
CBS Educational and Professional Publishing
A Division of CBS, Inc.
521 Fifth Avenue, New York, New York 10017 U.S.A.

0123456789 145 987654321

Printed in the United States of America

To Carl Beck

Dedicated to his memory
Inspired by his vision

PREFACE

International relations in 1980 look nothing like they did in 1950. Three times as many independent states, nearly three times as many nuclear powers, unprecedented recognition of the entire web of interdependencies that link governments and people across national boundaries and, occasionally, against their will, and a clear decline in the ability of once dominant superpowers to have their way casually with other states. In one region alone do things seem at first glance to be virtually as they were 30 years ago: East Europe. Yet, the fact is, of course, that politics and policy in East Europe are not the same, even though both formal and informal structures which act as formidable obstacles to change remain in place.

The states of East Europe enter the 1980s facing as different a milieu—domestic and international—as do most other states. But like other small states, the East European states have known for a long time what the major powers are only now coming to understand: that seeming absolutes, such as independence, sovereignty, and autonomy, are in fact relative, and a state's ability to choose a path or policy in domestic or international affairs, though formally residing in its sovereign government, in reality tends to be limited—even severely so—by forces external to that government and even to the country itself. All states formulate and execute their policies within parameters, the breadth and volatility of which they do not necessarily set themselves. For small, less powerful states that exist alongside large but nervous superpowers, these parameters can be quite narrow indeed. For students of East Europe, then, the fascinating phenomenon to observe has been and remains these states' attempts to deal with the needs and shifting demands of the domestic and international environment while not transgressing narrow but imprecisely known and externally determined parameters. The transgression of these parameters in domestic governance and the Draconian response it produced are well known and have been exhaustively studied. Less fully examined are these states' attempts to deal with their international environments, with all the dangers, opportunities, turbulence, and interdependencies therein, and their often asymptotic approaches to similar parameters. It is toward exploration in this area that the present volume is directed.

The idea of putting together a collection of this sort occurred to me when I was preparing a panel on comparative foreign policy and East Europe for the 1979 meeting of the International Studies

Association in Toronto. I was convinced that there were a number of people "out there" who were interested not only in studying the foreign policies of the East European states but in trying to do so in ways that were somewhat different, perhaps untried, broader in spatial setting or comparative basis; people who seemed interested in asking questions like, Of what more general phenomenon is this an instance? and, conversely, What can we learn about that general phenomenon from this instance?

Thus were my contributors searched out, suggested, solicited, entreated, and inveigled into participating in this effort. I owe my first thanks, then, to them, for their ideas, their enthusiasm for the project, their admirable patience, and their willingness to risk their reputations on such a venture. To a person, they responded quickly and conscientiously to my suggestions and concealed their true feelings toward a meddlesome editor.

I owe my thanks also to the Russian and East European Studies Program of the University of Pittsburgh whose grant made possible the purchase of the reprint rights for Bill Zimmerman's article from Slavic Review. I am indebted, of course, to the American Association for the Advancement of Slavic Studies for permission to reprint that article. I extend my sincere appreciation to Bob Donnorummo and Rose Krasnopoler of the Russian and East European Studies Program for their unselfish correspondence and assistance in handling my scribbled editorial reports to the contributors. A task equally burdensome, the typing of the Introduction, was discharged equally well by Kendall Stanley. My thanks go also to Betsy Brown, Associate Editor of Praeger Publishers, for her early support for the volume and her enduring patience in the course of its completion.

I'm sure I voice a feeling shared by all the contributors when I express my gratitude to those close to me for their understanding during this period. Any doubts I had that my family did not fully comprehend the nature of this profession were dispelled by my son Ethan (age three) who, when asked what Daddy does for a living, responded, "He types."

I hope, too, that another sentiment shared by the contributors, and by the profession as a whole, is adequately conveyed in the book's dedication, no less than its substance.

CONTENTS

THE
FOREIGN POLICIES
OF EAST EUROPE

1

INTRODUCTION: FOREIGN POLICY STUDIES AND EAST EUROPE

Ronald H. Linden

In a recent review of several volumes devoted to East Europe, Voytech Mastny called foreign policy "potentially the most consequential of the neglected topics of inquiry."[1] Indeed, Roger Kanet's statement in the conclusion to this volume, that "Western scholarship has not always kept pace with developments either within East Europe itself or in the relations of the states of the region with the outside world" is probably a generous understatement, as Kanet's own review articles in the field have demonstrated.[2] The "why's" of this neglect will be familiar to anyone who has labored in this particular vineyard for any length of time. Evidently convinced that the East European states' foreign policies were products of puppet strings held in Moscow and that therefore the foreign policy to be studied was that of the Soviet Union, students of East European politics have focused their attention predominantly on intra-polity developments. This seemed all the more appropriate since postwar experience in the region suggested that the Soviet Union, the most salient and threatening state from the standpoint of the United States, perceived the greatest danger to its own security and international position as emanating from domestic instability in East Europe and the possible alteration or dismantling of the regimes installed there. Thus, the substantial obstacles to exhaustive inquiry into closed communist systems plus the necessity of mastering new languages, cultures, and histories as part of the inquiry made attractive those areas where significant payoffs seemed most probable.

In addition, of course, the region remained caught in an image which assumed, if not total bloc unity, at most minimal and inconsequential foreign policy differences. When the public explosion of the Sino-Soviet dispute and its spillover into East Europe combined

1

with other equally public differences, such as those between Bucharest and Moscow, to destroy this image and put in its place a notion of communist polycentrism,[3] foreign policy nevertheless remained relegated to a residual category of analysis. Not even the "comparative communism" revolution, which brought with it calls for a new approach to the subject as well as a good deal of comparative empirical work, could stimulate much study of these states' foreign policies.[4]

It was nearly a decade after the emergence of the Sino-Soviet break before recognition of the greater diversity of the East European states stimulated investigations into their foreign policies that sought to bring to bear the concepts, methods or approaches of international relations or comparative foreign policy. This impact can be measured in the growth of the number of studies devoted to mapping the diversity in foreign policy actions and attitudes in the region.[5] But, as Roger Kanet has noted, much less attention has been given to examining the causes behind these differences.[6] This is true because, with the limited exception of Yugoslavia, the causes of these states' foreign policies in general have gone largely unexamined, either on an individual or region-wide, comparative, basis. Thus both differences from and adherence to Soviet foreign policy have been left to conventional wisdom or seemingly "obvious" factors, such as geography, to explain. Only the most public case of foreign policy divergence, that of Romania, has received any significant treatment.[7] In short, if one were looking for comprehensive, analytic treatments of the postwar foreign policies of virtually any of the East European states, one would be searching in vain.

Comparative work touching on all or even some of these states is similarly in short supply. There are volumes that scan these states' responses to a particular issue, for example, the Conference on Security and Cooperation in Europe (CSCE),[8] or their relations within the region's international institutions, for example, the Council for Mutual Economic Assistance (CMEA).[9] In addition, a number of works describe how the region has been treated as a foreign policy target of other states. Here, too, the work is skewed, with most focusing on Soviet-East European relations[10] and surprisingly little on U.S.-East European relations, especially for the recent past.[11] Somewhat more work has been done on West European relations—especially economic relations—with the region,[12] including, not surprisingly, a "bubble" in the chart for work on West German Ostpolitik.[13]

Finally, and most significantly for the authors of the pieces in this volume, the smallest cell is that which embraces those works which are conceptually guided or based. If work in this region is ever to move beyond, and at the same time make proper use of, the body of descriptive, narrative, and rather incomplete literature that exists at present, it would seem imperative that we bring both to the field and from it some gains relevant to the broader study of international relations and foreign policy. Heretofore, the study and understanding of the international relations of the East European states has been cast within one of three descriptive frameworks. First, it has been conceived of in terms of the region's relationship to the Soviet Union, that is, its role in Soviet foreign policy, especially the ideological penumbra thrown over these relations by the Communist Party of the Soviet Union.[14] Second, there has been the institutional focus, which hems inquiry in to the regional institutional arrangements sponsored and dominated by Moscow. The result of this, as Cal Clark says, has been to miss "where the action is" in comprehending the region's integration.[15] Finally, there has been the international milieu approach, which asks how contemporary situations, for example, detente, affect the region.[16] Though no one would deny the value of placing these states' international relations in such frames or fields of descriptive reference, there is certainly much to be gained from and given to the broader study of international relations and foreign policy by placing our work on these states into potentially more generalizable frameworks. There have been a few attempts to do so. Modelski's suggestion of a form of "communist international system" and Zimmerman's postulation of a "hierarchical regional state system" were designed to both explore and suggest propositions relating to interstate relations more generally.[17]

The benefits of approaching the study of these states with such an orientation are several. First, such work can bring to bear the conceptual refinements, analytic rigor, and substantive findings that have been produced in these broader fields. At the same time, rigorous, conceptually guided, empirical work in East Europe can make a real contribution to the study of international relations and foreign policies outside the region. The international relations of the East European states are conducted under certain circumstances which are relatively clear but by no means unique.[18] The states themselves are of a certain similar size, development, and political system. Because of their similarities, the states of East Europe are particularly useful for the development and testing of more generalizable ideas about foreign policy. Some factors, in the words of experimental science, would automatically be held "constant."[19] Yet their differences in both domestic and international politics are significant enough and appear with sufficient regularity to make investigation challenging, fruitful, and, not least, suggestive of further inquiry. In undertaking this inquiry, might there not be something to be gained from sifting through the results of broader foreign policy studies to consider their possible relevance for East Europe? Even more likely, might not one of the various analytic frameworks or conceptual schemes be adopted and adapted for the study of this region? The expectation here is that not only would these act as a guide to inquiry but they would be improved by any modification derived from work in this region.[20]

Nor is selecting such guides or tools from the existing general literature as formidable an undertaking as it might seem. Much of it would be inappropriate for use in East Europe for one reason or another. Much, for example, has focused on states with fundamentally different characteristics, thus failing on grounds of prima facie isomorphism. McGowan and Kean, for example, suggest that, "although most theorizing in international relations and in the comparative study of foreign policy purports to be general, and therefore applicable to all states, it is implicitly modeled on the behavior of 'great' powers."[21] This has, in addition, rendered much of the empirical work less transferable to states that do not fall into this category.[22] The states of East Europe would certainly fall into the non-superpower category, as would virtually every other state by definition. Thus, results from a study of East Europe would seem to have a wide impact potentially, especially in areas like great power-small power relations.

A good deal of international relations research has produced results which are inconclusive, insufficiently suggestive, or mindlessly inductive. But John Vasquez' depressing conclusion that almost 93 percent of all "correlational-explanatory" research conducted before 1970 produced weak or statistically insignificant results should serve not to prevent a mining of this field for us in East Europe but to push us toward results that do seem suggestive.[23] For example, Vasquez suggests that of the independent variables used in international relations research, strategies "focusing solely on subnational actors are the most successful in predicting behavior and the least employed."[24] Such a focus would seem particularly relevant in understanding the foreign policies of the East European states, especially given the rather constricted international parameters within which they operate. Furthermore, it seems likely that research on East Europe could make a contribution toward filling gaps in dependent variables studied. Vasquez notes, for example, that "not much research effort has been concentrated on trying to explain the political characteristics of the international system."[25] Examining international alliance patterns in East Europe, especially as they reflect or affect the global system, can certainly offer useful evidence bearing on questions like this.[26] In addition, some of the globally aggregated results—or nonresults—do yield certain positive, that is, non-null, findings for certain subsets or types of nations. Thus, for example, Wilkenfeld found a relation between some types of domestic conflict and foreign conflict behavior for nations with a "centrist" governmental structure, though the globally aggregated findings of both Rummel and Tanter had suggested a nonexistent or at best quite weak relationship.[27]

Certain approaches drawn from comparative foreign policy or international relations would seem implausible in some configurations but more likely to yield useful insights in other forms. For example, the "societal" approach to foreign policy, that is, looking for factors explaining foreign policy within a state's societal structure, or its public opinion, would likely be of little value in East Europe if one were searching for evidence that these states are sensitive to public views or preferences in foreign relations. Indeed, searching for such preferences or public views would likely be futile. Even in the Western liberal democracies results establishing a relation between public opinion and foreign policy have been scant and weak.[28] But the impact of other societal factors, such as level and scope of modernization or role and position of ethnic groups, might well be significant, and research in this area has yet to begin.[29]

Some approaches that seem promising—even greatly so—might have to wait until greater data availability and system openness makes their use possible. For example, the bureaucratic politics approach widely utilized in studying U.S. foreign policy,[30] though not without its critics,[31] has proven more difficult to exploit in studying the Soviet Union.[32]

However, even to have recognized all of these obstacles and problems of nonproductivity or non-isomorphism is still to leave much of the work in international relations, both theoretical and empirical, available and usable for work in East Europe. For example, systems theory has stimulated little empirical investigation compared, say, to an approach based on nation-state attributes. It is cast at the global level of analysis, whereas our desired focus is regional; and, in virtually all its formulations, the systems approach brings with it a host of theoretical and empirical problems.[33] Still, the systems approach does provoke at least one fascinating question which, when adapted for investigation in East Europe, poses a significant research problem: What is the regional (or subsystem) effect of a decided shift in the global system, say from bipolarity to multipolarity? Further, what impact does the direction, speed, and scope of this shift have on the nations making up the system? Does the regional subsystem mute or reinforce such an impact? What kind of global system is more advantageous for weaker states in the subsystem? That such an approach can be the catalyst for interesting questions and answers has already been demonstrated by William

Zimmerman's examination of the effect of an existing bipolar system with low expectations of violence on a regional hierarchical (sub)system.[34] Given the present disintegration or transformation of that system, questions such as those posed above might be addressed usefully and profitably, with the results benefiting both East European studies and general international relations theory.

It is unlikely, of course, that any one approach borrowed from the comparative study of foreign policy or international relations would fit perfectly into the field of East European studies. What is more likely is that certain broader concepts or frameworks would shed light on the shadowy and understudied field of East European foreign policies and, in return, improve our understanding of the overall phenomenon of interestate relations.

To what kinds of questions might such approaches be addressed? If we want to move beyond situational description, in what direction might we travel? The need for studies—especially comparative studies—of causation has already been noted. Of the particular questions waiting to be addressed, probably the most provocative—and most studied in relation to domestic politics—is the relation of these states' policies to the phenomenon they are most rhetorically committed to yet fundamentally terrified of: change. Actually, to be more precise, it is not change itself that is the bogyman for these governments; it is uncontrolled change. Like all entrenched governing bodies, they are fearful and suspicious of changes whose direction, power, and, most importantly, end result they can neither control nor predict. Having the power to govern but seeking the authority to do so, they are cautioned by both ideology and realpolitik to be on guard constantly against uncontrolled, unguided, undirected change. In domestic politics, none, with the complex exception of Yugoslavia, have significantly yielded their domestic position dominating the intellectual, cultural, economic, and especially political aspects of their nation's existence, though most do bear only a pale resemblance to Western models of "totalitarian" systems.[35]

Western scholarship, searching for an alternative to that discredited model, has proceeded in two directions, one utilizing an "interest group" approach, another investigating the sources and effects of change on communist systems. The former wilted rather quickly—probably prematurely—in its study of domestic politics, though some effort was made to apply it to the foreign policy of the Soviet Union.[36] The focus on change, conceived of variously as modernization or development, flourished, as the proliferation of volumes on this subject attests.[37] Yet, as with other work in the area, this attention has focused largely on domestic aspects, despite the obvious fact that these states' international environment—and their relationship to it—was also changing.

Nor can we expect to comprehend this relationship to external, "ecological" change simply by extrapolating from the states' domestic experience. To begin with, the nature and number of interactive factors involved is different, and includes inter alia the reactions of other states, international economic and ideological aspects, leadership perceptions, and transnational effects. Second, the degree of exposure to such changes varies from state to state, as does their attitude toward international change. A perusal of Bill Potter's chapter on East European reactions to Ostpolitik will verify this.[38] Third, their degree of external dependence varies by levels, degrees, and types, as described, for example, in Clark and Bahry's essay. Thus, their freedom to react to change presumably is enhanced or restricted variously. Finally, there is of course the fundamental difference, which all governments face, between domestic and foreign policies: so much of what goes on outside their boundaries is beyond their control, though it affects them nonetheless.[39] Compared to the relatively more malleable domestic milieu of the East European states, problematic enough, in the world beyond the river's edge the unknowns are greater, the insecurities more heightened, and for us who study them, the range of responses less well understood.

Thus we should be asking ourselves, for example, how have and how will these states react to their changing international environment? How do such changes affect them, and to what degree can they manipulate such changes to their advantage?[40] What factors explain their particular reactions? If, of course, we simply consider it axiomatic that they will react as mimics of the Soviet Union, or that they will all react alike, we need not address such questions. If, on the other hand, we cannot accept such fiats, we must take care to build change into our investigations of these states' foreign relations, as, for example, Clark, Korbonski, and Bahry and Clark do herein, and, conversely, to ensure that foreign policy is one of those phenomena examined when we investigate change (or modernization, or development) in East Europe.

Among those phenomena currently undergoing rapid change and receiving extraordinary attention in the study of other states is international interdependence. Although there is some debate among students of the subject as to whether or not worldwide interdependence is presently more or less intense and extensive than previously,[41] for East Europe there can be little doubt of its substantial interdependence with the external world and especially of the increase in its ties with the noncommunist world, developed and developing, in the last 20 years. The challenging question for us is how have and how will these states react to such interdependence and its consequences? And why? What mixture of economic, political, cultural, ideological and individual factors will produce the particular reaction each state demonstrates in the face of ties that bind as well as benefit? As interdependencies grow and fluctuate with noncommunist states, it will certainly not be enough to generalize from the region's earlier and continuing experience with Soviet dominance and dependence. It is quite unlikely that these new interdependencies will duplicate that relationship. Nor for that matter has that relationship remained static in either form, function, or effect, as Andrzej Korbonski's chapter illustrates.

Instead of using the automatic assumption of a mimicked past and overdetermined future, our assumption as to the future of such interdependencies will need a sounder empirical and theoretical base. The essays in this volume by Bahry and Clark and Sarah Terry are tentative steps (as the authors themselves see them) in that direction.

Of course, some may argue that while the relations of the East European states with those of the West or the Third World are examples of interdependence, their relationship with the Soviet Union is, as it ever was, one of profound dependence. That this is true, of course, can hardly be argued and has been empirically demonstrated by Paul Marer[42] and by Bill Zimmerman in this volume, among others. However, as both Marer and Korbonski (herein) demonstrate, this relationship is multifaceted and includes significant losses as well as gains to the dominating side (the Soviet Union). Thus we could still include it under the rubric of interdependence, conceiving of dependence as simply an assymetrical form of inter- (or mutual) dependence. [43] Alternatively, following most dependencia theorists, we could view it as a fundamentally different phenomenon, characterized by a fixed structural relationship between states and producing, in the dependent ones, internal economic, political, and social "distortions." [44] As Bahry and Clark (following Richardson) point out, the presence of some proven costs to the dominant state in this case would not remove it from consideration as a case of dominant-dependent relations. [45] As these authors (along with Zimmerman) see it, there exists no a priori reason why these states' relations with the Soviet Union cannot be case in the framework of (ahem) dependentsia. Doing so not only suggests new dimensions and dynamics for study in the empirical field but also offers improvements in the notion itself as an analytic concept. Moreover, what empirical work has been done on such relationships suggests the need for further refinement and qualification of the concept and further investigations of other regions and even subregions. [46] Combining the two ideas, of course, would suggest a picture of states' relations which are dependent with respect to some state(s) and interdependent with respect to others. The theoretical and empirical possibilities suggested either by this or by keeping the two notions separate remain to be explored.

Even were the relationship to and increasing importance of change and interdependence not a key question, even were we to posit a world of unyielding isolation and sameness in which to observe our "subjects," we would still want to know why they did what they did. There would still remain a host of unexplored pathways toward a more complete understanding of the causes and courses of these states' foreign policies. Despite all the attention to domestic aspects of politics and change, there remains open a broad area for investigation into what Rosenau called "linkages" between domestic and international politics.[47] This is true for both the international — national direction[48] and especially the national — international direction. Could not attention be profitably directed, for example, toward discovering the significance and impact on foreign relations of intragovernmental bargaining and interest groups, societal subgroups, economic factors such as level of development, decision making, individual personality factors, and perceptions? Who supports what kind of foreign policies in Poland and why? What influence do "attentive publics" have on Romania's external relations? Does it matter what the "cognitive map" of a Party leader (say, Ulbricht compared to Honeker) is?

Exploring this kind of question in depth could, of course, consume a whole book itself; but many of the essays in this volume do begin addressing such questions. Cal Clark examines linkages across countries, Richard Herrmann, the range of groups in one country, and Sarah Terry, the entire "loop" of impact, response, and feedback in key areas of Poland's international economic relations. All of the authors in the volume recognize the preliminary nature of their inquiries and see their work as suggestive of future directions for themselves or others. But, most importantly, all have been willing to push back the bounds of their inquiries just a little, to set these states in a broader empirical and/or conceptual setting in an attempt to learn more about both the foreign relations of these states and useful ways of studying those relations.

NOTES

1. Vojtech Mastny, "East European Studies at a Crossroads," Problems of Communism 28, no. 3 (May–June 1979): 63.

2. See Roger Kanet, "Other Needs, Other Areas, New Directions," Chapter 10; and idem, "Integration Theory and the Study of Eastern Europe," International Studies Quarterly 18, no. 18 (September 1974): 368–92.

3. See, for example, "Foreign Policy in a Polycentric World," Survey 58 (January 1966), special issue.

4. The examples of such work that did appear during this period are Jan F. Triska, ed., Communist Party States (New York: Bobbs-Merrill, 1969); and P. Terrence Hopmann, "International Conflict and Cohesion in the Communist System," International Studies Quarterly 11, no. 3 (September 1967): 212-36.

5. See Barry Hughes and Thomas Volgy, "Distance in Foreign Policy Behavior: A Comparative Study of Eastern Europe," Midwest Journal of Political Science 16, no. 3 (August 1970): 459-92; William R. Kintner and Wolfgang Klaiber, Eastern Europe and European Security (New York: Dunellen, 1971), chap. 13; Vilho Harle, "Actional Distance Between the Socialist Countries in the 1960s," Cooperation and Conflict 14, no. 3-4 (1971): 201-22; Harvey J. Tucker, "Measuring Cohesion in the International Communist Movement," Political Methodology 2, no. 1 (1975): 83-112; Ronald H. Linden, Bear and Foxes: The International Relations of the East European States, 1965-1969 (Boulder, Colo.: East European Quarterly, distributed by Columbia University Press, 1979).

6. Roger E. Kanet, "Is Comparison Useful or Possible?" Studies in Comparative Communism 8, nos. 1-2 (Spring-Summer 1973): 20-27.

7. See, for example, David Floyd, Rumania: Russia's Dissident Ally (New York: Praeger, 1965); and Aurel Braun, Romanian Foreign Policy Since 1965 (New York: Praeger, 1978).

8. Robert R. King and Robert Dean, East European Perspectives on European Security and Cooperation (New York: Praeger, 1974); Wolfgang Klaiber et al., Era of Negotiations (New York: Praeger, 1973).

9. Henry Schaefer, COMECON and the Politics of Integration (New York: Praeger, 1972); Paul Marer, "Prospects for Integration in the Council for Mutual Economic Assistance (CMEA)," International Organization 30, no. 4 (Autumn 1976): 631-48; Lawrence T. Caldwell, "The Warsaw Pact: Directions of Change," Problems of Communism 24 (September-October 1975): 1-19; Walter C. Clemens, Jr., "The European Alliance Systems: Exploitation or Mutual Aid?" in The International Politics of Eastern Europe, ed. Charles Gati (New York: Praeger, 1976), pp. 217-38.

10. See, for example, Ghita Ionescu, The Break-up of the Soviet Empire in Eastern Europe (Baltimore: Penguin, 1965); Nish Jamgotch, Jr., Soviet-East European Dialogue (Stanford: Hoover Institution Press, 1968); Roger Kanet and Donna Bahry, "Soviet Policy in East Europe," Current History 69, no. 409 (October 1975): 126-28, 54; Gati, op. cit., chaps. 2-4; Christopher D. Jones, "Soviet Hegemony in Eastern Europe," World Politics 29, no. 2 (January

1977): 216-41; Richard F. Staar, "Soviet Relations with East Europe," Current History 74, no. 436 (April 1978): 145-49, 184-85; J. F. Brown, "Soviet Relations with Eastern Europe" (Paper presented at the annual meeting of the American Political Science Association, Washington, D.C., August-September 1979).

11. Of the few pieces not focusing on the origins of the Cold War, see Bennet Kovrig, "The United States: 'Peaceful Engagement' Revisited," in Gati, op. cit., pp. 131-53; Robert F. Byrnes, "United States Policy Towards Eastern Europe: Before and After Helsinki," Review of Politics 37, no. 4 (October 1975): 435-63; Charles Gati, "The Forgotten Region," Foreign Policy 19 (1975): 135-45; Roy E. Licklider, "Soviet Control of Eastern Europe: Morality versus American National Interest," Political Science Quarterly 91, no. 4 (Winter 1976-77): 619-24; Stephen S. Kaplan, "United States Aid to Poland 1957-64: Concerns, Objectives and Obstacles," Western Political Quarterly 28, no. 1 (March 1975): 147-66.

12. See, for example, Louis J. Mnsonides and James A. Kuhlman, eds., The Future of Inter-Bloc Relations in Europe (New York: Praeger, 1975), esp. pts. 1 and 2; and "The Future of East-West Relations," Survey 22, nos. 3-4 (Summer-Autumn 1976), whole issue; Roger E. Kanet, "East-West Trade and the Limits of Western Influence," in Gati, op. cit., pp. 192-213; Charles Ransom, The European Community and Eastern Europe (Totowa, N.J.: Rowman and Littlefield, 1973); Avi Shlaim and G. N. Yannopoulos, The EEC and Eastern Europe (Cambridge: Cambridge University Press, 1978); Joint Economic Committee, Reorientation and Commercial Relations of the Economics of Eastern Europe (Washington, D.C.: Government Printing Office, 1974); and idem, East European Economies Post-Helsinki (Washington, D.C.: Government Printing Office, 1977), pt. 3; Richard Portes, "East Europe's Debt to the West: Interdependence Is a Two-Way Street," Foreign Affairs 55, no. 4 (July 1977): 751-82.

13. See, inter alia, Andrew Gyorgy, "Ostpolitik and Western Europe," in Gati, op. cit., pp. 154-72; Lawrence Whetten, Germany's Ostpolitik: Relations Between the Federal Republic and the Warsaw Pact Countries (London: Oxford University Press, 1971); William Griffith, The Ostpolitik and the FRG (Cambridge, Mass.: MIT Press, 1978). In addition see William Potter's notes in Chapter 4.

14. See Nish Jamgotch, Jr., "Alliance Management in Eastern Europe (The New Type of International Relations)," World Politics 27, no. 3 (April 1975): 405-29; Teresa Rakowska-Harmstone, " 'Socialist Internationalism' and Eastern Europe—A New Stage," Survey 22, no. 1 (Winter 1976): 38-54, and 2 (Spring 1976): 81-86;

R. Judson Mitchell, "A New Brezhnew Doctrine: The Restructuring of International Relations," World Politics 30, no. 3 (April 1978): 366-90.

15. Cal Clark, "The Study of East European Integration: A 'Political' Perspective," East Central Europe 2, no. 2 (1975):133-51.

16. See Andrzej Korbonski, "Detente, East-West Trade, and the Future of Economic Integration in Eastern Europe," World Politics 28, no. 4 (July 1976): 568-89; George Klein, "Detente and Czechoslovakia," and Richard C. Gripp, "Hungary's Role in Detente," both in From the Cold War to Detente, ed. Peter J. Potichnyj and Jane Shapiro (New York: Praeger, 1976). Other examples of this genre would be Jacques Levesque, Le Conflit sino-sovietique et l'Europe de l'est (Montreal: Les Presses de l'Université de Montreal, 1970); and a number of articles on the energy squeeze and Eastern Europe, for example, Christopher Joyner, "The Energy Situation in Eastern Europe: Problems and Prospects," East European Quarterly 10, no. 4 (Winter 1976): 495-516; John M. Kramer, "Between Scylla and Charybdis: The Politics of Eastern Europe's Energy Problem," Orbis 22, no. 4 (Winter 1979): 929-50; and William Zimmerman, "The Energy Crisis, Western 'Stagflation' and the Evolution of Soviet-East European Relations" (Paper presented at the Conference on the Impact of International Economic Disturbances on the Soviet Union and Eastern Europe, Kennan Institute for Advanced Russian Studies, Washington, D.C., September 24-26, 1978).

17. George Modelski, The Communist International System (Princeton, N.J.: Center for International Studies, 1960); William Zimmerman, "Hierarchical Regional Systems and the Politics of System Boundaries," International Organization 26, no. 1 (Winter 1972): 18-36. For a discussion and testing of some of Modelski's propositions, see Linden, op. cit., pp. 204-10; on Zimmerman, see below, Chapter 6.

18. As evidence, witness the various considerations of these states as exemplifying particular instances of larger phenomena, such as imperialism or dependency. See, for example, Paul Marer, "The Political Economy of Soviet Relations with Eastern Europe," in Testing Theories of Economic Imperialism, ed. James Kurth and Steven Rosen (Lexington, Mass.: D. C. Heath, 1974), pp. 231-60; and William Zimmerman's essay in this volume.

19. James N. Rosenau, "Comparison as a State of Mind," Studies in Comparative Communism 8, nos. 1-2 (Spring-Summer 1975): 57-61.

20. For examples, see the chapter by Terry in this volume, and Linden, op. cit., pp. 210-14.

21. James G. Kean and Patrick J. McGowan, "National Attributes and Foreign Policy Participation: A Path Analysis," in SAGE International Yearbook of Foreign Policy Studies, ed. Patrick J. McGowan, vol. 1 (Beverly Hills, Calif.: Sage, 1973), p. 246.

22. Indeed, Kean and McGowan, ibid., found that size and modernization were powerful, if indirect, factors explaining the variance in foreign policy participation across 114 states. But, as the authors themselves recognize, their results were much weaker for small states (57 of the 114) and less modern states (also 57). For similar conclusions about the necessity of disaggregating global results according to nation genotype, see James E. Harf, David G. Hoovler, and Thomas E. James, Jr., "Systemic and External Attributes in Foreign Policy Analysis"; David W. Moore, "National Attributes and National Typologies: A Look at the Rosenau Genotypes"; and Maurice A. East and Charles F. Hermann, "Do Nation-Types Account for Foreign Policy Behavior?" all in Comparing Foreign Policies, ed. James N. Rosenau (Beverly Hills, Calif.: Sage, 1974), pp. 235-304.

23. John A. Vasquez, "Statistical Findings in International Politics," International Studies Quarterly 20, no. 2 (June 1976): 171-218.

24. Ibid., p. 191.

25. Ibid., p. 193.

26. See Modelski, op. cit.; Hoppmann, op. cit.; and William Zimmerman, "The Transformation of the Modern Multistate System: The Exhaustion of Communist Alternatives," Journal of Conflict Resolution 16, no. 3 (September 1972): 303-17.

27. Rummel's findings, which have been reported and reprinted widely, are from "Dimensions of Conflict Behavior Within and Between Nations," General Systems Yearbook 8 (1963): 1-50; "The Relationship Between National Attributes and Foreign Conflict Behavior," in Quantitative International Politics, ed. J. D. Singer (New York: Free Press, 1968), pp. 187-214; and "Some Attributes and Behavioral Patterns of Nations," Journal of Peace Research 4 (1967): 196-206. Tanter's can be found in "Dimensions of Conflict Behavior Within and Between Nations," Journal of Conflict Resolution 10 (1966): 41-64. For Wilkenfeld's results, see Journal of Peace Research 1 (1968): 56-59. For a critical view of these studies, see Andrew Mack, "Numbers Are Not Enough," Comparative Politics 7, no. 4 (July 1975): 597-618. Of the globally aggregated studies, Mack states, "There is absolutely no reason to assume that the relationships that have been investigated should apply to the total sample of nations, and very good reasons why they should not" (p. 610).

28. See the discussion in Richard L. Merritt, "Public Opinion and Foreign Policy in West Germany," and Martin Abravanel and Barry Hughes, "The Relationship Between Public Opinion and Governmental Foreign Policy: A Cross-National Study," both in McGowan, op. cit., pp. 255-75 and 107-35, respectively.

29. For a preliminary discussion, see Bogdan Denitch, "The Domestic Roots of Foreign Policy in Eastern Europe," in Gati, op. cit., pp. 239-52.

30. The most complete statement of this approach is found in Graham Allison, Essence of Decision (Boston: Little, Brown, 1971).

31. See Stephen Krasner, "Are Bureaucracies Important?" Foreign Policy 7 (Summer 1972): 159-79; Robert J. Art, Bureaucratic Politics and American Foreign Policy: A Critique," Policy Science 4, no. 4 (December 1973): 467-90; Amos Perlmutter, "The Presidential Center and Foreign Policy: A Critique of the Revisionist and Bureaucratic Political Orientations," World Politics 28, no. 1 (October 1974): 87-106.

32. For an attempt to apply the model to Soviet foreign policy decision making, see Jiri Valenta, Soviet Intervention in Czechoslovakia 1968 (Baltimore, Md.: Johns Hopkins University Press, 1979). For an earlier critique of Valenta see Dimitri Simes, "The Soviet Invasion of Czechoslovakia and the Limits of Kremlinology," Studies in Comparative Communism 8, nos. 1-2 (Spring-Summer 1975): 174-80.

33. Many of these are discussed in Kenneth Waltz, Theory of International Politics (Reading, Mass.: Addison-Wesley, 1979), pp. 38-193.

34. Zimmerman, "Hierarchical Regional Systems."

35. For a comparative assessment of these states' level of "subsystem autonomy," see Jan F. Triska and Paul M. Johnson, Political Development and Political Change in Eastern Europe (Denver: University of Denver, 1975).

36. See Valenta, op. cit. For a less formal but highly effective discussion of such groups and their effect on foreign policy, see Carl A. Linden, Khrushchev and the Soviet Leadership, 1957-64 (Baltimore, Md.: Johns Hopkins University Press, 1966). The fullest explication for recent times is Walter C. Clemens, Jr., The USSR and Global Interdependence (Washington, D.C.: American Enterprise Institute, 1978). The seminal volume on the use of the interest group approach to the Soviet Union is H. Gordon Skilling and Franklyn Griffiths, eds., Interest Groups in Soviet Politics Princeton, N.J.: Princeton University Press, 1971). For a critical view of this approach, see William E. Odom, "A Dissenting View on the Group Approach to Soviet Politics," World Politics 28, no. 4 (July 1976): 542-67.

37. See, for example, Chalmers Johnson, ed., Change in Communist Systems (Stanford, Calif.: Stanford University Press, 1970); Charles F. Gati, ed., The Politics of Modernization in Eastern Europe (New York: Praeger, 1974); Jane P. Shapiro and Peter J. Potichnyj, eds., Change and Adaptation in Soviet and East European Politics (New York: Praeger, 1976); Jan F. Triska and Paul M. Cocks, eds., Political Development in Eastern Europe (New York: Praeger, 1977); Teresa Rakowska-Harmstone, ed., Perspectives for Change in Communist Societies (Boulder, Colo.: Westview, 1979).

38. See Chapter 4. See also William C. Potter, "Innovation in East European Foreign Policies," in The Foreign Policies of Eastern Europe: Domestic and International Determinants, ed. James A. Khulman (Leyden: A. W. Sijthoff, 1978), pp. 253-302.

39. See James N. Rosenau, "Foreign Policy as an Issue-Area," in Domestic Sources of Foreign Policy, ed. James N. Rosenau (New York: Free Press, 1967), pp. 11-50.

40. Conceptual frameworks for studying such questions are suggested by James N. Rosenau, "Foreign Policy as Adaptive Behavior," Comparative Politics 2, no. 3 (April 1970): 365-88; and Wolfram F. Hanrieder, "Compatibility and Consensus: A Proposal for the Conceptual Linkage of External and Internal Dimensions of Foreign Policy," in Comparative Foreign Policy, ed. Wolfram F. Hanrieder (New York: David McKay, 1971), pp. 242-64. Of particular interest for the study of East Europe is the modification of Rosenau's work for the situation of small states offered by Patrick J. McGowan and Klaus-Peter Gottwald, "Small State Foreign Policies," International Studies Quarterly 19, no. 4 (December 1975): 469-500.

41. See Kenneth Waltz, "The Myth of National Interdependence," in The International Corporation, ed. Charles Kindleberger (Cambridge, Mass.: MIT Press, 1970), pp. 205-23; Edward Morse, "Transnational Economic Processes," in Transnational Relations and World Politics, ed. Robert O. Keohane and Joseph S. Nye (Cambridge: Harvard University Press, 1972), pp. 23-47; Peter Katzenstein, "International interdependence: Some long-term trends and recent changes," International Organization 29, no. 4 (Autumn 1975): 1021-34; Richard Rosecrance et al., "Whither Interdependence?" International Organization 31, no. 3 (Summer 1977): 425-72. Waltz rejoins the argument in Theory of International Politics, pp. 129-60.

42. Paul Marer, "Has Eastern Europe Become a Liability to the Soviet Union?' The Economic Aspect," in Gati, The International Politics of Eastern Europe, pp. 59-81.

43. Thus James Caporaso writes, "Dependence refers to the condition under which the opportunities and behavior of one actor are affected by another actor. Dependence is a normal part of any social or exchange relationship. When dependence is a two-way street, such that two countries are roughly equally dependent on one another, we speak of interdependence. But when one country is affected strongly by another and the reverse is not true, we have a kind of relational inequality that we call dependence." "Methodological Issues in the Measurement of Inequality, Dependence, and Exploitation," in Kurth and Rosen, op. cit., p. 91. See also Robert O. Keohane and Joseph S. Nye, Power and Interdependence: World Politics in Transition (Boston: Little, Brown, 1977), pp. 8-11.

44. For a discussion of these concepts, see Raymond D. Duvall, "Dependence and dependencia theory: Notes toward precision of concept and argument," International Organization 32, no. 1 (Winter 1978): 51-78. On this point see also the discussion in Terry, Chapter 7.

45. See the chapter by Donna Bahry and Cal Clark in this volume, esp. pp. 135-36; compare Albert O. Hirschman, "Beyond asymmetry: Critical notes on myself as a young man and on some other old friends," International Organization 32, no. 1 (Winter 1978): 45-50.

46. See Patrick J. McGowan and Dale L. Smith, "Economic dependence in black Africa: An analysis of competing theories," International Organization 32, no. 1 (Winter 1978): 179-236; Robert Kaufman, Harry Chernotsky, and Daniel Geller, "A Preliminary Test of the Theory of Dependency," Comparative Politics 7, no. 3 (April 1975): 303-30.

47. James N. Rosenau, "Toward the Study of National-International Linkages," in Linkage Politics, ed. James N. Rosenau (New York: Free Press, 1969), pp. 44-63. See also Rosenau's (by now somewhat dated) review of linkage research, "Theorizing Across Systems: Linkage Politics Revisited," in Conflict Behavior and Linkage Politics, ed. Jonathan Wilkenfeld (New York: David McKay, 1973), pp. 25-56.

48. See, for example, Sarah Terry, "External Influences on Political Change in Eastern Europe: A Framework for Analysis," in Triska and Cocks, op. cit., pp. 277-314.

2

BALKAN COMMUNIST FOREIGN POLICIES: A LINKAGE PERSPECTIVE

Cal Clark

Through the early 1960s, the communist world (or at least the ruling parties thereof) seemed to form a monolithic entity. The Soviet Union, it was assumed, had constructed an "empire" of near-ly total dominance over the other "satellites." The Sino-Soviet split and the ensuing greater diversity among the foreign policies of the smaller communist states were generally viewed in terms of con-flicts with and deviations from the dominant Soviet model. A rough comparative framework emerged, then, classifying the communist states and movements according to whether they fit more closely into the Chinese or Soviet camp. This was still simply an extension of the large-power dominance thesis, though; and there was still no concerted attempt to view all communist states as individual units whose goals, strategies, and resources could be subjected to com-parative inquiry.

The four Balkan communist countries present an especially interesting field for comparative treatment because they developed radically different foreign policies within two decades despite sev-eral factors which suggested that they should evolve similarly after

An earlier version of portions of this paper was presented at the Seventeenth Convention of the International Studies Association, February 25-29, 1976, Toronto. Professor Robert Farlow's ideas have contributed greatly to the analysis herein; and Professors Ronald Linden, Jacques Levesque, and Vladimir Petrov have added valuable suggestions. They are, of course, not responsible for the scope of the material, the specific interpretations, or the various errors of omission and commission.

the communist takeover. First, the speed and ease with which the communist regimes gained power in the Balkans contrasted to the significantly more drawn-out process elsewhere in East Europe and, thus, seemingly would have augured more docile and dependable political prospects from the Soviet perspective, although the independent nature of the Yugoslav revolution might have suggested the potential for future patron-client conflict. Second, initially all four new Balkan regimes were committed to "hard line" orthodox ideological positions, providing another possible basis for compatibility.[1] Finally, these four states were the poorest in East Europe, a condition suggesting common external needs that should have maximized their dependence on the Soviet Union.

Yet, their foreign policies soon diverged. Yugoslavia, forcibly expelled from the Soviet bloc in 1948 for resisting Soviet penetration,[2] gradually worked out a policy of "nonalignment" oriented toward identification with and promotion of the interests of the Third World, while maintaining a shifting "balance between East and West." Albania used the 1948 Cominform break to escape Yugoslav tutelage by taking the Soviet Union as her new patron. When de-Stalinization in the Soviet bloc apparently encroached upon Albanian interests, the Sino-Soviet split was used to effect a new "realignment"—this time with the People's Republic of China. Finally, the Albanians and the post-Mao Chinese leadership have gone their separate ways. In the late 1950s and early 1960s, Romania became increasingly dissatisfied with Soviet political and economic policies toward her. This led to a foreign policy stance which Farlow has termed "partial alignment," in that the Romanians, while formally maintaining membership in the Soviet alliance system, exercise substantial independence in foreign affairs and seek to minimize the Soviet Union's political and economic leverage.[3] Bulgaria, in contrast to the varying "independent" foreign policies of her Balkan neighbors, has remained one of the most loyal and subservient of the Soviet Union's client states throughout the postwar period.[4]

The four Balkan states developed such radically different foreign policies that comparative theory would appear appropriate for explaining these various outcomes. Such a framework should incorporate two disparate features of the relations among communist states. First, the very fact of foreign policy diversity shows that, contrary to images of a communist monolith under great-power dominance, the smaller states do have significant room for maneuver and initiative in pursuit of their individual goals. Second, the conventional images of Soviet domination over East Europe certainly cannot be rejected completely either. Dramatic events, such as the invasions of Hungary and Czechoslovakia, quantitative studies of bloc cohesion using such indicators as trade, U.N. voting, and issue

agreement, and conventional works of diplomatic history and Kremlinology all strongly indicate that the Soviet shadow has affected
many events in East Europe. [5] These two presumptions, in turn,
suggest the applicability of Rosenau's "linkage perspective," which
views foreign policy as deriving from the interactions, or "linkages,"
between external and internal factors. [6] The next section, therefore,
outlines the major stages in the evolution of these nations' domestic
and foreign policies. Rosenau's linkage theory will then be presented as a suggestive first step toward a more comprehensive and
theoretical approach to comparing Communist foreign policies.

THE EVOLUTION OF BALKAN FOREIGN POLICIES

The basic assumption on which this essay is constructed is
that the linkage between external and internal influences on Balkan
foreign policies centers upon the actions and perceptions of the
Balkan states' national leaderships, who can be seen as pursuing
various political goals. Given these nations' substantial vulnerability to external forces, the political decisions of their elites must
necessarily include considerations of the threats and opportunities
provided by the international environment; so it is certainly reasonable to suppose that their foreign policies should reflect these factors. The following summary of postwar developments in the Balkans, then, will concentrate upon two factors: the factional struggles in each country that have been the major emphasis of the "conflict school" of communist politics;[7] and the stages through which
the four foreign policies have actually progressed. This section
will be primarily descriptive, with analysis and interpretation reserved for the following section.

Albania: Flights from Dependency

Along with Yugoslavia's expulsion from the Cominform, Albania's two reorientations in external ties from Yugoslavia to the
Soviet Union in 1948, and from the Soviet Union to China in 1961,
constitute the most dramatic changes in postwar Balkan foreign
policies. These foreign policy reversals were also clearly associated with bitter intraparty factional rivalries, as each brought
blood purges.

While there was some communist activity among Albanians
during the interwar period, the communist movement there was by
far the weakest in the Balkans. In fact, the Albanian Communist
Party (subsequently renamed the Albanian Party of Labor) was not

formed until November 1941 when, under the auspices of the Yugoslav Party, several separate groups were merged. The Party,
heavily under Yugoslav influence, formed the core of the wartime
resistance and outmaneuvered the non-Communist groups to seize
sole power at the conclusion of World War II.[8]

The Albanian Communists, even at their moment of victory,
suffered from several significant splits, such as those between "intellectuals" and "proletarians," pro-Yugoslavs and Albanian nationalists, and the Geg and Tosk ethnic groups. These tended to reinforce rather than crosscut and to pit the two most important figures
in the regime, Enver Hoxha and Koci Xoxe, against each other.[9]
After the war, the pro-Yugoslav Xoxe faction continuously gained
power as Albania became, in effect, a Yugoslav satellite. Just as
Xoxe appeared on the verge of total victory in early 1948, however,
the burgeoning Soviet-Yugoslav rift gave Hoxha a reprieve as he
liquidated his internal opposition and switched from Yugoslav to
Soviet patronage in external affairs.[10] Until the death of Stalin,
Albania's relations with the Soviet Union remained very good,
marred only by diplomatic indications of Albania's insignificance to
the Soviets.[11] While the new policies emanating from the Kremlin
after 1953 probably caused some concern for the leadership of Hoxha
and Mehmet Shehu, the Soviet Union did upgrade Albania's diplomatic status, perhaps to compensate and reassure the Albanians.
This "balance" was destroyed, from Hoxha's perspective at least,
when the continuing Soviet-Yugoslav rapprochement and Khrushchev's
"secret speech" denouncing Stalin at the Twentieth Congress of the
Communist Party of the Soviet Union (CPSU) played a large part in
stimulating a direct domestic challenge to Hoxha and Shehu in the
late spring of 1956.[12]

The Soviet response to the Polish and Hungarian revolutions
presented a welcome opportunity to Hoxha, who responded with the
strongest propaganda outbursts in the bloc, especially regarding
Yugoslavia, and with a purge of his domestic enemies. Unlike
Xoxe's execution in 1949, which apparently required Soviet approval,
the 1956 purge was carried out over Khrushchev's objections, indicating a substantial deterioration of the dependency relationship.[13]
The late 1950s, then, saw a muted divergence of Albania's position
from the Soviet Union on such issues as international detente, domestic de-Stalinization, and, most particularly, relations with
Yugoslavia, despite a sharp increase in Soviet aid to Albania.[14]

According to Pano, "The outbreak of the Sino-Soviet polemics
in April 1960, probably marks the point at which the Albanian leaders began seriously to reappraise their relationship with the Soviet
Union."[15] The Albanians generally backed the Chinese positions,
although with some moderation and pro-Soviet balance at first.

Soviet-Albanian relations rapidly deteriorated, culminating in late 1961 in the vitriolic denunciations of Albania at the CPSU's Twenty-Second Congress in October, and with the Soviet Union breaking diplomatic relations with Albania in December—an unprecedented event in the relations among communist states.[16] Albania thus became firmly entrenched as China's only European ally within the communist movement; and the PRC took over the burden of providing economic aid to Albania.[17]

The 1968 invasion of Czechoslovakia renewed the specter of Soviet aggression and "forced a sudden and drastic reappraisal of Hoxha's perceptions of the geopolitical realities in Europe." Albania began to cultivate broader relations with the West and especially with the other Balkan states, including former archenemy Yugoslavia, which was now seen as another country "under the wolf's mouth."[18] With the fading of direct threats to Albania's security in the mid-1970s, Hoxha's predilection for isolation and "ideological purity" was once again strongly reasserted. Albania has recently undergone substantial domestic purges and external strains in her relations with China because of the PRC's "moderating" stances in world affairs; and in July 1978, China terminated her assistance programs, marking "the formal end of the Sino-Albanian alliance."[19]

In sum, Albania has seemingly followed a foreign policy of "realignment" in which patrons have been successfully switched whenever external political penetration and threats to the dominant Hoxha faction became imminent. Until the mid-1970s, the Albanians evidently believed that they needed the support of a political and economic patron; but the latest move away from China suggests the possibility of a new "independence through isolation."

Bulgaria: Continuing Loyalty to the Soviet Union

With a few minor exceptions, Bulgaria has been the most faithful of the Soviet Union's client states in East Europe during the postwar period. As in Albania, relations with the Soviet Union appear highly correlated with the outcomes of intraparty conflicts since the factions or personalities backed by the Soviets have emerged triumphant in each of Bulgaria's succession crises.

The Bulgarian Communist Party was the oldest and strongest in the Balkans before World War II and had produced such internationally known figures as Dimitur Blagoev, Georgi Dimitrov, and Vassil Kolarov; yet, it was relatively weak during the war period. The unexpectedly rapid advance of the Red Army through the Balkans, though, allowed the BCP to seize almost complete control of the country at the beginning of the postwar period. When the party came to power, its leaders could be divided into two groups: exiles who had spent extended periods in the Soviet Union, such as Dimitrov and Kolarov, and men who were in Bulgaria during the Party's rapid rise to power, such as Traicho Kostov. Dimitrov, who returned to Bulgaria in late 1945, became Party leader and premier; and Bulgaria appeared to follow Soviet designs very well as Dimitrov became a leading advocate of the new "People's Democracies."[20] Kostov was probably the leading contender to succeed the aging Dimitrov and Kolarov, but the Soviets found a new protégé in the person of Vulko Chervenkov, who had lived in the Soviet Union for 20 years, although he never attained great importance among the Bulgarian exiles there. The Cominform break with Yugoslavia set off an extensive purge of "nationalists" and "Titoists" throughout the bloc, with Kostov being the most prominent Bulgarian victim. Following the deaths of Dimitrov and Kolarov, Chervenkov, with Moscow's obvious backing, succeeded to the leadership of both the Party and the government in 1950. He quickly replaced most of the older and more prestigious of the leadership group and, modeling himself upon his patron Stalin, became probably the most dominant and dictatorial leader in East Europe.[21]

Stalin's death led to the application of the "New Course" in Bulgaria, as elsewhere in East Europe; and Chervenkov relinquished his position as first secretary of the BCP in early 1954 to Todor Zhivkov, generally regarded as a secondary figure in the Bulgarian elite. Chervenkov subsequently became an early target of Khrushchev's efforts to remove Stalinists in East Europe, as Zhivkov now became the Soviet favorite. During the next eight years, Chervenkov gradually lost power and may well have been responsible for Bulgaria's brief flirtation with Maoism in the abortive "Great Leap Forward" campaign of 1958. He was not completely dropped from the leadership, though, until after the strongly anti-Stalinist Twenty-Second Congress of the CPSU in 1961. Zhivkov, for his part, was not able to gain supreme power until the Eighth BCP Congress in November 1962, when, following very evident Soviet intervention, his other major rivals were purged.[22] In the spring of 1965, Soviet security organs uncovered a primarily military plot against Zhivkov which both represented the last major political challenge to him and indicated his strong dependence on Soviet backing.[23]

After Zhivkov's victory, Bulgaria generally followed a policy of unbroken fealty to the Soviet Union, with one important exception. A limited rapprochement occurred with the West during 1965-66— one of the few independent initiatives in postwar Bulgarian diplomacy— presumably because of the benefits that were seen as accruing from increased economic interactions with the West.[24] Since then, however, the Bulgarians have clung much more closely to the positions of the Soviet leadership in the areas of relations with the West, intrabloc ties, and the role of the Soviet Union in the Communist movement.[25] In particular, Zhivkov and the Bulgarians have expressed interest in centering their economic and political integration with the Soviet Union alone rather than with the Council for Mutual Economic Assistance (CMEA) as a bloc. Soviet penetration of Bulgarian politics, hence, has resulted in a situation where the BCP leadership seemingly sees Soviet support as a vital element in the internal calculus of power.

Romania: A Gradual Assertion of National Power

Until the early 1960s, Romania was generally "cited as the most docile of Soviet satellites, as an example of Stalinism triumphant over nationalism, as a country that had lost its past and had no future."[26] The evolution of "partial alignment," though, brought the Romanian Communist Party into the unique position of exercising substantial foreign policy independence while retaining formal membership in the Soviet alliance system. As in Bulgaria, factional conflicts appear related to the subsequent foreign policies, but Romania is distinctive in that its first postwar leader, Gheorghe Gheorghiu-Dej, rose to power as a loyal Stalinist but preserved his power by ultimately defying the Soviet Union and charting Romania's semiautonomous course.

The Romanian Communist Party was very ineffectual in interwar politics, but Soviet troops gave the RCP effective control of Romania by 1945, although coalition governments in increasingly bogus forms were continued until 1947. The fact that the communists did not seize power directly made little difference to the fate of non-communist forces in Romania, but it may well have proved decisive in the struggle between the "Muscovites" and "home communists" within the RCP. In a strategic move before the arrival of the Red Army, the home communists were able to gain the position of party first secretary for their own leader Dej. With the return of the more trusted Muscovites, the position of the home communists fell, but Dej was able to use the continuing coalition government as a prop for his position within the RCP. He established himself as the intermediary linking the RCP and Moscow and built up his credentials as a devoted and trustworthy Stalinist. Thus, when the final intraparty showdown came in 1951-52, Dej was able to obtain Kremlin acquiescence in the downgrading of the Muscovites.[27]

Following the purge of the Muscovites, Dej increasingly championed Stalinist policies. This brought him into conflict with Khrushchev's new de-Stalinist line in the mid-1950s, but by 1957 he had gained sole control over the RCP.[28] Still, any Soviet-Romanian discord remained very muted as Soviet backing of the anti-Stalinists was not nearly as strong as in Bulgaria and Albania. In fact, when the RCP did begin to differ openly from the Soviet Union, it was over economic policy, not the fortunes of internal factions. Dej and the RCP wanted to pursue a Stalinist policy of rapid industrialization concentrated in heavy industry, to modernize Romania. Khrushchev, on the other hand, was attacking the "eaters of metal" at this time and was not happy about providing the massive aid necessary for the huge iron and steel complex the Romanians wanted at Galati.[29] This issue came to a head in the conflict over the nature of Comecon in the early 1960s when Romanian objections proved sufficient to veto the Soviet attempt to increase CMEA integration and to enforce a division of labor between Comecon's more and less developed members.[30] This also forced the RCP to turn elsewhere in order to support its industrialization plans; and there was a gradual but steady expansion of trade with the West beginning in the late 1950s.[31]

The independence of partial alignment emerged strongly in the mid-1960s. The Romanian Statement on the Stand of the Romanian Workers Party, issued in April 1964, is generally considered a "declaration of independence" in that it stressed the rights of sovereignty and domestic autonomy and made it clear that these principles should apply to Soviet-Romanian relations.[32] The death of Dej and his replacement by Nicolae Ceausescu in 1965 only accentuated the transformation of these principles into practice as Romania's separate road in foreign policy became more clearly defined. Internally, the Romanian regime remained orthodox and conservative, but the independence of partial alignment probably did much to increase "socialist patriotism" and the RCP's domestic popularity.[33] In contrast to the dramatic changes in the half-decade following the Statement, the 1970s have seen a stabilization in Romania's foreign relations. Ceausescu continues to emphasize relations with the West and China; Romania joined the General Agreement on Trade and Tariffs (GATT), the International Monetary Fund, and the World Bank; and Third World contacts have been pursued very aggressively. On the other hand, Romania's relations with the Soviet bloc stabilized as Ceausescu apparently realized that he had reached the limits of permissible independence within the framework of bloc membership, and as Romania's ability to finance trade outside the bloc became increasingly limited.[34] There is some disagreement among Western analysts about whether significant retrenchment has occurred in Romania's foreign policy autonomy since the early 1970s, but Linden makes a strong case for the continuation of substantial independence.[35]

Romania's policy of partial alignment, therefore, emerged from the victory of the Stalinist Dej faction at a time when the Soviet Union was committed to a policy of de-Stalinization throughout the bloc. Soviet pressure was not really applied, however, until after the power struggle within the RCP had been resolved; and subsequent Soviet-Romanian friction appeared to turn upon economic, rather than factional, concerns. The central tenet of partial alignment, in its ideal form at least, seems to be a balance of power approach in which power centers both inside and outside the bloc are used to counterbalance the Soviets' economic and political leverage.

Yugoslavia: Nonalignment as Coming in from the Cold

Yugoslavia's expulsion from the Cominform in June 1948 provided the dramatic first instance of open conflict among the ruling Communist states that was not to be repeated until the "revolutions" in Poland and Hungary and the emergence of the Sino-Soviet split. Initially forced to turn to the West for aid and protection, the Yugoslavs were able to establish a "balance between East and West" after Stalin's death, and, from the late 1950s on, Yugoslavia's foreign policy has been distinctive among the Balkan Communist states in that "nonalignment" has been officially centered on a non-communist group of nations—the developing "Third World."

While the Yugoslav Communist Party was relatively weak before the war,[36] Tito's partisans came to dominate the Yugoslav resistance. And, unlike the rest of East Europe's parties, the Yugoslav Communist Party came to power at the end of the war primarily because of its own strength, not that of the Red Army. With the rapid consolidation of communist power, Yugoslavia soon became considered "the most Stalinist of the satellites" by many observers. At the level of political action, however, increasing Yugoslav resistance to Soviet penetration of their internal organs led to the controversy between Moscow and Belgrade during the first half of 1948 that culminated in Yugoslavia's expulsion from the Cominform in June. The Cominform break forced a revolutionary reappraisal of the Tito government's foreign policy outlook; and gradually during 1948-50 the decision evolved to turn to the West for aid and support. Yugoslav ideological doctrine was also reworked extensively, both on the political and economic structures necessary for a truly Marxist society and on the nature of positive international "forces of socialism" which could justify Yugoslav ties to non-communist and even anti-communist nations.[37]

The newly renamed League of Communists of Yugoslavia could not have been particularly happy with their political and economic attachments to the West in the early 1950s. In any case, two developments occurred in the early 1950s which drew Yugoslavia toward the establishment of its own style of nonaligned external relations. First, the death of Stalin in 1953 led to a normalization of relations with the Soviet bloc and a policy of "balance between East and West," from the mid-1950s onward. The international bombshell of Khrushchev's 1955 visit to Belgrade brought a tremendous improvement in Soviet-Yugoslav relations; but the upheaval in Poland and Hungary began a substantial cooling of Soviet-Yugoslav relations, as indicated by Yugoslavia's refusal to sign the resolutions of the 1957 Moscow Conference of Communist Parties and by the harsh Soviet denunciations of the Yugoslav Party Program in 1958. This new "freeze" by the Soviets in their relations with Yugoslavia was spurred on by the Chinese and Albanians, but the extreme hostility of the Cominform break period was not revived. After the exacerbation of the Sino-Soviet split at the Soviet Union's Twenty-Second Party Congress, Belgrade's relations with the Soviet bloc improved rapidly and remained very cordial until the Czech invation of 1968.[38] Strains in Soviet-Yugoslav relations increased substantially after this demonstration of Soviet hegemony, but in the early 1970s the Yugoslav domestic reaction against nationalism and liberalism stimulated a strengthening in her ties to the Soviet Union. Since then the balance between East and West has fluctuated somewhat in response to various events, such as the discovery of Soviet intrigues in "Cominform plots" against the regime, the failure of the Soviet Union to deliver promised foreign aid credits, polemics with the Soviets about Eurocommunism, and internal preparation for the impending Tito succession. At present, the Soviet Union seems to be viewed as a larger threat to Yugoslav independence than the United States, and Yugoslavia is leading the opposition against the Cuban attempt to have the nonalignment movement proclaim a commonality of interests with the Soviet bloc.[39]

Second and probably more important was the evolution of the Yugoslav policy of nonalignment directed toward cooperation with the developing nations not tied to either Cold War camp. In the mid-1950s, Tito became one of the "Big Three" of nonalignment, along with Nasser and Nehru. The First Conference of Nonaligned States in Belgrade in 1961 demonstrated Yugoslavia's key role in promoting the development of nonalignment. While the nonalignment movement in general waned somewhat during the late 1960s, Yugoslavia still maintains nonalignment as the central theme of her foreign policy and continues to play a prominent role in the diplomatic initiatives of the Third World nations.[40]

The policy of nonalignment was not a sudden creation. Rather, it evolved somewhat uncertainly as the Tito regime reacted to the exigencies of Yugoslavia's ambiguous place in the international system. The most fundamental thread in nonalignment has been Yugoslavia's maneuvering to preserve her independence in the face of enticements and pressures from the Soviet and U.S. alliance systems. This fear of bloc domination has led Yugoslavia to advocate and promote the concerted activity of nonbloc or "nonaligned" nations. The core of nonalignment rests upon an appeal for democratic and egalitarian relations among nations, which are seen as the only means for containing the imperialistic and hegemonistic intrigues of the superpowers and for solving the problems of economic development and the "North-South" division in world affairs. More philosophically, the Yugoslavs also view their nonalignment policy as playing a key role in the development of socialism through its encouragement of progressive socialist forces in the Third World.[41]

After the period of the Cominform break, the factional struggles in the LCY appear little related to foreign policy as such, although the fall of Alexander Rankovic in 1966 and the 1971-72 purge of Croatian "nationalists" and political "liberals" probably led indirectly to better relations with the West and the Soviet Union, respectively.[42] Factional conflict appears much less linked to foreign policy than elsewhere in the communist Balkans, therefore. Two reasons may be advanced to explain this. First, the Cominform break ended Yugoslavia's strong dependence upon another Communist power, which lasted much longer in the other three countries. Thus, there was neither need nor opportunity to utilize "external" power bases in domestic politics. Second, the existence of several polarizing economic and nationality issues in the LCY creates a strong incentive to pursue nonalignment as a "compromise" foreign policy, removing one potentially explosive cleavage from intraparty conflict.[43]

A LINKAGE MODEL OF BALKAN FOREIGN POLICIES

One image of the Soviet bloc holds that it is still essentially monolithic, with the dominant Soviet Union severely constraining the latitude of the subordinate East European states in domestic and foreign policy: "Any deviation in domestic policy from the model considered by Moscow as the true socialist one, or any deviation from Soviet foreign policy would be declared a betrayal of socialist internationalism, as the Czechs have learned at their own expense."[44] The invasions of Czechoslovakia and Hungary certainly demonstrated that such limits of tolerance exist; and several recent analyses have argued that Soviet-East European relations may be best conceptualized in terms of dependency theory.[45] Still, the

Balkan cases reviewed here demonstrate that substantial initiative can remain for an East European state. Three of these four countries have displayed considerable independence in their relations with the Soviet Union. This section outlines some relevant variables for comparing and understanding Balkan foreign policies; it is followed by the empirical application of the model to the Balkan histories outlined above.

Conceptual Overview

East European foreign policies evidently derive from a combination of internal and external influences. Given the very different foreign policies that evolved in the Balkan states, these influences must have varied greatly among the four countries. What is needed, then, is a theoretical framework for identifying the principal influences on the foreign policies of these countries and for sketching the causal structure of their effects. Rosenau's "linkage theory" would seem especially appropriate for this purpose. Rosenau explicitly conceptualizes foreign policy as resulting from the connections between a state's domestic system and international environment, recognizes that the relative impact of internal and external factors vary greatly among nations, and constructs a typology of different external influences. This section attempts to apply Rosenau's abstract concepts to the concrete task of explaining the variations among the Balkan foreign policies.

A basic assumption of the linkage approach is that foreign policies and the internal-external linkages that cause them represent a process of national adaptation in which a country responds to potentially disturbing factors threatening to transform its geographic, political, economic, or social characteristics and structures beyond acceptable parameters. Rosenau delineates four foreign policy types that depend upon the relative need to adapt to internal or external pressures. First, promotive adaptation is possible when there are no strong impinging forces from either the internal or the external environment. Second, acquiescent adaptation occurs when there are strong external influences and few or no internal ones. Third, intransigent adaptation results when there are strong internal factors which must be accommodated in the absence of external pressures, which stimulates, in turn, a policy of manipulating the international environment in order to meet domestic needs. Fourth, preservative adaptation is forced on a state when it faces simultaneously strong internal and external pressures. Rosenau then ties the four types of adaptation policy to various internal and external phenomena as possible causes and consequences of these foreign policy strategies.[46]

Rosenau further argues that external influences upon a state's policy can be transmitted by three different types of linkage processes: (1) a "penetrative process" occurs when actors from one state in the environment directly participate in a nation's policy making; (2) a "reactive process" occurs when domestic policy is made in direct response to some stimulus from the environment; and (3) an "emulative process" occurs when the domestic policy takes essentially the same form as an environmental stimulus. He also emphasizes that single events are not very important in themselves but that linkages are formed only by the "recurrence of behavioral sequences."[47]

For small states, such as the Balkan Communist countries, penetration would be the strongest linkage to an external power since that power would have the opportunity to dictate their policies directly. In reactive linkages, the leadership in the subordinate state is at least autonomous in its decision-making processes, although it may well recognize that real constraints exist on the scope of decisions it can make without running the risk of unacceptable retribution (for example, invasion and the termination of energy exports). Finally, emulation represents the weakest level of linkage since it entails a policy similarity which, because it is voluntary, presumably is seen as advantageous by the regime in question. The problem, of course, is distinguishing true emulation from a policy similarity forced by penetrative or reactive linkages.

Rosenau's framework is valuable because it suggests that variations in foreign policy can be explained by the different factors impinging upon different states from their domestic and international environments. Figure 2.1 summarizes this framework in terms of a path diagram.

FIGURE 2.1

Rosenau Linkage Framework

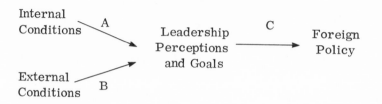

Source: Constructed by the author.

Foreign policy is depicted as the result of decisions by the political leadership, and these decisions, in turn, are conditioned by the leadership's perceptions of internal and external stimuli.[48] Rosenau's four categories of adaptation policies presume that the relative strengths of paths A and B determine path C, that is, the type of foreign policy pursued. His typology of linkage processes implies that the strength of path B will be affected by whether the dominant linkage is penetration, reaction, or emulation. This is still a fairly abstract formulation, though, and the variables in the model need further specification before it can be used to explain the differences among Balkan foreign policies.

Leadership goals and perceptions form the central element in Figure 2.1. This is based on the premise that the foreign policy of a nation is formulated by a narrow elite in order to further various goals, based upon their perceptions of domestic and international conditions. Probably the most basic goal of the Balkan political elites has been to maintain power, both in terms of communist party domination of the political system and their own domination of the communist party apparatus. Support for a communist regime can come from either internal or external sources. The domestic sources would include the positive support, or at least passive acceptance, of the rank-and-file party members and of broader segments of the population, while external military or political support can be obtained from stronger communist nations, such as the Soviet Union and the PRC. The process of building internal support or legitimacy can have many components. The two that seem most prevalent in East Europe are the improvement of people's living conditions and appeals to traditional nationalism.[49]

These two legitimacy motifs, in turn, imply several concrete policies: promotion of national-territorial issues; policies of rapid economic development and socioeconomic change; and, perhaps, economic and political decentralization and reform. Despite Marxism's emphasis on class rather than nationality, the Soviet Union has found appeals to nationalism and non-communist national symbols to be quite effective, and the continuing national rivalries that are endemic in East Europe suggest that nationalistic appeals could serve as a significant source of regime and governmental legitimacy. Marxist theory and Stalinist practice undoubtedly both motivated the East European elites to implement policies of forced-draft industrialization, but industrialization also opened the way for massive upward social mobility in all but the most highly developed East European states by creating many new managerial and professional positions and bringing a massive influx of peasants into the industrial sector.[50] Thus, increased regime legitimacy and the stability of the political system in these countries seemingly depends upon radical change in economic and social structures. The transformation brought on by industrialization and universal education also creates a much more sophisticated citizenry who might well be expected to demand greater participation; moreover, central control is made increasingly difficult by the growing complexity of political and economic structures. Thus, internal pressures are generated for general decentralization and reform.

These putative goals of the East European leaderships suggest, in turn, several influences from their domestic and international environments that would be especially important for their decisional responses. Internally, major factors affecting these goals should include: (1) domestic support for the communist party; (2) factional challenges to the leadership from within the party; (3) the economic base for industrialization; (4) the strength of nationalism; and (5) popular expectations related to standard of living and political participation. As Herrmann argues, actors and forces in the international environment can be seen as providing either a threat or opportunity for the pursuit of national goals.[51] The maintenance of power is probably the most fundamental objective of almost all political regimes, and a powerful foreign nation might be perceived either as a threat to national legitimacy or as a necessary support for a government that lacks strong domestic legitimacy. In many instances, national-territorial and economic development goals could also force a leadership to look outward for opportunities and threats in the international environment.

Figure 2.2 sketches these relationships. The elite goals are divided into the postulated basic goal of maintaining power and the three policies that might be implemented to increase domestic legitimacy and support. Path X, then, indicates that power goals could result in one or more of the policies listed in the lower block. The internal and external conditions affecting these goals and policies are denoted by paths A to E and F to I, respectively. Each of these influences can vary from nonexistent to very strong. The strength of the external factors (paths F through I) should be affected, in addition, by the form of their transmission, that is, via penetrative, reactive, or emulative linkages. Paths Y and Z denote the impact of the elites' power and policy goals upon foreign policy, as mediated by their perceptions of internal and external conditions. In sum, paths X, Y, and Z describe a state's foreign policy and are dependent, in turn, upon the linkages between paths A to E and F to I.

FIGURE 2.2

Revised Linkage Model for Balkan Foreign Policies

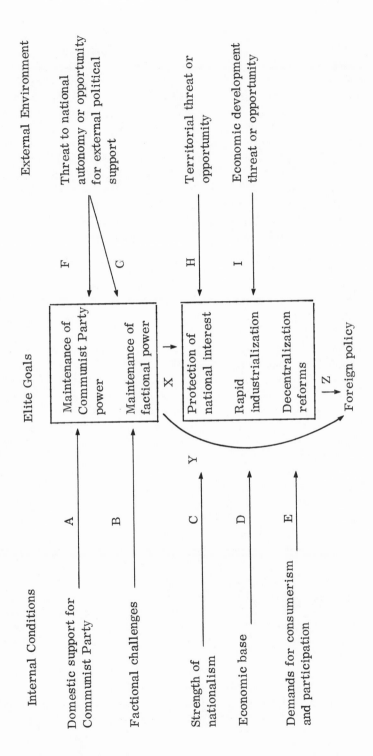

32

Applying the Model

<u>Power Goals</u>

The power goals of the Balkan elites form the central element in the theoretical model in Figure 2.2 in that they are assumed to be the primary determinant of foreign policy, either directly (path Y) or indirectly (paths X and Z). This implies that differences in the power positions of the Balkan regimes should influence their foreign policies; and, in fact, this appears to be the case. Following World War II, the new Balkan communist regimes had the same general goals—the maintenance of the new elites in power, the monopoly of political power by the communist party, and the transformation of backward societies into modern industrial states, to name a few. They did not bring the same set of opportunities and constraints to this "adaptive process," however. In particular, the new Balkan communist leaders and parties had very different levels of internal support and popularity. Thus, while all four states found themselves dependent upon external sources for a variety of political and economic supports, variations in external threats and internal strengths contributed to the formation of significantly different adaptive strategies.

Among the four countries, Yugoslavia was distinctive in that the Communist revolution was primarily brought about by indigenous elites, not an external force, such as the Red Army for Bulgaria and Romania and, to a lesser extent, the Yugoslav communists for Albania. As a result, domestic support (path A) was significantly stronger in Yugoslavia than in the other three states, and the Yugoslav party also suffered much less factional conflict (path B), probably because of the partisan experience. When the split with the Soviet Union occurred in 1948, for example, only a few men among the top leadership did not back Tito. At the same time, splits within the Romanian and Bulgarian communist elites were brewing, which led, in contrast, to extensive purges in the late 1940s and early 1950s. Factional conflict seemed the most extreme in Albania, where the outcome of the Hoxha-Xoxe rivalry would determine who would be stood up against the wall.

The differences in paths A and B, in turn, conditioned the way the Balkan elites viewed external sources of support (paths F and G). Yugoslavia had less need of outside support and, because of her much more unified leadership, should have been the most able to resist external penetration among the Balkan states. Initially, the ideological lenses of the Yugoslav communists made them view the Soviet Union primarily in terms of opportunities for external support (path F), even though external support was not vital to the regime's survival as it was elsewhere throughout East Europe.[52] When the Soviet Union demanded that Yugoslavia desist from any attempts to limit Soviet penetration of domestic Yugoslav institutions, the Soviet Union became perceived as a major threat. At this point the favorable Yugoslav position in terms of paths A and B gave the Yugoslavs the power to render fraudulent Stalin's boast that he could make Tito fall by shaking his little finger. During the 1948-52 period of danger, the Yugoslav turn to the West, especially the United States, for political support and economic and military aid can be seen as a case of path Y, that is, one in which the maintenance of power directly dictates foreign policy.

This was a situation, then, of strong external pressures combined with low-to-medium domestic ones. An "acquiescent foreign policy" of changing internal structures to meet external demands (for example, the overthrow of Tito) might have been predicted by the Rosenau framework, but it certainly did not occur. The Yugoslav regime, rather, responded by finding alternative sources of external support. This suggests that Rosenau's typology might be expanded somewhat to include multiple and contradictory sources of external pressures or stimuli. Furthermore, attention should be paid to the target of, as well as the pressure source for, foreign policy adaptation. In the Yugoslav case outlined above, pressure from the Soviet Union radically altered Yugoslavia's foreign policy course toward the "target" of the West and the United States and, in so doing, demonstrated that under the right conditions even a weak nation can successfully manipulate the international environment.

After Stalin's death, the threat of direct intervention waned, and the Yugoslavs, already alerted to the dangers of being a small state in a great power's alliance system, moved toward the nonalignment policy. This policy of trying to organize the less powerful into a potent force in world affairs required the absence of both an immediate foreign threat to Yugoslavia and internal pressures strong enough to force recourse to external support; that is, as observed earlier, Yugoslav domestic politics, while far from tranquil, have been only marginally related to foreign policy. Thus, nonalignment is a "promotive foreign policy" determined by interests of the Yugoslav leadership not involved in the power considerations denoted by path Y. To some extent, as will be discussed below, one can discern an indirect relationship through paths X and Z, but apparently these objectives primarily reflect factors not explicitly included in the model in Figure 2.2. They could be pursued because neither internal nor external forces entailed strong foreign policy imperatives.

The weakness of the Romanian and Bulgarian parties after World War II made them see Soviet support as a vital external opportunity which was a virtual prerequisite for continuing communist rule. Soviet support was also vital to the outcome of the factional struggles. Thus the Dej and Chervenkov regimes probably viewed Soviet domination as an opportunity in the intraparty squabble, too, although the fate of their purged comrades also spotlighted the threat that inevitably accompanies dependency, whatever the momentary opportunities. Thus, low internal support and substantial factional infighting forced these parties to rely on Soviet political support. Their penetration by and subservience to the Soviet Union, then, represents a direct impact of power needs on foreign policy (path Y). Their strong reliance upon the Soviet Union, in turn, allowed the two regimes to pay little attention to most domestic constituencies. Thus their foreign policies at this time can certainly be considered "acquiescent," that is, responding primarily to an external power.

Following Stalin's death, both the Stalinist and subservient Dej and Chervenkov regimes were clearly threatened by Khrushchev's de-Stalinization program of the mid-1950s. The Bulgarian and Romanian responses to this crisis were diametrically different, and their divergence can be explained by differences in the regimes' internal power positions. First, Dej was a "home communist" who maintained power by his own strategems and ability to curry Stalin's favor, while Chervenkov was a "Muscovite" propelled to the top by Soviet decision. Second, by the mid-1950s Dej had purged the top leadership circles of potential rivals, thereby forging a unified Romanian party, while the Bulgarian politburo was clearly riven by severe factionalism. This difference in the strength of path B, in turn, determined the effects along path G. The weak position of the Bulgarian party greatly facilitated Soviet intervention in the domestic power struggle as Zhivkov rode Khrushchev's support to supreme power and, in return, continued Bulgaria's generally "acquiescent" foreign policy. For Zhivkov, if not for his rivals, therefore, Soviet support represented an opportunity.

In Romania, on the other hand, Khrushchev presented a dire threat to Dej's political position, and Soviet plans for bloc integration also directly threatened Romanian economic autonomy and development. Romania's relatively favorable, or weak, position on path B, then, allowed Dej and subsequently Ceausescu to negate the threat along path G. To use Rosenau's terminology, Dej's consolidation of power within the RCP by the mid-1950s transformed Soviet-Romanian linkages into "reactive" processes, in contrast to the continued Soviet "penetration" of Bulgaria's internal politics. The increasing assertion of Romanian independence from the Soviet Union also appealed to traditional anti-Russian feelings among the population and doubtlessly increased domestic support for the regime (path A) by imbuing it with nationalistic legitimacy. The partial alignment policy, hence, appears an "intransigent" one in that external pressures were resisted and adjusted in order to accommodate the internal political order. The primary cause of this intransigence, however, was not the relative strength of the domestic and international pressures upon the Romanian regime, the latter being very probably greater, but was the regime's commitment to maintaining several political values: its own power (path Y) and the nationalistic and developmental policies it saw as central to its legitimation (the indirect power-foreign policy linkage through paths X and Z). The Romanian case, then, supports McGowan's contention that leadership, as well as external and internal stimuli, should be placed in the equations for determining national adaptation strategies. [53]

Factional conflicts in Albania during 1945-47 were probably the strongest in East Europe at that time. Yugoslav penetration thus constituted an overwhelming threat to the Hoxha-Shehu faction and an opportunity for the Xoxe faction. As with Tito in Yugoslavia, Hoxha used the Cominform crisis to reorient Albania's external ties to the most logical alternative for support against the external threat—the principal enemy of Albania's potential dominator. Albania, hence, chose penetration by the Soviet Union over Yugoslavia because the former was seen as potentially less destructive to both national identity and the dominant faction in the APL. Like the party leadership in Romania and Yugoslavia but unlike that in Bulgaria, Hoxha and Shehu were in general command of the party after the purge of Xoxe. The attempts to topple them in 1956 and 1960, which are generally attributed either directly or indirectly to the intrigues of Khrushchev and Tito, made ending the Albanian dependency on the Soviet Union much more urgent for Hoxha than for the stabler Dej regime and probably accounted for the much more radical Albanian position on the Sino-Soviet dispute. Albania's realignments away from Yugoslavia and the Soviet Union were motivated by a high level of threat from the patron to the dominant APL group, but the latest break with the PRC seems more likely to have come from perceptions of diminishing opportunities for ideological and economic succor.

Characterizing Albania's foreign policy in terms of Rosenau's four adaptive types seems complex. The escape from Yugoslavia's clutches can be called "preservative" since the Hoxha faction faced extreme internal and external threats, while the Chinese switch in 1961 seems similar to Dej's "intransigence." The recent break with the PRC indicates that Albania no longer perceives any grave threat from the external or internal environment necessitating reliance on an external patron. Evidently the Albanians have learned that dependence may begin with an external opportunity but ultimately produces a disastrous threat. Technically, this should be a "promotive" foreign policy, but Albania's retreat from international ties in order to preserve Hoxha's view of the world really does seem to merit the title of "intransigent."

Domestic Policies

In addition to the direct impact of power considerations on foreign policy, the three domestic policies enumerated above (promotion of nationalistic objectives, rapid industrialization, and decentralization reforms), which might be used to build domestic legitimacy, can also have significant implications for foreign policy. These linkage relationships, then, are indirect ones following the route of paths X and Z in the model sketched in Figure 2.2.

The Balkans are notorious for national conflicts, both within and between states, and for overlapping territorial claims by its nation-states.[54] The former Romanian province of Bessarabia was incorporated into the Soviet Union during World War II; Bulgaria casts jealous eyes on Yugoslav Macedonia on the ethnic grounds that Macedonians are really Bulgarians as well as on ancient historical-territorial grounds; and Yugoslavia also contains a large Albanian irredenta in the Kosovo area. (The number of Albanians in Yugoslavia equals nearly 50 percent of Albania's population.) All four Balkan states, therefore, presented their communist regimes with ample opportunities to press nationalistic appeals, and all four have taken advantage of this legitimizing motif. The Dej and Ceausescu regimes gained popular approval by standing up to Romania's gigantic Slavic neighbor; Hoxha's anti-Yugoslav policy probably reaped a like benefit, although Albanian-Yugoslav relations have improved appreciably over the last decade; Bulgaria, while making no direct territorial claims, has pursued the Macedonian question fairly consistently since the late 1940s; and Yugoslavia successfully combatted extreme pressure during the Cominform crisis and has pursued a nonalignment policy that has given her a much larger role in the international arena than her meager resources would naturally warrant. The leaderships in all four Balkan states, then, reacted to threats and opportunities in the external environment in a manner that made them appear as spokesmen for traditional national interests, thus contributing to their domestic support.

The industrialization drives of these four states (even Albania's percentage of national income coming from industry and construction jumped from 4 percent in 1938 to 16 percent in 1950 and 53 percent in 1970)[55] almost certainly helped legitimize these regimes by creating large classes of people whose upward mobility gave them a stake in the system. The principal external economic threat to development affecting Balkan foreign policy in the postwar period was formed by the Soviet integration plan, which the Romanians successfully resisted on the grounds that it would stifle their own industrialization. Even for Romania, though, the Soviet Union has presented an opportunity to obtain vital raw material imports. (For example, despite Soviet opposition to the Galati steel complex, they have still supplied most of Romania's coke and iron ore.) This advantage of exchanging generally lower quality industrial goods for vital raw materials is even more pronounced for Bulgaria, which lacks Romania's rich oil resources. And Bulgaria's political loyalty has been rewarded by high Soviet aid relative to the rest of East Europe.[56] Albania's realignments to the Soviet Union and to the PRC also brought economic opportunity. After the Cominform crisis, Freedman's study showed that while "the USSR was extracting resources from the other East European nations in the form of raw materials and machinery, it was extending economic assistance to Albania and compelling its satellites to do so as well."[57] The PRC also supplied substantial aid to Albania following her break with the Soviet Union, much to the chagrin of the post-Mao leadership. Albania's recent break with the PRC, however, indicates that Hoxha decided that the opportunity for economic aid from a patron was not sufficient to offset the political benefits of his own brand of isolation. Somewhat similarly, Yugoslavia has received large amounts of aid from both East and West (substantially more from the West), but her strong pursuit of nonalignment indicates that she values economic aid less than political independence and stature.[58] In sum, with the exception of massive Soviet exploitation under Stalin, external sources of support seem to represent more of an opportunity than a threat to the Balkan countries, through the provision of either aid or vital imports, especially energy and raw material products.[59]

The implementation of decentralization reforms to win domestic support is not a popular strategy in the Balkans. Yugoslavia is by far the most liberal communist country in the world, but the other three have retained essentially orthodox Stalinist internal polities. For Yugoslavia, reform, if more than marginally related to foreign policy, is probably more a consequence than a cause since the break with Stalin resulted in a radical reappraisal of what domestic policies were consistent with true communism rather than Stalinist bureaucracy.[60] In Bulgaria, too, external penetration by the Soviet Union appears a prime determinant of domestic orthodoxy. Hoxha's brand of Stalinism, in contrast, evidently influenced the Albanian external reorientations away from the Soviet Union and the PRC when first one and then the other began to follow a different political tack.

Finally, the domestic orthodoxy of Dej and Ceausescu in Romania seems related only indirectly to foreign policy specifically, except for the possibility that foreign policy appeals to nationalism have been substituted for internal concessions as a means for maintaining political loyalty. In fact, Romanian independence from the Soviet Union in foreign policy has been accompanied by an emulation of the Soviet domestic system, presumably because it is in the interest of Ceausescu's maintenance of power. To the degree that this domestic orthodoxy provides Ceausescu with both domestic support and a unified party with which to resist Soviet pressure, foreign and domestic policy are related, though not in the expected direction.

CONCLUSIONS

The wide variation in the foreign policy of the four Balkan states certainly validates Gitelman's contention about the need for developing a truly comparative theoretical approach to analyzing East European foreign policies.[61] As argued here, Rosenau's linkage theory appears very suggestive for delineating the central variables in such a framework. This "linkage perspective" views Balkan foreign policy as deriving from a combination of internal and external factors: the domestic strength and policy goals of the four regimes, intraparty factional conflicts, and the types of foreign forces that were brought to bear upon these regimes. In many cases, competing factions set the dominant tone in domestic and foreign policy by appealing to (or fighting against) external power bases. A sketch of some internal-external linkages was presented in Figure 2.2, and this model was then applied to the foreign policies of the four Balkan Communist states with special reference to Rosenau's types of adaptation strategies. The Balkan experiences also indicated that modification and expansion of Rosenau's typology might be in order.

The model in Figure 2.2 is built around the political power needs of the East European elites. This variable is viewed as a function of both domestic support and pressures emanating from the international environment. Power position, in turn, affects foreign policy both directly and indirectly through domestic policies, which possess foreign policy implications. The Balkan nations differ substantially in terms of the various posited external and internal factors, and these variables go far in explaining the major differences that evolved in the Balkan states' external orientations.

One notable change in these relationships over time has been in the relative impact of the direct and indirect effects of power needs upon foreign policy. Initially, all the regimes were fairly weak except Yugoslavia, and here the Cominform crisis certainly put Tito's position on the line. Under these conditions, power considerations were quite salient and exerted a direct impact upon foreign policy. The political situations in the Balkans have since become much more stable as there have been no leadership changes since the mid-1960s. Thus, as these regimes' positions have become much less precarious, the links between power variables and foreign policy have changed from primarily direct to indirect (although succession crises, especially in Yugoslavia, might change this). The decline of direct threats to regime existence has also been vital to Romanian and Albanian foreign policy since the early 1960s. Albania's conflicts with the Soviet Union and the PRC could only have been carried out in the absence of direct military threats, while Romania's partial alignment has demonstrated a fairly wide latitude of Soviet tolerance for Romania's independent actions.

The Balkan histories also confirm the impression of declining Soviet potency in its East European relations. During Stalin's "Soviet embassy" system of ruling East Europe, there was little room for independent action, except for excommunicated Yugoslavia. With the loosening of the Soviet bonds after Stalin's death, Albania and Romania used the new reactive linkages to proclaim their independence (in quite different degrees) from the regional hegemon, while Bulgaria, in contrast, remained penetrated and subservient. As Romania's continued application of Soviet orthodoxy in domestic politics shows, furthermore, emulation does not necessarily denote direct influence. Yugoslavia and Romania are also quite distinctive from the rest of East Europe in their attempts to influence the character of the international environment rather than be penetrated by or simply react to a dominant foreign center. This also differs from Albania's independence-through-isolation policy. Thus, the Yugoslav and Romanian experiences suggest adding another category to Rosenau's typology of linkage relationships—"initiating linkages"—to describe such situations. Again, the Balkan regimes appear worthy of being considered individual actors in the international system, responding to differing pressures and opportunities in their internal and external environments as they pursue their own idiosyncratic objectives.

NOTES

1. Hugh Seton-Watson, The Pattern of Communist Revolution (London: Methuen, 1953), pp. 248-56, presents a typology of the stages in communist takeovers. For a more detailed political history of this period, see Zbigniew K. Brzezinski, The Soviet Bloc:

Unity and Conflict (Cambridge, Mass.: Harvard University Press, 1967), chaps. 1-7; and Hugh Seton-Watson, The East European Revolution (New York: Praeger, 1956).

2. Adam Ulam, Titoism and the Cominform (Cambridge, Mass.: Harvard University Press, 1951); and Vladimir Dedijer, The Battle Stalin Lost: Memoirs of Yugoslavia, 1948-1953 (New York: Viking Press, 1971), give excellent discussions of the Cominform break.

3. Robert L. Farlow, "Romanian Foreign Policy: A Case of Partial Alignment," Problems of Communism (December 1971).

4. Cal Clark and Robert L. Farlow, Comparative Patterns of Foreign Policy and Trade: The Communist Balkans in International Politics (Bloomington: International Development Research Center, Indiana University, 1976), provides a comparative treatment of these four foreign policies focusing upon the relationship between foreign trade and foreign policy.

5. William R. Kintner and Wolfgang Klaiber, Eastern Europe and European Security (New York: Dunellen Press, 1971); Ronald Haly Linden, Bear and Foxes: The International Relations of the East European States, 1965-1969 (Boulder, Colo.: East European Quarterly and Columbia University Press, 1979); and William C. Potter, "Innovation in East European Foreign Policies," in The Foreign Policy of Eastern Europe: Domestic and International Determinants, ed. James A. Kuhlman (Leyden: Sijthoff, 1978), contain major quantitative studies. For diplomatic-historical analyses, see Brzezinski, op. cit.; Robin Alison Remington, The Warsaw Pact: Case Studies in Communist Conflict Resolution (Cambridge, Mass.: MIT Press, 1971); Francois Fetjo, A History of the People's Democracies (New York: Praeger, 1971); and Ghita Ionescu, The Break-up of the Soviet Empire in Eastern Europe (Baltimore, Md.: Penguin, 1965).

6. James N. Rosenau, "Toward the Study of National-International Linkages," pp. 307-39 in James N. Rosenau, The Scientific Study of Foreign Policy (New York: Free Press, 1971).

7. For example, Myron Rush, Political Succession in the USSR (New York: Columbia University Press, 1965).

8. For a summary of this period, see Nicholas C. Pano, The People's Republic of Albania (Baltimore, Md.: Johns Hopkins University Press, 1968), pp. 26-58.

9. William E. Griffith, Albania and the Sino-Soviet Rift (Cambridge, Mass.: MIT Press, 1963), pp. 12-14.

10. Ibid., pp. 14-21; and Pano, op. cit., pp. 60-87.

11. Pano, op. cit., p. 108. "With the exception of East Germany, Albania was the only satellite state which by 1952 did not possess a treaty of mutual assistance with the Soviet Union. Soviet-Albanian relations were still conducted at the ministerial level."

12. Ibid., pp. 111-17; and Griffith, op. cit., pp. 22-24.

13. Griffith, op. cit., p. 90. Khrushchev claimed after the Soviet-Albanian break that the Soviet Union had objected also to the execution of Uri Gega while she was pregnant.

14. Ibid., pp. 24-32; and Pano, op. cit., pp. 117-34.

15. Pano, op. cit., p. 135.

16. For a comprehensive study of this period, see Griffith, op. cit., chaps. 2-4. Also, see Pano, op. cit., pp. 135-57.

17. Griffith, op. cit., chap. 5; and Pano, op. cit., pp. 157-58. Another stark indicator of Albania's radical reorientation of foreign policy is trade: in 1960, 54 percent of her trade was with the Soviet Union and 7 percent with the PRC; in 1962, it was 0 percent and 50 percent, respectively.

18. Griffith, op. cit., pp. 168-70; Nicholas C. Pano, "The Evolution of Albanian Foreign Policy: The 1960's" (Paper presented at the Northwest Slavic Conference, Montreal, May 5-8, 1971); and Peter R. Prifti, "Albania's Expanding Horizons," Problems of Communism (January-February 1972).

19. Nicholas C. Pano, "Albania," in Communism in Eastern Europe, ed. Teresa Rakowska-Harmstone and Andrew Gyorgy (Bloomington: Indiana University Press, 1979), p. 210.

20. J. F. Brown, Bulgaria Under Communist Rule (New York: Praeger, 1970), chap. 1. For a more detailed analysis of the pre-war Communist Party, see Joseph Rothschild, The Communist Party of Bulgaria: Origins and Development, 1888-1936 (New York: Columbia University Press, 1959); and Nissan Oren, Bulgarian Communism: The Road to Power, 1934-1944 (New York: Columbia University Press, 1971).

21. Brown, op. cit., pp. 20-24.

22. Ibid., chaps. 2-8; Robert R. King, Minorities Under Communism: Nationalities as a Source of Tension among Balkan Communist States (Cambridge, Mass.: Harvard University Press, 1973), pp. 58-68, 187-99; and Nissan Oren, Revolution Administered: Agrarianism and Communism in Bulgaria (Baltimore, Md.: Johns Hopkins University Press, 1973), pp. 69-70, 104-5, 135-47.

23. Brown, op. cit., chaps 6, 8.

24. Ibid., pp. 283-88. For example, Bulgaria was the only Eastern bloc country besides Romania not to send an official negative response to Erhard's "peace note" of March 1966. The quantitative analysis of Linden, op. cit., chaps. 2 and 3, for 1965-69 found that while Bulgaria ranked high on the conformity of her attitudes about international affairs, she deviated much more in terms of interactions with various areas of the world.

25. F. Stephen Larrabee, "On the Eve of the 10th BCP Party Congress: Problems and Prospects," Radio Free Europe Research (April 16, 1971): 13-15; and Brown, op. cit., pp. 287-97.

26. Stephen Fischer-Galati, The New Rumania: From People's Democracy to Socialist Republic (Cambridge, Mass.: MIT Press, 1967), p. vii.

27. For a summary of the development of the RCP through 1952, see ibid., chaps. 1, 2.

28. Ibid., chap. 3.

29. R. V. Burks, "The Rumanian National Deviation: An Accounting," in Eastern Europe in Transition, ed. Kurt London (Baltimore, Md.: Johns Hopkins University Press, 1966), pp. 97-100.

30. John Michael Montias, Economic Development in Communist Rumania (Cambridge, Mass.: MIT Press, 1967), chap. 4, provides an excellent analysis of Romania's struggle against expanding CMEA's supranational power and freezing the East European division of labor.

31. Clark and Farlow, op. cit., pp. 49-55. For example, Western trade jumped from 15 percent to 25 percent of Romania's total trade between 1955 and 1963.

32. Fischer-Galati, op. cit., pp. 100-3. For text in English, see William E. Griffith, Sino-Soviet Relations, 1964-1965 (Cambridge, Mass.: MIT Press, 1967), pp. 269-96.

33. In foreign affairs, the Soviet Union was attacked for her past interference in Romanian affairs; the RCP strenuously opposed further economic and military integration in the bloc; relations were greatly improved with "deviant" socialist states as Romania became a neutral in the Sino-Soviet dispute; economic and political ties to the West were greatly strengthened; and, most spectacularly, Romania was the only Warsaw Pact member not to participate in the invasion of Czechoslovakia, even experiencing some fears of invasion herself. Regarding internal affairs, Kenneth Jowitt, Revolutionary Breakthroughs: The Case of Romania, 1944-1965 (Berkeley: University of California Press, 1971), constructs a most insightful model of the development of the RCP's domestic policies.

34. J. T. Crawford and John Haberstroh, "Survey of Economic Policy Issues in Eastern Europe: Technology, Trade, and the Consumer," in Joint Economic Committee, Reorientation and Commercial Relations of the Economies of Eastern Europe (Washington, D.C.: Government Printing Office, 1974), p. 37.

35. Ronald H. Linden, "Romanian Foreign Policy in the 1980's," mimeographed, 1979.

36. Ivan Avakumovic, History of the Communist Party of Yugoslavia (Aberdeen: Aberdeen University Press, 1964).

37. A. Ross Johnson, The Transformation of Communist Ideology: The Yugoslav Case, 1945-1953 (Cambridge, Mass.: MIT Press, 1972); and M. George Zaninovich, "The Yugoslav Variation

on Marx," in Contemporary Yugoslavia: Twenty Years of Socialist Experiment, ed. Wayne S. Vucinich (Berkeley: University of California Press, 1969).

38. See John C. Campbell, Tito's Separate Road (New York: Harper & Row, 1967), for a good summary of this phase of Yugoslav foreign policy.

39. Robin Alison Remington, "Yugoslavia," in Rakowska-Harmstone and Gyorgy, op. cit., pp. 238-40.

40. Alvin Z. Rubinstein, Yugoslavia and the Nonaligned World (Princeton, N.J.: Princeton University Press, 1970), provides the best summary of the evolution of Yugoslavia's policy of nonalignment.

41. For an exposition of the principles of nonalignment, see ibid.; Johnson, op. cit.; and John Geoffrey Peters, "Yugoslav Foreign Policy Toward the Nonaligned World" (Ph.D. diss., American University, 1970).

42. Both these upheavals, though, appear to be primarily the result of domestic factors. See Dennison Rusinow, The Yugoslav Experiment, 1948-1974 (Berkeley: University of California Press, 1977), chaps. 5-8.

43. Alvin Z. Rubinstein, "Whither Yugoslavia?" Current History (May 1973): 202-3.

44. Wladyslaw W. Kulski, The Soviet Union in World Affairs: A Documented Analysis, 1964-72 (Durham, N.C.: Duke University Press, 1974), pp. 297-98.

45. William Zimmerman, "Dependency Theory and the Soviet-East European Hierarchical Regional System," Slavic Review (December 1978); and Cal Clark and Donna Bahry, "Dependency in the Soviet Bloc: A Reversal of the Economic-Political Nexus" (Paper presented at the Annual Convention of the International Studies Association, Toronto, March 20-24, 1979).

46. James N. Rosenau, The Adaptation of National Societies: A Theory of Political System Behavior and Transformation (New York: McCaleb-Seiler, 1970). Also see Patrick J. McGowan and Klaus-Peter Gottwald, "Small State Foreign Policies," International Studies Quarterly (December 1975), for further conceptual elaboration of these four policy types.

47. Rosenau, "Toward the Study of National-International Linkages," pp. 318-22.

48. Potter, op. cit., p. 260, presents a fairly similar model of three elements, which he labels "operational environment," "psychological environment," and "adaptation strategy."

49. These two policies are suggested by the insightful discussion of political legitimacy in East Europe by Zvi Gitelman, "Power and Authority in Eastern Europe," in Change in Communist

Systems, ed. Chalmers Johnson (Stanford, Calif.: Stanford University Press, 1970), and by Alfred Meyer, "Legitimacy of Power in East Central Europe," in Eastern Europe in the 1970's, ed. Sylvia Sinanian, Istvan Deak, and Peter C. Ludz (New York: Praeger, 1972). Gitelman argues that "national performance: and "authentic participation" represent two major legitimacy motifs of communist regimes in response to their inevitable "authority crises." Performance and conformity to national culture are two of the primary criteria discussed by Meyer.

50. Walter D. Connor, Socialism, Politics, and Equality (New York: Columbia University Press, 1978).

51. Richard Herrmann, "Comparing World Views in Eastern Europe: Contemporary Polish Perceptions," Chapter 3 in this volume.

52. For example, see Milovan Djilas, Conversations with Stalin (New York: Harcourt, Brace, 1962).

53. Patrick J. McGowan, "Adaptive Foreign Policy Behavior: An Empirical Approach," in Comparing Foreign Policies: Theories, Findings, and Methods, ed. James N. Rosenau (New York: Halsted Press, 1974).

54. King, op. cit., shows that the imposition of the socialist commonwealth has not eradicated these hostilities.

55. Pano, "Albania," p. 204.

56. Clark and Farlow, op. cit., chap. 8.

57. Robert Owen Freedman, Economic Warfare in the Communist Bloc (New York: Praeger, 1970), p. 60.

58. Stephen C. Markovich, "American Foreign Aid and Yugoslav Foreign Policy," in From the Cold War to Detente, ed. Peter J. Potichnyj and Jane P. Shapiro (New York: Praeger, 1976).

59. Paul Marer, "Has Eastern Europe Become a Liability to the Soviet Union—The Economic Aspects," in The International Politics of Eastern Europe, ed. Charles Gati (New York: Praeger, 1976); Clark and Bahry, op. cit. discuss the relationship between terms of trade and commodity composition in Soviet-East European trade.

60. Johnson, op. cit. describes this ideological transformation.

61. Zvi Gitelman, "Toward a Comparative Foreign Policy of Eastern Europe," in Potichnyj and Shapiro, op. cit.

3

COMPARING WORLD VIEWS IN EAST EUROPE: CONTEMPORARY POLISH PERCEPTIONS

Richard K. Herrmann

Like most of the literature analyzing the foreign policy of states, studies of the foreign policies of East European states, whether focused individually or comparatively, have relied heavily upon Western scholars' descriptions and interpretations of these states' international positions and upon these same analysts' views of the options and prospects available to policy makers. Though these views have offered valuable insights on a number of signifi- cant issues, for example, European security, relations with the Soviet Union, integration among the Socialist states, and relations with Western countries, these studies have rarely made efforts to examine systematically how various East European states interpret their own situation and options.[1] Students of the subject have tended to derive the contemporary viewpoint of the East Europeans more from historical projection than from contemporaneous em- pirical research.[2] As Charles Gati describes it, the focus has been primarily on " 'the view from the outside,' that is, how East Europe is perceived rather than 'the view from the inside,' meaning how East Europe perceives the outside world. "[3]

Whatever the limitations on the formulation of foreign policies in the East European states, it is the East European leaders them- selves who must formulate and execute these policies, based on

I am appreciative for a three-month travel and study grant from the University Center for International Studies at the Univer- sity of Pittsburgh and the University of Pittsburgh's exchange pro- gram with the Polish Institute of International Affairs which allowed me to study in Poland in April-June 1977.

their perceptions of the international circumstances and their options within them. Therefore, it may be fruitful and important to study their interpretations and understandings of political "reality." This chapter will outline an approach to the study of the foreign policies of the East European states based on an analysis of these perceptions and applicable to empirical work both on individual countries and in comparative inquiry.

The present work will discuss the use of <u>perceptual analysis</u> in the study of the foreign policies of the East European states and, in doing so, will comment on the usefulness of examining perceptions and suggest an approach to the study of these perceptions. To illustrate the approach, the essay will describe several contemporary Polish points of view, or perceptions, of two key countries: the Soviet Union and the Federal Republic of Germany. Beyond the empirical task of establishing these differing perceptions, this work will endeavor to connect these and the analysis that yields them to the broader context of Polish foreign policy. Thus, in the final section, an interpretive outline of contemporary Polish foreign policy based on perceptual analysis will be presented as an example of the judgments that might be inferred from a study of perceptions.

THE STUDY OF PERCEPTION IN FOREIGN POLICY ANALYSIS

Why bother analyzing perceptions at all? The answer to this question is offered by the place the study of perceptions occupies in the broader analysis of foreign policy. One of the major problems in analyzing foreign policy is the interpretation of motivation. Motivational attribution (that is, the imputing of certain motives or goals to foreign policy actors) is perhaps the key assumptional base from which a state's foreign policy is interpreted and understood in a politically meaningful context. A state's policy can be described, but, if it is to be understood and presumably responded to, a causal motivation must be determined that allows for the predictions of trends and actions. Therefore, a major question in the study of foreign policy seems to be, how can motivation be inferred from empirical evidence rather than simply postulated? Further, how can we move beyond both the implicit attribution of foreign policy motives as "common sense" or "natural" and the monocausal theoretical assumptions of state actions as being based on power, economic interest, messianism, or defense? What is needed is a method of inferring motivation that is empirically derived and does not rest on a monocausal theoretical assumption nomothetically applied.

The present approach to the problem of motivational inference in foreign policy analysis is founded on the study of perceptions. Perception is defined here as the construction of the reality in which foreign policy decisions are made. The concept of perception can be used in the inference of motivation by defining the concept so that it is easily connected to the major attribution of defensive or imperialistic motives. This can be accomplished by defining sets of indicators that suggest and discriminate between perceptions of threat and perceptions of opportunity. By applying the operational indicators to the actions of a state one might be able to infer the predominance of certain perceptions of threat or opportunity and thereby have a basis for suggesting a general motivational scheme for the state's foreign policy.

The perceptual approach to the study of foreign policy motivation that I will employ operates at two distinct levels of analysis. First, the approach aims to identify and describe the various and competing world views held by elite spokesmen in a state. Secondly, the approach attempts to identify and describe the prevailing world view in the state, that is, the view that is most harmonious with the state's actual strategic actions. By comparing the resemblance of the different competitive world views with the prevailing view, the approach seeks to identify empirically the spokesmen who apparently exert the greatest influence in formulating the state's foreign policy.

This dual-level perceptual analysis yields two empirical bases for the inference of a motivational system that best describes the state's foreign policy. First, by examining the perceptions of prevailing spokesmen, one can determine if they are operating from a vision of threat or opportunity with respect to the policy toward a foreign state. From this perceptual analysis one can then infer whether the state's policy toward the foreign state is primarily directed by defensive or imperialistic (opportunistic) motives. Second, by identifying the prevailing spokesmen's role and key values, more specific motives can be attributed to the state's foreign policy. For example, if economic elites apparently prevail over the state's policy toward a specific foreign country, motives such as vested interest in trade, investment, or resources, might be imputed. Should ideological or religious elites prevail, messianism might be a probable motive; and if governmental or military spokesmen prevail, bureaucratic vested interests or national power would be a likely motivational attribution.

In this chapter I will concentrate on analyzing competitive world views and presenting a scheme for the analysis of perceptions. I will employ the perceptual scheme to describe and analyze (infer perceived threat and perceived opportunity) competitive Polish spokesmen's views of the Soviet Union and of the Federal Republic of Germany. This will illustrate how the analysis of competitive world views might be coupled with a study of prevailing views to yield both empirically derived patterns of influence and a basis for the construction of a motivational outline of Polish foreign policy. Since the major focus will be upon the analysis of Polish percep- tions, the concluding sections illustrating the broader scheme for foreign policy analysis will be brief and designed simply to highlight the possible resultant output (that is, an empirically derived moti- vational outline) of perceptual analysis.

There are several well-known methods of studying percep- tions,[4] including operational coding,[5] belief systems and attitudinal study,[6] and cognitive mapping.[7] The approach to perception that I will suggest follows a tradition that rests on the notions of "image" and "stereotypes."[8]

The most explicit and clear presentation of this approach is Richard Cottam's Foreign Policy Motivation,[9] although others, such as W. Gamson and A. Modigliani, have also developed the notion of using perception to infer motivation.[10]

The approach employed here rests on the Gestalt assumption that people tend to simplify and organize the world they sense and see into whole images.[11] Since I assume that a person's view of a foreign country will tend toward a whole image, I posit four per- ceptual concepts that can be grouped into patterns and then used to describe this complex psychological phenomenon. The four con- cepts are (1) perception of threat; (2) perception of opportunity; (3) perception of cultural differences; and (4) perception of capabil- ity differences.[12] In this study the following perceptual patterns will be used as ideal types to serve as referents in the empirical identification, description, and measurement of the actual points of view of salient political spokesmen in the European countries. In other words, the following four patterns are posited as "ideal" extreme views, which act as identification points or parameters with which one can compare the actual views held by various East European spokesmen.

The Enemy Image. A perception of threat from a state perceived to have similar capability and as possessing a culture of com- parable quality.[13]

The Ally Image. A perception of opportunity derived from coopera- tion with a state that is perceived to have similar capability and as possessing a culture of comparable quality.

The Hegemonic Enemy Image. Primarily a perception of threat from a country that is perceived as overwhelmingly more power- ful, yet culturally inferior.

<u>The Hegemonic Ally View</u>. Primarily a perception of opportunity
   from a country that is perceived as overwhelmingly more powerful and culturally inferior.

   To derive operational indicators for each ideal perceptual
pattern, I will rely on a basic psychological theory suggested by
Fritz Heider and commonly known as "balance theory."[14] Trans-
lating Heider's balance theory, I will assume that perception of
threat and perception of opportunity are mutually interdependent
with those characteristics a subject consciously recognizes as descriptive of the object perceived. At the level of international
politics, I assume that a subject's perception of threat or perception of opportunity from a foreign country will tend toward a harmonious, balanced state with the descriptive characteristics the
subject consciously associates with the state. In other words, a
subject's conscious descriptive picture of a foreign state will tend
toward a "balanced condition" that will allow the subject to respond
vigorously to perceived threat and perceived opportunity—even with
actions normally considered reprehensible—without feeling uncom-
fortable or guilty about his or her actions. In this chapter I con-
tend that it is possible to construct deductively the "stereotype"
that would be a balanced conscious description for each ideal typical
perceptual pattern. Consequently, to operationalize each ideal
pattern I will present a stereotype and stereotypical strategic
choice of action which follows from the image held. A subject's
perception of a foreign country will therefore be inferred by first
examining both his description of the country and the strategy for
dealing with the country that the subject advocates. These are then
compared to the stereotypical patterns. The logic of this perceptual
approach and the relevant perceptual patterns are summarized in
Table 3.1.
   In order to evaluate the tendency of a person's perceptions
to approach the stereotypical patterns outlined in Table 3.1, it is
necessary to establish an operational pattern that will serve as a
base point from which tendencies toward the stereotypes can be
gauged. It will label this base point "complex."[15] Like the stereotypes, the complex pattern is not assumed to be reality but only a
description of a view that is sufficiently complex to prevent the
clear identification of any single stereotypical pattern. The operational characteristics of the complex pattern as described by
Richard Cottam are systematized across four dimensions and
include:

<u>Motivation</u>. Individuals holding "complex" perceptual patterns will
   grant the observed government motivational complexity. There

will be little tendency to ascribe a judgment of good or bad to the policy thrust associated with motivations. Defense is likely to be perceived as a significant aspect of motivation.

Capability. Capability judgments will be made on the basis of empirical estimates of industrial and resource base, armed forces, equipment, and training rather than on estimates of aggressive will and cunning from which power advantage derives.

Style and Decisional Locus. A highly diversified decisional process will be seen, with decisions made incrementally rather than coldly rationally in accordance with a detailed and preordained plan.

Domestic Forces Interaction. Those domestic compatriots and political competitors of the subject who disagree with the subject's description of the target foreign government will be described by the subject in complex motivational terms and as patriots.[16]

TABLE 3.1

Summary of the Logic behind the Perceptual Approach

Concepts	Deductive Logic	Operational Indicators
Perceptual patterns	Psychological balance theory	Stereotypical descriptions and strategic choices
If this pattern is a good description of the subject's view of of a foreign state	then	The subject will consciously use this descriptive stereotype and make this strategic choice
Threat Similar capability Comparable culture		Enemy
Threat Greater capability Inferior culture		Hegemonic enemy
Opportunity Similar capability Comparable culture		Ally
Opportunity Greater opportunity Inferior culture		Hegemonic ally

Source: Constructed by the author.

An operational stereotype and strategic choice has been deduced for each of the four ideal typical perceptual patterns. As noted, balance theory provides the central guide to this deductive process, and consequently the set of operational indicators for the ally patterns are designed to be harmonious with a subject's inclination to seize fully the perceived opportunity. Similarly the operational indicators for the enemy patterns are designed to be harmonious with a subject's inclination to respond vigorously to the perceived threat.

The following are the ideal typical patterns, the operational indications, or what the holder of such a view says about the target state, and the strategic choice of action that flows from this image.

The Ally Image

Theoretical pattern: perceived opportunity; perceived similar capability; perceived comparable culture.

Operational Indicators:

(a) Stereotype:

Motivation: Represented in a rather simple fashion focusing only on a defensive motive. In addition, there is a willingness to judge quickly the observed state's motives to be benign, justified, and morally good.

Capability: Described as superior to that which empirical study might indicate, emphasizing the additional strength accruing from the good will, skill, and morale of the leadership and from the popular public support the government enjoys.

Decisional style: Presented with a degree of complexity and with an appreciation of the incremental nature of decision making and of the limitations this has on quick planning and expedient execution of policy.

Decisional locus: Described as a diversified assembly of a variety of dissimilar decisional elements representing a complex assortment of different and often competitive or contradictory interests and world views.

Description of domestic opposition: People adhering to this perceptual pattern will describe those in their own state who disagree with their view of the observed state as traitors, as possible agents of a foreign power, and as attempting to weaken the defense of the home state by sowing discord between itself and the states which are its partners in the common cause of defense.

(b) Strategic Choice:

The strategic choice for this pattern is <u>alliance</u> and active <u>military and economic cooperation</u>. It includes mutual cooperation in order to expand all aspects of the power bases of both the target state and the home state. It advocates building the capability of both states similarly.

The Enemy Image

Theoretical Pattern: perceived threat; perceived similar capability; perceived comparable culture.

Operational Indicators:

(a) Stereotype:

Motivation: Represented in an extremely simple fashion (usually a monocausal explanation will be advanced) emphasizing the aggressive drive for expansion and power. In this pattern there is a quick and convinced judgment that the motives of the observed state are evil and unjustified.

Capability: Described as a derivative of the weakness of one's own state. In other words, the observed state derives strength from other's weakness and if directly met with strong opposition will be exposed as an inherently weak "paper tiger."

Decisional style: Described as extremely rational and conspiratorial; able to plot in advance and execute sinister plans of enormous complexity.

Decisional locus: Depicted as a complete monolith united in common cause.

Description of domestic opposition: People holding this pattern will describe those who disagree with their view of the observed state as traitors and suspect of being "agents" of the foreign observed state.

(b) Strategic Choice:

The strategic choice is "containment" and seeks through coalition construction to isolate the enemy state in world politics and surround it by states allied to the observer's state. The strategy calls for consolidating and increasing all dimensions of potential power, in order to build superior capability with respect to the enemy. To make the home state stronger and able to defeat without unacceptable damage any potential attack the enemy might conceivably launch by maximizing at any expense all of the home state's capabilities and by actively seeking to destroy, hinder, limit, constrain, and in every way minimize all of the enemy's capabilities

The Hegemonic Enemy Image

Theoretical Pattern: perceived threat; perceived greater capability; perceived inferior culture.

Operational Indicators:

(a) Stereotype:

Motivation: Described in very simple terms as aggressively imperialistic and expansionistic and immediately judged as immoral and absolutely evil. The primary motive of the state is described as the desired exploitation of the observer's own state's resources, and transformation of his nation into a pliant destroyed people ready to be assimilated easily into the larger state's hegemonic sphere. The state is characterized as possessing an inferior culture and as aiming to destroy the superior culture of the observer's own state so as to facilitate assimilation.

Capability: Described as superior to that which empirical study might indicate, emphasizing the presence of overt military forces and covert coercive agents as well as the leverage accruing from the observer's own government's political dependence upon the observed state and from its forced economic and technological "integration."

Decisional style: Described as rational and conspiratorial; able to plot and execute well-constructed plans to efficiently further its aims with masterful sophistication and deceit.

Decisional locus: Seen as a hierarchal monolith with only a handful of persons at the top and a highly obedient rigid "machine" throughout the rest of the state (each element of which only plans its designated role in carrying out the decisions reached by those above).

Description of domestic opposition: The observer will describe those who disagree with his description as morally weak and lacking in integrity, willing to sacrifice the culture, traditions, and dignity of the nation for personal material gain and career success.

(b) Strategic Choice:

The strategy calls for the mobilization of national resistance and, in time, the simultaneous revolt of all of the nationalities and states controlled within the empire of the observed state. The strategy calls for the resistance of all efforts to assimilate the country and its culture into the superpower's culture and political system. The maintenance and continued existence of the national culture and identity is posited as absolutely central in the long-term resistance to assimilation.

The Hegemonic Ally Image

Theoretical Pattern: perceived opportunity; perceived greater capability; perceived inferior culture.

Operational Indicators:

(a) Stereotype:

Motivation: Described in very simple terms. It is seen as selflessly devoted to the promotion of peace and prosperity and is very quickly judged to be morally good. The observed state is labeled as a "great" or "leading" ally that accepts significant self-sacrifice in order to ensure that the observer's state is secure, free, and prosperous. The state is described as selfless and as offering disinterested assistance out of a humane internationalist concern.

Capability: The most distinguishing element of this view is that it describes the observed state as providing absolutely vital assistance to the observer's own state. The "fraternal ally" is described as responsible and unquestionably necessary for the survival and prosperity of the observer's state. The capability is described as somewhat greater than empirical indicators may suggest, owing to the goodness and justness of the people and the government.

Decisional style: Defined as democratic, as clearly expressing the overwhelmingly popular will of the people, and as basically practical and reality-oriented, if somewhat unsophisticated and lacking in forethought and complexity.

Decisional locus: Identified as highly diversified and as encompassing the expression of the popular will of all of the people.

Description of domestic opposition: Labeled as traitors and paid agents of an enemy superpower promoting that enemy's imperialism and their own potential dictatorship and tyranny.

These opponents are described as self-interested demagogues, having no real following and as constituting only a very tiny radical fringe.

(b) Strategic Choice:

The strategic choice is total alignment and commitment to the observed superpower and maximum cooperation politically, militarily, and economically.

By using these ideal type perceptual patterns as referents, a mapping scheme can be devised to facilitate the representation and comparison of the perceptions of various spokesmen. Further, by mapping a spokesman's perception of several states on one graph, a systemic picture of that spokesman's "world view" is presented. The mapping scheme thus illustrates various spokesmen's relative perceptual tendencies as derived from the extent to which their descriptions and strategic choices approach the referent stereotypes. A subject's perceptions are presented by plotting his or her tendencies toward the ideal patterns along the various lines defined by the center point ("complex") and the ideal typical poles. An actual subject's perception of a country is very unlikely to tend toward just one ideal typical pattern and will probably include aspects of at least two images and some dimensions of the complex pattern. Consequently, most spokesmen's perceptions will be mapped in the quadrant defined by the complex center point and the two stereotyped images. For example, if a subject's perception of a state resembles the hegemonic enemy image yet also includes aspects of the enemy image, this would be mapped near point 1 in Figure 3.1. If, on the other hand, the subject's perception most closely resembles the enemy image but has some aspects of the hegemonic enemy image (for example, reflecting a perception of somewhat greater capability but not hegemonic) it would be mapped near point 2 in Figure 3.1.

FIGURE 3.1

Mapping Scheme for Perceptual Patterns

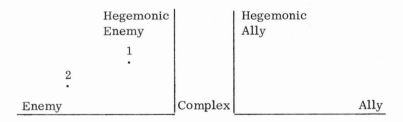

AN ANALYSIS OF POLISH WORLD VIEWS

The period 1977-78 is particularly auspicious for studying the politically competitive "world views" of various Poles. During this time a number of factors coalesced to bring the basic assumptions on which Poland's international position rests into visible debate. In 1976, the government's efforts to include a clause in the Polish constitution formally recognizing Poland's membership in the Socialist community and Poland's fraternal alliance with the Soviet Union not only provoked significant opposition but also seemed to bring into question the implicit assumption that there was a basic agreement among the Poles on the country's international position and its fundamental foreign policy aims.

While the constitutional debate perhaps sensitized the attentive public in Poland to the potential differences in foreign policy aims, the political argument remained primarily an elite phenomenon. In the summer of 1976, however, the government attempted to insitute a rather dramatic increase in prices that sparked an angry reaction among urban industrial workers.[17] The political force of the strikes and violence that erupted in June brought about a speedy rescission of the price increases which effectively deflated a large part of the immediate political action (although not dissatisfaction) revolving around standard-of-living issues. The social disturbances seemed to stimulate enough political uncertainty in the government to allow the already sensitized attentive elite, both secular and Catholic, which had sympathized with the worker's economic dissatisfaction and had been repulsed by the brutality of the government's retaliation, to engage the government in debate on fundamental political and social issues.

As the debate on the causes of Poland's economic problems continued, some intellectuals moved directly to a discussion of Poland's political order and the country's international position. The intellectuals attempting to channel general economic dissatisfaction into political pressure identified the fundamental cause of Poland's economic plight as its nonliberal, nondemocratic political order and the lack of state independence with respect to the Soviet Union. Therefore, in the discussion on the "roots" of Poland's economic dilemma, very basic foreign policy issues were introduced and perceptions revealed in a growing underground information media, which had been regularly exempted from easy visibility due to government censorship. Throughout 1977 and 1978, the voicing of disparate foreign policy opinions and descriptions continued in Poland with increasing intensity.[18] Recognizably different views became visible in the legal censored media, and by late 1978 there were no less than 20 underground, or "samizdat" papers being published fairly regularly.[19]

Therefore, from sources both legal and illegal, official and unofficial, a number of distinct competing world views, or pictures of the international situation, within which Poland operates, can be discerned. The world-view patterns presented herein are "model views" describing in aggregate form the perceptions of many Poles and do not necessarily depict perceptions inferred from the descriptions and actions of any single individual. Rather, the modal views are inferred from the descriptions and policy preferences expressed by representative spokesmen for each pattern.

This chapter will seek to describe four competitive world-view patterns salient in contemporary Polish politics. I will label these four patterns: conservative Communist; reform Communist; non-Communist Catholic; and democratic-socialist. While the four world-view patterns I have chosen to study as modal views certainly present only a partial and simplified picture of the spectrum of different viewpoints being voiced in Poland today, they are designed to reflect the central perceptual differences in contemporary Polish politics. Other patterns reflecting various mixtures of the defining tendencies of the conservative Communist, reform Communist, non-Communist Catholic, and democratic-socialist views could surely be identified and based on different visible representative spokesmen. For example, the conservative Communist view may not describe well the perceptions of Poles who previously were attracted to the nationalistic Communism of Mieczyslaw Moczar and the "partisans." Since 1974, when F. Szlachcic left the Politburo, it may be more difficult to identify a visible spokesman for a nationalistic communistic world-view pattern, but certain organs within the army might be suggestive. The reform Communist pattern could also be complemented by views derived from Communists preferring significantly greater "reform," such as W. Bienkowski[20] or J. Strzelecki.[21] A variety of views might be inferred from the different Catholic-oriented spokesmen, ranging from the socialistic Pax publications, through the publications of the Polish Club of Catholic Intelligentsia (PKIK) emerging after the 1976 constitutional debate, to the original spokesmen of ZNAK, such as S. Stomma.[22] Also a world-view pattern could perhaps be inferred from the descriptions and preferences expressed by the Movement for Human and Civil Rights (ROPCO) in its journal Opinia.[23]

Before describing the four world-view patterns I have labeled conservative Communist, reform Communist, non-Communist Catholic, and democratic-socialist, it seems appropriate to identify clearly the people and sources I have used as the representative spokesmen for each view. Additionally, so as to better explain my choice of labels, it will be useful to present some of the major domestic policy choices on which the spokesmen also express clearly disparate preferences.

Conservative Communist

This world-view pattern is derived from the descriptions and policy preferences expressed in two Warsaw daily papers, Trybuna Ludu (the main organ of the Polish United Workers' Party [PUWP]) and Zycie Warszawy. The variations in presentation that appeared within these two papers was not considered significant, and a single world-view pattern inferred using both as a common "spokesman." In these two papers there seemed to be a consistent preference for strong authority in the form of centralized and unified command leadership by the PUWP as well as a significant interest in increasing production through the utilization of science and the enforcement of labor discipline. These ideal spokesmen reflected a moderate interest in the immediate material welfare of the Polish people and very little concern with liberal freedoms or tolerance. While I did not examine individuals, P. Jaroszewicz, E. Babiuch, and J. Szydlak are the prominent Polish politicians mentioned most often who seem to tend toward the conservative Communist view.

Reform Communist

This world-view pattern is derived from the descriptions and policy preferences expressed in the Polish weekly Polityka and from a number of scholars and politicians who align themselves closely and promote the views expressed in Polityka.* As a representative spokesman, Polityka generally expressed a primary interest in "rationalizing" the PUWP's leadership by introducing reforms directed from within the PUWP that would decentralize authority, introduce a good deal of flexibility into commands, and make full use of technological and managerial sciences. Polityka reflected a preference for greater but still limited liberal freedoms and expressed a significiant interest in economic welfare. I used two individuals as "spokesmen" for the reform Communist view: Mieczslaw F. Rakowski, editor-in-chief of Polityka, and Politburo member and former foreign minister Stefan Olszowski. Olszowski, although rather young, often seems to be considered a major voice of reform within the PUWP and a significant figure in Poland's effort to improve rapidly its relations and economic trade with Western Europe, and especially the FRG, in the early 1970s (when he was foreign minister).

---

*Interviewed by the author in Warsaw during the spring of 1977.

Non-Communist Catholic

This world-view pattern is derived from the descriptions and policy preferences expressed by the Primate of Poland, Cardinal Stefan Wyszynski, and from individuals who seem to follow the cardinal's guidance closely.[24] Cardinal Wyszynski and the representative spokesmen for the non-Communist Catholic view express a predominant preference for the integrity and independence of the Polish nation and the Polish nation's inseparable bond to God and Catholicism. This preference for nation and church is coupled with a significant respect for authority and firm leadership that encourages moral integrity and communal dignity. The cardinal has recently expressed a very strong preference for liberal freedom of speech, assembly, and press, as well as an interest in immediately improving the public welfare and standard of living. The cardinal appears interested in improving production but primarily as a way to raise the immediate standard of living.

Democratic-Socialist

This world-view pattern is derived from the descriptions and policy preferences expressed by the Social-Self-Defense Committee, previously the Committee for the Defense of the Workers,[25] (KSS-KOR) and three of its prominent members: Edward Lipinski,[26] Jacek Kuron,[27] and Adam Michnik.[28] The spokesmen on whom I base the Democrat-Socialist view voice a very strong preference for national independence and for parliamentary democracy with free elections and a separation of powers among the judiciary, legislature, and executive. Additionally, these spokesmen express the highest priority for liberal freedoms and tolerance and favor immediate improvements in the standard of living over maximizing production potentials.

In each of the four world-view patterns studied, it is the perceptions of two states, the Soviet Union and the Federal Republic of Germany that will be examined. For comparative purposes I will first present the different perceptions of the Soviet Union that seem to be characteristic of each world-view pattern and then do the same for the perceptions of the FRG. This analytical dissection is useful for comparative purposes but may produce some distortion since each world-view pattern is conceived of as a psychologically balanced system. Therefore, after comparing each spokesman's perceptions of the Soviet Union and the FRG, I will present a summary picture of the spokesman's overall world view.

Descriptions of the Soviet Union

Conservative Communist

In Trybuna Ludu and Zycie Warszawy, the Soviet Union is consistently described as a peace-loving and generous ally devoted to the preservation of peace and extension of the principles of Socialism and justice.[29] Throughout 1977-78, these spokesmen consistently attributed only benign, selfless, and morally correct motives to Soviet foreign policy and praised the generous Soviet support for its fraternal ally Poland. In these descriptions the Soviet Union is depicted as responsible for the emergence of modern Polish independence and as responsible for continuing Polish security and prosperity.[30] The report of the PUWP Politburo to the Second National Conference of the PUWP argued that the October Revolution and subsequent merging of national and social revolutions in Poland following World War II were the prerequisites for obtaining "unshakable guarantees of permanent independence, full sovereignty, inviolable security, and the successful development of Poland."[31]

The conservative Communist view not only describes the Soviet Union as generous and vitally responsible for Poland's security and prosperity but also makes the strategic choice of political unity and economic integration with the Soviet Union. In Zycie Warszawy, for example, Jerzy Sieradzinyki presented a rather typical formulation:

> We see the highest raison d'état and the highest national need in the strengthening of our friendship, alliance and cooperation with the fraternal Soviet Union, thanks to which Poland has saved its independence, scored a historic victory, and found reliable guarantee for its security, inviolability of its borders and peaceful development.[32]

J. Szydlak's report in Trybuna Ludu also suggests that Poland must tighten its links to the Soviet Union:

> In drawing up plans for the country's further development, we should increasingly link them to tighter cooperation with the Soviet Union and other CMEA countries. This is a basic premise for further developing Poland's economic potential, increasing its power, and strengthening its sovereignty.[33]

The PUWP Politburo not only endorses the strategy of unity with the Soviet Union but raises its promotion to a defining principle of Polish patriotism:

> Patriotism is manifested today in sound work, respon-
> sibility for the country, caring for the good name and
> future of Poland, and in bringing in closer together
> the internationalistic unity with the fraternal socialist
> nations, above all with the Soviet Nation, our chief
> ally and friend.[34]

Trybuna Ludu also endorses the strategy of cooperation with the Soviet Union and calls for "unequivocal unity" among all the parties and states in the "Communist family." In the controversial debate among European Communist parties, Trybuna Ludu made its position relatively clear in two rather long articles stating that "the movement's unity is a supreme goal."[35]

Reform Communist

In Polityka, the Soviet Union's foreign policy is consistently attributed defensive motives but is not necessarily attributed such features as generosity or selflessness. The spokesmen for the reform Communists describe the Soviet Union in terms which students of international politics might call "realist."[36] Spokesmen for this view present a picture of a Soviet Union as defending its own national interests and concerned primarily with the stable preservation of its security and economic development. In Polityka, the Soviet Union is always presented as necessary for Poland's security but not necessarily as responsible for Poland's independence or development. Usually the Soviet Union is not described by spokesmen for this view as responsible for either Poland's development or Poland's problems but is depicted as a superpower which can be a useful ally since it shares many interests with Poland. In this picture, Poland's development and political stability is in the Soviet Union's "national interest," both defensively and economically, and can help Poland greatly as long as Poland remains a faithful and "tested" ally.

The strategic choice preferred by these spokesmen is the promotion of a close security alliance with the Soviet Union and engagement in mutually beneficial economic cooperation with the Soviet Union. These spokesmen do not endorse full unity and economic integration with the Soviet Union as enthusiastically and prefer a close but "equally beneficial" set of relationships with Poland's major ally. While reform Communists do not favor the integration strategy preferred by the conservative spokesmen, they also reject the actions of "romantics," whom they see as over-emotional in blaming the Soviet Union for Poland's troubles. For example, Michal Radgowski wrote in Polityka:

> To us romanticism means a philosophical vision of history, of human fate of the fatherland. Its component is idealism, which assumes that much can be achieved by ignoring reality; in politics, this means ignoring the actual alliance of forces, and in didactics—aiming at something that far exceeds the concrete possibilities. [37]

While the spokesmen in Polityka see the Soviet Union's security interests as setting certain parameters for Poland's actions, they simultaneously express the conviction that there is ample latitude in Polish-Soviet relations to allow Poland to solve its problems efficiently and effectively and pursue self-determined national interests. In their view, the Soviet Union will accept and even encourage Poland's effort to "rationalize" its economy and introduce limited liberties as long as these reforms promote domestic stability and do not threaten to sever the fraternal tie to the Soviet Union. [38] In this regard, Polityka responded very differently than the conservative Communist spokesmen did to the Soviet attack on S. Carrillo and Eurocommunism. Polityka published a small portion of the second Novoye Vremya article on Carrillo, and the excerpt seemed to have been selected carefully; it mentioned only the Soviet's willingness to tolerate differences and the Soviet's right to defend their position when attacked.

> Faithful to the principles and policies mapped out by its 20th-25th Congresses, the CPSU has not organized and is not organizing any campaigns against fraternal parties, has not "excommunicated" anyone from the Communist movement, and is unable to do anything of the kind as this is contrary to its principles. [39]

Non-Communist Catholics

Spokesmen for this view describe the Soviet Union as an aggressive state with imperialistic motives. These spokesmen consider the Soviet Union not only as an immoral and despotic state bent on foreign domination and exploitation but also as the major contemporary symbol of evil due to its atheistic and communistic system. They describe the Soviet Union as aiming to destroy traditional Polish culture and heritage in an effort to assimilate the

Poles and absorb the Polish nation into the Russian empire. They depict the Soviet Union as purposefully attempting to devastate the Polish educational system and striving to limit the Poles from retaining a national identity so as to create a pliant and servile population that could be assimilated more easily into the Soviet state.

The picture of the Soviet Union as an imperialist state aiming to absorb the Polish people after having decimated their national consciousness and traditional heritage and culture is not openly expressed by Cardinal Wyszynski or by the censored Tygodnik Powszechny. Some of these sentiments were carefully hinted at, however, in the primate's pastoral Letter, read to the Polish nation over the Vatican's radio on October 2, 1977:

> Today, God's charity is also needed by our christened
> nation which is being led away from God's love and
> which is often doubting whether there is still justice
> between nations. Not everyone has the courage to
> claim for the nation the right to have God, the right to
> charity, the right to the freedom of conscience, to the
> history of culture and heritage. Not everyone feels the
> duty to defend so many threatened values of our Christian
> culture in regard to which attempts are being made to
> grind it in the mill of soulless materialistic dialectic.
> It is impermissible to stay silent when the national cul-
> ture, its literature and art, its Christian morality and
> the links between Poland and the Roman Church and with
> the values of the Gospel, the Cross, and the Supernatural
> forces brought to Poland are being pushed right to the
> back in the plan for the education of the young genera-
> tion. . . .
> Our dignity demands that we should resist this pre-
> sumption with which everything that is Polish is being
> treated with disregard at the expense of imports which
> are so alien to us. If you want to show justice to our
> fatherland we should not abandon it at the moment of
> trial but remain courageously on guard over our com-
> mon values elaborated over the centuries.[40]

Cardinal Wyszynski and the Catholic hierarchy in Poland seem to prefer a strategy of national resistance designed to limit Soviet control and to ensure the preservation and continuity of Polish heritage and national consciousness. In reaction to the proposed constitutional change in 1976, the church hierarchy stressed the following among other themes:

> The fact that the constitution may not contain anything
> that would limit the sovereignty of the nation and of the
> Polish state. . . . The nation cannot be absorbed into
> any supernational or suprastate body. . . . The right
> of the nation and of the state to preserve complete sov-
> ereignty in the domain of national culture, economic
> freedom, and of its own aims should be emphasized
> and guaranteed by the constitution. [41]

The strategy of national resistance outlined by those spokesmen emphasized the continual teaching of uncensored national history and the establishment of educational opportunities free from
state control and devoted to the preservation of national consciousness and the personal will for national independence. The aim of
this strategy is to ensure the existence of a vibrant Polish nation
and people in generations to come which will be imbued with a
desire for national independence and the will to take advantage of
every opportunity for increasing the nation's latitude in self-
determination. The strategy of national resistance and the preservation of national spirit is cast within a fairly long time-frame,
however. The non-Communist Catholic spokesmen argue that
presently the Soviet Union is overwhelmingly more powerful and
that any short-range effort to change Soviet-Polish relations would
be disastrous. In late 1977, Cardinal Wyszynski "stressed that
the bishops regard it as their task to prevent any sort of 'mini-
revolution' in their country . . . in an evident effort to avoid any
bloodshed that might cost Polish lives."[42]

Democratic-Socialist

The spokesmen of KSS-KOR, such as Lipinski, Kuron, and
Michnik, describe the Soviet Union as a basically imperialist state
determined to preserve its exploitative position and ensure that the
status quo in East Europe prevails. They depict the Soviet Union
as engaged in a world contest for power and as dedicated to retaining and enhancing its already advantageous position. While
they rarely elucidate the specific motives underlying Soviet foreign
policy, their general picture is clear: "The sovereignty of the
East European nations is violated in the name of the imperialist
interests of the USSR."[43]

The spokesmen of KSS-KOR directly reject the argument that
the Soviet Union is necessary or responsible for either Poland's
peace and security or Poland's economic development. In fact,
they assert Poland would have been much better off without the
Soviet Union's involvement.[44] Not only is the Soviet Union's

"pressure" described by KSS-KOR spokesmen as the major cause of Poland's problems, but they label that pressure as "the source of ultimate evil." "The Polish State is not sovereign, and in the minds of our people this is the evil at the root of our political life."[45]

In the picture of Soviet-Polish relations presented by spokesmen of the democratic-socialist view, Poland is clearly subordinate to the Soviet Union and its "totalitarian" hierarchical bureaucracy. There is no question in the minds of those holding this view, Kuron, for example, that the Soviet's control is ever-present in Poland and imposed by the constant threat of the use of force. "The system's stability is guaranteed by the readiness of the Soviet Union, which has been displayed three times already, to reimpose it by force on any nation attempting to free itself."[46]

Despite this threat of Soviet retaliation, Poland is seen as capable of utilizing considerable leverage with respect to the Soviet Union. Lipinski, for example, argues that positive changes, even if gradual, are possible if the leaders of the Polish state had the "courage, character and political wisdom to act with the aim of increasing our independence."[47]

The analysis of the Soviet Union's willingness and interests in intervening militarily in Poland is a crucial aspect of both the KSS-KOR's description of the Soviet Union and its view of the relative leverage and latitude Poland can exercise in domestic and foreign policy. Both Kuron and Michnik have addressed this issue at length:

> The fundamental factor which constrains the social action towards democratization is consciousness of Soviet military power. . . . Poles may win sovereignty only in combined effort with other captive nations of the Soviet empire, . . . but this programme cannot be realized today. I am convinced that this quadrature of the circle can be resolved, that is, totalitarianism may be overcome without risk of a suicidal clash with the military power of the USSR. . . . Social and economic crisis, dependence on the West and on Japan permits the inference that the Soviet leadership fears armed intervention in Poland. But that does not imply that such intervention is impossible, rather it implies that Moscow would be prepared to make many concessions.[48]

The KSS-KOR advocates a strategy of "evolutionism" designed to obtain greater national independence gradually through active national resistance and oppositional pressure. Michnik argues, "It is unrealistic in Poland today to think of a change in the government while the political structure of the USSR remains what it is," and suggests that the only policy for dissidents is to struggle unceasingly and exert pressure for "evolution" in domestic and foreign relations.[49] Kuron elaborates a basic program of national resistance based on the coordination of peasants, workers, the Catholic clergy, and the liberal intellectuals. His program emphasizes the Catholic and secular intelligentsia's vital task in preserving and passing on to the new Polish generation a sense of dignity, freedom of conscience, and personal identity with the national culture and heritage. In this respect the establishment of underground educational opportunities like the "flying university" are an important aspect of the KSS-KOR's strategy.[50]

The KSS-KOR strategy is designed to unite the political leadership in Poland with the whole of Polish society in confronting Soviet pressure and exercising self-determined national prerogatives. As Kuron explains, "This way it could no longer be the party on its own but Polish society in almost all its entirety who could bargain from the Russians a status similar to that of Finland."[51] In his "Reflections on a Program of Action," Kuron concludes by returning to the notion of a sort of "Finlandization" for Poland. "We should aim to achieve a status similar to that of Finland: a parliamentary democracy with a limited independence in the foreign policy field where it touches directly upon the interests of the USSR."[52]

Descriptions of the Federal Republic of Germany

Conservative Communist

The spokesmen in Trybuna Ludu and Zycie Warszawy describe the FRG as a country with a tremendous potential for aggression, expansionism, and imperialism. They present a picture of the FRG that highlights the "red hot" and "growing intensity" of the domestic struggle over foreign policy which divides the country into two camps: those "realistic," peaceful-minded Social Democrats who favor the territorial status quo in Europe and those "chauvinistic" nationalists in the Christian Democratic Union (CDU)/Christian Social Union (CSU) who aggressively press for an "expansionistic revision" of the present territory of the FRG.

In early 1977, Trybuna Ludu and Zycie Warszawy began to emphasize increasingly the mounting danger from "neo-Hitlerite chauvinists" who claim to be the "heirs of the German Reich in 1937." While acknowledging that they did not believe that the present government in the FRG was responsible for the nationalists and chauvinists, the spokesmen in these papers did say that Poland needed to be deeply concerned with this aggressive trend that represented half of the West German community and the largest political groups.[53] The "imperialistic, Great German chauvinism and nationalism" was described in Zycie Warszawy as attempting to saddle Poland with the responsibility for Germans' postwar situation and as manifesting itself in a "conspiracy of rightist forces to stroke chauvinism and nationalism" in Germany and "reinstitute the legitimacy of the Reich and Hitler's aggression."[54]

In Trybuna Ludu Ryszard Wojna explained that the Germans were striving to blame Poles for imaginary crimes so as to "justify their own aggression." He contended that the reemergence of "German arrogance" must cause fearful concern throughout Europe as the revisionist, chauvinist forces become increasingly influential in the FRG attempt "to exploit their state's potential for expanding its position in Western Europe and the world."[55]

Since the domestic pressure in the FRG is described as intensifying, spokesmen in Trybuna Ludu and Zycie Warszawy identify the containment of the FRG as a necessary condition for peace and detente in Europe. The existence of two German states is always described by spokesmen in these two papers as the basic political reality of Europe, as is the U.S. obligation to constrain its number one European ally, the FRG, and the Soviet Union's commitment to ensure the integrity and security of its fraternal ally, the German Democratic Republic. Polish spokesmen for this view reacted very bitterly to President Carter's statements in West Germany in July 1978 reaffirming a commitment to eventual unification of Germany.[56] They severely criticized the president's "bad service" and indirect "promotion of potential German aggression" and argued adamantly that two German states must remain intact and that all German ambitions to alter the territorial status quo must be contained. While these spokesmen said they favored normalization, they emphasized that recognition of the territorial status quo and the inviolability of borders in Europe is a "precondition" for peace and detente in Europe.

> The existence of the two German states is one of the most important elements of the postwar status quo in Europe. The recognition of this state of affairs has been one of the preconditions for European detente. . . . He who questions Europe's territorial status puts in doubt the very principle of detente. It is hard to assume that anyone in Europe would like to sacrifice detente for the sake of fulfilling the great power daydreams entertained by some West German politicians.[57]

Reform Communists

Mieczyslaw F. Rakowski, editor-in-chief of Polityka, describes the FRG as basically peaceful, as primarily "realistic" in its recognition of the status quo of Europe, and as sincere in its commitment to the normalization of relations with Poland. Rather than accenting the possible hostility toward Poland in the FRG, Rakowski highlights the authority of the Social Democratic Party (SPD) and Helmut Schmidt and emphasizes the irreversible movement in FRG policy toward the peaceful recognition of Poland's borders and the normalization of relations. In Rakowski's opinion, Schmidt and the FRG are striving to achieve not just normalization but also partnership, neighborly relations, and perhaps someday even friendship.[58] He apparently believes that very real chances for the achievement of these aims "exist not only because Helmut Schmidt wants that or because some politicans in the Federal Republic want to establish such relations," but "the chances also exist because this is the only way to go for both nations."[59]

Rakowski contends that Poles must assess the relations between Poland and Germany with "realism" as "the most important political category." He suggests that "the realism I have mentioned prevents the Polish leaders from regarding the West German opposition as a political force that is uniformly hostile or unsympathetic to the process of normalizing FRG-Polish relations."[60] While Rakowski recognizes that "many CDU/CSU politicians have been sabotaging the normalization machinery," he discounts this factor in the light of the many possibilities that are based on the "enduring foundation" of cooperation that derives from "the conviction shared by many Germans and Poles that in view of all the tragic experiences that have been the lot of the two nations, the road we are now treading is the only correct road."[61] The empathy in Rakowski's recognition that both nations have suffered "tragic experiences" and his suggestion that Poland's "inability to erase from our people's collective memory the horrible crimes of Hitlerism"[62] has been responsible for some of the difficulties in normalization of relations is a somewhat different approach than that taken in Trybuna Ludu and Zycie Warszawy. The two conservative Communist spokesmen stress exclusively the German guilt for Polish suffering, demand recognition of complete Polish innocence, and place all blame for difficulties in normalizations upon German chauvinism and neo-Hitlerite forces in the FRG.

Rakowski does not stress the necessity of containing the FRG but instead points out that Poland's alliance to the Soviet Union and the recognized existence of the GDR already define the "realistic" parameters of West German foreign policy. He rejects comparing contemporary Polish-German relations with the prewar period, arguing that Poland's position in Europe today is fundamentally different; furthermore, for the FRG, Poland today is an "interesting partner" in trade and economic cooperation. Thus, Poland ought to adopt a strategic policy toward the FRG that will promote "further cooperation between the two governments and nations in politics, economy, and culture."[63]

Non-Communist Catholics

The non-Communist Catholic view describes the FRG as essentially nonaggressive and legitimately pursuing peace and development without endangering Poland's security or territorial interests. Spokesmen for this view emphasize the positive influence the United States has had on the FRG in the postwar era, especially in the establishment of a stable democratic system, which in their view minimizes the potential internal pressures for aggression. They argue that totalitarianism has historically demonstrated an inner logic and predisposition for aggression and expansion, and, since democracy now prevails in the FRG, the tendency toward an imperialist national policy is much less significant. Non-Communist Catholics attribute FRG's military capability and involvement in NATO to predominately defensive motives, such as ensuring the FRG's independence versus Soviet hegemony and influence. In the picture presented by the "ideal spokesmen" of the non-Communist Catholic view, the FRG appears as a defensive state democratically directed by a stable majority of citizens who favor detente and normalization of relations with Poland, the Soviet Union, and the GDR for a variety of reasons, not the least being economic opportunities and a desire to improve the living conditions and "human rights" of the German people throughout East Europe and the Soviet Union.

Since the late 1960s, Cardinal Wyszynski has emphasized repeatedly that Polish-West German relations should be based on mutual forgiveness and empathy and not unilateral accusations of guilt and justified punishment. In 1965, in the "Letter of the Polish Bishops Inviting the German Prelates to the Millenium Festivities in Poland," the bishops explained that "after all that has happened in the recent past, it is not surprising that Poland needs elementary security and still considers the neighbor to the West with suspicion." They further explained, however, to their "Dear German Brethren" that this enumeration" is to be less an accusation than our own justification."[64] In the same letter, the bishops not only explicitly expressed sympathy for the suffering of millions of German refugees following World War II[65] but also accepted indirectly a measure of responsibility for this suffering: "We extend our hands to you granting forgiveness, and asking for forgiveness. We take your extended hands with brotherly respect."[66]

This acceptance of a measure of Polish responsibility for German suffering brought an angry reaction from the political authorities in Poland and led to a significant controversy in church-state relations. Cardinal Wyszynski, however, refused to withdraw any portion of the letter or admit that it was either poorly worded or contrary to Polish national interests. Moreover, the cardinal refused to see those Catholic intellectuals who attempted to offer conciliatory speeches, explanations, or rewordings of the bishops' message for the Polish authorities in the Sejm.[67]

In September 1978, Cardinal Wyszynski embarked on a symbolically significant visit to the FRG, the first by a Polish primate to West Germany since the end of World War II. While in West Germany, the cardinal emphasized the common Christian heritage of Poland and Germany and Poland's historic attachment to Catholic culture and Western traditions. He recalled the foundations for cooperation among all "Christian nations" and seemed to call for an explicit alliance of Christian nations to re-Christianize Europe. The cardinal proclaimed:

> We need such cooperation now when we are faced with the task of re-Christianizing Europe. . . . Our churches have the duty to build cooperation and the collaboration of nations on the foundations of the principles of Christian morality. We must not continue to look back and recall the past, although we must keep it in mind in order not to repeat mistakes. Just as cooperation between our churches is necessary, there must also be cooperation between our nations, one that is comprehensive and sincere and that results in mutual enrichment.[68]

While not inferring too much from the cardinal's statements, we can at the very least conclude that his strategic preference regarding the FRG is primarily one of rapprochement and cooperation, if not partial alliance. This is not to suggest that the cardinal does not also favor the present international circumstances that may contain FRG policies but rather that he apparently does not prefer any further extension or intensification of Poland's present efforts to contain the FRG.[69]

Democratic-Socialists

The spokesmen of KSS-KOR describe the FRG as primarily a defensive country concerned about the threat of Soviet hegemony and limited in its actions by the influence of the United States, which ensures the status quo in West Europe. Most KSS-KOR spokesmen recognize a wide spectrum of opinion in the FRG and reject "the chauvinist and anti-Polish circles of the German right wing which challenges the continued existence of the Polish state" but seem to believe that this point of view in the FRG is relatively limited in popularity and political influence. In "A Programme for Poland," the Polish League for Independence directly challenged the Polish government's fear of German revisionism:

> German-Polish relations still suffering from the hor-
> rors of the last world war are aggravated by another
> factor. The Moscow-directed Party propaganda exag-
> gerates the danger of German revisionism. It conceals
> from the public that a far-reaching change is occurring
> in political thinking in West Germany and that an un-
> derstanding between us is indeed possible. This fact
> has to be suppressed because the Polish people have
> to be convinced of the need for constant military read-
> iness. This involves the costly alliance with the USSR
> and the maintenance in Poland of a large contingent of
> the Red Army said to be necessary for our own safety.[70]

Adam Michnik accents the number of friends Poland has in the FRG who not only recognize Poland's security but have supported Polish efforts to ensure full respect for human rights in Poland. Michnik explains that he associates with: "Friends of Poland in the Federal Republic who have struggled for years for the recognition of Poland's western borders and for normalization of Polish-West German relations, and who have recently raised their voices in support of respect for human rights in Poland."[71]

With respect to human rights, Michnik not only describes liberal opinion in the FRG as friendly but also calls on the Western governments to support human rights in Poland. He argues that Western involvement in this regard cannot be interpreted as a viola-tion of national sovereignty since human rights is legitimately an "internationalized problem." While Michnik argues that a policy of detente in international relations is a vital necessity, he calls on the governments of West Europe and the United States to recognize the "human rights" movement in Poland as a central actor and perhaps implicit ally in developing a peaceful and justified rap-prochement with the Communist government of Poland.[72]

Jacek Kuron also voices support for detente and has called on both the FRG and U.S. governments to aid Poland in overcoming Soviet hegemony and interference.[73] He explains that only the

support of great powers like the United States and the FRG can offset the Soviet Union's principle of interference in East Europe and
calls on these Western powers to ally themselves with the interests
of human rights in Poland in their pursuit of detente. Kuron explains that the "so-called Socialist camp headed by the Soviet Union
basically is economically dependent on the West" and necessarily
needs detente in all fields. Consequently, Kuron suggests that the
United States and the FRG can exert significant leverage on the
Communist leadership in both the Soviet Union and Poland and significantly contribute to the cause of democracy and national independence in Poland.

While the KSS-KOR spokesmen thus see strategic value in
detente and the official policies of Western governments, their primary appeal and pledge of allegiance goes to the West European
democratic-socialists and so-called Eurocommunist parties, especially the Spanish Communist Party. In the FRG the KSS-KOR has
appealed to and been supported by such German intellectuals as
Guenter Grass, Heinrich Boell, and Wolf Biermann.[74]

Descriptions of Domestic Opposition

In describing the various pictures of the Soviet Union and the
Federal Republic of Germany held by the modal spokesmen, this
work has described three aspects of their descriptions: motivation,
capability, and decisional style and locus. This section focuses on
a fourth dimension of descriptive simplification: the portrait they
present of those in Poland who hold contrary points of view.

Conservative Communist

Polityka and spokesmen for the reform Communist view are
generally treated in Trybuna Ludu as naive and thus vulnerable to
the disguised and devious means Poland's enemies will use in their
efforts to destroy Socialism and Polish development. Michael
Misiorny, in an article in Trybuna Ludu[75] responding to a previous
comment in Polityka by M. F. Rakowski,[76] for example, openly
warns against allowing the adversaries of Poland to "take advantage
of one's credulity."

The spokesmen of the non-Communist Catholic view are
treated moderately in Trybuna Ludu and Zycie Warszawy. B.
Rolinski, the editor of Zycie Warszawy, who is very critical of
KSS-KOR spokesmen, openly praises the "sensible attitude of the
Polish clergy who are conscious of their civic responsibilities as
Poles."[77] Conversely, both Trybuna Ludu and Zycie Warszawy

have viciously attacked the KSS-KOR and its spokesmen as traitors, anti-Polish, quasi-Poles, and paid agents of the most chauvinistic and nationalistic West German revisionists.[78] Spokesmen in both of these papers have described KSS-KOR members as a "peripheral handful of implacable enemies" who are interested only in personal power and attention and who are servile allies of the "heirs of the Third Reich" implementing the orders and plans they receive from Munich.[79] Rolinski links the KSS-KOR spokesmen to still another international movement that he sees as anti-Polish, namely "Zionism."[80]

Reform Communist

M. Rakowski in Polityka generally describes those in Zycie Warszawy or Trybuna Ludu who disagree with his picture of the Soviet Union and FRG as overly fearful of both ideological competition with the West and the intentions of Western politicians. He explains that the spokesmen of the conservative view fail to make allowance for the fact that Western leaders are basically realists and therefore well aware of the limits in international relations. At times, however, Rakowski seems to insinuate that some spokesmen in Zycie Warszawy and Trybuna Ludu may be dogmatic, rigid, and unimaginative and may have succumbed to the "fascination of the possibilities created by being in power."[81]

The spokesmen for the non-Communist Catholic view are treated in Polityka with a fairly significant degree of tolerance. They are depicted as mature, responsible, and above all else "realistic" leaders in the Polish nation.

Rakowski does not label the spokesmen of KSS-KOR as traitors or agents of any foreign state. He explains quite clearly, "For me the entire movement of dissidents is part of our history. . . . I consider all this the struggle of various forces for a life we are building together."[82] While Rakowski may consider KSS-KOR spokesmen as part of Polish society, he nevertheless describes them as "naive," "irresponsible individuals," who represent only themselves and who are "politically immature" and "fascinated by publicity." Consequently, Rakowski refuses to "directly polemicize" with the views of KSS-KOR spokesmen since he does not want them to think that he regards them as "serious" partners in the discussion of Polish affairs. In Polityka Rakowski argues that KSS-KOR spokesmen have "naive ideas about the balance of power in the world" and suggests that they "should subject their emotional gestures of solidarity to a more rational consideration." Rakowski concludes that he cannot engage in a dialogue with KSS-KOR spokesmen because a "serious discussion about Polish affairs" can only be conducted among "people who accept Poland's basic political principles and development concepts that the main political forces active in our country (Poland) have adopted."[83]

Non-Communist Catholic

The non-Communist Catholic view generally describes the political authorities now prevailing in Poland as morally weak, spiritually void "careerists," who sacrifice the integrity of their "personality" and the interests of their nation in order to achieve certain material benefits. Spokesmen for this view tend not to differentiate among points of view within the political leadership but describe the personal spokesmen of both the conservative and reform Communist views as essentially "careerists" who are committed to varying degrees to achieving professional position and personal gain at the expense of the nation. Non-Communist Catholics hesitate to label the prevailing political figures in Poland as either traitors or as agents of the Soviet Union but insist that they are better described as "careerists" whose personal interest in achievement and material gain, coupled with weakness and an absence of spiritual strength, make them pliable and servile figures both within the Polish political system and with respect to the Soviet Union.

Cardinal Wyszynski and the clergy in Poland spoke out in defense of KSS-KOR spokesmen throughout 1976-78. The cardinal repeatedly criticized the brutality with which the police attacked the KSS-KOR and warned the political leadership that "peace in a community depended on respect for basic human rights and that contemporary abuses of these rights could bring about new riots in the future."[84] While the cardinal sympathized with the KSS-KOR spokesmen and clearly accepted them as children of the Polish nation, he described some of their tendencies as "hot-headed" and cautioned them against endangering the nation's present international latitude and biological substance.

Democratic-Socialist

KSS-KOR spokesmen like Adam Michnik have argued that despite the present Polish leaders' servility with respect to Moscow in the current situation, they are not simply Soviet agents. "For the Polish leaders, Soviet military intervention would mean reducing their role to that of mere guardians of the Soviet empire, whereas at present they are still rulers, even though only with limited sovereignty but they are nonetheless governing a country of 34 million inhabitants."[85]

Moreover, Michnik contends that the KSS-KOR must distinguish "between different tendencies manifesting themselves inside the regime" so as to calculate strategies that do not "ignore the realities of the situation" and fall into "extremism" or "political adventurism."[86] In this vein, Michnik differentiates the "careerist," who is driven solely by personal achievement and power (for example, the spokesmen for the conservative Communist view), from the "pragmatist," who is a proponent of realpolitik (the spokesmen of the reform Communist view). Michnik describes the "pragmatists" as "believers in economic reform," the "imperatives of economic efficiency," and the "development of science" and as preferring "professional competence to high-flown ideological criteria." He adds, however, that "pragmatists" are not interested in democratic or liberal changes and that they accept a limited political pluralism only because it is more effective in political control than brutal repression. Consequently, Michnik concludes that while the "pragmatist" might become a "partner" in a "political compromise with the democratic opposition" he will never become its "ally."[87]

In the pursuit of greater civil liberties and national independence the KSS-KOR has attempted to cultivate a cooperative relationship with the Catholic Church in Poland. Michnik has been especially active in seeking an accommodation between the liberal Marxist dissidents and the Catholic Church and typically describes the actions of the church as "centered on the defense of religion and human rights and on the maintenance of traditions of independence." He explains that the church "embraces the majority of the population" and is an authority for almost all citizens, irrespective of their religion.[88] Apparently Michnik is hopeful that the church will affirm the social and political efforts of the KSS-KOR and alter its historical anti-Communist attitude (which previously led the church to reject a number of social reforms) into an attitude of "anti-totalitarianism."[89]

Contemporary Polish Perceptions of the
Soviet Union and FRG

A major premise of the approach utilized in this work is that the perceptual pattern which describes the view of reality held by a person making foreign policy decisions can be inferred from the descriptive picture and strategic choices he presents. Thus, one can compare the above spokesmen's descriptions and strategic preferences with the deductively created stereotypes (see above) that serve as operational referents and, in so doing, infer a partial picture of that spokesmen's "world view." Thus, it is appropriate at this point to compare the descriptions and strategic choices relating to the Soviet Union and FRG, presented by the various Polish spokesmen, to the referent stereotypes. The spokesmen's views are mapped on the graphs in Figures 3.2-5. The comparison of the actual descriptions and choices with those of the operational stereotype is judgmental, and the placements on the graphs relative and approximate. The perceptions of each of the ideal spokesmen, derived from their descriptions of the Soviet Union and FRG, are mapped using as parameters the stereotypical views they appear to resemble most closely.

FIGURE 3.2

Conservative Communist World View

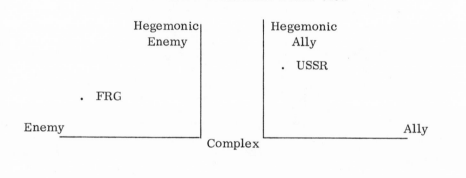

FIGURE 3.3

Reform Communist World View

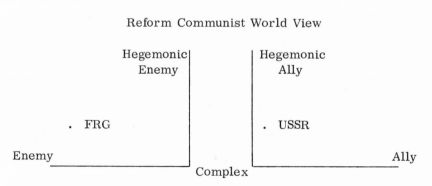

FIGURE 3.4

Non-Communist Catholic World View

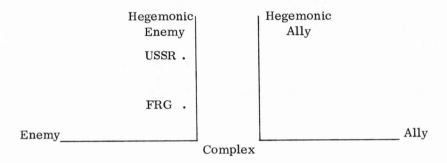

FIGURE 3.5

Democratic-Socialist World View

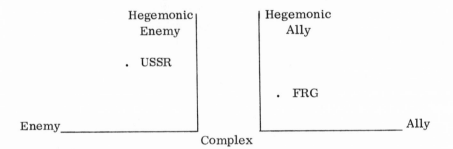

The perceptions of the Soviet Union and FRG that these graphs present are as follows:

In the conservative Communist view (Figure 3.2) the Soviet Union is perceived as presenting a tremendous opportunity and as a state that is not only overwhelmingly more powerful than Poland but upon which Poland is wholly dependent for security and prosperity. In the conservative Communist view the FRG is seen as a significant threat and as rather more powerful than Poland.

In the reform Communist view (Figure 3.3) the Soviet Union is perceived as presenting an opportunity (but of significantly less magnitude than that perceived in the conservative Communist view) and as a state upon which Poland is dependent for both security and prosperity. In the reform Communist view the FRG is perceived as a threat (but less of a threat than in the conservative Communist view) and as possessing less of a capability advantage than in the conservative Communist view.

In the non-Communist Catholic view (Figure 3.4) the Soviet Union is perceived as a highly threatening state which is not only overwhelmingly more powerful but largely in control of Polish politics. The FRG in this view is perceived as a very slight threat and as a state which enjoys a notable capability advantage.

In the Democratic-socialist view (Figure 3.5) the Soviet Union is perceived as a highly threatening state with an overwhelming capability advantage, but in this view the capability distance between Poland and the Soviet Union is not perceived to be as great as that perceived in the non-Communist Catholic view. In the democratic-socialist view the FRG is perceived as presenting a very slight opportunity as an implicit ally and as enjoying a moderate capability advantage.

These graphs present a partial picture of the "international reality" within which the spokesmen operate. By themselves these graphs are a useful comparative tool, a heuristic—if admittedly incomplete—picture of the world view of certain attentive publics, and a step toward inferring the motivation of foreign policy decision makers. This, of necessity, is only the initial part of a study of Polish foreign policy. It may be productive at this point to outline how such an approach might proceed further and what the possible yields mught be from an expanded perceptual analysis of competing Polish world views. To move in this direction requires some further explication of the methodology.

THE ANALYSIS OF PREVAILING VIEW

The prevailing view in a country is that construction of reality on which the country's foreign policy decisions appear to be based. Prevailing view can be inferred from the foreign policy actions of the state by comparing those actions to the strategic choices deduced as operational indicators of each perceptual pattern. By identifying the strategic choice toward which the state's foreign policy actions seem to tend, a student can infer the perceptual tendencies that constitute the components of prevailing view. In the present case, for example, we could identify the prevailing view of the Soviet Union and FRG in Poland from inferences drawn from Polish foreign policy actions.

The task of inferring the prevailing view of the Soviet Union in Poland begins with the proposition that the prevailing view is basically described by the hegemonic ally pattern. If the prevailing view of the Soviet Union is usefully described with this hegemonic ally pattern, then, according to the deduced strategic choice serving as an operational indicator, Poland's foreign policy actions should resemble a strategy of "integration" with respect to the Soviet Union. To test this proposition concerning prevailing view, a student must therefore measure the extent to which Polish foreign policy does resemble integration with the Soviet Union. There are a variety of measures of integration, but for purposes of inferring prevailing view perhaps broad measures of military, economic, and political-normative integration would be sufficiently suggestive. In the main, it appears that militarily Poland is substantially integrated with the Soviet Union and Warsaw Treaty Organization members, although there is evidence that Poland has resisted full integration in certain areas, such as the planning of defense budgets.[90] In the economic sphere, Poland is for the most part well integrated with the Soviet Union and Council of Mutual Economic Assistance, although in terms of total trade apparently somewhat less so than most other East European states except Romania. In the political sphere, a strategy of integration might be seen most easily in Polish policies that stress the "unity" and mutual responsibility of Socialist internationalism. Poland consistently supports both the unity of the Socialist movement and Socialist internationalism but has recently done so with recognizably less vigor than have some other East European states. At the 1976 Berlin Conference of Communist and Worker's Parties, Poland appeared to stress the unity of goals and principles of Marxism-Leninism less than the GDR, Bulgaria, or the Soviet Union itself. More recently, in the discussion among European Communist parties over the phenomenon labeled "Eurocommunism," Poland has been significantly more reserved in its criticism than Czechoslovakia, Bulgaria, the GDR, or the Soviet Union. These examples of Polish behavior surely do not offset the basic thrust of rather major political agreement with the Soviet Union but perhaps do suggest that Poland's foreign policy actions do not conform to a "pure" strategy of integration.

Naturally a far more sophisticated set of indicators for relevant aspects of an integration would need to be applied to Polish foreign policy actions before the prevailing view could be inferred. The very brief consideration of Polish policy presented in this paper suggests that strategically Poland is substantially integrated with the Soviet Union and that therefore the hegemonic ally pattern is probably appropriate for describing prevailing view. It also appears, however, that Polish actions do not conform precisely to those predicted from an ideal integration strategy and therefore, while prevailing view may reflect a significant tendency toward the hegemonic ally view, it does not indicate the pure pattern.

To infer the prevailing view of the FRG in Poland, a student might start with the proposition that the prevailing view is the enemy view. Since the enemy view suggests a strategic choice of containment, if this is the appropriate conceptual pattern then Poland's foreign policy actions ought to match or tend toward an ideally defined set of containment policies. In major respects Poland's actions regarding the FRG do follow the pattern expected in containment. Poland demands recognition of its borders and the legitimacy of the GDR, although to date not with complete success (both the 1970 treaties and the Helsinki Final Act include clauses allowing for the change of boundaries and allowing disparate inter-pretation on the status of the FRG-GDR relationship). Poland re-jects the notion of German reunification and in a variety of arms control and disarmament proposals (most recently in the force re-duction talks in Vienna) has sought to establish a ceiling on West German military might. Poland seems to be committed to the continuation of U.S. and Soviet influence on their respective German allies.

While Poland's policies seem to fit an expected containment pattern, there are a number of recent actions that do not completely coincide with such a description. The major policy that seems to qualify such a judgment is Poland's enormous increase in trade, economic, and technological exchanges with the FRG. For exam-ple, the U.S. Congress's Joint Economic Committee's Report describes Polish trade with the FRG as increasing from $767 mil-lion in 1972 to $1,547 million in 1975, with the respective Polish deficit leaping from $375 million to $3,050 million over the same time period.[91] As with measuring Polish integration with the Soviet Union, measuring Polish containment policy toward the FRG must be carried out with rigor and care. The purpose here is simply to illustrate how this endeavor might be undertaken and prevailing view inferred. From the brief overview of Poland's actions, which may resemble a containment policy, I might suggest that the prevailing view of the FRG in Poland is indeed an enemy view but with the tendency toward this pattern rather moderate.

If for illustrative purposes I might suggest a propositional prevailing view for Poland in 1977-78, it would be mapped with the competing world views as shown in Figure 3.6.

FIGURE 3.6

Propositional Prevailing View, Poland, 1977-78

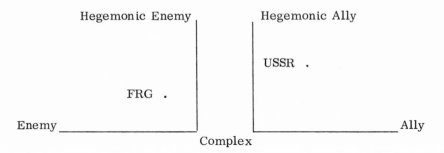

THE INFERENCE OF MOTIVATION AND POLAND'S FOREIGN POLICY

One of the major purposes in conducting a perceptual analysis is to create an empirically derived basis from which motivation can be inferred. The constructed ideal perceptual patterns each suggest a basic perception of either opportunity or threat, which is meant to serve as the fundamental guide in motivational analysis. The basic motivational thrust of a state's foreign policy can be inferred, therefore, from the analysis of its prevailing view. In the illustrative case of Poland, the inference would be that the basic thrust of Poland's policy with respect to the Soviet Union is based on a moderate perception of opportunity (suggested by the hegemonic ally view) and that the basic thrust of Poland's policy toward the FRG is based on a moderate perception of threat. In the Polish case the prevailing view of neither the Soviet Union nor the FRG is very close to the ideal patterns, and therefore the motivational compound is likely to be rather complex and mixed.

The more specific motives of Polish policy toward the Soviet Union and FRG can be inferred from an analysis of the roles and values of the Polish spokesmen that seem to prevail (that is, the spokesmen whose world views most closely resemble the prevailing view). Working with the propositional prevailing view suggested above, both the reform Communist and conservative Communist spokesmen could be identified as major influences on Polish foreign policy. Consequently, it is from an analysis of the primary values of these two sets of spokesmen that the specific motives of Polish policy toward the Soviet Union and FRG could be inferred. Constraints on time and space prevent a systematic study of the role and political preferences of these spokesmen, although I have tried to give the flavor of their chief concerns in my brief introduction to the four basic orientations (see above). Concerns of the conservative Communists, such as those related to preservation of the PUWP's authority, and concerns of the reform Communists, such as those related to the rationalization of the economy, can be used to provide a specific motivational content to the general picture inferred from the prevailing view. In the following outline I have attempted to demonstrate how the general thrust inferred from the prevailing view (in the Polish case, defensive toward the FRG and moderately opportunistic toward the Soviet Union) can be combined with an analysis of the values of the prevailing spokesmen.

In the following illustrative outline, the major aims I infer are used to organize Poland's general foreign policies with respect to their purposes and relative priority. The order of presentation of major aims is meant to suggest the relative priority attributed to the aim and relevant policies. In this outline I present only general policy lines related to the key general strategies. Many policies and specific actions could be added to elaborate on each of the major policies described.

The aims and general policies of Polish foreign policy toward the Soviet Union and FRG in 1977-78 can be outlined as follows:

I. Defend the territorial security of Poland.
   A. Contain any potential German effort to revise the territorial status quo of Poland.
      1. Deter Germans from using force to threaten Poland's territorial status quo.
         a. Strategically integrate Poland's military forces with the Soviet Union's military and communicate to the FRG the impression that revision of German territories would be intolerably expensive.
         b. Preserve a balance of forces in Central Europe between the Warsaw Treaty Organization and North Atlantic Treaty Organization and communicate the impression to the FRG and United States that any territorial encroachment led by the FRG would be intolerably expensive for both the FRG and United States.
            1. Work to ensure a balance of political legitimacy and recognition between East and West European states.
               a. Strive to secure international recognition of the legitimacy, integrity, and inviolability of boundaries of Poland on the Oder-Neisse.

        b.   Strive to secure international recognition of the legitimacy and independence of the German Democratic Republic.

        c.   Strive to secure international recognition of the legitimacy of Socialism as a social system and the political principles of "peaceful coexistence."

    2. Work to ensure a balance of military forces between WTO and NATO.

        a.   Work to maintain a balance of military forces in the Central European Theater sufficient to deter potential West German encroachment.

        b.   Support the existence of a strong Soviet strategic nuclear force well integrated into Poland's and the WTO's security system so as to communicate to the United States the idea that it has a vital interest in restraining any German desire to revise the status of Polish boundaries or the GDR's state sovereignty.

2. Prevent Germans from acquiring political and military influence sufficient to threaten the territorial status quo in Europe.

    a.   Encourage the United States and Soviet Union to remain immediately involved in German relations, with the United States restraining the FRG and the Soviet Union ensuring the position of the GDR.

    b.   Work to prevent German reunification.

        1. Oppose all potential Western initiatives toward reunification.

        2. Strive to convince the Soviet leadership that a USSR-FRG rapprochement should not be allowed to jeopardize the Soviet Union's relationship with a loyal and tested ally like Poland.

    c.   Encourage the establishment of internationally recognized limits on West German military capability.

        1. Work to prevent West German acquisition of nuclear weapons.

        2. Work through arms control and disarmament negotiations to establish "ceilings" on West German military capabilities.

B. Prevent active Soviet military intervention in Poland by appeasing perceived Soviet demands and staying within perceived parameters of Soviet tolerance.

1. Accept the principles of "Socialist internationalism" as superseding the principles of peaceful coexistence (and interstate relations adopted in Helsinki 1975) in Polish-Soviet relations.

2. Preserve the PUWP's leading position in Polish politics and ensure that the PUWP's leadership is acceptable to Moscow.

II. Keep the PUWP's leadership position stable by satisfying the Polish public's demand for an increase in the material standard of living.

    A. Establish relations with major Western industrial states that will provide economic and technological benefits to Poland.

    B. Seek to rationalize and make more efficient and beneficial to Polish economic production and welfare the economic cooperation and integration among the CMEA states.

III. Strive to acquire an increasing degree of independence and freedom of maneuver with respect to the Soviet Union in pursuing nationally defined concerns.

    A. Promote detente between the superpowers and strive to reduce fear and tensions in Moscow that compel the Soviet Union to enforce "bloc discipline."

        1. Encourage the United States not to threaten the Soviet Union and instead to seek mutual accords with the Soviet Union, such as strategic arms limitations.

        2. Oppose the foreign policy thrust of the People's Republic of China.

           a. Oppose the PRC's efforts to threaten the Soviet Union by mobilizing U.S. support.

           b. Oppose the PRC's anti-detente policy and especially condemn China's support for German reunification and territorial revision.

    B. Strive to create a new political order in Europe to supersede the bipolar bloc division of Europe.

        1. Develop strong bilateral relations with West European countries and the United States that may provide Poland with an increment of additional political leverage with respect to the Soviet Union.

        2. Encourage the development of an all-European consciousness and an all-European system of international cooperation. Encourage the development of an all-European security system that will supersede the two mutually antagonistic alliances (WTO and NATO). By including all the European states and both superpowers in a common security system, obtain greater national

latitude for Poland. By linking Poland to major Western powers and especially the United States within a multilateral security system develop a counterweight to offset Soviet influence that in the present bilateral relationship imposes Soviet hegemony over Poland.

The above outline of Poland's aims and general strategic policy toward the Soviet Union and the FRG is based on the analyses of the prevailing view and the prevailing spokesmen and does not take into account the views or strategies of the non-Communist Catholics or democratic-socialists, since their world views were not significantly reflected in the prevailing view. The relative lack of influence on foreign policy exerted by the spokesmen of the non-Communist Catholics and democratic-socialist views is not a sufficient reason to ignore their perceptions, however, since they represent a locus of dissatisfaction and potential pressure for change within Polish politics. Moreover, the non-Communist Catholic and democratic-socialist views both provide clearly developed perceptions and strategic choices which might easily become patterns toward which the views of many Poles might migrate should a major crisis or disruption occur affecting Poland's international situation. More broadly, such an analysis suggests potential changes in Polish foreign policy that might result from the continuing domestic interaction among a variety of competitive world views. For example, while containing the FRG seems to have retained its high priority in Polish policy, it appears to have become less salient in 1977-78, as more pressing domestic issues demand increasing attention. In 1977-78, the desire to increase the standard of living in order to keep the PUWP's position stable spurred accommodation and economic relations with the West and especially the FRG and seemed to overshadow the commitment to containment. Spokesmen for the reform Communist view have been particularly important in raising the salience of trade with the West and minimizing attention to the more traditional postwar Polish aim of containing Germany. Should the influence of the spokesmen of the reform Communist view continue to increase and should they continue to perceive only moderate threat from the FRG—seeing it as already adequately contained—then it seems likely that the Polish efforts to build further economic, technological, and cultural interdependencies with the FRG will intensify. Nor would this prospect be necessarily contradictory to the other primary security aim of Poland, that is, preventing active Soviet military-political intervention. The spokesmen of the reform Communist view stress that their attention to trade and relations with the West in no way contradicts Poland's fundamental alliance with the Soviet Union, nor do these spokesmen question the leadership role of the PUWP. Moreover, the Soviet Union itself is moving rapidly toward increasingly positive and interdependent relations with the FRG. Additionally, if the Soviet Union were to face mounting tensions in the Far East, it may well prefer a Polish leadership that is stable and that facilitates rather than hinders Soviet efforts to ensure FRG neutrality in the Sino-Soviet conflict.

While the possible changes in Polish foreign policy resulting from an increase in the influence of the spokesmen of the reform Communist view may not directly challenge the fundamental underpinnings of Polish-Soviet relations, changes emanating from the pressure of spokesmen of the non-Communist Catholic and democratic-socialist views might. Spokesmen typifying the former view seem to accept the high priority attributed to Polish efforts to avoid active Soviet military intervention but demand that the third major Polish aim of increasing independence with respect to the Soviet Union be granted not only significantly more attention but perhaps even higher priority than other aims, for example, containing the FRG. The pressure exerted by the spokesmen of the democratic-socialist view, if it were to become effective, would probably increase the priority of obtaining greater Polish independence, accenting in particular policies providing Poland with more Western allies and leverage with respect to the Soviet Union.

This chapter has suggested an approach to the study of foreign policy which utilizes the analysis of perceptions as a key empirical guide to the critical attribution of motivation. The essay has endeavored to demonstrate the approach by identifying and describing four competitive Polish world views and by proceeding through an illustrative case study of Poland's contemporary foreign policy (toward the Soviet Union and FRG). It is hoped that this brief illustration indicates how the study of perceptions and world views might be useful in the broader task of analyzing the motives and general strategic policies of the other East European states. While the Polish case study presented makes use of only four ideal type perceptual patterns and operational stereotypes, the use of other conceptual patterns and operational stereotypes would allow the basic approach to be employed comparatively in an analysis of competitive world views in other East European states and the Soviet Union. Cross-state comparisons of the range and content of competitive world views as well as a cross-state comparison of prevailing views may then be possible. Cross-state comparisons of these types might be very useful in approaching the salient multinational issues of East Europe, such as the prospects for political integration in the region, relationships between the Soviet Union and other East European states, and security and cooperation in Europe.

NOTES

1. An exception, though one devoid of theoretical basis, would be Robert King and Robert Dean, eds., East European Perspectives on European Security and Cooperation (New York: Praeger, 1974). Compare Robert King and James Brown, eds., East Europe's Uncertain Future (New York: Praeger, 1977).

2. For example, see Peter Bender, East Europe in Search of Security (Baltimore, Md.: Johns Hopkins University Press, 1972).

3. Charles Gati, ed., The International Politics of Eastern Europe (New York: Praeger, 1976), p. vi.

4. For a general overview of perception and international politics, see Robert Jervis, Perception and Misperception in International Politics (Princeton, N.J.: Princeton University Press, 1976).

5. Nathan Leites, The Operational Code of the Politburo (New York: McGraw-Hill, 1951); Ole Holsti, "The Operational Code Approach to the Study of Political Leaders," Canadian Journal of Political Science, no. 3 (1970): 123-57; David McLellan, "The Operational Code Approach to the Study of Political Leaders," Canadian Journal of Political Science, no. 4 (1971): 52-75.

6. Thomas Hart, The Cognitive World of Swedish Security Elites (Stockholm: Esselte Stadium, 1976), R. B. Byers, D. Leyton-Brown, and P. V. Lyon, "The Canadian International Image Study," International Journal (special volume, "Image and Reality") 32, no. 3 (Summer 1977): 606-71.

7. Robert Axelrod, ed., The Structure of Decision: The Cognitive Maps of Political Elites (Princeton, N.J.: Princeton University Press, 1976); G. M. Bonham and M. J. Shapiro, eds. Thought and Action in Foreign Policy: Proceedings of the London Conference on Cognitive Process Models of Foreign Policy (Stanford, Calif.: Center for Advanced Study in the Behavioral Sciences, 1977).

8. Kenneth Boulding, The Image (Ann Arbor: University of Michigan Press, 1956); Kenneth Boulding, "National Images and International System," Journal of Conflict Resolution 3 (June 1959): 120-31; Ralph K. White, Nobody Wanted War: Misperception in Vietnam and Other Wars (Garden City, N.Y.: Doubleday, 1970); Ralph K. White, "Images in the Context of International Conflict: Soviet Perceptions of the U.S. and the USSR," in International

Behavior: A Social-Psychological Analysis, ed. H. C. Kelman (New York: Holt, Rinehart and Winston, 1965), pp. 238-76. Also see Gordon Allport, The Nature of Prejudice (Reading, Mass.: Addison-Wesley, 1954).

9. Richard W. Cottam, Foreign Policy Motivation: A General Theory and a Case Study (Pittsburgh: University of Pittsburgh Press, 1977).

10. W. Gamson and A. Modigliani, Untangling the Cold War (Boston: Little, Brown, 1971).

11. For an introduction to the background of this very basic assumption of the Gestalt psychologists, see M. Deutsch and R. M. Krauss, Theories in Social Psychology (New York: Basic Books, 1965), pp. 14-36. For a broad review of basic cognitive theories in social psychology, see R. B. Zajonc, "Cognitive Theories in Social Psychology," in The Handbook of Social Psychology, ed. G. Lindzey and E. Aronson, 2d ed. (Reading, Mass.: Addison-Wesley, 1968), pp. 320-411. For an interesting new approach to the use of "whole patterns" on social psychology, see R. Abelson, "Script Processing in Attitude Formation and Decision Making," in Cognition and Social Behavior, ed. J. S. Carroll and J. W. Payne (New York: John Wiley, 1976).

12. See Cottam, op. cit., p. 63.

13. D. J. Finlay, O. R. Holsti, and R. R. Fagen, Enemies in Politics (Chicago: Rand McNally, 1976); and White, Nobody Wanted War, op. cit., have also considered this image.

14. Fritz Heider, The Psychology of Interpersonal Relations (New York: John Wiley, 1958).

15. See Cottam, op. cit., pp. 65-66.

16. These dimensions are taken from Cottam, op. cit., p. 64. J. G. Stoessinger, Nations in Darkness: China, Russia and America (New York: Random House, 1971), p. 5, also suggests four categories for the analysis of perception, including self-image, character of adversary, intentions, and capability.

17. For a general overview of Polish politics in 1976, see Adam Bromke, "A New Juncture in Poland," Problems of Communism (September-October 1976): 1-17. For a Socialist view of Poland's political circumstances and the 1976 crisis, see Peter Green, "The Third Round in Poland," New Left Review 101-2 (February-April 1977): 69-108.

18. See Adam Bromke, "The Opposition in Poland," Problems of Communism (September-October 1978): 37-51. For a history of political opposition in Poland and a very useful review and collection of some of the statements of prominent contemporary opposition groups in Poland, see Peter Rains, Political Opposition in Poland, 1954-1977 (London: Poets and Painters Press, 1978).

19. Ibid., p. 49.

20. W. Bienkowski, a former minister under Gomulka, has become an outspoken critic who appears to be on the outermost periphery of reform efforts within the PUWP. For example, see "An Open Letter to the Authorities of the Polish People's Republic on the Normalization of Relations with the Soviet Union" in Dissent in Poland, 1976-1977, ed. A. Ostoja-Ostaszewski (London: Association of Polish Students and Graduates in Exile, 1977), pp. 38-43. Also see "Appeal by W. Bienkowski, October 1976," Labour Focus on Eastern Europe 1, no. 1 (March-April 1977): 11-12.

21. Jan Strzelecki, among other past party officials signed a letter to Gierek and the PUWP leadership critical of present policies. See Der Spiegel 16 (January 1978) in Foreign Broadcast Information Service-Eastern Europe, 1978, no. 30 (FBIS-EEU-78-39).

22. Znak refers to a loose group of Catholic intellectuals who tend to identify with the weekly Tygodnik Powszechny and the monthly Znak. Their views were represented in the Sejm by a so-called Znak circle. See Stefania Sdek Miller, "The Znak Group: Priests or Jesters?, 1956-1970," The Polish Review 21, no. 4 (1976): 80; and Thomas E. Heneghan, "The Loyal Opposition: Party Programs and Church Response in Poland," Background Report, no. 45, Radio Free Europe Research (February 28, 1977).

23. The Movement for the Defense of Human Rights was established in March of 1977. Some of its most prominent members included former Christian Democratic Party Leader Stefan Kaczorowski, prewar general M. Borula Spiechowicz, and two younger members, Leszek Moczulski and Andrzej Czuma, who were former members of "Ruch," an opposition association visible in 1968. In November of 1978, ROPCO apparently split with Moczulski and several allies, separating from the movement. See Dziennik Polski (December 27, 1978), in FBIS-EEU-79-19.

24. I base this view on the views expressed by non-Communist Catholics in personal interviews with the authors.

25. The Committee for the Defense of the Workers expanded its purpose and adopted a broader program as the Committee for Social Self-Defense in the spring of 1977.

26. Edward Lipinski is a prominent economist and was a Social Democrat prior to World War II. His outspoken criticisms surely did not begin in the 1970s, but were significant throughout the 1960s. He, among other protesters, joined in the "Letter of 59," criticizing the constitutional changes in 1976, and was a founding member of the Committee for the Defense of the Workers.

27. Jacek Kuron was expelled from the PUWP and his university position in 1965, following his writing with Karol Modzelewski of "An Open Letter to the Party Leadership," which was subsequently published in English in Revolutionary Marxist Students Speak Out, ed. George L. Weissman (New York: Merit Publishers, 1968), pp. 15-90.

He spent 1965-67 in prison and was arrested again in 1968 and held until 1971 for "instigating" during the 1968 student demonstrations. He, like Lipinski, signed the "Letter of 59" and was a founding member of KOR.

28. Adam Michnik enrolled in Warsaw University in 1965 and studied under Jacek Kuron, his tutor, and Leszek Kolakowski, and was evidently impressed by liberal Marxism. He became a visible figure in the 1968 student movement and from 1968 to 1970 spent 18 months in prison for his involvement. In 1972, he became the personal secretary of the Polish writer Antoni Slonimski. He signed the "Letter of 59" and, while not a founding member of KOR, is a prominent member and spokesman.

29. See, for example, Trybuna Ludu (April 21, 1977) (editorial), in FBIS-EEU-77-79; Zycie Warszawy (April 19, 1978); A. W. Wysocki, "For the Good of Nations: In the Interests of Peace," in FBIS-EEU-78-78.

30. Address by J. Szydlak, reported in Trybuna Ludu (November 7, 1978), in FBIS-EEU-78-217.

31. Report of the PUWP Central Committee Politburo to the Second National Conference of the PUWP (January 9, 1978), broadcast by Warsaw Domestic Service in Polish January 9, 1978. Reported and translated in FBIS-EEU-78-7, p. G29.

32. Jerzy Sieradzinyki, "Unity of Views and Unity of Action," Zycie Warszawy (April 19, 1978), in FBIS-EEU-78-78.

33. J. Szydlak, op. cit. For a similar view, see Trybuna Ludu (November 7, 1978), (editorial), in FBIS-EEU-78-217.

34. See the Report of the PUWP Central Committee Politburo, op. cit.

35. "For the Implementation of the Berlin Conference Decisions," Trybuna Ludu (June 30, 1978), in FBIS-EEU-78-132. Jerzy Kraszewski, "In Connection with S. Carrillo's book 'Eurocommunism and the State'—The Movement's Unity is a Supreme Goal," Trybuna Ludu (August 3, 1977), in FBIS-EEU-77-153.

36. See H. J. Morgenthau, Politics among Nations (New York: Knopf, 1973).

37. Michal Radgowski, "Impressions on Attitudes," Polityka (August 21, 1977), cited in "Poland Situation Report number 5," Radio Free Europe Research (February 17, 1978).

38. In personal interviews, spokesmen argued that the Soviet Union would accept a Polish leadership devoted to significant economic and domestic reforms as long as Soviet security interests were not jeopardized. They suggested that the Soviets would accept any regime in Poland that led to stability and preserved the position of the PUWP. As evidence of Soviet acceptance they pointed to the friendly and prominent reception given Stefan Olszowski in Moscow.

39. Polityka (July 25, 1977) reports second Novoye Vremya article on S. Carrillo, in FBIS-EEU-77-142.

40. Pastoral Letter from Primate Cardinal Stefan Wyszynski (October 2, 1977), in FBIS-EEU-77-191.

41. "Explanatory Statement by the Secretariate of the Polish Hierarchy Regarding the Proposed Changes to the Constitution," in Dissent in Poland, op. cit., pp. 21-22.

42. "Poland Situation Report number 4," Radio Free Europe Research (February 17, 1978), p. 11.

43. In "A Programme for Poland" of the Polish League for Independence (a group predating the establishment of KOR but whose views are very similar to those expressed by E. Lipinski), the Soviet motives are not attributed to national interests but directly to greed and stupidity. "The Russian government must realize that the present situation tends to only increase the dislike, even hatred, felt by Poles toward Russia and that present tensions may easily lead to tragedy. The interests of the two countries are not necessarily at variance; only greed and stupidity of the government makes them so." The Polish League for Independence, "A Programme of Poland," Survey 22, no. 2 (Spring 1976): 188.

44. Edward Lipinski, "An Open Letter to Comrade Edward Gierek," Survey 22, no. 2 (Spring 1976): 196.

45. Jacek Kuron, "Reflections on a Program of Action," The Polish Review 22, no. 3 (1977): 54, 64. The Social Self-Defense Committee explains, "The deepest cause underlying the crisis in our country is that the citizens are deprived of their rights and the state of its sovereignty." The Social Self-Defense Committee, "A Programme of Action" (October 10, 1978), in Labour Focus on Eastern Europe 2, no. 6 (January-February 1979): 14.

46. Kuron, op. cit., p. 54.

47. Lipinski, op. cit., p. 203. Others call for the struggle for democracy and national independence to begin "here and now." See Declaration of the Democratic Movement, in Labour Focus on Eastern Europe 1, no. 5 (November-December 1977): 18. This declaration of the Democratic Movement was signed by 110 people, most of whom were KSS-KOR members or sympathizers. The document explicitly calls for active cooperation with the KSS-KOR.

48. See Jacek Kuron in Dissent in Poland, 1976-1977, op. cit., p. 176. Adam Michnik summarizes the situation this way:

One may conclude that for the Soviets the decision to intervene militarily in Poland would literally mean a war with her. Militarily, the Poles would lose such a war, but it would bring no political victory to the Soviet Union. It would be a national massacre for Poland, but also a political defeat for the Soviet Union. . . . I do not say that Soviet intervention in Poland is impossible. On the contrary, I think that it could become inevitable if on the one hand the governments in Moscow and Warsaw, and on the other hand the Polish people, were to lose their sense of reality and their grasp of good sense. The Polish democratic opposition should admit that transformations in Poland have to be made at least in their first stage, in line with the "Brezhnev doctrine."

Adam Michnik, "The New Evolutionism," Survey 22, no. 3-4 (Summer-Autumn 1976): 273-74. KSS-KOR has clearly attempted to form initial relations with representatives of similar movements in other "captive nations of the Soviet empire" as Kuron calls them. There have been several meetings between KSS-KOR leaders and Charter 77 leaders from Czechoslovakia. These two groups have sent letters expressing solidarity and encouragement to similar groups in Bulgaria, East Germany, Hungary, Romania, Armenia, Estonia, Latvia, Georgia, the Ukraine, and Russia. See Jiri Pelikan, "Dissidents of the East Unite," in L'Espresso (November 12, 1978), in FBIS-EEU-78-224. Also see W. Robinson and P. Moore, "New Links Forged by Polish and Czechoslovak Dissidents," Background Report number 210, Radio Free Europe Research (September 26, 1978).

49. Michnik, "The New Evolutionism," op. cit., pp. 272-73.

50. The "Flying University," (Uniwersytat Latajacy, UL) officially established by the Educational Courses Society, has a historical predecessor in a similarly named educational system operating at the turn of the century in the Polish areas of the Russian empire, which were designed to avoid the official policies of "Russification." See "Poland Situation Report number 4," Radio Free Europe Research (February 17, 1978).

51. Kuron, in Dissent in Poland 1976-1977, op. cit., p. 175.

52. Kuron, "Reflections on a Program of Action," op. cit., p. 69.

53. Ryszard Wojna, "Poland and the FRG: For Honest Normalization," Trybuna Ludu (March 12-13, 1977), in FBIS-EEU-77-55.

54. A. W. Wysocki, "Who Is Calling Up Spirits? Zycie Warszawy (March 19-20, 1977), in FBIS-EEU-77-56.

55. Ryszard Wojna, "In Connection with President Carter's Visit to the FRG," Trybuna Ludu (July 18, 1978), in FBIS-EEU-78-140.

56. Ibid. President Carter, in response to a question during his town meeting in Berlin on July 15, 1978, said that eventual German reunification is "a commitment I believe should be carefully preserved." New York Times, July 16, 1978. Carter's later statement in Frankfurt, West Germany, however, was perhaps more upsetting to Poles since it included the following phrase: "So we pray for the unification of Germany as the expression of will by the people of your great nation." "President Carter's Remarks at Frankfurt City Hall July 15, 1978," in Department of State Bulletin 78, no. 2018 (September 1978): 9.

57. Janeusz Reiter, "Bad Service," Zycie Warszawy (July 19, 1978), in FBIS-EEU-78-141.

58. Interview with M. F. Rakowski, in FBIS-EEU-77-230.

59. Ibid.

60. M. F. Rakowski, "Realism and Emotion," Polityka (December 3, 1977), in FBIS-EEU-77-238.

61. Ibid.

62. Ibid.

63. Ibid.

64. "Letter of the Polish Bishops Inviting the German Prelates to the Millennium Festivities in Poland," in T. N. Cieplak et al., Poland Since 1956 (New York: Twayne, 1972).

65. Ibid.

66. Ibid., p. 162.

67. Stefania Szlek Miller, "The ZNAK Group: 'Priests or Jesters?' 1956-1970," The Polish Review 21, no. 4 (1976): 80.

68. "Statement by Primate of Poland Cardinal Stefan Wysznski on his visit to the FRG made in Cologne" (September 25, 1978), Slowo Powszechne (October 3, 1978), in FBIS-EEU-78-196.

69. Adam Bromke also explains that former Catholics like S. Stomma, who once felt Soviet containment of Germany was vital, have increasingly reappraised this judgment and now no longer favor any further efforts in this direction. Bromke suggests they may now even accept German reunification if it might facilitate greater Polish independence with respect to the Soviet Union. Adam Bromke, "Czechoslovakia 1968-Poland 1978: A Dilemma for Moscow," International Journal 33, no. 4 (Autumn 1978): 759-62.

70. The Polish League for Independence, "A Programme for Poland," op. cit., p. 189.

71. See "Poland Situation Report number 12," Radio Free Europe Research SR/12 (May 11, 1977), p. 2.

72. Adam Michnik, "Only Political Means Can Resolve the Crisis of the Society," Le Monde (October 25, 1977), in FBIS-EEU-77-207.

73. Interview with Jacek Kuron, in FBIS-EEU-77-103.

74. International Herald Tribune, July 19, 1977.

75. Michael Misiorny, "The Exorcists of Past Tense," Trybuna Ludu (August 8, 1977), in FBIS-EEU-77-155.

76. M. F. Rakowski, "Proportions are Important," Polityka (June 11, 1977), in FBIS-EEU-77-120.

77. B. Rolinski, "All Antennas Zeroed in on Poland," Zycie Warszawy (May 28-29, 1977), in FBIS-EEU-77-108. The clergy is described moderately, but this surely does not mean it is free from criticisms and restrictions. The church is provided very limited access to communication media, and in the spring of 1977 the ZNAK group was criticized by Secretary Kakol (Secretary of State for Religious Affairs) for both being too close to the Workers' Defense Committee and failing to come out firmly enough against the actions of "revanchist" forces in the FRG. Le Monde (April 23, 1977), in FBIS-EEU-77-82.

78. Jozef Baracki, "The Continuation of Anti-Polish Activities: Wrong Address," Trybuna Ludu (March 28, 1977), in FBIS-EEU-77-61, and comment Zycie Warszawy (April 9, 1977), in FBIS-EEU-77-70.

79. Editorial, "Against the People's Interest—Pitfalls of Provocation," Trybuna Ludu (May 20, 1977), in FBIS-EEU-77-101, and Vys, "Thanks to National Zietung," Zycie Warszawy (April 9-11, 1977), in FBIS-EEU-77-74.

80. Interview with B. Rolinski, "Anti-Semitism Here Is a Foreign Press Image," in Svenska Dagbladet (June 11, 1977), in FBIS-EEU-77-74.

81. Rakowski, "Proportions Are Important," op. cit.

82. Interview with M. F. Rakowski (June 15, 1977), in FBIS-EEU-77-117.

83. Rakowski, "Proportions Are Important," op. cit.

84. Cardinal Wyszynski, "Corpus Cristi Address," Broadcast from Vatican City to Poland, reported in FBIS-EEU-77-113.

85. Michnik, "The New Evolutionism," op. cit., p. 273.

86. Ibid., p. 276.

87. Ibid.

88. Michnik, "Only Political Means Can Resolve the Crisis of the Society," op. cit.

89. Michnik, "The New Evolutionism," op. cit., pp. 274-75.

90. New York Times, January 9, 1979.

91. Gary R. Teske, "Poland's Trade with the Developed West: Performance and Prospects," in Joint Economic Committee, East European Economies Post-Helsinki (Washington, D.C.: Government Printing Office, 1977), p. 1315.

4

EXTERNAL DEMANDS AND
EAST EUROPE'S *WESTPOLITIK*

William C. Potter

Most observers of Soviet and East European affairs concur
that over the past 25 years significant changes have taken place in
the external behavior of the Warsaw Pact states. Increased trade
with the West, rapprochement with West Germany, and collabora-
tive efforts with the West to control the proliferation of nuclear
weapons are examples of significant shifts in the Warsaw Pact
states' foreign policy behavior. Much less consensus exists, however, as to the causes of Soviet and East European foreign policy
change.

This lack of consensus is not surprising given the failure of
most approaches to and "theories" of foreign policy to address the
issue of how and why foreign policies change. A neglect of the dynamic element in foreign affairs is especially pronounced in the
field of East European studies, where traditional wisdom has emphasized the acquiescent nature of East European states' foreign
policies to Soviet demands. To the extent that changes in these
policies are acknowledged, they are generally attributed to shifts
in Soviet external behavior.

There is little reason to doubt the continued importance of
Soviet demands on the conduct of East European foreign policy.

I wish to express my thanks to Alexander Dallin and Andrzej
Korbonski for their comments on an earlier version of this essay,
which was presented at the meeting of the Western Slavic Association, Reno, February 16-18, 1978. The thoughtful editorial suggestions of Ronald Linden are also gratefully acknowledged.

The question of whether the designation "acquiescent" still portrays the behavior of most East European states, however, is more difficult to answer. This essay addresses that question with respect to a specific foreign policy issue: the Warsaw Pact states' relations with West Germany. In particular, an effort is made to assess the extent to which changes in East European policy toward the FRG were responses to changes in demands and incentives from the regional hegemon, the Soviet Union.[1]

EAST EUROPE'S WESTPOLITIK:
THE VIEW FROM MOSCOW

The prime characteristic of acquiescent adaptation, James Rosenau maintains, "is a readiness to adjust external behavior and internal institutions to the demands emanating from at least one segment of the environment (usually the nearest superpower)."[2] Officials of states pursuing an acquiescent strategy of national adaptation, Rosenau implies, concern themselves primarily with "reaffirming the commitments and implementing the decisions" desired by the regional hegemon. The foreign policy orientation of East European states as acquiescent states, therefore, may be expected to reflect changes in Soviet foreign policy behavior toward West Germany (or other states). A finding that the behavior of one or several East European states has not consistently mirrored Soviet foreign policy toward West Germany may be indicative of several things: (1) the preponderance of domestic over external demands (a sign of nonacquiescent behavior from Rosenau's perspective); (2) the presence of conflicting external demands and incentives from different actors in the international system (a sign that the external determinants of acquiescent behavior may be more complex than, but not necessarily inconsistent with, Rosenau's formulation); and (3) the absence of clear and resolute behavior on the part of the regional hegemon (again, a possibility not considered by but not inconsistent with Rosenau's adaptation framework). In order to determine the correspondence between Soviet and East European policy toward West Germany and to account better for differences in Soviet-East European policy when they do occur, it is first necessary to trace briefly the evolution of Soviet foreign policy toward Bonn.

The word "evolution" is perhaps a misnomer for the development of Soviet-German relations, if it implies a process of continuous and unidirectional change toward a more complex and desirable state of affairs. This is not to deny the fact that Soviet relations with West Germany have improved remarkably since World War II. The path toward rapprochement, however, has been anything but constant and as often as not has been marked by retrogression as well as progress. Nor have Soviet foreign policy objectives with regard to West Germany been clear or consistent. Indeed, one of the fundamental dilemmas that has faced Soviet decision makers for the past three decades has been the conflicting policy choices that arise from "fear and suspicion of Germany on the one hand and hopes of seducing her on the other."[3]

Until Adenauer's retirement in the fall of 1963, a hard-line policy based upon a fear and suspicion of West Germany generally prevailed over attempts to seduce Bonn. This was particularly evident in Khrushchev's preoccupation with the problem of preventing West German acquisition of a nuclear role through the North Atlantic Treaty Organization (NATO). Following the installment of a new West German government in October 1963, however, a new drift in Soviet German policy emphasizing accommodation rather than containment became evident. Initial Soviet overtures toward the Bonn leadership took the form of encouraging an Erhard-Khrushchev meeting, increasing economic ties, and more favorable newspaper coverage of the new German chancellor. Soviet interest in improving relations with West Germany gained additional public exposure in July 1964, when Khrushchev's son-in-law, Aleksei Adzhubei, journeyed to the Federal Republic on a 12-day goodwill mission. Adzhubei's account of his visit, published in a series of articles in Izvestia (August 9, 11, 13, and 16) conveyed a picture of a changing West Germany whose leadership was more realistic and whose image of contemporary international relations was becoming more reasonable. In early September, following a meeting of Warsaw Pact foreign ministers (to which East German leaders apparently were not invited and during which Khrushchev expressed his readiness to visit the Federal Republic), Bonn announced that Khrushchev would visit West Germany sometime in December. This trip and the prospects for a major improvement in Soviet-West German relations, however, were interrupted in October 1964 with Khrushchev's ouster.

Khrushchev's successors, preoccupied with consolidating their position at home, quickly shelved the idea of a top-level visit to Bonn. Statements by Brezhnev and Gromyko in November and December 1964, however, suggest that although Moscow was inclined for the time being to eschew foreign policy initiatives, especially those hatched in the latter days of Khrushchev's rule, it did not seek to exclude the eventual improvement in Soviet-West German relations.[4] At the same time, the Brezhnev regime displayed little interest in West German rapprochement and did not develop a clear or well-coordinated Warsaw Pact policy on the German issue. This was apparent in the divergent East European responses to Bonn's March 1966 Peace Note and the Soviet failure to establish a common Warsaw Pact line on the German issue at the July 1966 Bucharest Conference. Despite attempts by Ulbricht at the conference to make West German recognition of the GDR a precondition for any Warsaw Pact state's further normalization of relations with West Germany, the conferees agreed only to urge Bonn to "accept the existence of two German states," "to respect the existing boundaries in Europe," and "to refrain from possession or co-possession of nuclear weapons."[5]

Soviet, Polish, and East German pressure to formulate a united Warsaw Pact stance on the issue of relations with West Germany was further blunted by the fall of Erhard's government in late 1966 and the formation of the CDU-SPD Grand Coalition. By including specific proposals for increased contacts in economic, cultural, and technical fields, denouncing the Munich Agreement, and advocating "respect" for the Oder-Neisse frontier and a partial abandonment of the Hallstein Doctrine, the Kiesinger Ostpolitik offensive effectively divided the Warsaw Pact states into as many divergent positions as there were members.[6]

Prior to 1967, the Soviet leadership appeared unable to reconcile its own interest in fostering better relations with Western Europe with its desire to maintain cohesion of the Warsaw bloc. The issue of East European diplomatic relations with West Germany was particularly sensitive given the precedent of Soviet-West German diplomatic relations and genuine Soviet interest in expanding economic and technological cooperation with the industrialized countries of Western Europe. In the wake of the establishment of diplomatic relations between Bucharest and Bonn in January 1967, however, a shift in Soviet policy gradually emerged. This was reflected initially in support by the Soviet leadership of Ulbricht's hard line following a meeting of Warsaw Pact state foreign ministers in February, and in Moscow's strong backing of Polish and East German efforts to counter Bonn's Ostpolitik at the Karlovy Vary Conference of European Communist Parties in April. Moscow also demonstrated its solidarity with the Ulbricht regime by supporting a drive to conclude (and in some instances renew ahead of schedule) a series of bilateral defense treaties between countries of the Warsaw Pact. At the same time the Soviets allowed East Germany gradually to escalate restrictions on West German access to Berlin.

It should be emphasized that although Moscow shared Pankow's interest in applying "salami tactics" to diminish West German and Allied rights in Berlin and probably realized that a heating up of the Berlin situation might be advantageous in enforcing Pact discipline regarding developments in Czechoslovakia, Kremlin leaders did not appear to want a full-scale Berlin crisis which would altogether immobilize Soviet-West German relations and jeopardize the likelihood of Bonn's signing the nuclear nonproliferation treaty. Indeed, as Wolfe points out, "Even though Soviet attitudes toward West Germany hardened perceptively in 1967 and the early months of 1968, the Soviet leadership had not closed its mind completely to the potential advantages of a more flexible [German] policy."[7]

Whatever prospects existed for bilateral rapprochement between Moscow and Bonn in 1968 were temporarily quashed by events in Czechoslovakia. Not surprisingly, the Soviet-led invasion produced second thoughts in Bonn regarding the desirability of a rapprochement, which might weaken the NATO alliance and jeopardize the security of Berlin. It also convinced West German leaders that any future effort at rapprochement with East Europe would have to proceed in concert with or follow an improvement in relations with the Soviet Union.

Although events in Czechoslovakia during 1968 demonstrated that the Soviet leadership placed a higher priority on control in East Europe than on detente with the West, by early 1969 a number of domestic and international events (including declining growth rates, resolution of the Czechoslovak crisis, and the Ussuri River clashes with the PRC) prompted the return of a more accommodating Soviet policy toward West Germany. Moscow's renewed interest in rapprochement with the Federal Republic became particularly apparent after the new Brandt government assumed office in October 1969 and signed the nuclear nonproliferation treaty the next month. Following an extraordinary meeting of top Warsaw Pact party and governmental officials in Moscow on December 3-4, 1969, at which time the new departure in Soviet Westpolitik was endorsed, the Soviet Union began bilateral talks with West Germany on a renunciation of force agreement and other cooperative endeavors. The first major tangible result of these negotiations was the conclusion in February 1970 of a commercial agreement providing for Soviet deliveries of natural gas in return for West German credits of over one billion DM to finance the export of large diameter gas pipes to the Soviet Union.[8] In the same month Moscow agreed to reopen four-power talks in Berlin, the first Big Four discussion of the subject since Geneva in 1959. Then, on August 12, 1970, the cornerstone of Moscow's new Westpolitik and Bonn's revived Ostpolitik was set in place with the signing in Moscow of the Soviet-West German treaty on the renunciation of force. Besides formally recording the mutual desire of the two countries "to improve and extend cooperation between them, including economic relations as well as scientific, technological, and cultural contacts," the treaty pledged both parties to "settle their disputes exclusively by peaceful means and . . . to refrain from the threat or use of force." In addition, the treaty recorded "the realization" on the part of the Federal Republic of Germany and the Union of Soviet Socialist Republics that "the frontiers of all states in Europe [are] inviolable such as they are on the date of signature of the present Treaty."[9] Although the East German leadership did its utmost to prevent any further progress in the development of Soviet-West German relations, on September 3, 1971, the Soviet Union, the United States, Great Britain, and France signed the Quadripartite Agreement on Berlin, thereby removing one of the major stumbling blocks to further improvement of East-West relations. Writing shortly after the Berlin Agreement had been signed, Pravda's major foreign policy commentator, Yury Zhukov, summarized the recent change in Soviet Westpolitik: "We are approaching in Europe the boundary between two stages—the post war stage, which was characterized by the atmosphere of the 'cold war' and the arms race, and a new stage, the stage of all-Europe businesslike cooperation."[10] Within two years of Zhukov's statement, and approximately three and one-half years following the Soviet-West German renunciation of force agreement, Poland, East Germany, Czechoslovakia, Hungary, and Bulgaria had joined the Soviet Union and Romania in establishing formal diplomatic relations with the Federal Republic of Germany.

The German Democratic Republic

The influence of Soviet pressure on changes in Warsaw Pact state policy toward West Germany is most clear in the case of the German Democratic Republic where it appears that East Germany modified its Westpolitik to the extent that Soviet policy demanded it. There is ample evidence, for example, that the August 12, 1970 Moscow Treaty provoked considerable anguish and embarrassment among the East German leadership. East German pronouncements in the late summer of 1970 indicate how hard it was for the Ulbricht regime to adapt to the new situation and how the East German leadership sought to influence East-West developments after the Moscow Treaty in accordance with their own preferences. As Karl Birnbaum demonstrates, three areas of contention were particularly prominent: (1) the failure of the Moscow Treaty to recognize East Germany's demand for West German diplomatic recognition; (2) re-affirmation of Four Power responsibilities in Berlin, which implied a threat to East German insistence on a link between ratification of the Moscow Treaty and the satisfactory conclusion of a Berlin settlement; and (3) the prospect that a "new dynamic stage in East-West relations" symbolized by the Moscow agreement might lead to increased West German penetration into Eastern Europe without prior stabilization of the GDR's international position.[11] Birnbaum notes that the divergence in Soviet and East German interests was apparent when Ulbricht attempted to deduce from the Moscow agreement that both Bonn and third parties were "now obliged to establish full diplomatic relations with the GDR." Moscow indicated its displeasure with the East German position by omitting the pertinent sentences in the Russian translation of the GDR's declaration. East German attempts to frustrate East-West rapprochement also included explicit condemnation of proposals for economic and technical cooperation between the two German states and implicit East German rebuttals of Moscow's stand on West German links to Berlin at the Four-Power talks.[12]

For a short time in December 1970, the East German leadership appeared to gain increased room for foreign policy maneuver as a consequence of the Polish riots along the Baltic coast. Ulbricht made an attempt, and may have been temporarily successful, at convincing Soviet leaders that the domestic weakness of the Polish (and by inference also the East German) elite argued against adoption of foreign policy changes that might further erode the political legitimacy of the East European regimes. By February 1971, however, thanks in part to Gierek's support for West German rapprochement, Moscow's foreign policy line was reconfirmed and movement restored to its Westpolitik.[13] The Twenty-Fourth CPSU Congress, which convened from March 30 to April 9, 1971, lent further support to Brezhnev's Western policy and possibly served as the forum for planning how to deal with East Germany's uncompromising Westpolitik. In any case, within a month Walter Ulbricht was ousted from his leadership post in the GDR and replaced by Erich Honecker. Lacking Ulbricht's personal authority and most likely under substantial Soviet pressure, Honecker quickly adopted positions, both on the Berlin negotiations and the issue of international recognition of the GDR, which were much more in harmony with the Soviet stand than were those of his predecessor. As Peter Ludz points out, from the vantage point in Moscow, "Ulbricht—in his prime a master maneuverer for political gain—had become so inflexible that he simply could not adjust to the change in the international climate and the consequent shift in Soviet objectives. . . . In this [changed international] situation, the Soviet leadership could not afford to run the risk of allowing Ulbricht's rigid attitudes—equated with GDR policies so long as he was at the helm—to spoil the show. It was time to downgrade Ulbricht and to call the East German junior partner to heel."[14]

One cannot say with absolute confidence whether the new regime's steps to align its foreign policy on the German issue with that of the Soviet Union were due to demands emanating from the Soviet Union, to a pragmatic reassessment of East German interests, or to a combination of the two factors. What is clear is that the Honecker regime, while continuing Ulbricht's policy of <u>abgrenzung</u> (demarcation of the two Germanies), abandoned Ulbricht's demand that recognition of the GDR be a precondition for any dialogue with Bonn. Honecker also acknowledged for the first time the "special political status" of West Berlin. This crucial change in East German policy, coupled with the prior Soviet-West German renunciation of force agreement and the recently concluded Four-Power Berlin accord, cleared the way for the first formal inter-German political negotiations in the history of the two states. The most important product of those talks, the Treaty on the Basis of Relations between the Federal Republic of Germany and the German Democratic Republic, was signed on December 21, 1972.

Poland

The role of external demands, in the form of policy guidance from Moscow, in shaping Polish policy toward West Germany is more ambiguous than in the East German case. Changes in Warsaw's interest in improving relations with Bonn in 1955 and after 1969 parallel rather closely shifts in Soviet policy preferences. In 1964, however, during Khrushchev's rapprochement initiative, Polish policy toward the Federal Republic became noticeably more intransigent rather than more accommodating.

Polish interest in improving relations with West Germany was first apparent in March 1955, shortly after the Soviet Union expressed its readiness to normalize relations with Bonn. In October, one month after the Soviet Union and West Germany established diplomatic relations, Polish Prime Minister Jozef Cyrankiewicz again expressed Poland's readiness "to extend friendly relations as soon as possible to the whole of Germany."[15] The timing of these overtures was consistent with an interpretation that Poland in 1955 was very responsive to Soviet policy changes. Events in 1956, however, suggest that Polish interest in rapprochement with West Germany at that time may have been motivated by considerations other than Soviet preferences. Gomulka's return to power in October 1956, and the pronounced deterioration of relations between Poland and East Germany, for example, also may be viewed as precipitants for renewed Polish efforts to normalize relations with West Germany. As Melvin Croan points out, "Both governments [in 1956] shared a common antipathy to the staunchly Stalinist Ulbricht regime."[16] The Hungarian Revolution and the Polish October encouraged the Adenauer government to believe that economic assistance to the new Polish regime might promote the further erosion of the Communist bloc in East Europe. Gomulka, for his part, probably saw rapprochement between Poland and West Germany as a means of acquiring economic support to shore up the domestic foundations of his regime and thereby achieve increased freedom of maneuver internationally. These promising developments were stymied not because of Soviet pressure on Poland but because in October 1957 Marshall Tito extended Yugoslav diplomatic recognition to East Germany. The issue of Polish-West German relations immediately became entangled with the Hallstein Doctrine and the question of whether Bonn should continue diplomatic relations with Yugoslavia. The decision of the West German leadership to retain the Hallstein Doctrine intact led not only to the severance of West German relations with Yugoslavia but to the collapse of the anticipated rapprochement with Poland. [17]

If the favorable change in Polish-West German relations in 1955 represents a marginal case of Polish acquiescence to Soviet policy preferences, the hardening of the Polish position on relations with West Germany in 1964 constitutes a contrary example. In that year and at the same time that Khrushchev began to explore a major change in Soviet-West German policy, "the Poles, who had hitherto been willing to overlook the interests of the German Democratic Republic for the sake of improving relations with the FRG," aligned themselves with the GDR against the FRG. [18] Indeed, if Nicholas Bethell's account of Polish-Soviet interaction in 1964 is correct, Gomulka's response to Khrushchev's announcement that he would shortly go to Bonn to seek some form of Soviet-West German reconciliation was first one of terror and then active opposition (with Ulbricht) to Khrushchev's initiative. [19] The later convergence of Polish and Soviet positions on the German issue resulted not from Polish acquiescence to Soviet demands but from Khrushchev's removal and the new regime's abandonment of his scheme for rapprochement.

Perhaps the strongest case for an explanation of Poland's Westpolitik based on external determinants involves the last major reversal in Polish-West German relations in 1969. Again, however, evidence of Polish acquiescence to external pressures from the Soviet Union is circumstantial in nature and involves the parallel development of Soviet and Polish initiatives (and the response to West German overtures) for improving relations with Bonn.

In March 1969, a meeting of the Political Consultative Committee of the WTO in Budapest dropped its standard denunciation of West German revanchism and called for an all-European security conference to discuss the German issue. At the same time, more favorable accounts of West German society began to appear in Polish newspapers. Then, on May 17, 1969, shortly after Kiesinger's personal envoy returned from exploratory talks with Soviet leaders in Moscow, Gomulka delivered a major speech acknowledging the diminished German threat and the need to reevaluate Polish national interests with respect to West Germany. By December 1969, Soviet-West German negotiations on a renunciation of force agreement were in progress, and two months later formal negotiations between Poland and West Germany were begun. An extraordinary number of high-level consultations between Polish and Soviet decision makers took place during 1969-70. Undoubtedly the question of East European relations with Bonn was often the topic of discussion during these meetings.[20] The Polish decision to emulate Soviet behavior with regard to West Germany, however, was not necessarily the result of Soviet pressure. Given the change in West German leadership and Brandt's more flexible Ostpolitik, Gomulka had good reason to reevaluate the propriety of existing Polish-West German relations and to conclude independently that rapprochement was in the best interest of the Polish nation. Ambitious economic development goals, disappointment over the level of East German economic assistance, and the potential for economic modernization through an influx of West German financial and technological resources, in particular, were probably significant considerations in the Polish regime's decision to revise its Westpolitik. With the coming into force of the Eastern treaties, Polish foreign policy, which previously had been obsessed with the unsettled territorial question, might now, in the words of one Polish observer, "be determined by the same factors as in the case of other countries."[21] According to another Polish commentator, Poland was "faced with a completely new situation in which Poland's pro-Russian course is no longer incompatible with other international associations. . . . Our participation in the Eastern bloc provides us with an opportunity to reach a Polish-West German reconciliation and to revive our traditional friends in the West."[22]

Czechoslovakia

The role of external factors, in the form of demands from Moscow, is apparent during several stages in the evolution of Czechoslovak foreign relations with West Germany. External demands are most prominent in the period between the establishment of diplomatic ties between West Germany and Romania (January 1967) and the fall of Novotny (January 1968), the immediate aftermath of the August 1968 invasion, and in the period after the August 1970 Soviet-West German renunciation of force agreement.

Contrary to the Soviet charges against Dubcek made after the 1968 invasion, a cautious movement toward Czechoslovak-West German rapprochement began near the end of the Novotny regime and prior to a major change in the composition of the Czechoslovak leadership.[23] The trigger event appears to have been not any specific economic crisis or change in Soviet policy but rather the declaration of the Kiesinger government on December 13, 1966, that the 1938 Munich agreement had been made under the threat of force and therefore was invalid. This moved Bonn closer to the position held by every Czechoslovak government since World War II, that the Munich Pact was invalid ab initio, not simply no longer valid. In January 1967, Czechoslovak-West German consultations regarding diplomatic relations began in Prague. Like Romania (which established diplomatic relations with the FRG in January 1967), but unlike the other Northern Tier states, Czechoslovakia apparently was interested in establishing diplomatic ties without demanding as a quid pro quo West German recognition of either the GDR or the permanence of the Polish-German frontier.[24] Before these talks could produce tangible results, however, the Romanian-West German Treaty was signed, and the Czechoslovak leadership chose to retreat in the wake of East German, Polish, and Soviet demands for a tougher and more coordinated German policy. This démarche was apparent shortly after the February conference of Warsaw Pact foreign ministers, when Czechoslovakia concluded bilateral treaties with Poland and the GDR, both of which contained direct references to West Germany as a potential aggressor and pledges to consult on "all important international questions which involve the international interests of both sides."[25] The retrenchment in Czechoslovak policy was also noticeable during and after the April conference of European Communist parties at Karlovy Vary, when Czechoslovak statements on the conditions for improving relations with Bonn fell more in line with those of other Northern Tier states and included demands for West German recognition of the GDR, acknowledgment of the permanence of the Oder-Neisse border, and acceptance of the invalidity of the Munich Agreement ab initio.[26] The results of the February Warsaw Pact consultations and the treaties with Poland and East Germany were effectively to rule out independent Czechoslovak initiatives or responses to overtures by West Germany.[27]

During the brief tenure of the Dubcek regime, the Czechoslovak leadership displayed a greater disregard for the policy preferences of decision makers in Moscow and radically altered their responsiveness to domestic demands. This shift in decision-maker responsiveness to internal and external demands did not lead to a dramatic or immediate change in Czechoslovakia's Westpolitik, although by April 1968 the Dubcek regime had clearly expressed its intention to improve relations with all states regardless of their social system.[28] Although one cannot be sure, a more rapid improvement in Czecho- slovak-West German relations probably was deterred by the Dubcek regime's reluctance to further provoke Moscow and by the Bonn gov- ernment's equal reluctance to appear too eager to interfere in the unstable Czechoslovak situation. Unfortunately, the Czechoslovak leadership's estimate of what constituted prudent policy innovation did not correspond to the prevailing Soviet judgment. The August 1968 invasion was the consequence.

Given the Soviet Union's reliance on the threat of West Ger- man imperialism as one rationale for the invasion of Czechoslovakia, it is not surprising that in the immediate post-invasion period the Czechoslovak leadership found it necessary to demonstrate its loyalty to the Warsaw Pact by repudiating Bonn's Ostpolitik. Preoccupied with the tasks of reestablishing domestic political control and gain- ing the trust of the other Warsaw Pact states, the Czechoslovak leadership was in no position either domestically or internationally to accelerate rapprochement with West Germany. Significant move- ment toward improved relations with Bonn began only after some degree of "normalization" had been achieved domestically and after Moscow had demonstrated its own inclination to improve relations with the new Brandt government.

At the same time that the Husak regime maintained a constant polemical campaign against West German "revanchist tendencies," it was ambiguous on the subject of normalizing relations. In June 1970, for example, in a speech to the Central Committee plenum, and several months before the conclusion of the Soviet-West German treaty, Husak is reported to have expressed disappointment in the Ostpolitik's failure to bring about a change in relations between Bonn and Prague.[29] After the signing of the Soviet-West German treaty on August 12, 1970, and consultation with the Soviet leader- ship at a Warsaw Pact Political Consultative Committee meeting in Moscow one week later, the Husak regime expressed approval of Bonn's Ostpolitik and indicated its desire to resolve points of differ- ence through negotiations.[30] Preliminary negotiations began in Prague in October 1970, and the first round of top-level talks were initiated in March 1971.

Somewhat surprisingly, in view of West Germany's successful negotiation of treaties with the Soviet Union (August 1970), Poland (December 1970), and the German Democratic Republic (December 1972) and the Husak regime's own expressed interest in resolving points of dispute with the FRG, negotiations with Bonn dragged on for over three years, the principal stumbling block being Czecho- slovak insistence on abrogation of the Munich Agreement ab initio.[31] The available evidence suggests that the deadlock was broken only in late 1972, when Moscow finally tired of Czechoslovak intransigence on this issue. Signs of Soviet influence in revising the Czechoslovak position are evident in November 1972, when Soviet communiques at the conclusion of Todor Zhivkov's visit to Moscow and Brezhnev's visit to Hungary both omitted the standard ab initio formula. Shortly thereafter, the Czechoslovaks also relinquished their heretofore scrupulous adherence to the ab initio postulate and instead began to use the term "void." The final treaty document, initialed on June 20, 1973, and signed on December 11, 1973, incorporated this Czechoslovak concession and left to the contracting parties the interpretation of the term "void" used to describe the abrogation of the Munich Agreement of September 29, 1938.[32]

Romania

The circumstances responsible for the reorientation of Romanian foreign policy in the early 1960s are especially complex and not easily separated into economic, ideological, idiosyncratic, and systemic determinants. Nor is it easy to assign a specific date to the transformation of Romanian foreign policy. As Michael Montias and Kenneth Jowitt document, even in the realm of economic differences with the Soviet Union, the widening of the conflict was incremental, not sudden, and evolved amidst a combination of domestic and intrabloc conflict, in reaction to a series of challenges.[33] Thus, although one can point to Khrushchev's Comecon integration proposal as a plausible contributing factor in the Romanian leadership's decision to pursue a more active and autonomous Westpolitik after 1962, the economic irritant in Soviet-Romanian relations must be viewed within the context of the Romanian elite's growing commitment to certain foreign policy principles previously articulated but rarely adhered to by Soviet decision makers (for example, national sovereignty, equality, and independence in interparty and interstate relations) and the opportunities for foreign policy innovation afforded by the Sino-Soviet rift, Bonn's interest in promoting polycentric tendencies within the Warsaw Pact, and the absence of a clear Soviet or coordinated Warsaw Pact policy regarding East European relations with West Germany.

The lack of specific Soviet guidelines for East European-West German relations may have been important in the Romanian decision to establish diplomatic ties with Bonn and certainly facilitated the defense of this policy in the wake of Polish and East German criticisms.[34] The failure of Soviet efforts to preempt the German issue through a coordinated Warsaw Pact policy and the strength of the Romanian position are evident in the sequence of events beginning in the spring of 1966, and ending with the establishment of Romanian-West German diplomatic ties in January 1967. Among the more significant events were Ceausescu's May 7, 1966 statement reproving the Soviet Union for past transgressions and expressing satisfaction over the development of closer Romanian-West German relations,[35] Soviet concessions to the Romanian position regarding East German attacks on Romanian foreign policy at the June 1966 Warsaw Pact foreign ministers conference in Moscow, and Romanian diplomatic successes at the July 1966 Warsaw Pact Political Consultative Committee (PCC) meeting in Bucharest. At the latter meeting, not only was the subject of Warsaw Pact organizational reform shelved, but the lengthy conference communique tempered a strong denunciation of militaristic and revanchist forces in West Germany by noting "as a positive feature the presence of circles in the Federal Republic of Germany that come out against revanchism and militarism."[36] The Bucharest Declaration also expressed the view that the establishment of an effective security system in Europe must be based on the achievement of normal relations between states regardless of social systems (implying that bilateral diplomatic relations could develop between Warsaw Pact states and West Germany). The fact that the Soviet Union withheld public condemnation of the Romanian-West German treaty for several weeks suggests that initially the Soviets may also have shared—or at least were reluctant to challenge—the Romanian interpretation. This indecision (and possible divergence of opinion on the German issue within the Kremlin) was indicated by Soviet Premier Kosygin's comments at a London news conference on February 9, 1967—over a week after the establishment of Romanian-West German relations—and during the February meeting of WTO foreign ministers in Warsaw, at which the Soviet Union was reported to have sided with the Poles and East Germans on the German question.[37] In response to a reporter's query as to whether the Romanian move was a step in the right direction, Kosygin replied that "this is a question that could best be answered by the Romanian leaders."[38] The continuation of Hungarian and Bulgarian interest in improving relations with West Germany throughout much of February 1967 also suggests that even after January 31, 1967, the Soviet leadership was undecided on an appropriate response to Bonn's first major Ostpolitik triumph and/or that other Warsaw Pact states were reluctant to endorse Ulbricht and Gomulka's demand for a harsh anti-West German stand. Although Soviet support for the Polish and East German position appears to have developed by mid-February, harsh polemics against the Romanian interpretation of the Bucharest Declaration did not begin until April.

Romanian behavior throughout 1967 (including the defense of Israeli sovereignty and opposition to the U.S.-USSR-sponsored nuclear nonproliferation treaty, in addition to diplomatic recognition of Bonn) suggests that Ceausescu was able to accommodate his regime to external challenges it faced without compromising its basic foreign policy principles. Accommodation without compromise, Jowitt argues, was successfully carried out because Ceausescu was aware of the limits of Soviet tolerance and judiciously mixed concessions (for example, reaffirmation of the centrality of the world socialist system in the RCP's foreign policy) with the defense of Romania's commitment to the development of friendly relations with all states.[39] Evidence of the limits of Romanian foreign policy autonomy and the readiness of Romanian decision makers, at times, to adapt to Soviet external demands includes the temporary change in Romania's Westpolitik following the Soviet-led invasion of Czechoslovakia.

Romania's treatment of developments in Czechoslovakia prior to the August invasion was consistent with Bucharest's oft-stated commitment to the principles of national independence, equality, and noninterference in the internal affairs of other states. Thus, although the nature and extent of domestic reforms were undoubtedly repugnant to the Romanian leadership, Ceausescu upheld Czechoslovakia's right to pursue her own internal course. Ceausescu's initial harsh condemnation of the Soviet-led invasion as "a flagrant transgression of the national independence and sovereignty of the Czechoslovak Republic . . . [and as] an act in complete contradiction with the fundamental norms that must govern relations between socialist countries and Communist parties" also underlined the important role of principle in Romanian foreign policy.[40] As J. F. Brown points out, the initial Romanian condemnation reflected the tenuous position of Romania in the aftermath of the Czechoslovak invasion and was designed to magnify the risk of Soviet intervention in the eyes of Kremlin decision makers by warning that Romanian resistance would be much stronger than the Soviets encountered in Czechoslovakia.[41] Having established this position in strong and unmistakable terms, however, Romanian condemnation of the Soviet-led invasion was muted after August 26, 1968, and Romanian interaction with West Germany diminished. These changes in Romanian policy followed Ceausescu's August 25th meeting with Soviet Ambassador Basov in Bucharest. It is uncertain whether the Soviet ambassador issued an explicit warning that further provocation would lead to armed intervention or whether Basov attempted to instruct Ceausescu in how such action could be avoided.[42] In any case, immediately following this meeting and at the same time that the Soviet Union began to attack Romania publicly for failing to recognize the West German threat and for being "soft on revanchism," the Romanians began to emphasize the need for closer cooperation among socialist states and to downplay the development of closer relations with West Germany. [43] A return to specific condemnation of the intervention and renewed encouragement of rapprochement with West Germany occurred only in early 1969, after the Soviet threat to Romania had subsided and Moscow had demonstrated its own interest in improving relations with Bonn. Support for the Romanian position on Germany and an indication that intrabloc conflict over Czechoslovakia had subsided were evident in the March 1969 "Budapest Appeal," which omitted the standard condemnation of revanchist forces in West Germany and instead stressed the prospects for peace, good neighborness, detente, and coexistence. [44] By the middle of 1969, therefore, it was apparent that the Romanian leadership, through the "judicious use of concessions"[45] and an awareness of the environmental constraints on their policy innovation, had not only survived the threat of Soviet military intervention but had seen the vindication of their German policy.

Hungary

The evolution of Hungary's foreign relations with West Germany is consistent with a model of foreign policy adaptation that emphasizes greater decision-maker responsiveness to external rather than domestic demands but allows for the independent formulation of foreign policy in the absence of a clear and forceful stand by the regional hegemon. Prior to mid-February 1967, and before the Moscow leadership indicated that it had made up its mind regarding the dangers of Ostpolitik, Kadar demonstrated a readiness to improve relations with West Germany matched only by the Romanians and perhaps the Bulgarians. This was evident in Hungary's non-polemical reply to Bonn's March 1966 Peace Note, media commentary emphasizing the traditional cultural, economic, and even political bonds between the two countries, and the reluctance of the Kadar regime to abandon efforts to establish diplomatic relations with West Germany despite the strong criticism of Hungary's position by the German Democratic Republic in late 1966. [46] Hungarian interest in rapprochement with the Federal Republic also continued for a short time after the formal establishment of diplomatic relations between Romania and the FRG. [47] Once the Soviet Union took a firm stand on the German issue, however, Kadar repressed whatever doubts he may have entertained and quickly endorsed Moscow's hard-line position. [48]

Developments in Czechoslovakia in 1968 further reduced Kadar's room for foreign policy maneuver. Because of historical circumstance (that is to say, memories of 1956), domestic economic problems, proximity to Czechoslovakia and the West, and the existence of greater cultural freedom than in most Warsaw Pact states, events in Czechoslovakia during Dubcek's tenure accentuated existing demands within Hungary for more radical internal reform and external autonomy. Hungary's political, geographic, and strategic position, however, realistically ruled out either a "Prague Spring" or a Romanian national independence solution. Instead, the potential for counterrevolution in Czechoslovakia and the prospect of reconciliation between Prague and Bonn heightened Kadar's need to demonstrate to the Soviet Union and its allies that there would be no repetition in Hungary of 1956 and that in the realm of foreign policy Hungary would not sacrifice common Pact interests for a bilateral improvement of relations with Bonn.[49]

This concern with the preferences of other Warsaw Pact states also is reflected in Hungary's relations with West Germany after August 1968. Although ironically the Soviet invasion mitigated Hungary's immediate "security dilemma" and made possible the revival of interest in rapprochement with Bonn (reflected particularly in an improvement in economic relations after 1968), Kadar moved cautiously so as not to provoke his Warsaw Pact allies. In policy terms this meant delaying Hungarian treaty negotiations with West Germany until Bonn's problems with the other Warsaw Pact states had been resolved. This decision to act "in harmony with our allies" on the German question[50] was publicly announced by Foreign Minister Janos Peter on January 5, 1970, two weeks after a Warsaw Pact summit in Moscow and less than one month after the signing of the Warsaw-Bonn treaty. Peter emphasized that although there were new possibilities for the establishment of diplomatic relations between West Germany and Hungary, before this question could be taken up there should be a "settlement of relations between the Federal Republic and the GDR in conformity with the principles of international law."[51] One year later, in March 1971, the Hungarian ambassador to Czechoslovakia indicated that there were additional conditions to Hungarian-West German rapprochement. Although he acknowledged that there were no important unresolved questions between the two countries, he said that no step would be taken in the direction of establishing diplomatic relations "without prior consultation with the Socialist allies, in particular those which have important problems to resolve." More precisely, he noted that "only when diplomatic contacts with Poland, the GDR, and the CSSR have been established will there be no obstacle to the establishment of diplomatic relations between Hungary and the Federal Republic."[52] Again, in February 1973, after the signing of the Treaty on the Basis of Relations between the FRG and the GDR, Jeno Fock, the Hungarian prime minister, acknowledged that the establishment of diplomatic relations with the Federal Republic would be in Hungary's interest as this would "open up possibilities for further economic advantages" but emphasized that "the international standpoint of the Hungarian Party and Government [on this question was] decisive." He pointed out:

> Earlier, we made this question of diplomatic relations
> dependent on the ratification of the Soviet-West German
> and the Polish-West German treaties, then on the treaty
> with the GDR and the agreement on West Berlin. Today
> it depends on solving the problem of the invalidity of the
> Munich Agreement. When this has happened, we will,
> together with Bulgaria, after consultation with our
> friends, establish diplomatic relations with Western
> Germany—certainly not before.[53]

These frequent acknowledgments by top Hungarian officials concerning the lack of outstanding political problems between Bonn and Budapest and their belief that economic benefits would accompany the establishment of diplomatic ties suggest that Hungary's delay in normalizing relations with West Germany stemmed from external constraints (a Soviet veto, if not orchestrated Warsaw Pact policy) rather than domestic policy considerations. This interpretation also is supported by the speed with which Hungarian-West German ambassadors were exchanged once the Bonn-Prague treaty was signed in December 1973.

Bulgaria

The findings of most analyses of Bulgarian foreign policy are compatible with J. F. Brown's observation that "Bulgaria has seldom ventured into the foreign field without an anxious, eastward look over her shoulder."[54] As the 1971 draft program of the Bulgarian Communist Party emphasized, "The fraternal friendship and cooperation of the Bulgarian Communist Party with the Communist Party of the Soviet Union and the ever broader and deeper alignment of Bulgaria with the Soviet Union will remain the immovable cornerstone of the entire work and the domestic and foreign policy of our party."[55] A general readiness to adjust foreign policy behavior to the regional hegemon's preferences, however, should not be interpreted to mean automatic Bulgarian emulation of Soviet foreign policy behavior. Following the fall of Khrushchev in October 1964, and

before the Soviet enunciation of a firm anti-Ostpolitik program at
Karlovy Vary (April 1967), Bulgarian foreign policy toward West
Germany exhibited a degree of self-interest and autonomy not im-
plied by the designation "acquiescent."

The first indications of movement in Bulgaria's Westpolitik
appeared in 1964, with the signing of a long-term trade agreement
with Bonn, increased Bulgarian trade with the West and West Germany, and a doubling over the previous year of the number of Bulgarian treaties signed with NATO countries as a percentage of total
bilateral treaties. Although the new Brezhnev-Kosygin team immediately indicated their solidarity with Ulbricht and abandoned
Khrushchev's initiative for West German rapprochement, between
1964 and 1966 the Bulgarian leadership showed little concern over
the dangers of "creeping revanchism" and proceeded to develop
closer economic ties with Bonn at the same time that it moved to
reduce its economic dependency on the Soviet Union. By 1966, new
highs had been reached in Bulgarian trade with the Federal Republic
and the West, while trade with the Soviet Union as a percentage of
total Bulgarian trade dropped under the 50 percent mark for the first
time in ten years. The first major signal of Bulgarian disagreement
with her Northern Tier neighbors over Westpolitik also came in 1966,
in the form of Bulgaria's handling of Erhard's March 1966 Peace
Note proposal to exchange renunciation of force agreements with all
East European states but East Germany. While Poland and Czechoslovakia joined the Soviet Union in rejecting the peace note outright
and the Hungarians published a cool but not entirely negative reply,
the Bulgarians (like the Romanians) published no official response.[56]
A more positive gesture of the Bulgarian leadership's responsiveness to Bonn's initiative occurred in the fall of 1966, with the invita-
tion of West German State Secretary Rolf Lahr to visit the Plovdiv
Fair. The Bonn-Sofia flirtation intensified in December 1966, with
the launching of Kiesinger's Ostpolitik offensive and led to speculation
that Bulgaria (as well as Hungary) might soon follow Romania in establishing diplomatic relations with West Germany. But the signing
of the Romanian-West Germany treaty in January 1967 doomed the
prospects for a more flexible Bulgarian policy toward Bonn. It is
significant, nevertheless, that even after the February 1967 meeting
of Warsaw Pact foreign ministers in Warsaw, at which time the
Soviet Union and Czechoslovakia gave support to the Polish and East
German demand for a tougher stand against Bonn, Bulgaria continued
to hold open the possibility of improving relations with West Germany.
As late as March 1967, for example, Ivan Bashev, the Bulgarian
foreign minister, pointed out that although West Germany would have
to recognize the realities of postwar Europe, this demand was intended as a general principle for normalizing relations and not as a

precondition for an improvement in relations.[57] Even at Karlovy Vary when it became apparent that the Bulgarians had acquiesced to Soviet preferences for a common Warsaw Pact German policy, the Bulgarian delegation joined Kadar in challenging the Polish and East German position that an aggressive West Germany remained incorrigible as long as its social system remained unaltered. Although the Bulgarians and the Hungarians condemned the militaristic and revanchist aims of the West German leadership, they attributed the "obstacle to peace" only to contemporary West German policy and not to the inherent structure of the West German government.[58]

A final indication of Bulgaria's reluctance to abandon its Westpolitik despite pressure from its other Warsaw Pact allies is the delay in the signing of a Bulgarian-East German friendship treaty. Promoted by the Soviet Union as a means of reassuring East Germany of the solidarity of the Warsaw Pact, a series of bilateral treaties were concluded between the GDR and Poland (March 15, 1967), the GDR and Czechoslovakia (March 17, 1967), and the GDR and Hungary (May 18, 1967). Only on September 7, 1967, almost six months after the initial Polish-East German treaty, did Bulgaria and East Germany sign a mutual assistance pact. Moreover, unlike the East German treaties with Poland and Czechoslovakia, which singled out as the enemy "the forces of West German militarism and revanchism," identification of the West German threat in the Bulgarian treaty (and also the treaty with Hungary) was less specific, additional reference being made to "other military revanchist forces."[59] The failure of the Bulgarian leadership to take a more hostile anti-West German stand led Ulbricht, on a visit to Bulgaria for the signing of the Bulgarian-East German friendship treaty in September 1967, to remind Sofia that "whoever held his tongue about the aggressive designs of the West German imperialists would make himself an accomplice in whatever crimes they might commit."[60]

Admittedly, the initiative and autonomy shown in Bulgaria's Westpolitik between 1964 and 1967 was uncharacteristic of Sofia's general foreign policy behavior, and in the end it was Bulgaria and Hungary—the two states with the fewest historical impediments to rapprochement—who were the last to sign treaties with the Federal Republic of Germany. It would be a mistake, therefore, to conclude on the basis of its Westpolitik that Bulgaria can ignore, for a sustained period, Soviet preferences once Soviet decision makers have made up their minds. As Phillip Windsor put it, Bulgaria's "flexibility . . . is strictly confined by a pragmatic regard for the reactions of the Soviet government; the Bulgarians are independent enough to disregard Herr Ulbricht, but their independence is based on a cautious policy of neighborliness."[61]

THE INFLUENCE OF THIRD PARTIES

Attempts to sort out the determinants of East European foreign policy usually begin with an assessment of the influence exerted by the Soviet Union. This is not an unreasonable starting point given the unequal relationship between the East European states and the regional hegemon in terms of geographic area, population size, economic resources, military capability, and so forth and the conformity on the part of most East European states (less apparent for Romania since the mid-1960s) to Soviet foreign policy preferences on many foreign policy issues. A focus on East European responsiveness to Soviet demands, however, should not preclude the consideration of alternative external influences on East European foreign policy behavior. In particular, it would be a mistake to conclude a discussion of the external determinants of East European policy toward West Germany without saying something about the effect of West German behavior itself on East European policy.

It is not surprising that prior to October 1963 and Adenauer's retirement little progress occurred in East European-West German relations. As the first chancellor of the postwar Federal Republic of Germany and chief architect of West German foreign policy, Adenauer "chose to forgo the pursuit of West German interests in the East, especially reunification, in favor of the country's political objectives in the West."[62] As Robert Dean points out, the net effect of Adenauer's policy was clear: "economic, political, and military rehabilitation that was little short of miraculous" but also policy stagnation with regard to Ostpolitik.[63] Not only was West Germany's Ostpolitik under Adenauer fundamentally passive and negative, but, because of Adenauer's conviction that the East European states possessed little in the way of foreign policy independence, it also was directed almost exclusively toward Moscow. This assumption of East European impotence combined with the need to secure the trust of the United States, a legalistic and rigid view of East Germany (epitomized by the Hallstein Doctrine), and extreme sensitivity to the demands of expellee organizations effectively precluded any sustained West German initiative for rapprochement with the East European states.[64] The one exception to the generally unimaginative and passive West German stance before 1963 on the issue of relations with East Europe is, in a sense, the deviant case which demonstrates the general tendency. The deviant case concerns Polish-West German relations between 1955 and 1958.

As previously discussed, in March 1955, shortly after Moscow expressed its readiness to establish diplomatic relations with Bonn, the Polish leadership followed suit. Gomulka's assertion of Polish autonomy in October of the following year and the concurrent popular uprising in Hungary also encouraged critics of Adenauer's Ostpolitik to believe that a more active approach to Bonn's Eastern neighbor might reinforce the development of fissiparous tendencies in the Warsaw Pact. The Adenauer government itself, however, displayed little eagerness in responding to Poland's initiative and adopted a wait-and-see attitude despite the United States' approval of economic aid to Poland and a demand from the Bundestag for an explanation for the lack of West German responsiveness. While Bonn tarried, Yugoslavia acted. In October 1957, President Tito recognized East Germany and thereby entangled Polish-West German relations in the web of the Hallstein Doctrine by raising doubts in Bonn that "if a conciliatory policy (including extensive economic aid) toward the most independent of the Communist East European states (that is, Yugoslavia) had failed to gain tacit respect for fundamental German rights, how could it succeed elsewhere?"[65] Whatever prospects may have existed for Polish-West German rapprochement in 1957 ended shortly after the Yugoslav move and Bonn's retaliatory severance of relations with Belgrade. Poland, frustrated by Bonn's continued rebuff to its initiatives, hardened its position by attaching preconditions to its offers of reconciliation. One can deduce from this deviant case of temporary movement in Polish-West German relations at least one simple but important conclusion: A change in East European policy toward Bonn might have been necessary but was most certainly not a sufficient condition for rapprochement with West Germany.

In the absence of West German interest in an active Ostpolitik— an interest notably lacking during the Adenauer government—Warsaw Pact-West German political relations remained basically static. Only in the realm of foreign trade was some movement apparent, the most tangible result being the signing in March 1963 of a trade agreement with Poland calling for the establishment of a West German trade mission in Warsaw without consular rights.

Under the new Erhard-Schroeder government, which assumed office in 1963, Bonn began to advocate an improvement in West German relations with East Europe. Initially, this took the form of trade mission diplomacy. Trade agreements were reached in short order with Romania in October 1963, Hungary in November 1963, and Bulgaria in March 1964. Attracted by the prospects of economic cooperation with West Germany, all the WTO states except Czechoslovakia abandoned their position that the establishment of diplomatic relations must precede the exchange of trade missions.

The coincidence in time of the Erhard-Schroeder initiative, growing detente between the United States and the Soviet Union, the increasingly public rift in Sino-Soviet relations, and Khrushchev's own West German gambit make it difficult to identify with confidence the source(s) of motivation for the favorable response by Poland, Romania, Hungary, and Bulgaria to Bonn's initiative or to determine the extent to which most of these states would have been receptive to even more radical overtures by Bonn. Only in the case of Poland is there much evidence (relating mainly to Gomulka's negative reaction to Khrushchev's West German initiative) that a West German move to open diplomatic ties would have been flatly rejected. Indeed, one might argue that, because of Khrushchev's own interest in improving relations with Bonn, the years 1963-64 might have been an opportune time (internationally) for Bonn to have pursued further diplomatic negotiations with East Europe. When the Erhard government finally decided that trade mission diplomacy was inadequate to resolve the outstanding political issues between Bonn and her Eastern neighbors and began in August 1965 to explore the possibility of diplomatic ties with Romania, the international climate had changed, and Moscow was no longer sympathetic to West German rapprochement. In fact, in 1965, coincident with the holding of a Bundestag session in West Berlin and President Johnson's decision to use U.S. ground troops for offensive action in Vietnam, the Soviet Union had begun to escalate their joint harassment (with the GDR) of Western air and land communications with Berlin.[66] Whether because of German domestic opposition to the Schroeder initiative,[67] or Bonn's disagreement with Romania over the question of Berlin (probably aggravated by the Soviet show of support for the East German regime),[68] or, more likely, due to a combination of these domestic and external factors, no agreement was reached, and the FRG withdrew its proposed diplomatic exchange.

The next chapter in Bonn's Ostpolitik began in March 1966, with the Erhard government's peace note proposal to exchange renunciation of force agreements with all the East European states, excluding East Germany. The replies revealed the diversity of East European views on the subject. Poland and Czechoslovakia responded in a harsh and negative manner. Hungary's response, although not enthusiastic, was more moderate and less polemical. Romania and Bulgaria, on the other hand, refrained from any formal reply. That Bonn's peace note had served as a stimulus for Soviet and East European reconsideration of the German question and the need (from the perspective of the Northern Tier countries) for a common Warsaw Pact policy was indicated both by the lengthy list of Soviet counterproposals on Westpolitik and European security in its formal reply to Bonn on May 18, 1966,[69] and by the intensified East German and Polish efforts in the spring and summer of 1966 to halt any Romanian attempts to promote the further improvement of East European relations with West Germany.[70]

An active West German Ostpolitik, cautiously initiated by Foreign Minister Schroeder in 1963-64, received an important boost in
late 1966, with the formation of the government of the Grand Coalition. Although the two partners in the coalition did not agree fully
on all aspects of Ostpolitik (the principal difference involving Bonn's
relations with East Berlin), the thinking of the CDU/CSU and the
SPD was sufficiently close to facilitate a major breech with past
policy. In particular, as Karl Birnbaum points out, the Kiesinger-
Brandt government recognized "the need to adapt to the general
detente policy of the West, if Bonn were to avoid isolation within its
own camp."[71] From a policy standpoint this meant abandonment of
the view that rapprochement between East and West could be achieved
only as a consequence of progress toward German reunification. The
new attitude was manifest in Kiesinger's declaration to the Bundestag
on December 13, 1966, in which he asserted that West Germany
wanted "to improve economic, cultural, and political relations with
[her] Eastern neighbors who have the same wish—wherever conditions permit—and even to take up diplomatic relations."[72] Kiesinger
also emphasized that Bonn no longer regarded the Munich Agreement as valid and recognized "Poland's desire to live within a state
of secure boundaries."[73]

The immediate impact of the Grand Coalition's revived Ostpolitik was to aggravate Moscow's difficulties with its Warsaw Pact
allies by adding to the disarray in German policies of the East European states. The East German response to the Kiesinger offensive
was predictably quick and unambiguously negative. The initial reactions of the other Warsaw Pact states, however, including the
Soviet Union, were either ambiguous or positive.[74] Even the Polish
position, which previously had been very closely linked to that of the
Ulbricht regime, was at first quite moderate and displayed a willingness to acknowledge the new spirit of Kiesinger's remarks.[75]
The Czechoslovak response was also initially cautious and reflected
an interest in improving relations with Bonn—an interest which preceded the Dubcek regime. Like Hungary and Bulgaria, the Czechoslovaks sought to distinguish between normalization of relations
with the FRG, which they regarded as a bloc affair (that is, defer-
ence to the interests of the GDR was necessary), and diplomatic relations, which might be worked out bilaterally. The seriousness of
Czechoslovakia and Hungary's response to the Kiesinger offensive
was indicated by the fact that both countries went so far as to receive envoys from Bonn in January 1967 to discuss the possibility
of establishing diplomatic ties. As might be expected, the Romanian
response to Kiesinger's declaration was even more favorable, and,
when it appeared as though the Kiesinger-Brandt government might

prefer to court Hungary before establishing diplomatic relations with Romania, it was the Romanians who insisted on haste.[76]

An immediate consequence of the Grand Coalition's revived Ostpolitik was to reinforce the position of the East European advocates of German rapprochement and to highlight the ambiguity of Soviet policy toward Bonn. By the middle of February, however, a firmer Soviet position began to emerge as the Soviet leadership recognized the impossibility of maintaining even a semblance of Warsaw Pact solidarity in the absence of an unambiguous Soviet stance on the issues of Westpolitik and European security.[77] Thus, if Bonn's revised Ostpolitik in late 1966 aggravated Moscow's difficulties with its Warsaw Pact allies and encouraged the further assertion of Romanian independence, it also contributed to the hardening of the Soviet position on relations with West Germany and heightened Soviet, Polish, and East German fears of domestic developments in Czechoslovakia. In short, the Soviets had interpreted the Kiesinger-Brandt Ostpolitik as promoting the very divisive tendencies within the Warsaw Pact that it had sought to overcome.

Events in 1967 and 1968 demonstrated that Bonn's Ostpolitik could not succeed in the face of determined Soviet opposition. After August 1968, therefore, Bonn was careful to accord priority in its Ostpolitik to relations with Moscow and to avoid any actions that might be interpreted as interference in the Eastern alliance. The most important change in West Germany's Ostpolitik after the Czechoslovak invasion, however, did not take place until October 1969, when the Brandt-Scheel administration took office.

Although the Kiesinger-Brandt Ostpolitik had represented a significant departure from the policies of Adenauer and Erhard, it had shared with them an unwillingness to pursue any policy that sanctified or implied acceptance of the coexistence of two sovereign political regimes on German land. The policy declaration of the new Brandt-Scheel government in October 1969, which explicitly acknowledged the existence of the GDR as a separate state on German soil, therefore, marked an important watershed in the evolution of Bonn's Ostpolitik. Not only did this policy change strengthen the hand of East European advocates of rapprochement, who could now defend diplomatic negotiations with Bonn without appearing to abandon the interests of the GDR, but it placed the Ulbricht regime in the awkward situation of having to reconsider the logic of its own opposition to rapprochement. The precarious position of East Germany increased in December 1969, when the new Brandt government reached agreement with both Moscow and Warsaw on initiating bilateral negotiations for normalizing relations. In this situation of Soviet and Polish recognition of and favorable response to the "more realistic" foreign policies of the Brandt government, the East German government itself submitted a proposal to Bonn that inter-German negotiations begin in early January 1970. Although this East German initiative by no means signaled the end of Ulbricht's efforts to obstruct Bonn's Ostpolitik, it reflected the diminished support within the Pact for Ulbricht's hard-line position and the major reorientation that had taken place in the Pact's approach to Westpolitik since Karlovy Vary (April 1967).

The major revisions in Bonn's Ostpolitik, most apparent in 1963, 1966, and 1969, by themselves did not lead to the reorientation of East Europe's Westpolitik. A simple action-reaction interpretation of events ignores the variety of domestic demands and external constraints under which different East European decision makers formulated their positions toward West Germany. It also obscures the instances in which one side's overtures went unanswered or produced a contrary response. Attention to the evolution of West Germany's Ostpolitik and its interaction with the Westpolitik of the East European states, however, illustrates the permeability of even the most hierarchical of regional systems and is a useful corrective to a "system dominant" view of international relations, which focuses on the foreign policy responsiveness of subordinate states to "the demands emanating from one segment of the environment."[78]

INTERACTION EFFECTS

One thing that has been apparent in the discussion of change in East European policy toward West Germany is the difficulty of attributing policy change to only one factor. This is generally the case both across nations and for any one nation over time. There are, however, several exceptions to this multi-factor rule. Further examination of these "deviant cases" may provide insight into the conditional nature of the relationship that generally exists between external demands and foreign policy change. A comparison of the ways in which these special cases differ from (and resemble) other instances of policy transformation also may assist one in formulating in more general terms the necessary and sufficient conditions for foreign policy change in East Europe.[79]

The major instances in which a single factor appears to account for much of the variation in East European foreign policy toward West Germany are the shift toward Warsaw Pact solidarity (excluding Romania) on the German issue in the spring of 1967, a similar emergence of Pact solidarity following the invasion of Czechoslovakia in 1968, and a shift in the direction of a more accommodating stand by the East Germans in the spring of 1971. From the standpoint of theory development, what is striking about all three "deviant cases" is the presence in each case of a clear and resolute Soviet stance on the German issue.

In the first two instances the Soviet stand was one of active opposition to Bonn's Ostpolitik. As such, it coincided with the East German and Polish positions and therefore cannot be regarded as a source of or stimulus to policy change. In the case of Hungary and Bulgaria (and to a lesser degree Czechoslovakia), however, Soviet preferences clearly were at odds with the policy objectives of the leadership of the East European regimes. Due to mounting domestic economic demands, overtures of economic assistance by West Germany following Adenauer's retirement, and the lack of a clear and resolute Soviet policy between 1963 and 1967 regarding the question of East European relations with Bonn, decision makers in Budapest, Sofia, and Prague viewed with increasing favor the prospect of expanded contacts with the Federal Republic. In the case of Hungary and Bulgaria, movement toward improved relations with the FRG also was facilitated by the absence of outstanding political problems or historical animosities between the respective nations. Only after the establishment of West German–Romanian diplomatic relations in January 1967, and in anticipation of similar treaties with Hungary, Bulgaria, and Czechoslovakia (which threatened a serious breach between the Soviet Union and the East German regime), did the Soviet Union take a firm stand in opposition to East European relations with West Germany. This new and more resolute Soviet posture was apparent at the February 1967 meeting of Warsaw Pact foreign ministers and at the April 1967 Karlovy Vary conference of European Communist parties and was also reflected in the series of bilateral anti-West German defense treaties renewed or initiated between March and September of 1967. When this form of summit diplomacy proved insufficient to deter the Czech leadership from elevating domestic political considerations above Soviet policy preferences (including the renewal of interest in improving relations with West Germany at a time when Soviet-West German relations had deteriorated), the Soviet-led military intervention was taken to restore bloc solidarity. In short, both in the spring of 1967 and the summer of 1968, a deterioration of Soviet-West German relations and a resolute Soviet stand on the German issue preceded and adequately accounts for the shift in Bulgarian, Hungarian, and Czechoslovak Westpolitik.

The third occasion in which explicit Soviet policy preferences appear to account for a change in East European policy toward West Germany involves the shift in East German policy in 1971, and differs from the previous two cases in that the Soviet commitment was in favor of rather than against rapprochement. This case also is different from other instances of East European policy change in that economic incentives for a more conciliatory policy toward Bonn were not clearly evident (and actually may have argued against rapprochement) from the perspective of the East European state.[80] Its similarity to other uni-factor explanations resides in the assumption that Soviet pressure in the spring of 1971 was responsible for the removal of Walter Ulbricht, his replacement by Erich Honecker, and East Germany's subsequent adoption of a more flexible West-politik in accord with the Soviet stand. Admittedly, the grouping of this policy change in the uni-factor category is based on circumstantial evidence. One cannot dismiss altogether the possibility that idiosyncratic differences between Ulbricht and Honecker were responsible for the differences in their Western policies.[81] It also is conceivable that the East German policy shift resulted from a pragmatic reassessment of East German interests begun under Ulbricht and in response to policy changes of the Brandt government (for example, the more flexible position regarding recognition of the GDR as a separate state on German soil). Nevertheless, the coincidence of Ulbricht's removal and the immediate shift in East German policy in accordance with Soviet preferences (as well as Soviet treatment of Ulbricht's demotion and prior disagreement with Pankow over the German issue) support the contention by Peter Ludz that when Ulbricht failed to adjust to the change in international climate and the shift in Moscow's objectives, the Soviet Union acted "to downgrade Ulbricht and to call the East German junior partner to heel."[82]

The utility of single-factor explanations and the appearance of East European acquiescence to Soviet policy preferences is less apparent in the remaining cases of East European foreign policy change toward West Germany. This is not to say that the example of Soviet behavior was generally negligible. It most likely contributed to the improvement of Polish-West German relations after 1955, and undoubtedly reinforced Polish, Czechoslovak, Hungarian, and Bulgarian interest in rapprochement with Bonn in the 1969-73 period. These changes in East European policy, however, as well as other cases involving more open defiance of Soviet Westpolitik preferences, cannot be explained adequately without introducing additional variables. For example, in those cases involving a change in the direction of improved East European-West German relations, domestic economic considerations and accommodating behavior by Bonn appear to have been particularly important. The case of Romania in the early 1960s is the clearest example of the significance of these factors, although they also appear to have been important in Czechoslovakia (first half of 1968), Hungary (1964 to early 1967), and Bulgaria (1964 to early 1967).[83] When change was in the opposite direction, West German inflexibility, ideological considerations, and active Soviet opposition tended to be present. In several instances, a change in elite attributes, elite turnover, and/or a commitment to certain foreign policy principles also interacted with economic, idiosyncratic, and international systemic factors to encourage foreign policy change. [84]

Illustrative of the complex and interactive nature of domestic and external demands is the conciliatory position on the German question taken by Poland in 1955-56. Although the initial impetus for the Polish expression of interest in normalizing relations with Bonn in March 1955 may well have been the Soviet precedent established earlier in the year, there were a number of other domestic and external incentives for the reorientation of Polish policy. Externally, Khrushchev's revelations at the Twentieth Party Congress unleashed forces which found expression in the Hungarian Revolution and the Polish October. These developments, in turn, encouraged Bonn to take a closer look at the role that West German economic assistance might play in stimulating further East European assertiveness. Domestically, the rise to power of Gomulka and his personal animosity toward the Stalinist Ulbricht regime contributed to a deterioration in Polish-West German relations and a certain congruence of Polish-East German interests (that is, my enemy's enemy may be my friend). The declining rate of Polish industrial growth after 1954 also enhanced the appeal of closer economic ties with the West in general and the Federal Republic in particular. The combination of these factors and the absence of active Soviet opposition increased the freedom to maneuver of Polish foreign policy decision makers and made realistic the extension of conciliatory Polish overtures to West Germany. Similarly, in 1969 in Poland (and also in Hungary, Bulgaria, and Czechoslovakia), domestic economic difficulties, the promise of West German economic assistance in the form of hard currency loans and technology transfer, the more conciliatory stance taken by the Brandt government on such issues as recognition of the Oder-Neisse boundary and the existence of two states on German soil, the atmosphere of superpower detente, and the removal of the danger of contagion from the Czechoslovak heresy combined with a Soviet interest in improving relations with Bonn to stimulate East European movement toward rapprochement. Thus, while a resolute Soviet stand on the German issue proved to be a sufficient condition for East European policy change in 1967 (Bulgaria, Czechoslovakia, Hungary), 1968 (Czechoslovakia), and 1971 (GDR), the absence of active Soviet opposition to improved East European relations, while perhaps a necessary condition, was not sufficient for movement toward rapprochement to occur in 1955-56 (Poland), 1963+ (Romania), 1964 (Hungary, Bulgaria), and 1969+ (Hungary, Bulgaria, Czechoslovakia, and Poland).

The extent to which the absence of active Soviet opposition to rapprochement is a necessary condition for a positive change in East European-West German relations is difficult to determine on the basis of our study. The readiness of Bulgarian and Hungarian decision makers to abandon their pursuit of closer ties with Bonn in the face of active Soviet opposition suggests the importance of the "Moscow factor." On the other hand, in at least one and possibly two cases of Westpolitik change, movement toward rapprochement accelerated in the face of Soviet opposition. The clear case of defiance is Czechoslovakia in early 1968, where the shift in foreign policy can be attributed primarily to domestic economic and political considerations. The second and less obvious instance of defiance is the Romanian effort to improve relations with the Federal Republic in the mid-1960s. The ambiguity of this case stems not from the absence of explicit indicators of Romanian foreign policy innovation but from the difficulty of pinpointing the time of change in Romania's Westpolitik. If one accepts Kenneth Jowitt's date of 1962, then clearly the Romanian change came during a peak period of Soviet-West German animosity. [85] If, on the other hand, one selects the 1963-64 period as the turning point in Romania's independent course, at least in regard to the German issue, Gheorghiu-Dej's policy was not contrary to that of Khrushchev. Finally, if one identifies the early post-Khrushchev period as the major point of change in Romanian-West German relations, there still existed no firm Soviet position on the issue of East European-West German contacts, although the Kremlin's attitude toward Bonn had hardened somewhat. Improvement in relations between Bucharest and Bonn during the later period, therefore, would not constitute a case of open defiance of Moscow's preferences. Regardless of the role of Soviet demands, identification of the sources of the change in Romania's Westpolitik is further complicated by the interaction at approximately the same time of changes in Bonn's Ostpolitik, the emergence of a strong Romanian commitment to certain foreign policy principles (national independence, state sovereignty, and noninterference in the party affairs of other states), and a change in Romanian elite attributes and leadership. All of these changes, in combination with the Romanian elite's refusal to abandon its industrial developmental goal in the face of Soviet challenges, enhanced the appeal of improved ties with West Germany and contributed to the reorientation of Romania's foreign policy.

CONCLUSIONS

The question was raised at the beginning of the essay as to whether or not the designation "acquiescent" still portrays the

foreign policy behavior of the East European states. If by acquiescent behavior one means a readiness to regularly subordinate domestic demands to the policy preferences of the nearest superpower
(Rosenau's definition), then the behavior of the East European states
with regard to the German question does not appear to fit the designation "acquiescent." All East European states, including those
countries frequently regarded as foreign policy extensions of the
Soviet Union (for example, Bulgaria and East Germany), engaged in
foreign policy activity with respect to West Germany for an extended
period of time which was not supported by and did not correspond to
Soviet policy. In different instances, this divergence of Soviet and
East European behavior toward West Germany was interpreted to
mean (1) the likely preponderance of domestic over external demands; (2) the presence of conflicting demands and incentives from
more than one segment of the external environment; and (3) the absence of clear and resolute behavior on the part of the Soviet Union.

In most contexts it would hardly be surprising to discover the
inadequacy of single-factor explanations of observed behavior. International relations scholars increasingly have called attention to
the abundance and importance of situations in the global arena involving nonadditive, interactive relationships. The findings that an
explanation of foreign policy change in East Europe also is dependent upon interaction effects is striking only in the context of the
legacy of uni-factor commentary on East European affairs.

To be sure, our study of East Europe's Westpolitik does not
dispute the important role played by Soviet policy preferences. Indeed, the only cases in which East European foreign policy change
toward West Germany can be attributed to a single factor are occa-
sions of active Soviet opposition to or support of Bonn's Ostpolitik.
The extent of East European policy nonconformity and change with
respect to the issue of Westpolitik, however, also indicates that
Soviet ability to define the boundaries of permissible foreign policy
change does not imply an ability or willingness to prescribe Warsaw
Pact state behavior within a rather wide range of activity, at least
for certain foreign policy issues. Indeed, an important implication
of our study is that an exclusive concentration on Soviet policy preferences not only can distort one's perception of the foreign policy
objectives of the East European states but can conceal the extent of
change in East European foreign policy behavior over time.[86]

The issue of Warsaw Pact state relations with West Germany
makes clear that the mix of domestic and external demands affecting
East European foreign policy objectives and behavior can vary substantially from country to country. As a consequence of this variabil-
ity, those interested in explaining (and/or influencing) East European
foreign policy must direct more attention to the policies of individual

East European states without losing sight of the similarities across states.[87] Recognition of the desirability of this context-dependent but comparative approach provided the focus and orientation for this study.

NOTES

1. For a discussion of the Soviet Union as a regional hegemon, see William Zimmerman, "Hierarchical Regional Systems and the Politics of System Boundaries," International Organization 26, no. 1 (Winter 1972): 18-36.

2. James Rosenau, The Adaptation of National Societies: A Theory of Political System Behavior and Transformation (New York: McCaleb-Seiler, 1970), pp. 5-6. Rosenau suggests in his "foreign policy as adaptive behavior" framework that there are four basic orientations or strategies a nation may pursue in order to adjust to internal and external demands. These are acquiescent adaptation, intransigent adaptation, promotive adaptation, and preservative adaptation, and they are distinguished by their relative responsiveness to change and demands emanating from the domestic and external environment.

3. Thomas W. Wolfe, Soviet Power and Europe, 1945-1970 (Baltimore, Md.: Johns Hopkins University Press, 1970), p. 112.

4. Both Brezhnev and Gromyko, for example, failed to mention any demands regarding the status of West Berlin in several speeches discussing a German peace settlement. See ibid., p. 282.

5. Neues Deutschland, July 7, 1966. See also Laszlo Görgey, Bönn's Eastern Policy, 1964-1971 (Hamden, Conn.: Shoe String Press, 1972), p. 97.

6. Fritz Ermath, Internationalism, Security, and Legitimacy: The Challenge to Soviet Interests in East Europe, 1964-1969, RM-5905-PR (Santa Monica, Calif.: RAND Corporation, 1969), p. 41. There were even more positions if one counts intranational differences.

7. Wolfe, op. cit., p. 322.

8. See Karl Birnbaum, East and West Germany: A Modus Vivendi (Lexington, Mass.: Lexington Books, 1973), p. 8.

9. The text of the treaty is reprinted in ibid., pp. 109-10.

10. "Program of Peace in Action," Pravda, September 23, 1971.

11. Birnbaum, op. cit., pp. 56-57.

12. Ibid., pp. 57-58.

13. An indication of this movement was Moscow's tacit acceptance of the link between ratification of the Moscow and Warsaw treaties and the Berlin accord.

14. Peter Ludz, "Continuity and Change Since Ulbricht," Problems of Communism (March-April 1972): 58. For a discussion of the Soviet role in Ulbricht's dismissal, compare David Childs, "East German Foreign Policy: The Search for Recognition and Stability," International Journal (Spring 1977): 350-51; and Gerhard Wettig, Die Sowjetunion, die DDR und die Deutschland-Frage, 1965-1976 (Stuttgard: Verlang Bonn Aktuell, 1976), pp. 101-4.

15. Cited by Hansjacob Stehle, The Independent Satellite (New York: Praeger, 1965), p. 249.

16. Melvin Croan, "Moscow-Bonn-Pankow: Reality and Illusion in Soviet-German Relations," Survey (October 1962): 23.

17. See ibid., pp. 23-24, for a discussion of the Yugoslav-Polish-West German linkage.

18. Zvi Gitelman, "Toward a Comparative Foreign Policy of Eastern Europe," in From the Cold War to Detente, ed. Peter Potichnyj and Jane Shapiro (New York: Praeger, 1976), p. 152. West German recognition of the GDR, for example, was added as a precondition for the improvement of Polish-West German relations.

19. Nicholas Bethell, Gomulka: His Poland and His Communism, rev. ed. (Middlesex: Penguin Books, 1972), p. 242.

20. Lawrence Whetten reports that either before or after every important negotiating session with the FRG, leading Soviet and Polish officials would confer, in accordance with what a Polish delegate claimed were the resolutions of the December 3, 1969 Warsaw Pact Moscow Conference. See Whetten, Germany's Ostpolitik: Relations Between the Federal Republic and the Warsaw Pact Countries (London: Oxford University Press, 1971), p. 165. Reference to possible Soviet-Polish coordination also is provided in J. F. Brown, Relations Between the Soviet Union and Its Eastern European Allies: A Survey, R-1742-PR (Santa Monica, Calif.: RAND Corporation, 1975), pp. 83-84; Andrew Gyorgy, "Ostpolitik and Eastern Europe," in The International Politics of Eastern Europe, ed. Charles Gati (New York: Praeger, 1976), p. 161; and Louis Ortmayer, Conflict, Compromise, and Conciliation, Monograph Series in World Affairs, vol. 13 (Denver: University of Denver, 1976), pp. 44-45.

21. Ernest Skalski, "Victoria Consumata," Kultura (June 1972), cited by Robert Dean, "Foreign Policy Perspectives and European Security: Poland and Czechoslovakia," in East European Perspectives on European Security and Cooperation, ed. Robert King and Robert Dean (New York: Praeger, 1974), p. 124.

22. Andrzej Micewski, "Historyczne Warianty i Teranzniejszosc Polityki Polskiej," Zycie Warszawy, December 27, 1970, cited by Adam Bromke, "A New Political Style," Problems of Communism (September-October 1972): 15. See also a number of

articles in Zycie Warszawy in March and April 1969, by Polish
correspondent Ryszard Wojna emphasizing the risks to Polish interests of continued inflexibility in viewing Bonn as a political monolith whose policy was static. These articles are discussed in A.
Ross Johnson, "A New Phase in Polish-West German Relations,
Part I: The Background to Gomulka's May 17 Proposal," Radio
Free Europe Research (RFER hereafter), Poland/13, June 20, 1969.

23. Major changes in the leadership's composition began on
January 3, 1968, and continued during successive months. See
Yearbook on International Communist Affairs, 1968 (Stanford, Calif.:
Hoover Institution Press, 1968), p. 166.

24. Czechoslovakia was careful to distinguish between normalizing relations with West Germany, which was still regarded as im-
permissible, and establishing diplomatic relations which, in light of
Bonn's renunciation of the Munich agreement, was now feasible.
See J. F. Brown, "Eastern Europe and the Kiesinger Offensive,"
RFER, Bloc, February 4, 1967, pp. 4-5, for documentation of this
point.

25. Robert Dean, "West German-Czechoslovak Relations:
Problems and Prospects," RFER, Czechoslovakia, October 9, 1970,
pp. 4-5.

26. See, for example, the text of President Novotny's address
to the Karlovy Vary conference reprinted in Rude Pravo, April 25,
1967.

27. Dean, op. cit., p. 5. One possible indication of continued Czechoslovak interest in the improvement of relations with Bonn,
at least in the economic sphere, was the signing in Prague on August 3, 1967, of an agreement with West Germany on the exchange of
trade missions and a three-year trade and payments agreement.

28. See, for example, the Czech position on West Germany
in the April 8, 1968 Action Program of the CCP, and the more detailed discussion of the government's position in the declaration of
April 24, 1968. See documents 16 and 20 in Robin Remington, ed.,
Winter in Prague (Cambridge, Mass.: MIT Press, 1969). The
static nature of Prague's policy toward West Germany during the
reform period of 1968 is emphasized by H. Gordon Skilling,
Czechoslovakia's Interrupted Revolution (Princeton, N.J.: Princeton University Press, 1976), pp. 647-50.

29. Husak's speech as reported by Ceteka International Service, July 14, 1967, cited by Dean, op. cit., p. 9. See also the
article by T. Rok, "In the Light of the New Czechoslovak-Soviet
Treaty: Topical Problems of the Relations between the Czechoslovak
Socialist Republic and the Federal Republic of Germany," Pravda
(Bratislava), June 3, 1970. Rok notes that under the Brandt government the dialogue on mutual relations between West Germany

and the socialist states "has reached the stage where signs of the possibility of progress in solving individual problems in mutual relations are beginning to appear."

30. See the speech by Prime Minister Lubomir Strougal, reported in Pravda (Bratislava), September 10, 1970, and articles in Rude Pravo, August 19 and 21, 1970.

31. Initially the Czechs also insisted on abrogation of the agreement "with all ensuing consequences." This demand was dropped in September 1971. See Brown, op. cit., pp. 66-67, for a discussion of possible motives for Czechoslovak intransigence.

32. See Documentation Relating to the Federal Government's Policy of Detente (Bonn: Press and Government of the Federal Republic of Germany, 1978), pp. 67-69.

33. Kenneth Jowitt, Revolutionary Breakthroughs and National Development: The Case of Romania, 1944-1965 (Berkeley: University of California Press, 1971), esp. pp. 210, 252; and J. Michael Montias, "Background and Origins of the Romanian Dispute with COMECON," Soviet Studies (October 1964): 125-51.

34. See, for example, the vitriolic front page editorial in Neues Deutschland, February 3, 1967, and the equally scathing Romanian reply in Scinteia, February 4, 1967.

35. See Scinteia, May 8, 1966. Among Soviet transgressions noted by Ceausescu were CPSU domination of the Romanian Communist Party during the Comintern period and Soviet economic exploitation after World War II.

36. See the Bucharest Declaration, as reprinted in Survival (September 9, 1966): 289-94.

37. The ministers met February 8-10, presumably to coordinate their policies toward Bonn. In protest, Romania sent only a deputy foreign minister. The conference was originally scheduled to take place in East Berlin but reportedly was shifted to Warsaw after the Romanians threatened to boycott the meeting if it were held in East Germany.

38. UPI London, February 9, 1967. See also Moscow IASS International Service in English, 1035 GMT, February 10, 1967.

39. See Jowitt, op. cit., pp. 254-55, for a discussion of Ceausescu's skill in selecting the most favorable interpretation of the facts and evidence of his "accommodation without compromise" tactics.

40. Ceausescu's speech to the National Assembly, Scintiea, August 23, 1968.

41. J. F. Brown, "Rumania Today," Problems of Communism (March-April 1969): 39. In a speech to the National Assembly, for example, Ceausescu emphasized that should those who today see a danger of counterrevolution in Czechoslovakia tomorrow see a

similar danger in Romania, "we answer to all that the Romanian people will not permit anyone to violate the territory of the Fatherland." See Scinteia, August 23, 1968.

42. See Brown, "Rumania Today," p. 35, for speculation on this meeting.

43. It is interesting to note that on August 24, 1968, one day before Ceausescu's meeting with Basov, Tito and Ceausescu conferred. The Tanjug account of their meeting indicated that both leaders agreed that the alleged excuse for the invasion—the threat from West Germany—was absurd. Both leaders condemned the invasion and agreed to pursue parallel efforts to deter a similar Soviet move against Yugoslavia and/or Romania. Brown, ibid., p. 35, suggests that Tito may have cautioned Ceausescu against pursuing too provocative a stance. See Izvestia, August 24, 1968, and Pravda, August 25, 1968, for Soviet charges of Yugoslav-Romanian collusion.

44. The appeal was issued by the seven active members of the Warsaw Pact following the summit meeting in Budapest on March 17, 1969. An English version of the communique appears in Survival (May 1969): 159-61.

45. The phrase is applied to Romanian foreign policy by J. Arthur Johnson, "Rumanian Foreign Policy Since the Ninth Party Congress," RFER, Romania, August 7, 1969, p. 9.

46. See Görgey, op. cit., p. 86, for a discussion of Hungarian media commentary. East German dissatisfaction with the position initially taken by Hungary (and Bulgaria) on the issue of West German-Romanian diplomatic ties appears to have persisted even after the conference of Warsaw Pact foreign ministers in early February. See, for example, Ulbricht's February 13 speech to the Berlin SED party aktiv, in which he expressed gratitude to the CPSU and our "Polish and Czechoslovak friends" for their "clear statement" on the West German danger. No thanks were extended to the Hungarians or the Bulgarians. East Berlin ADN Domestic Service in Germany, 1452 GMT, February 15, 1967.

47. See, for example, the Radio Budapest broadcast to Europe in English on February 2, 1967, 1930 GMT. This broadcast, two days after the establishment of West German-Romanian diplomatic relations, applauded the fact that "an important feature of the present situation is the fact that it is the German Federal Republic that has made the effort to develop contacts" and that "it can be inferred that West Germany is interested in adjusting its relations with Hungary and the other European Socialist countries." Hungarian receptiveness to Bonn's Ostpolitik also was reported by Belgrade's TANYUG International Service on the day of the opening of the Conference of Warsaw Pact State Foreign Ministers (February 8, 1967, 1316 GMT, in English).

48. See, for example, Kadar's speech at the April Karlovy Vary conference (Radio Budapest broadcast in English to Europe, 1930 GMT, April 26, 1967). An earlier indication of Kadar's decision to support a harder line toward Bonn is provided in an election rally speech on February 22, 1967 (Radio Budapest, February 22, 1967, 1630 GMT, cited by William Robinson, "Hungary and European Security: Hunting with the Hounds," in King and Dean, op. cit., p. 153).

49. Even in 1966, before there was any indication of the Prague Spring to come, Kadar had been careful to stress that "political understanding with the Federal Republic cannot be brought about on a purely bilateral basis." See Nepszabadsag, August 2, 1966, and Görgey, op. cit., p. 91.

50. These were the words used in the communique of Hungarian-West German relations of the HSWP Central Committee on June 15, 1972, cited by Robinson, op. cit., p. 157.

51. Keesings Contemporary Archives (February 25-March 3, 1974): 26366.

52. Ibid.

53. Ibid. The remarks were made at a press conference during Fock's visit to Czechoslovakia on February 16, 1973.

54. J. F. Brown, Bulgaria Under Communist Rule (New York: Praeger, 1970), p. 203. The major exceptions are Barry Hughes and Thomas Volgy, "Distance in Foreign Policy Behavior," Midwest Journal of Political Science (August 1970): 459-92, and Ronald H. Linden, Bear and Foxes: The International Relations of the East European States, 1965-1969 (New York: Columbia University Press, 1979).

55. Rabotnichesko Delo, March 14, 1971, cited by F. Stephen Larrabee, "Bulgaria's Politics of Conformity," Problems of Communism (July-August 1972): 42.

56. Brown, "Eastern Europe and the Kiesinger Offensive," op. cit., p. 2.

57. Press conference in Copenhagen, March 6, 1967, reported in Neue Zucher Zeitung, March 8, 1967, and cited by Birnbaum, op. cit., p. 62.

58. See Karl Birnbaum, Peace in Europe (London: Oxford University Press, 1970), p. 67, for a discussion of this point.

59. The treaties are published in Freundschaft, Zusammenabeit, Beistand (East Berlin: Eietz Verlag, 1968).

60. Cited by Philip Windsor, Germany and the Management of Detente (London: Chatto and Windus, 1971), p. 127.

61. Ibid. For an interesting quantitative analysis of Bulgarian deviance from the Warsaw Pact norm, see Linden, op. cit., esp. pp. 18-19, 45-49, 170-73.

62. Dean, West German Trade, p. 17.

63. Ibid., pp. 17-18.

64. Ibid., pp. 18-19.

65. Ibid., p. 23.

66. See Wolfe, op. cit., p. 284.

67. See Dean, op. cit., p. 29.

68. See Robert King, "Bucharest, Bonn, and East Berlin: Rumania and Ostpolitik," RFER, Romania, December 18, 1970, p. 8.

69. See Pravda, May 19, 1966.

70. Highlights of this intra-Pact dialogue over relations with Bonn include Ceausescu's May 7, 1966 speech, Brezhnev's hurried trip to Bucharest three days later, the acrimonious June 1966 pre-summit meeting of Warsaw Pact foreign ministers in Moscow, and the July 1966 Bucharest Conference.

71. Birnbaum, East and West Germany, p. 29.

72. Cited by Brown, "Eastern Europe and the Kiesinger Offensive," p. 2, my emphasis.

73. Kiesinger's Munich statement went beyond Erhard's formula that the agreement no longer had territorial significance. The reference to Poland's desire for secure boundaries stopped short of unequivocal West German recognition of the Oder-Neisse frontier.

74. See Brown, "Eastern Europe and the Kiesinger Offensive," for a description of Warsaw Pact state reactions to the Kiesinger offensive.

75. William Griffith suggests that the Polish leadership may have been divided over the issue of Bonn's initiative and identifies General Mieczyslaw Moczar, leader of the so-called Partisans Faction, as Gomulka's chief antagonist. See Griffith, The Ostpolitik of the Federal Republic of Germany (Cambridge, Mass.: MIT Press, 1978), pp. 153-54.

76. This interpretation relies heavily on Ermath's account of events provided to him by "informed West German observers." See Ermath, op. cit., p. 47.

77. One can detect signs of Soviet anxiety over Bonn's Ost-politik before the conclusion of the West German-Romanian treaty. See, for example, Pravda, January 14, 29, 1967. It is probably wise to distinguish, therefore, between the apparent indecision by the Soviet leadership on an appropriate response to Bonn's Eastern initiative and the more likely decision-maker consensus that something had to be done to prevent further defections. I am thankful to Ronald Linden for alerting me to this possibility.

78. Rosenau, op. cit., p. 5 (my emphasis).

79. See Alexander George and Richard Smoke, Deterrence in American Foreign Policy (New York: Columbia University Press, 1974), pp. 514-15, for a discussion of deviant case analysis.

80. As an industrialized state whose economic performance generally has been impressive, the leaders of the GDR have been spared many of the demands for drastic domestic reform that have plagued other East European regimes like Czechoslovakia and Poland and which at times enhanced the appeal of closer economic cooperation with West Germany. In the case of the GDR, moreover, success for Bonn's Ostpolitik was apt to do little to improve trade turnover, which already was substantial, and would jeopardize East Germany's special access to the Common Market (because of formal EEC and GATT recognition of inter-German trade as domestic German trade) and decrease East European dependency on East German technology.

81. Reference to the possible connection between Honecker's background and belief system and his responsiveness to Soviet policy preferences is made by Stephen R. Bowers, "Contrast and Continuity: Honecker's Policy Toward the Federal Republic of West Berlin," World Affairs (Spring 1976): 310-11.

82. Ludz, op. cit., p. 58. See also Griffith, op. cit., pp. 200-6.

83. See William Potter, "Continuity and Change in the Foreign Relations of the Warsaw Pact States, 1948-1973: A Study of National Adaptation to Internal and External Demands" (Ph.D. diss., University of Michigan, 1976), pp. 100-44.

84. Ibid., pp. 218-25.

85. Jowitt, op. cit., pp. 200-7.

86. For an attempt to measure East European policy change and assess the determinants of foreign innovation, see William Potter, "Innovation in East European Foreign Policies," in The Foreign Policies of Eastern Europe: Domestic and International Determinants, ed. James A. Kuhlman (Leyden: Sijthoff, 1978), pp. 253-302.

87. The need to examine East European foreign policies for their intrinsic interest and importance is argued persuasively by Gitelman, op. cit., pp. 144-65.

5

POLITICAL CONFORMITY AND ECONOMIC DEPENDENCE IN EAST EUROPE: THE IMPACT OF TRADE WITH THE WEST

Donna Bahry
Cal Clark

The relationship between economic dependency and political conformity would appear to be clear-cut, at least superficially. Both concepts refer to linkages between a dominant center and its subordinate satellites which are by their very nature unequal or "asymmetric."[1] Yet, while the logic is clear enough, there are several competing perspectives on the precise connection between the two.

Albert Hirschman, in his classic study, argued that economic dependence can generate an "influence effect" in which economic leverage is used to extract economic and political concessions.[2] The dependencia school extended this premise by arguing that the structure of Third World economic relations with capitalist centers forces less-developed countries (LDCs) to accept externally dictated policies at variance with their economic and political self-interest. Dependence breeds exploitation, stunted developmental opportunities, and enforced political accommodation to a dominant patron. According to dependencia scholars, then, dependency—which is created and maintained by a combination of political, economic, and military means that are explicitly or implicitly coercive—fosters both economic exploitation and political conformity.[3]

One need not accept all of these assumptions, though, to postulate a strong link between dependency and conformity. As

A previous version of this chapter was presented at the 1978 annual meeting of the American Association for the Advancement of Slavic Studies, Columbus, Ohio. We are very grateful for comments by Ronald Linden and William Potter, which proved invaluable for our revisions.

Richardson observes, economic relations that are <u>disadvantageous</u> to the superordinate power can be used to increase the dependency of subordinate states (and, thus, their vulnerability to political "influence effects") by making it very costly for the less powerful partner to sever them regardless of the center's coercive capabilities. In such situations, Richardson argues, political compliance may be "viewed [by subordinate states] as partial payment in exchange for the maintenance of benefits they derive from their economic ties to the dominant country."[4]

In theory, then, the relationship between dependency and compliance would seem firmly established. Yet, empirical verification is still scanty. Richardson, for example, found that countries economically dependent on the United States were somewhat more likely to vote with the United States in the United Nations, although this relationship had decayed almost entirely by the early 1970s. He also found little relationship between degrees of dependence and conformity <u>among</u> these countries.[5] In the Soviet bloc, contradictory findings have emerged: Kintner and Klaiber conclude that a strong link exists between dependence and conformity, while Linden has argued that this relationship is much more attenuated.[6]

Thus, investigation into the linkage between dependency and conformity would still seem warranted, especially among communist states. Since these intrabloc relations ostensibly differ from the capitalist type, which invite most studies of dependency, they should provide an interesting comparative perspective. In addition, the Soviet bloc is marked by much tighter ties and controls than is the United States' far-flung set of dependencies (see, for example, Travis for a comparative quantitative evaluation),[7] although the putative effects on the dependency-conformity relationship are unclear. On the one hand, tighter control by the dominant power might intensify the connection, enabling the center to extract greater political concessions from somewhat reluctant satellites. On the other hand, differences among members of a semi-monolithic bloc might be small and fairly random, in which case there should be little or no association between conformity and dependence. The special nature of the Soviet bloc, then, makes it particularly attractive for such an analysis.

In this chapter, we develop indices of economic dependence on and political conformity to the Soviet Union among the six East European members of the Warsaw Pact and Council for Mutual Economic Assistance— Bulgaria, Czechoslovakia, the German Democratic Republic, Hungary, Poland, and Romania. In addition to observing the correlation between these two variables at two points in time, we also relate them to the East European nations' relative degree of trade with the West. Since declining economic growth rates in East Europe have stimulated trade with (and indebtedness to) the Western industrial nations, the West figures prominently in East European politics and economics. A consideration of this factor is therefore central to understanding the connection between dependence and conformity in the Soviet bloc.

THE POLITICAL ECONOMY OF THE SOVIET BLOC

During the initial period of Stalinist hegemony in East Europe, the Soviet Union behaved in the manner of classical capitalist imperialists as outlined by the dependencia school. Extreme political penetration of the local polities resulted in a "Soviet embassy" system of rule. Contacts among the satellites were kept to a minimum, and a massive transfer of economic resources from East Europe to the Soviet Union resulted from forced war reparations, the imposition of very unfavorable terms of trade, and the creation of "joint stock companies."

One very significant deviation from the normal structure of imperialism did occur, however, in the Soviet command that all the East European states pursue rapid industrialization, a drive that bred a dramatic economic transformation. Thus, contrary to the normal assumption that dependency reinforces underdevelopment, Soviet penetration promoted rapid growth. In the process, it produced an anomaly in the conventional dependency framework, making more developed countries more, rather than less, dependent on the dominant power. As East European industrial production expanded, most countries found themselves increasingly dependent upon Soviet-supplied imports of raw materials and also found the Soviet Union a primary purchaser of East European industrial products that were not easily salable on the world market. These two factors created what Hirschman calls "exclusive complementarity,"[8] molding trade and domestic economic structures in East Europe around the Soviet market and raising the costs for any bloc state seeking to change either its economic priorities or its external ties.

The post-Stalin period witnessed a gradual reversal of Soviet policy toward East Europe. In the political realm, Soviet control became much looser. The invasions of Hungary and Czechoslovakia notwithstanding, Romania pursued an increasingly independent foreign policy from the early 1960s onward; the "Prague Spring" endured for six months; Hungary's New Economic Mechanism deviated substantially from the orthodoxy of command economies elsewhere in the bloc; the Polish Gierek regime in the 1970s seemed to achieve a degree of autonomy in domestic policy; and even the normally conformist East Germany actively resisted Soviet accommodation with West Germany in the late 1960s and early 1970s.[9]

The change from Stalin's exploitative policies was even more dramatic in the economic sphere. Thus, for example, even though the Soviet Union was clearly in a position to dictate the terms of trade within CMEA and to extract benefits as Stalin had, instead it helped to create a price structure that undervalued primary products sold in the bloc and relatively overvalued manufactured goods. This put the Soviet Union at a serious disadvantage as a major exporter of raw materials and importer of manufactures. Price revisions from 1975 onward have been geared toward redressing the imbalance, but the gap still has not closed completely.[10] Thus it appears that the gross exploitation of the Stalinist period is clearly a thing of the past and that the Soviet Union may have subsidized her East European clients during much of the post-1960 period.[11]

The Soviet model thus imposed a set of economic priorities and a pattern of growth that made client states increasingly dependent on the Soviet Union as they industrialized. It also brought to East Europe the same problems with innovation and declining productivity that have concerned Soviet planners since the 1950s. In response, bloc states, like the Soviet Union, have turned to imports of sophisticated Western goods to boost productivity. The resulting rise in trade with the West, however, has created new problems of vulnerability to the world market and cross pressures derived from increased contacts with the West.[12]

The cross pressures on both the Soviets and the East Europeans are now substantial. For East Europe, what was once a virtual subsidy from the Soviet Union (based on an elaborate intrabloc pricing formula designed in theory to adjust for market disturbances) has been eliminated, with the Soviets now charging their client states what the market will bear. Ultimately, this change could benefit client states by encouraging the long-term rationalization of trade (that is, promoting exchange based more closely on comparative advantage). But higher costs of imports from the Soviet Union also pose a dilemma for East Europe. They cut into the resources available to buy Western goods and technology at a time when East Europe's technological lag is growing ever more costly.[13]

The Soviet Union, too, faces a dilemma: if prices of goods sold to East Europe are kept well below world market levels (as they were up until recently), they create a high opportunity cost to the Soviet Union, which could use its raw materials exports to finance its own purchases of goods and technology from the West. Yet, higher prices for Soviet raw materials create economic dislocations (inflation, shortages of consumer goods) in East Europe, which in turn threaten political stability. The dislocations might be offset if East Europe were to acquire Western technology; but increased contact with, and reliance on, capitalist countries—assuming that strictly economic barriers, such as East Europe's increasing debt and low ability to penetrate Western markets, can be overcome—imply a lessening of Soviet influence in the bloc.

There is, then, a tension between economic imperatives and the Soviet desire to promote intrabloc unity. In J. F. Brown's terms, the Soviet Union and its client states face a conflict between viability and cohesion. The first he defines as a combination of "confidence, credibility, and efficiency in Eastern Europe that would increasingly legitimize Communist rule there and consequently reduce Soviet need for a preventive preoccupation with the region." Bloc countries must thus adapt to rapidly changing environments and resolve a variety of political and economic problems, among them, sustaining economic growth and delivering on the longstanding promise to improve consumption. At the same time, the Soviet Union seeks to promote cohesion: "a general conformity of both domestic and foreign policies, as well as an identity of the institutions implementing these policies."[14] Though each of these is important, they may well be incompatible, since a common set of institutions and pressure to conform are at odds with the need for flexible responses to specific local problems.

The dilemma seems most pronounced where contact with the West is involved, in the sense that the one major source of promoting economic viability may also serve to destroy cohesion. The problem is not the existence of contact or trade with the capitalist countries per se but what it implies. As Robert Dean argues, East Europe's quest for Western goods and know-how can broaden beyond the trading of commodities and acquisition of licenses to other, more complex forms of interaction, such as cooperation agreements and foreign investment in East European firms.[15] These represent more direct and extensive Western involvement in bloc countries' domestic affairs and could, in turn, lead the East Europeans to seek expanded political ties with the West in order to underwrite and broaden economic relations. Bloc states might also reorient planning along more decentralized, "market" lines, that is, in directions that lead away from the standard Soviet model. In fact, some movements may already be seen in this direction.[16] The result is to complicate what Dean terms a Soviet strategy of "standardizing institutions and practices" in order to cement East European loyalties.[17]

The key assumption in this argument is that an inverse relationship exists between interaction with the West and bloc cohesion.

The quest for influence in East Europe is conceived as a zero-sum game between the Soviet Union and the West. Indeed, cohesion itself is frequently measured by the extent of trade and/or diplomatic contacts between bloc countries and capitalist states. While the assumption is logical enough, there has been little empirical research to test it—to determine whether greater East European involvement with Western nations actually means lessened Soviet influence or lessened East European conformity to Soviet policy. This paper offers a partial test, focusing on the connections between client states' economic dependence and political conformity to the Soviet Union and their economic interactions with the West.

MEASURING DEPENDENCE AND CONFORMITY IN THE SOVIET BLOC

East European economic dependence on the Soviet Union should be a product of (1) the level of trade conducted with the Soviets; (2) the relative importance of trade to the client state's domestic economy; (3) the concentration of goods sent to and received from the Soviet Union; and (4) the nature of the goods. The first two factors require little elaboration: the greater the volume of transactions with the dominant power and the greater the weight of the transactions in a bloc country's economy, the more costly it will be for the client state to weather an adverse shift in Soviet policy. And the greater the cost, the less inclined the East Europeans should be to depart from Soviet expectations. The concentration of goods traded exerts a similar influence on East European dependence: the less diversified the product mix (that is, the more heavily a bloc state relies on one or a few products in dealing with the Soviet Union), the less the client country's ability to shift among goods or partners when terms of trade with the Soviet Union change. Thus, the more concentrated the trade, the more the bloc state should conform to Soviet policy.[18]

The effects of the composition of trade are less obvious and, in fact, suggest a different pattern than that described in the literature on dependency. Dependence and corresponding vulnerability are typically associated with less developed countries—systems that produce and export a few primary products with little opportunity to diversify the domestic economy.[19] Yet Soviet-sponsored development in East Europe has fostered a reversal of the relationship, as outlined above. By promoting rapid industrialization in their own image, the Soviets have helped transform the East European economies into modern industrial systems. But the transformation has also meant that East Europe's industrial products

are often substandard and thus not competitive on the world market
and that its growth has depended on cheap supplies of fuels, minerals, and raw materials from the Soviet Union. As a result, client
states with more primary products ("hard" goods, those that can be
sold outside the bloc for hard currency) at their disposal should be
less dependent on the Soviet Union and thus under less pressure to
adhere to Soviet policy.[20]

Accordingly, export composition, that is, the degree to which
a bloc country sells "hard goods," is one measure of relative vulnerability with respect to the Soviet Union, and it should strongly
influence economic links with the Soviet Union (as represented by
the trade percentage, trade/GNP, and trade concentration indicators discussed above). To use the conceptual language of Keohane
and Nye, then, the greater the "vulnerability" of an East European
state, the greater should be Soviet economic penetration and thus
the greater the "sensitivity dependence."[21]

Economic dependence, in turn, should influence East European
conformity to the Soviet Union because Soviet economic leverage can
be applied to enforce adherence to Soviet policy. Finally, trade
with the West should be a function of both the "potential" for dealing outside the bloc (measured by a country's hard goods position),
and a given regime's political orientation (with the most conformist being the least inclined to venture into Western markets). It
should also "feedback" by reducing economic dependence on the
Soviet Union.

Figure 5.1, then, depicts our basic hypothetical model with
the presumed feedback effects of Western trade denoted by broken
arrows. Ideally, the test of the model would depend on multiple
regression and path analysis techniques. However, because of the
small number of cases and because of the crude and partial measurement of most of the variables, we have relied on rank order
correlations (Spearman's rho) to indicate the rough magnitude of the
relationships. Our basic analysis is cross-sectional, correlating
the ranks of the East European states on these variables for each of
two years, 1965 and 1975. This seems adequate for testing most
of our hypotheses. Some of these presumed relationships also have
a significant longitudinal dimension, however, since changes in the
absolute level of a factor over time should influence the absolute
level of other items for all the client states regardless of their
relative rank (such as the feedback effects of Western trade upon
political and economic dependence). Unfortunately, while the data
seem adequate to rank the countries at one point in time, comparisons of absolute levels for most of the variables between the two
time frames are much more problematic. Thus, the statistical
analysis is limited to cross-sectional results, while longitudinal
trends and relationships are presented in a more tentative fashion.

FIGURE 5.1

Model of Relationships among Dependency, Conformity,
and Western Trade

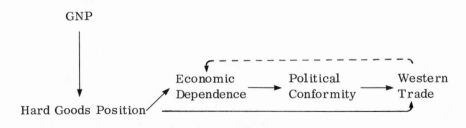

The measures we employ are partial in several senses.
Ideally, for example, the importance of foreign trade (and thus the
degree of economic penetration) should be measured by comparing
imports or exports to gross national product (GNP). The degree of
concentration should be estimated by a weighted average of all
products traded, and the degree of conformity should be determined
by comparing Soviet and East European positions and actions on all
issues of joint concern. In reality, however, East European countries report data on foreign trade and on domestic economic activity
in different prices, and offer no complete measure of GNP, so that
we have had to rely on estimates of exports/GNP derived from several sources (see Table 5.2). The East Europeans also fail to give
a complete breakdown of exports and imports (up to 20 percent of
each major category may be reported as a lump sum without break-
downs by commodities). This has led us to develop an alternative
to the standard measure of concentration more appropriate to the
bloc: the share of exports to the Soviet Union accounted for by the
top 20 commodity groups.[22] Using these three variables, we have
calculated an index of economic dependence on the Soviet Union,
according to the formula: (percent exports to the Soviet Union +
concentration score) x (percent of exports in national income).
    Admittedly, these measures of economic dependence are
limited since they focus only on trade. Other types of economic
interaction, such as joint investments, cooperation agreements,
and the export of labor, also help tie East European countries to a
"patron." Their impact, however, is extremely difficult to measure. For example, there is fragmentary evidence on the number
and types of agreements and joint ventures,[23] but none on their
value or their effect on the host country. Thus, while a complete

measure of economic interactions and dependence would require data on all such activity, the available information limits us to a consideration of trade relationships. (Some of the impact of cooperation and joint ventures may in fact be included in trade data, though the precise share is difficult to estimate. [24])

Political conformity poses additional measurement problems. The Soviet Union and East Europe provide little information on their policy differences; it is difficult to know how frequent and intense disagreements within the bloc are. We have relied here on a measure of public divergences between the Soviet Union and its client states over foreign affairs, derived in part from the earlier study of Kintner and Klaiber for 1965, and in part from a survey of the East European press and of Western reports of East European policy for 1975. [25] We summed the number of issues on which there was public disagreement in the bloc for each year studied and then ranked countries according to the number of deviations from the Soviet Union's position (on issues ranging from condemnation of the PRC to reforms within CMEA).

The measure clearly has its limitations. First, by focusing only on instances of dissension, it obscures a great number of issues on which all of the bloc states agree and thus may overemphasize the extent of conflict within the bloc. And, since contested issues change from year to year, the number of deviations may differ, too, making it difficult to compare conformity over time. Yet, what interests us is the relative incidence of disagreements in the bloc in a given year, that is, whether Poland is more apt than Hungary to diverge from Soviet policy. And, if so, do economic relationships with the Soviet Union and the West influence their actions? A second limitation on our measure is that all issues are treated equally in this index when in fact their significance may differ radically. Still, for the two years in our analysis, there do not appear to be any such gross differences; so issues and deviations are simply combined in an unweighted summation. There is, finally, a third limitation: we have relied on Western sources for data on Soviet and East European policy divergences, and Western sources are obviously selective in their coverage. Nonetheless, our measure of conformity basically fits assessments by other authors using other types of data and thus appears to measure what we want. [26]

Our other two variables are measured more directly and thus pose relatively few problems. The hard goods composition of trade is indicated by the value of fuel, metal, and mineral raw material exports (CTN 1 in Comecon trade nomenclature) minus imports divided by total exports; and trade with the West is measured by the percentages of total imports coming from and exports going to the "Western capitalist" countries. (For sources of trade data, see Appendix.)

DEPENDENCE, CONFORMITY, AND
EAST-WEST TRADE

We begin our empirical analysis by presenting the East European states' scores and ranks on the variables outlined in the preceding section. Rank order correlations are then used to test the
model presented in Figure 5.1, with correlations that are statistically significant at $p \leq .05$ identified by an asterisk. Finally, the
implications of the statistical results for the relationships among
dependence, conformity, and trade with the West are discussed.

Table 5.1 summarizes each bloc state's hard goods position
and also presents figures on GNP per capita. (A score of zero in
columns one or two here represents an exact balance of hard goods
exports and imports, while a positive score indicates a hard goods
surplus and a negative one a hard goods deficit.) The data suggest
several things. First, the rankings remain stable over the 1965-75
decade. East Germany and Hungary exchange places at the low end,
and Czechoslovakia's rank improves somewhat, but the overall correlation between the hard goods rankings for the two years is .77.
Second, as would be expected, level of development seems to be
inversely related to hard goods position, at least for 1965. The
two least developed countries, Romania and Bulgaria, ranked first
and second on hard goods position in 1965, and first and third in
1975, respectively. In comparison with the rest of the bloc, they
were thus in a better position to trade outside CMEA and to parry
Soviet economic pressure. For the six countries as a whole, level
of development (as measured by GNP) was negatively correlated
with hard goods position for both years, though the correlation attenuated by 1975. (The values were $-.83*$ and $-.23$, respectively.)

Though there are differences among bloc countries, overall,
East Europe is in a relatively disadvantaged position in terms of
hard goods, and this position has been deteriorating over time. In
1965, for example, Romania and Bulgaria had surpluses, while in
1975 all the East European states had deficits, ranging from 6.4 percent for Romania to 32.2 percent for Hungary, and all except East
Germany had registered a decline in hard goods composition, with
Bulgaria and Romania, which had had surpluses in 1965, experiencing the most dramatic changes. Thus, client states' general vulnerability to external pressures and penetration increased over the
decade.

The components of the index of economic dependence on the
Soviet Union are presented in Table 5.2. The overall index combines the share of each country's exports going to the Soviet Union
plus the extent to which these exports are concentrated among a few
products and weights this sum with a measure of the importance of

TABLE 5.1

East European "Hard Goods" Position and GNP Per Capita, 1965 and 1975

Country	Deficit (-) or Surplus (+) in Hard Goods[a]				GNP Per Capita (dollars)			
	1965	Rank	1975	Rank	1965[b]	Rank	1975[c]	Rank
Bulgaria	10.4	2	-12.7	3	1,085	5	2,184	3.5
Czechoslovakia	-6.4	4	-10.9	2	2,120	1	3,116	2
East Germany	-33.5	6	-24.4	5	2,053	2	3,379	1
Hungary	-22.9	5	-32.2	6	1,402	3	2,105	5
Poland	-6.0	3	-17.4	4	1,298	4	2,184	3.5
Romania	18.1	1	-6.4	1	1,032	6	2,024	6

[a]Exports minus imports of fuels, minerals, and raw materials, divided by total exports.
[b]This estimate of GNP is based on 1972 dollars.
[c]The data in this column are based on 1973 dollars.
Sources: See Appendix.

TABLE 5.2

Indicators of East European Economic Vulnerability, 1965 and 1975

Country	Exports to Soviet Union ÷ All Exports				Exports ÷ National Product[a]				Commodity Concentration[b]				Composite Score[c]			
	1965	Rank	1975	Rank	1968	Rank	1975	Rank	1965 (percent)	Rank	1975 (percent)	Rank	1965	Rank	1975	Rank
Bulgaria	52.1	1	55.5	1	16.5	3	23.4	1	84	1	70	2	225	1	294	1
Czechoslovakia	38.0	4	33.0	4	17.4	2	15.3	4	58	6	60	5	167	3	143	3
East Germany	42.7	2	37.8[d]	3	13.8	4	15.6	3	60	5	58	6	142	4	142	4
Hungary	34.8	6	38.9	2	18.9	1	22.9	2	66	4	66	3	191	2	238	2
Poland	35.1	5	31.5	5	8.9	6	11.8	5	68	3	65	4	92	6	108	5
Romania	39.8	3	19.9	6	9.5	5	10.9	6	78	2	76	1	112	5	105	6

[a]The magnitudes for the two years may not be strictly comparable, since data on national product for 1975 are more inclusive.
[b]Measured as the percent of exports to the Soviet Union accounted for by the 20 largest commodity categories.
[c]Calculated by adding the percent of exports going to the Soviet Union to the concentration score and multiplying this sum by the percent of exports in national product.
[d]1973.

Sources: See Appendix.

of exports in each nation's economy. In other words, we are assigning equal weight to the extent of exports and to concentration, since each may offset the other.

Bulgaria stands out as having by far the highest proportion of trade in the bloc with the Soviet Union; and Romania's 1965-75 change in proportion of exports sent to the Soviet Union clearly reflects her commercial reorientation away from the Soviet Union.[27] The export proportions of the other states changed marginally: Hungary became more dependent on the Soviet Union, while the other three became less so.

As columns 3 and 4 reveal, the importance of foreign trade increased for five of the East European nations (excepting Czechoslovakia). Indeed, given that the data in 1965 overstate the ratio by excluding some items from the estimate of national product, the change between the two years is in all likelihood somewhat greater than that indicated in columns 3 and 4. As for commodity concentration, four of the six nations experienced a drop between 1965 and 1975, though the decrease was marginal for all but Bulgaria. Taken together, the trade data in Table 5.2 thus suggest that East Europe as a whole has become more vulnerable to external pressure over time, though by comparison with dependent states elsewhere the East European countries have well-diversified export structures and lower levels of commodity concentration.[28]

As with our first two variables, the composite index of economic dependence on the Soviet Union is stable over time with a correlation of .90* between 1965 and 1975. The pattern of individual changes, however, is mixed. Hungary, Bulgaria, and Poland increased their dependence scores; East Germany stayed the same; and Romania and, somewhat surprisingly (in view of the 1968 Soviet invasion), Czechoslovakia experienced a decrease. Thus, despite the growing economic vulnerability throughout East Europe, different combinations of political and economic factors evidently have produced several patterns of change.

There is little association between these rankings and development level: the correlations between GNP per capita and the composite score are .14 for 1965, and .20 for 1975. This might seem surprising since dependence theory and interdependence theory both posit a strong relationship here, albeit in different directions. The dependence literature argues that less developed countries are economically weaker and thus more vulnerable,[29] while interdependence theorists believe that the more industrially advanced nations are the ones most integrated into the economic and communications "global village" and thus less capable of withstanding economic pressure.[30] Our data suggest, however, that neither theory is wholly adequate to describe East Europe. Though the

more developed nations among Soviet client states are somewhat
more vulnerable to external pressure, they are not necessarily more
economically dependent on the Soviet Union. As we explain below,
other variables intervene to influence each country's economic ties
to the Soviet Union.

Table 5.3 presents political conformity rankings for each of
the six countries. They are less stable over time than are the economic variables, with a correlation between 1965 and 1975 of only
.44. Three countries kept exactly the same rank in both years: East
Germany tied for most conformist, Czechoslovakia tied for third,
and Romania appeared the least conformist. Hungary registered the
biggest change, dropping from third in 1965 to fifth in 1975, as it
adopted a relatively "pro-market" position in intra-Comecon debates,
in contrast to Soviet emphasis on supranational planning.[31] Bulgaria
moved in the opposite direction, from a tie for third to a tie for
being the most conformist satellite. It had displayed some mildly
independent foreign policy initiatives in the mid-1960s as part of an
abortive attempt to expand economic contacts with the West[32] but by
1975 seemed disinclined to stray from Soviet preferences. Poland
also moved from fifth to a tie for third in the conformity rankings,
but this is primarily a reflection of Hungary's changing orientation.

TABLE 5.3

East European Conformity to Soviet Policy,
1965-66 and 1975-76

Country	1965-66	1975-76
Bulgaria	3	1
Czechoslovakia	3	3
East Germany	1	1
Hungary	1	4
Poland	5	3
Romania	6	6

Note: Countries are ranked from most (1) to least (6) conformist. Reported instances of disagreement for a two-year span
have been combined in order to account for potential lag in the
effect of economic conditions. For method of calculating these
rankings, see Note 25.

Sources: Kintner and Klaiber, Eastern Europe and European
Security, Keesings Contemporary Archives, Joint Publications Research Service, Survey of the East European Press.

Finally, turning to Table 5.4, we can see that trade with the West during the 1965-75 decade grew virtually across the bloc. East Germany experienced the biggest change, overcoming traditional suspiciousness of the West and using the mechanism of intra-German trade as an entree to the European Economic Community. Poland also registered a marked change, as the new Gierek regime tried to raise the Polish standard of living through imports of Western technology and consumer goods. Romania and Bulgaria, in contrast, registered less change, with Bulgaria's share of exports to Western countries actually dropping between 1965 and 1975. As Table 5.4 illustrates, Romania had already established relatively extensive economic ties to the West in 1965, and expanded these moderately in the following decade.[33]

TABLE 5.4

Share of Trade Conducted with the West, 1965 and 1975
(percent)

Country	1965			1975		
	Exports	Imports	Rank	Exports	Imports	Rank
Bulgaria	11.0	17.4	(4.5)	6.5	19.3	(6)
Czechoslovakia	14.8	13.9	(4.5)	17.1	19.4	(5)
East Germany	7.4	9.7	(6)	22.0	22.7	(3.5)
Hungary	17.0	17.9	(3)	19.2	24.6	(3.5)
Poland	26.3	19.1	(2)	26.8	41.5	(1)
Romania	23.6	28.6	(1)	27.0	32.9	(2)

Source: U.S. Department of Commerce, Bureau of East-West Trade, Selected Trade and Economic Data of the Centrally Planned Economies (Washington, D.C.: Department of Commerce, annual).

The rankings for the two years on trade with the West are fairly similar ($r_s = .60$), although this variable is not as stable over time as hard goods composition or economic dependence. East Germany accounted for the major changes in the rankings by rising from last to a tie for third. Most other countries also significantly expanded trade with the West during the detente era, though relative magnitudes for each country have remained roughly constant.

TESTING THE MODEL

  Rank order correlations among these variables offer a crude test of the model outlined in Figure 5.1. These correlations are presented in Figure 5.2 for 1965 and Figure 5.3 for 1975. All of these coefficients are in the expected direction, but they vary from strong to negligible, suggesting that some parts of the model may need to be revised.

FIGURE 5.2

1965 Relationships

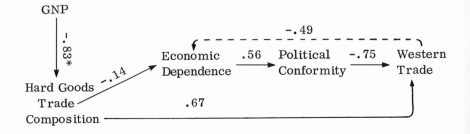

FIGURE 5.3

1975 Relationships

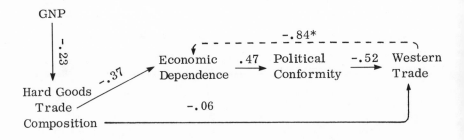

  For the first part of the model, level of development in 1965 was strongly related to our measure of vulnerability (hard goods position), but the latter was not significantly related to economic dependence on the Soviet Union. This pattern had changed, however, by 1975. Given the worsening hard goods position for all six East European nations, level of development no longer correlated with rankings for hard goods. But the connection between hard goods position and economic dependence on the Soviet Union grew stronger. Thus, as raw materials grew more costly in the 1970s, countries most able to weather the change were somewhat less likely to be economically reliant on the Soviets. The modest correlation (-.37), however, indicates that other factors—including the political pro-clivities of each bloc state—are also important influences on economic dependence.

These might help to explain some of the divergent ranks in Tables 5.1 and 5.2. For example, Bulgaria is the most economi-cally dependent on the Soviet Union, in spite of a relatively favorable hard goods position, and this might be explained by her heavy re-liance on Soviet political backing. In other words, there may be different factors at work producing high levels of economic depen-dence: a "voluntary" political one and a less voluntary economic one.

Turning to the connection between economic dependence on the Soviet Union and conformity with Soviet policy, we find that there is a moderate correlation (r_s = .56 for 1965, and .47 for 1975). Again, the reasons for the modest relationship may be political. East Germany, for example, was more conformist in 1965 than its economic position would seem to warrant—largely because of its political dependence on the Soviet Union. Bulgaria, on the other hand, was less conformist than we would predict on strictly eco-nomic grounds, in part because of the efforts to expand economic contacts with the West, noted earlier. In another instance, eco-nomic dependence would appear to account for a conformity score but does not seem to supply the best substantive explanation: Hungary in 1965 was high on both dependence and conformity. But this may have stemmed less from direct Soviet economic leverage (to which Hungary was extremely vulnerable because of a high de-gree of economic dependence) than from a conscious political trade-off by the Kadar regime, tendering foreign policy support to the Soviet Union in order to gain greater latitude for the domestic re-forms that accompanied the beginning of the New Economic Mecha-nism.[34] These cases suggest that domestic political factors, in addition to purely economic ones, may help explain differences in political conformity to Soviet policy. In fact, there appears to be a significant domestic factor that we might term "political dependence" mediating both the degree of economic dependence on, and conform-ity to, the Soviet Union.[35] In other words, some client states look more readily to Moscow rather than to domestic sources for sup-port and legitimacy, and this in turn may shape both the extent of their economic contact with the Soviets and their willingness to follow the Soviet lead in foreign policy.

How does trade with the West fit in? The "fit" is essentially what we anticipated, although it grows weaker between 1965 and 1975 for some of our predicted linkages, and the drop is most dramatic for one of the factors (hard goods position) we expected to be significantly related to Western trade. As Figure 5.1 illustrated, political conformity should be negatively related to Western trade, and hard goods position should be positively related to it. Both correlations do in fact run in the predicted directions for 1965 ($r_s = -.75$ and $.67$ respectively). Western trade should also be inversely correlated with economic dependence on the Soviet Union, and this, too, is borne out by the data ($r_s = -.49$), though with only a weak correlation. Equally important, there are two significant deviations in rankings between economic dependence, conformity, and trade with Western countries: in one case, Bulgaria's trade with the West is lower than might be expected from her hard goods position; and, in another, Hungary's high rank on ties with the West clashes with a high conformity score. Both emphasize, again, the role of domestic political factors in shaping relations within and outside the bloc.

By 1975, the links between economic dependence, political conformity, and Western trade changed. The 1965 correlation of .67 between Western trade and hard goods position dropped to -.06, at precisely the time that raw material scarcity was having an explosive impact on both the world and CMEA markets. Moreover, the correlation between political conformity to the Soviet Union and trade with the West also dropped (from -.75 to -.52). But the link between Western economic ties and economic dependence on the Soviet Union grew stronger (from -.49 to -.84*). Thus, by 1975, countries with the most extensive dealings in Western markets were the ones over which the Soviet Union enjoyed the least economic leverage. Soviet leverage, however, by no means prevented some highly dependent countries from open divergence with Soviet policy.

To sum up, our data indicate that an association does exist between trade with the West and a syndrome of economic dependence on and political conformity to the Soviet Union. But parts of the relationship are weaker than we had originally expected. For example, our measure of vulnerability to external penetration (hard goods position) indicates that some of the countries that are least susceptible to economic dependence on the Soviet Union may nonetheless be highly dependent. Thus, economic vulnerability is at best only a partial explanation for the extensive economic ties that exist between some bloc countries (such as Bulgaria) and the Soviet Union. A more complete explanation would have to include what we have termed "political dependence," or the extent to which a client country's party looks to Moscow rather than to domestic political sources for support.

IMPLICATIONS

The picture that emerges is thus more complex than our initial formulation and many studies of East Europe suggest. The negligible link between economic vulnerability and economic dependence on the Soviet Union, and the modest correlation between economic dependence and political conformity indicate that there may be meaningful choices open to East Europe in pursuing economic ties with the Soviet Union and in supporting Soviet foreign policy initiatives. This is not to say that client states are completely autonomous. Nonetheless, they can decide how closely to follow the Soviet lead.[36] The very different courses of the Husak and Kadar regimes, for example, show that even Soviet invasions do not have inevitable results in terms of the successor regimes.

If bloc states do exercise meaningful choices, there are at least two possible explanations. The first is that the Soviet Union may be less insistent on strict conformity than it is reported to be.[37] The second is that the Soviets may simply be unable or unwilling to press home the advantages they derive from East Europe's economic dependence. Where Soviet leverage is greatest, the potential disruption from a Soviet reprisal is also the highest. The Soviet Union may be reluctant to use extensive economic pressure on highly dependent bloc states for fear of the economic and political problems it can unleash.

Whatever the reasons, Soviet client states in East Europe clearly have more room to maneuver with respect to the Soviet Union than any assessment of economic vulnerability alone would imply. The data thus bear out Galtung's observation that the elite or "center" in a dependent state may exercise considerable discretion in developing ties to a center nation. It can thus mediate both the degree and the ultimate effects of dependence.[38]

Our results also suggest a somewhat more complex trade-off between viability and cohesion than the one we discussed earlier. For example, to the extent that the Soviet Union encourages East European viability through trade with the West, it does undermine the economic leverage it can bring to bear against bloc countries. But its economic leverage is no guarantee that each bloc state will conform wholly to Soviet policy. So an increase in East European trade with the West need not signal a corresponding drop in intra-bloc cohesion. In fact, an increase might actually reinforce the Soviets' dominant position. As Mark Allen argues, high levels of East European indebtedness to the West may make Western countries unwilling to offer new credit to some bloc states unless the Soviet Union offers to guarantee repayment.[39] Thus, paradoxically, Soviet client countries could find themselves relying on Soviet good will to assure a continuing flow of credit for purchases in the West.

On the other hand, it is also possible that a <u>drop</u> in East Europe's trade with the West—and a drop in the availability of Western credit—might threaten intrabloc cohesion. Since bloc economies are often more competitive than complementary in trade with the West, any drop in Western credits to or trade with East Europe could reduce cohesion by stimulating economic competition for financing and for capital goods that are unavailable in the bloc.[40]

Finally, the trade-off between viability and cohesion within East Europe is also less clear-cut than we had originally anticipated. It is not at all clear, for example, that the two are mutually exclusive. If there are different degrees of "political dependence," then each bloc country may have a different stake in intrabloc cohesion. The most politically dependent can be threatened by a precipitous drop in cohesion (as was East Germany at the time of the 1968 crisis in Czechoslovakia), while too great cohesion could topple the more independent regimes (as in the cases of Hungary's economic policy, Poland's relations with the Catholic Church, and most certainly Romania's foreign policy). The very question of cohesion, then, can create conflicts of interest among bloc countries. Some may view a high degree of bloc unity as necessary for their own viability, while others may view it as anathema.

The Soviet bloc, then, faces some underlying tensions that the political stability of the 1970s and the secureness of the Soviet hold may obscure. This is not to say that the Soviet Union's East European empire is about to collapse like a moldy house of cards. Rather, East Europe seems to be a more complex problem for both analytic theorists and policy planners than would be suggested by most of the conventional images that have been used to describe it.

APPENDIX: SOURCES FOR TABLES 5.1 and 5.2

<u>Vneshniaia Torgovlia SSSR</u> (Moscow: Statistika, 1961, 1974, 1975), passim; <u>Statisticheski Godishnik na Narodna Republika Bulgaria</u> (Sofia: Durzhavno Upravlenie za Informatsia, 1970, 1975); <u>Statisticka Rocenka Ceskoslovenske Socialisticke Republike</u> (Prague: Federal Statisticky Urad, 1970, 1975); <u>Statistisches Jahrbuch der DDR</u> (Berlin: Staatsverlag der DDR, 1972, 1975); <u>Statistical Yearbook</u> (Budapest, Hungarian Central Statistical Office, 1974, 1976); <u>Statistical Pocket Book of Hungary</u> (Budapest: Hungarian Central Statistical Office, 1973); <u>Rocznik Statystyczny</u> (Warsaw: Glowny Urzad Statystyczny, 1973, 1976); <u>Concise Statistical Yearbook of Poland</u> (Warsaw: Central Statistical Office, 1974); <u>Anuarul Statistic</u> (Bucharest: Central Statistical Board, 1970, 1975); <u>Statistical Pocket Book of the Socialist Republic of Romania</u> (Bucharest: Central Statistical Board, 1970).

G. E. Zhelev, Problemy Vosproizvodstva i Mezhdunarodnogo Razdeleniia Truda v Stranakh-Chlenakh SEV (Moscow: Ekonomika, 1971); U.S. Department of Commerce, Bureau of East-West Trade, Selected Trade and Economic Data of the Centrally Planned Economies (Washington, D.C.: Government Printing Office, annual).

NOTES

1. Robert O. Keohane and Joseph S. Nye, Power and Interdependence: World Politics in Transition (Boston: Little, Brown, 1977), pp. 8-19.

2. Albert O. Hirschman, National Power and the Structure of Foreign Trade (Berkeley: University of California Press, 1945), pp. 30-32.

3. Johan Galtung, "A Structural Theory of Imperialism," Journal of Peace Research 8 (September 1971): 81-98; Andre Gunder Frank, Capitalism and Underdevelopment in Latin America (New York: Monthly Review Press, 1969); Paul A. Baran and Paul M. Sweezy, Monopoly Capitalism (New York: Monthly Review Press, 1966); Pierre Jalee, The Pillage of the Third World (New York: Monthly Review Press, 1968); and Theotonio Dos Santos, "The Structure of Dependence," American Economic Review, Papers and Proceedings 60 (May 1970): 231-36.

4. Neil R. Richardson, Foreign Policy and Economic Dependency (Austin: University of Texas Press, 1978), p. 64.

5. Ibid., chaps. 4, 5.

6. Compare William R. Kintner and Wolfgang Klaiber, Eastern Europe and European Security (New York: Dunellen Press, 1971), chap. 13, with Ronald Haly Linden, Bear and Foxes: The International Relations of the East European States, 1965-1969 (New York: Columbia University Press, 1979), pp. 50-52, 158-60, 208.

7. Tom C. Travis, "Toward a Comparative Study of Imperialism" (Paper presented at the annual convention of the International Studies Association, Washington, D.C., February 20-22, 1975).

8. Hirschman, op. cit., p. 32.

9. Robin Alison Remington, The Warsaw Pact: Case Studies in Communist Conflict Resolution (Cambridge, Mass.: MIT Press, 1971), provides an excellent comparative analysis of these events (excepting the Gierek regime in Poland). For other comparative studies of East European foreign policies, see Zbigniew K. Brzezinski, The Soviet Bloc: Unity and Conflict (Cambridge, Mass.: Harvard University Press, 1967); Charles Gati, ed., The International

Politics of Eastern Europe (New York: Praeger, 1976); Kintner and Klaiber, op. cit., and Linden, op. cit.

10. Martin J. Kohn and Nicholas R. Lang, "The Intra-CMEA Foreign Trade System: Major Price Changes, Little Reform," in U.S. Congress, Joint Economic Committee, East European Economies Post-Helsinki (Washington, D.C.: Government Printing Office, 1977), pp. 135-51; and Martin J. Kohn, "Soviet-East European Economic Relations since the 1975 Price Changes" (Paper presented at the convention of the American Association for the Advancement of Slavic Studies, Columbus, Ohio, October 1978).

11. Paul Marer, "Has Eastern Europe Become a Liability to the Soviet Union? The Economic Aspect," in Gati, op. cit., pp. 59-81; and Cal Clark and Donna Bahry, "Dependency in the Soviet Bloc: A Reversal of the Economic-Political Nexus" (Paper presented at the annual convention of the International Studies Association, Toronto, March 20-24, 1979). Paul Marer, in "Statement before the Subcommittee on Europe and the Middle East of the House International Relations Committee," mimeograph (September 1978), provides the most recent evaluation and concludes (p. 16), "At this point I would conclude that it is very difficult to draw up an accurate balance sheet of who benefits and how much in Eastern Europe's trade with the USSR. We may also wonder whether the CMEA countries themselves know how these matters stand" (p. 37).

12. Thomas Wolf, "East-West European Trade Relations," in Joint Economic Committee, op. cit., pp. 1042-54; and Philip Hanson and Michael Kaser, "Soviet Economic Relations with Western Europe," in Soviet Strategy in Europe, ed. Richard Pipes (New York: Crane, Russak, 1976), pp. 224-301, provide good summaries of East-West trade relations.

13. Alfred Zauberman, "The East European Economies," Problems of Communism 27 (March-April 1978): 55-69.

14. J. F. Brown, Relations between the Soviet Union and Its Eastern European Allies: A Survey, Report R-1742-PR (Santa Monica, Calif.: RAND, 1975), focuses primarily on the need for East European autonomy to promote viability; and one element of autonomy would be to depart from Soviet norms in planning and allocating resources. Robert Dean, "Moscow and Eastern Europe: A New Look," Problems of Communism 26 (July-August 1977): 83-88, argues, however, that in theory at least the bloc could well guarantee viability through closer cooperation and/or integration of politics and planning.

15. Dean, op. cit., p. 84.

16. Hanson and Kaser, op. cit., p. 256. Some reorientations are already apparent. Bulgaria, Hungary, and Romania, for example, allow foreign firms to invest directly in domestic enterprises as minority shareholders.

17. Dean, op. cit., p. 86.

18. This is a normal assumption in dependency analysis. For example, see James Caporaso, "Methodological Issues in the Measurement of Inequality, Dependence, and Exploitation," in Testing Theories of Economic Imperialism, ed. Steven J. Rosen and James A. Kurth (Lexington, Mass.: D. C. Heath, 1974), pp. 103-5.

19. Galtung, op. cit., pp. 85-86.

20. The concept of "hard" and "soft" goods on the CMEA market is still somewhat controversial. Marer, "Statement," provides a good overall summary of some of the intracies involved.

21. Keohane and Nye, op. cit., p. 8.

22. A commodity group is defined here as one of the three digit categories of the CMEA trade nomenclature (CTN). The categories are explained in Paul Marer, Soviet and East European Foreign Trade, 1946-1969 (Bloomington: Indiana University Press, 1972), pp. 309-41.

23. Carl H. McMillan, "East-West Industrial Cooperation," in Joint Economic Committee, op. cit., pp. 1175-1224.

24. Harry Trend, "East European Indebtedness to the West," in Eastern Europe's Uncertain Future, ed. Robert King and J. F. Brown (New York: Praeger, 1977), pp. 244-47.

25. Kintner and Klaiber, op. cit., chap. 13. Instances of disagreement were coded as a "1," and instances of agreement were coded as a "0." Then the numbers were summed for each country in each year. The issues included, among others, acknowledgment of the "leading role" of the Soviet Union in the international Socialist movement, the "correctness" of Chinese policy, and the structure of CMEA. A full list of the issues and the coding used is available from the authors.

26. As a partial test of the validity of our conformity index, we correlated it with indices produced by Linden, op. cit., and by William Potter, "Continuity and Change in the Foreign Relations of Warsaw Pact States" (Ph. D. diss., University of Michigan, 1976), p. 51. The correlation between our 1965 index and Linden's data (covering 1965-69) is .88*; the relationship between our 1975 index and Potter's data (for 1970) is .70.

27. Cal Clark and Robert L. Farlow, Comparative Patterns of Foreign Policy and Trade: The Communist Balkans in International Politics (Bloomington: International Development Institute of Indiana University, 1976), chap. 5, provides a more detailed analysis.

28. Donna Bahry and Cal Clark, "A Dependence Theory of Soviet-East European Relations: Theory and Empirical Testing"

(Paper presented at the Conference on Integration in Eastern Europe and East West Trade, Bloomington, Indiana, October 1976).

29. Galtung, op. cit., pp. 85-86.

30. Edward L. Morse, "The Transformation of Foreign Policies: Modernization, Interdependence, and Externalization," World Politics 22 (April 1970): 371-92.

31. Henry Schaefer, Comecon and the Politics of Integration (New York: Praeger, 1972), discusses the differing policy positions of the CMEA nations concerning their economic relations.

32. Linden, op. cit., chap. 2, provides a good quantitative assessment of this trend.

33. Clark and Farlow, op. cit., pp. 49-55.

34. Bennett Kovrig, "Hungary," in Communism in Eastern Europe, ed. Teresa Rakowska-Harmstone and Andrew Gyorgy (Bloomington: Indiana University Press, 1979), pp. 93-95.

35. Linden, op. cit., pp. 206-10, and Clark and Farlow, op. cit., chap. 9, offer similar conclusions on the importance of political considerations for intrabloc economic ties.

36. The idea that the East European states have significant policy options within fairly wide parameters is also supported, according to Russett, by the pattern of defense spending in the Warsaw Pact, which switched in the mid-1960s from one evidencing "Soviet coercion" to one suggesting a more "voluntary" distribution in the assumption of defense burdens. See Bruce M. Russett, What Price Vigilance? The Burdens of National Defense (New Haven: Yale University Press, 1970), pp. 112-16.

37. Kulski has argued, for example, that "any deviation" from Moscow's view of true socialism or from Soviet foreign policy "would be declared a betrayal of Socialist internationalism, as the Czechs have learned at their own expense." The Soviet Union in World Affairs: A Documentary Analysis, 1964-72 (Durham, N.C.: Duke University Press, 1974), pp. 297-98.

38. Galtung, op. cit., pp. 83-84. For a similar conclusion, see Keith Orton and George Modelski, "Dependency Reversal: National Attributes and Systemic Processes" (Paper presented at the annual meeting of the International Studies Association, Toronto, March 1979).

39. "The Bulgarian Economy in the 1970s," in Joint Economic Committee, op. cit., pp. 695-96.

40. Thomas Wolf, "East-West European Trade Relations," in U.S. Congress, Joint Economic Committee, op. cit., p. 1054.

6

DEPENDENCY THEORY AND THE SOVIET-EAST EUROPEAN HIERARCHICAL REGIONAL SYSTEM: INITIAL TESTS

William Zimmerman

Throughout the post-World War II period, the prevailing paradigm of international politics among Western scholars has assumed that the major task confronting the decision makers of all states is achieving security in an anarchic state system. It follows from this assumption that relations between relatively equal superpowers constitute, in Arnold Wolfers's phrase, "the relationship of major tension" in the postwar world. In the 1970s, however, there has been a revival among Western scholars of an alternative perspective on world politics: the theory of economic imperialism, or, as it is usually labeled in the 1970s, "dependency theory." It is a perspective which focuses on unequal relations between states. In that perspective, "the basic model of international politics [is] the imperialist system that was centered upon states of unequal economic development," where "the relationship of major tension was between the developed and underdeveloped economies."[1]

There is much to be said for recent dependency theory. (Granted immediately that, like the Leninist theory of imperialism from which it draws its intellectual inspiration, dependency theory

I am grateful to David Abernathy, Harold K. Jacobson, Jan Triska, Barbara Zimmerman, and an anonymous reviewer for helpful comments, and to the Rockefeller Foundation for financial assistance. An earlier version of this paper was presented at the annual meeting of the American Association for the Advancement of Slavic Studies, October 6-8, 1976, in St. Louis, Missouri.

Reprinted from the Slavic Review: American Quarterly of Soviet and East European Studies 37, no. 4 (December 1978).

has often produced a melange of unfalsifiable propositions and rhetorical bombast.) Dependency theory is, among other things, a theory of interstate behavior which has an identifiable core that contains important propositions about explanations of the foreign-policy behavior of states, conditions for national autonomy, and linkages between the international environment and economic or political development. [2]

Among dependency theorists there exists a general disposition to regard independence as intrinsically good (perhaps even the primary value for a state and its citizenry) and a corresponding tendency to regard imperialism and dependency with opprobrium. (This is not as trite as it may seem at first glance; there are several reasons for viewing dependence favorably.) Whereas traditional approaches to international politics have been concerned primarily with relations among more or less equal states, dependency theory focuses on the inequality of states. Furthermore, dependency theorists adopt what is, in Kenneth Waltz's classic categorization, a second-image explanation of the foreign-policy behavior of states. [3] It is the socioeconomic system—capitalism—of the states in the international system, not the nature of man and not the security dilemma, which impels states to behave as they do. Economics provides the driving power that prompts the conduct of foreign policy of states. Moreover, the link between economics and politics is thought to be mutually reinforcing. Political domination by a large, developed, manufactured goods producing, metropolitan power results in economic dependence on the part of a small, underdeveloped, primary goods producing, small state. This domination is manifested in trade concentration, which in turn leads to political dependence and to the perpetuation of an asymmetrical relation between metropole and satellite that inhibits economic and political development in the satellite state. The result is that international relations among capitalist states—especially where some capitalist states are developed and others relatively underdeveloped—create dependency relationships resulting in the exploitation of the undeveloped, primary goods exporting, smaller states and the thoroughgoing penetration of their economies and societies by multinational corporations and the like from the metropolitan power. Consequently, in such conditions, the lesser states not only are unable to pursue an independent foreign policy, but their leaders are unable "to exert substantial influence over basic discussions affecting their national economies; the issue of what to produce, how to produce, and for whom, are all shaped directly or indirectly by international structures and processes." [4] Furthermore, the best of the recent literature on dependency theory has been preoccupied with conceptual clarity and operationalism, which permeated the social sciences in the 1960s and 1970s. There have been several efforts at concept specification and, in several instances, index construction and relationship testing, making it possible to bring dependency theory out of the realm of dogma and into an arena where the canons of science obtain.

What the dependency theorists have not undertaken, however, is a systematic comparison of relations among states across socioeconomic systems. This is unfortunate, because the only way in which hypotheses linking the nature of the socioeconomic system of states and the character of relations between those states can be verified (or falsified) is by comparing relations between states that have, in this instance, capitalist socioeconomic systems and those that do not.[5] Moreover, there exists an international system—which is well known to readers of this volume—whose constituent members have socialist, rather than capitalist, socioeconomic systems. I have in mind, of course, the Soviet-East European regional system.[6]

The purpose of this paper is to take some preliminary steps in the direction of applying dependency theory to relations among socialist states.[7] My goals are threefold: First, I will test, or in several instances, suggest how we might proceed to test, dependency theory.[8] This can be done by comparing interstate relations within the Soviet-East European regional system with those observed in the U.S.-Latin American context (defined here as the Organization of American States), that is, a comparison of a hierarchical regional system composed of socialist states with a hierarchical system composed of a developed capitalist state and a host of relatively undeveloped states to which dependency theorists often refer. (I also include several comparisons with the North Atlantic Treaty Organization in which the majority of the members of the system are developed capitalist states.) Second, I will illustrate how readily available data about the Soviet Union and Eastern Europe can be utilized to construct indicators whose relationships plausibly approximate important concepts. Third, I hope to suggest how some of the notions central to dependency theory facilitate the effort to systematize our understanding of Soviet-East European relations.

Specifically, I will focus on what seem to me and others[9] to be the key phenomena that dependency theorists associate with capitalist interstate relations: namely, the hypothesized association of capitalism with inequality, penetration, exploitation, and dependence. The following hypotheses, which should obtain if dependency theory has high explanatory power, are addressed:

(1) Inequality among states is more marked in a regional system composed of developed and less-developed capitalist states than in a system made up of socialist states, and the degree of inequality should increase over time.

(2) The penetration of the polity and society of lesser states that are members of a capitalist international system is greater than that of states that are members of a socialist international system.

(3) Exploitation as a phenomenon which characterizes relations among states is an attribute of relations primarily between developed, diversified, manufactured goods producing, capitalist states and primary goods producing less-developed states, in which the latter are exploited by the former.

(4) Under capitalism, the lesser states (especially underdeveloped states) of a regional international system are more dependent on the international market than are their counterparts in a regional system of socialist states. This dependency is reflected in more highly concentrated trade relations with a few states, especially the dominant states of the regional international system.

A central concept in the writings of dependency theorists is that of inequality among states. Relations between the United States and France and relations between the Soviet Union and China are unequal. We also know that relations between the United States and Chile and the Soviet Union and Czechoslovakia are unequal, and we feel intuitively that the latter pairs of relationships are more unequal than the former. There are two reasons why U.S.-Chilean relations and Soviet-Czechoslovak relations are unequal in greater degree than U.S.-French and Soviet-Chinese relations. First, the relative power, however made operational, of France and China vis-à-vis the United States and the Soviet Union, respectively, is greater than that of Chile and Czechoslovakia. The second reason, however, is equally important and somewhat less obvious. France and China benefit in their relations with the United States and the Soviet Union by the fact that they are direct participants in the overall international system, a system characterized by two or more great powers, a host of intermediate powers, and innumerable lesser states. The existence and behavior of the Soviet Union constrains U.S. behavior toward France and the existence and actions of the United States constrain the Soviet Union in its behavior toward China. By contrast, U.S.-Chilean relations and Soviet-Czechoslovak relations take place mainly within hierarchical regional systems, that is, within regional international systems composed of a single great power and a number of relatively small states. Within such systems, inequality in the relationship between a relatively great power and a lesser state is magnified by the structural characteristics of the system. The degree of inequality is a function of both the overall inequality of the system and of the permeability of the regional system's boundaries to influences from the dominant international system.

I have suggested elsewhere[10] how the boundaries of a hierarchical regional system can be defined. Scholars and policymakers alike employ several criteria in defining those borders. The boundaries may be defined geographically. Marked discontinuities in transnational flows—trade patterns, communications flows, and so forth—may serve to set off the regional system from the general international system, as may common membership in formal international organizations. Boundaries may be established by behavioral criteria, most notably by styles of conflict management and resolution, which are specific to a group of states. The permeability of the system boundaries may be said to increase as discontinuities in transnational interchanges decline, or as the norms for the system become less differentiated from those of the dominant international system. Since the leverage which the regional hegemon has over a small state decreases as the regional system's boundaries become more permeable, independently inclined small states pursue, inter alia, policies designed to increase the permeability of the system.

Thus, for approximately 15 years Rumanian elites have pursued policies with this evident intention. The Rumanian leadership has insisted that regional relations correspond to general international norms or, even better, to the Soviet Union's idealized characterization of general international relations: that peaceful coexistence should characterize relations among socialist states. In the Rumanian perspective, "respect for national independence and sovereignty, equality, noninterference in internal affairs, and mutual benefit" are principles which ought to be of "universal character and validity." The Soviet Union, by contrast, has never departed from the position that relations within Eastern Europe are distinct from those between socialist and capitalist states and are to be governed by the higher principle of proletarian internationalism. The Rumanians have intensified their ties with non-communist international organizations, including the Danube Commission, the European "group of nine" small states, the United Nations and its auxiliary conferences such as UNCTAD, the International Monetary Fund (the international organization whose formal decision-making structure is most open to charges of capitalist domination), and the conference of nonaligned states. In the latter case, the Rumanian

leadership has asserted that "Romania started from the idea that
the essential thing is not affiliation or non-affiliation with various
systems of military alliance, but the position and action each state
takes to support and put into practice the new principles governing
international relations," and that "Romania . . . , although a socialist country, is still a developing country from the economic
point of view."[11] Finally, with regard to transnational flows, the
Rumanians have taken steps to reduce the discontinuities between
the Soviet-East European regional system and the more general
international system. Trade figures vividly bear this out and indicate how generally insular Eastern Europe has been. A comparison
of East European trade within Comecon, as a fraction of the total
trade turnover, for the years 1960 and 1972 (see Table 6.1), shows
two striking phenomena: the magnitude and constancy of intra-
Comecon trade during that time period for all East European countries except Rumania, and Rumania's reorientation in trade.

In efforts to measure inequality in the Soviet-East European
hierarchical regional system, we can take advantage of prior work
by several scholars to devise measures of inequality. Assuming as
a first approximation that gross national product adequately summarizes the power of a state, I employed a measure suggested by
James Caporaso to compute the inequality of the Warsaw Treaty
Organization states qua system.[12] That equation is

$$\text{Con} = \sqrt{\frac{\sum_{i}^{n} P_i^2 - 1/N}{1 - 1/N}}, \tag{6.1}$$

where concentration is represented by Con, P_i stands for the proportion of GNP of each state in the total gross product of the regional
system, and N represents the number of actors in the system. By
inspection, it follows that the higher the concentration, or system
inequality, the more nearly Con approaches unity. Using this measure, I have compared the inequality of the East European regional
system over time with that of the Organization of American States
and the North Atlantic Treaty Organization. The results are summarized in Table 6.2. Although these numbers should be treated
with caution, they seem to indicate that the Soviet-East European
system, although clearly hierarchically configured, is somewhat
less unequal than the Organization of American States and somewhat
more unequal than NATO. This is not an earthshaking conclusion.
What is more interesting is that the figures also seem to suggest
that inequality is decreasing over time in the regional systems made
up of "capitalist" states not only in the system of (largely) developed

TABLE 6.1

East European Intra-Comecon Trade, 1960–72,
as a Proportion of Total Trade
(percent)

Country	1960	1972
Bulgaria		
Turnover	80	80
Imports	80	80
Exports	80	80
Czechoslovakia		
Turnover	63	66
Imports	64	65
Exports	63	66
GDR		
Turnover	67	67
Imports	66	63
Exports	69	65
Hungary		
Turnover	62	64
Imports	64	63
Exports	61	65
Poland		
Turnover	56	59
Imports	58	58
Exports	55	60
Rumania		
Turnover	67	46
Imports	68	45
Exports	66	47

Source: J. T. Crawford and John Haberstroh, "Survey of Economic Policy Issues in Eastern Europe," in Reorientation and Commercial Relations of the Economies of Eastern Europe, Joint Economic Committee, Congress of the United States, 93rd Congress, 2nd Session (Washington, D.C.: Government Printing Office, 1974), p. 41.

states but also where there is a single highly developed power and a host of smaller developing states. On the other hand, the degree of inequality may be increasing somewhat in the socialist hierarchical regional system where, we are told with excessive regularity, "international relations of a new type" are emerging. If future research should confirm that inequality decreases over time in regional international systems of capitalist states, while under socialism "the rich get richer and the poor get poorer," dependency theory would be in grave trouble.

TABLE 6.2

Measures of Interstate Inequality in Regional Systems

International Organization	1957	1965	1972
OAS	.882	.877	.867
	.891[a]		.877[a]
NATO	.618	.615	.584
	.616[a]		.485[a]
WTO	.685	.712	.717
	.678[b]		

[a]Inequality scores for the seven members with the largest GNP from each alliance.

[b]Includes Albania.

Sources: GNP figures are drawn from: Bruce Russett et al., World Handbook of Political and Social Indicators (New Haven: Yale University Press, 1964); Charles L. Taylor and Michael C. Hudson, World Handbook of Political and Social Indicators, 2nd ed. (New Haven: Yale University Press, 1972); and U.S. Arms Control and Disarmament Agency, World Military Expenditures and Arms Trade, 1963-73 (Washington, D.C.: Government Printing Office, 1974).

Applying the concept of the "penetrated system" to Soviet-East European relations long preceded the attention given to dependency theory in the 1970s. (My notion of a penetrated system corresponds to that of James Rosenau, that is, a system in which "non-members of a national society participate directly and authoritatively . . . in either the allocation of its values or the mobilization of support."[13]) Zbigniew Brzezinski has demonstrated superbly that the takeovers in East Europe at the end of World War II involved the creation of a Stalinist state system made up of little Soviet Unions.[14] During the years of high Stalinism, for its East European members, the bloc was a multiple sovereignty system in name only. Like the republics of the Soviet Union, the East European states were national in form and socialist in content; they were totally penetrated systems and little more than front organizations. As in the Soviet Union, controls were exerted primarily by the informal mechanisms of the party, the secret police, and above all by Stalin himself. The death of Stalin and the ramifications for East Europe of the Twentieth Party Congress produced important changes in the system of East European states and resulted in wide variation in degree of penetration. The Rumanians (and before them the Chinese and the Yugoslavs) have amply demonstrated that Stalinism as a state system had a fatal flaw. An international system composed of little Soviet Unions—hierarchical mobilization systems based on individual autarkic economies—contained within itself the seeds of its own decay. After Stalin died, the informal control mechanisms became ineffective, and it then became relatively easy for an autarkic, politically cohesive, mobilized Rumania to apply the Leninist model— which is ideally suited to resist penetration by an imperialist great power—to a strategy for countering the penetrative efforts of a socialist great power, the Soviet Union.

Given the attention that students of Soviet-East European relations have traditionally devoted to the phenomenon of penetration, it is surprising how few efforts there have been to compare systematically the penetration of Eastern Europe by the Soviet Union and the penetration of Latin America, Canada, and Western Europe by the United States (including its multinationals). Indeed, it is surprising how little attention has been given to the assessment of evolving patterns of Soviet political, economic, and cultural penetration of Eastern Europe since 1956, much less to systematic comparison.

Considerations of space and time preclude either effort in this study. In particular, I have made no attempt to compare the penetration of Eastern Europe by the CPSU with the penetration of Latin America, Canada, and Western Europe by American multinationals. Instead, I have limited myself to the presentation of a few examples of what might be done. On a larger and comparative basis, examples such as these could give students of communist affairs a more subtle appreciation of the current links between the Soviet Union and Eastern Europe and could shed more light on the general problems of the linkages between socioeconomic system and degree of penetration. I should stress, however, that I do not believe that there is a simple one-to-one relationship between the magnitude and scope of the penetration of a state's economic and political system and a state's ability to control its own destiny. The examples of Yugoslavia and Thailand—outside the scope of a paper focusing on Soviet-East European relations—amply illustrate the possibilities decision makers have to increase the permeability of a state's borders by plural influences and thereby to increase the state's national autonomy.[15]

One area of relevance for dependency theory is a comparative study of cultural penetration as a partial indicator of the presence of the hegemonic power over the lesser states. In the Soviet-East European context, for example, there are potentially comparable data: using the proportion of Russian translations as a percentage of total translations for various East European countries, and the proportion of translations (and Russian translations, specifically) of the overall production of books in Eastern Europe, it can be shown quite strikingly that Russian cultural presence has steadily diminished in Eastern Europe over the years (see Tables 6.3 and 6.4; Yugoslavia is included for comparison).

Similarly one could show that, after all these years, there is still a continued Soviet presence in East European cultural matters. Table 6.5 compares a randomly determined expected frequency with which East European states publish translations of Russian and English books with the observed pattern of translation. Obviously, the next step would be to compare expected and observed frequencies with those for English translations in Latin America and Western Europe.[16]

An important indicator of the penetration of one state by another is the impact of the latter on the formal constitution of the former. This is also a promising area for comparison. The American role, both direct and indirect, in the writing of the constitutions of Latin American states, Japan, and other countries could be compared with the Soviet role in East European constitutions. Even within Eastern Europe, important nuances can be discerned, as vividly illustrated by the exciting dialogue in Poland in the winter of 1975-76 over the phraseology of the new constitution. The most interesting dimension of this dialogue for our purposes was the formulation which referred to the Soviet Union. At one end of a continuum of allegiance to the USSR, the 1971 Bulgarian constitution refers to "developing and strengthening friendship, cooperation, and mutual assistance with the Soviet Union and the other socialist countries," and the 1974 East German constitution affirms that the GDR is "forever and irrevocably allied with the USSR . . . [and] is an inseparable component of the socialist community of states." At the other end of the continuum, there is no reference to the USSR by name in the 1965 Rumanian constitution, which declares that

TABLE 6.3

Russian-Language Books of the Total Number of Books Translated in East European Countries
(percent)

Year	Albania	Bulgaria	Czechoslovakia	GDR	Hungary	Poland	Rumania	Yugoslavia
1954	—	66	64	—	59	70	—	7
1955	—	69	52	—	48	57	47	21
1956	—	63	47	—	40	47	53	23
1957	—	63	31	—	16	30	32	10
1958	57	50	24	—	27	22	43	10
1959	44	49	26	—	25	20	44	10
1960	61	54	26	—	30	23	44	10
1961	48	57	24	—	23	26	49	13
1962	39	51	24	—	30	27	37	9
1963	34	53	23	—	22	23	34	13
1964	58	46	16	—	20	23	24	13
1965	26	43	16	—	16	23	11	—
1966	16	37	11	—	13	25	9	11*
1967	26	33	12	—	15	23	8	11
1968	19	34	15	—	13	20	8	12
1969	25	37	8	—	10	19	5	8
1970	28	39	9	—	11	21	10	13
1971	17	36	13	41	10	19	5	12
1972	7	44	18	73	11	17	10	8
1973	10	44	24	42	11	16	6	7

*1965–66 combined.
Sources: United Nations, Statistical Yearbooks, various years.

TABLE 6.4

Publication of Books and Translated Works, East European Countries, 1954–73

Translated Work as Percent of Total Book Production

Year	Albania	Bulgaria	Czechoslovakia	Hungary	Poland	Rumania	Yugoslavia
1954	–	24.8	29.7	–	–	–	14.9
1955	–	17.4	33.5	12.9	14.8	12.6	14.4
1959	14.1	17.8	17.1	5.9	10.4	–	16.8
1964	16.3	18.3	19.8	16.1	8.8	12.7	20.3
1969	–	16.0	17.6	19.8	8.7	10.2	11.6
1973	–	10.2	16.7	14.2	8.9	–	14.6

Translated Russian Work as Percent of Total Book Production

Year	Albania	Bulgaria	Czechoslovakia	Hungary	Poland	Rumania	Yugoslavia
1954	–	16.9	19.1	–	–	–	1.09
1955	–	12.1	17.5	6.6	8.5	5.9	0.8
1959	6.2	8.7	4.4	1.4	2.0	–	1.7
1964	9.4	8.4	3.3	3.2	2.0	2.9	2.5
1969	–	6.2	1.4	1.9	1.6	0.53	0.98
1973	–	4.5	4.0	1.5	1.4	–	1.0

Sources: United Nations, Statistical Yearbook, 1957, 1958, 1962, 1966, 1971, 1972, 1975, 1976.

TABLE 6.5

Observed and Expected Frequency of Translated Russian and English Works, 1973

Country	Russian Observed	Russian Expected[b]	English Observed	English Expected[c]	Totals (Expected or Observed)
Total[a]	3,006	3,006	17,879	17,879	20,885
Albania	8	4	18	22	26
Bulgaria	182	31	30	181	212
Czechoslovakia	349	76	176	449	525
GDR	745	150	297	892	1,042
Hungary	120	34	118	204	238
Poland	160	56	226	330	386
Rumania	53	20	85	118	138
Yugoslavia	106	59	307	354	413
Rest of world (excluding USSR)	1,283	2,576	16,622	15,329	17,905

[a]The USSR translates a large number of books from Russian into other languages. Soviet published translations are excluded from the table. The figures given by the United Nations for total works translated from Russian and English in the world during 1973 are 5,113 (from Russian) and 18,350 (from English).

[b]Expected frequency = individual country's total translation x 3,006/20,885.

[c]Expected frequency = individual country's total translation x 17,879/20,885.

Source: United Nations, Statistical Yearbook, 1976.

Rumania "maintains and develops relations of friendship and fraternal collaboration with the socialist countries." Against this backdrop, Polish elites with an aspiration to weaken Poland's link with
the USSR understandably opposed the announced intent to write into
the constitution a clause which referred to Poland's "unshakable
fraternal bond with the Soviet Union,"[17] and it is apparent from the
formulation adopted that their protests had some impact. The
final text "simply states that 'Poland strengthens its friendship and
cooperation with the Soviet Union and other socialist states.'"[18]

A study by Valerie Bunce and John Echols—on social service
expenditures and investment by the Soviet Union, East Germany,
Poland, and Rumania—can be cited as a third illustration of what
might be done on a comparative basis. Utilizing widely available
budgetary data, Bunce and Echols documented the reemergence
of domestic priorities in Eastern Europe by examining social service expenditures and investment outlays over the 1950-72 period.
They found that there was a "shifting degree of subordination of the
budgets of Eastern European states" to the USSR. In comparison
with the pattern observed in the 1950s, "the correlations between
the Soviet pattern of social expenditures and that of the Eastern
European states was much reduced in the 1960s and very early
1970s, especially in the Brezhnev period."[19]

These sketchy outlines of attempts to contrast the penetration
of polity and society within regional systems permit no conclusions
about whether penetration is more characteristic of relations among
capitalist states than among socialist states, as one would expect
logically from most formulations of dependency theory. Even this
brief survey, however, suggests that, although penetration is decreasing over time in the Soviet-East European system, penetration
of the polities and societies of lesser states has been such an overriding theme in Soviet-East European relations as to render suspect the argument that penetration of weaker states in an international system has causal roots in the capitalist nature of the socioeconomic system of the dominant state or states of that international
system.

Operationalizing the notion of exploitation poses much more
acute problems than are posed, for example, in the case of inequality. Unfortunately for thoroughgoing empiricists, the concept
of exploitation is invariably linked to perceptions and frames of
reference. In Yugoslavia, Albanian nationalists in Kosovo—who
have a standard of living that is much higher than that of their compatriots in Albania—consider themselves to be exploited because
Kosovo is discernibly less developed than other regions in Yugoslavia. Meanwhile in Croatia, Croatian nationalists are also
exercised and bitter; their frame of reference is Western Europe—

if Croatia were not held back by the Yugoslav south and by Serbian-dominated banks, export and import companies, and the federal government, Croatia could be at the same level as Sweden in a decade. An analogous situation is found in the Soviet Union: for Albanians substitute Uzbeks, for Croatians read Lithuanians.

Globally, since the discourse over exploitation has been more substantive than eristic, the focus has been on competing claims for the advantages of trade, and for the terms of trade. The advantages of trade are generally endorsed by economists and others from developed states while the asymmetrical effects of the terms of trade are more often noted by dependency theorists.

The prevailing view of dependency theorists is that there is a long-term continuing tendency for the prices of primary goods to decline vis-à-vis the prices of manufactured goods. Consequently, in the long run, the Marxist pauperization thesis obtains on an international scale. The developed, diversified manufacturing states develop even further on the backs of monoculturally oriented, raw material and primary goods producing, less-developed countries. It is further argued that policies of the advanced countries compound that trend:

> Some of the blame . . . [for exploitation] must be placed on the political forces shaping the commercial policy of the advanced countries. Among the components of this commercial policy are domestic agricultural protectionism in most of the advanced countries, [and] tariff systems that discriminate against semi-processed and manufactured goods, and increase protection against the labor-intensive exports of less developed nations.[20]

Students of Soviet-East European relations have something to say about exploitation—even in terms used by dependency theorists. Paul Marer has done the most thorough examination of the early post-World War II period. There can be no question that in those years the Soviet Union used its preeminent political and military position to exploit its East European clients economically, paying particular attention to disadvantaging what became the German Democratic Republic. Marer draws a careful, but necessarily partial, balance sheet, which does "not include uranium shipped by Czechoslovakia and Hungary and the maintenance of Soviet troops in Hungary and Romania . . . [nor the costs] of unfavorable prices on commercial exports during the early postwar years, except on Polish coal." On that basis, he concludes that "the size of . . . [the net] flow of resources from East Europe to the USSR [was] of

the same order of magnitude as the flow of resources from the
United States to West Europe" under the Marshall Plan.[21]

The story of exploitation in more recent relations between the
Soviet Union and the states of Eastern Europe is, however, much
more intricate. Fortunately, it has been treated by a number of
Western economists, particularly Marer and Edward Hewett. The
consensus of Western economists is that, at a minimum, it was an
open question as to who was exploiting whom during the years 1956-
73. Most Western economists have, in fact, been generally inclined
to give some credence to Soviet claims that the USSR, an exporter
chiefly of primary goods, was being exploited economically in return for political gains which were reflected in bloc loyalty and
cohesion. The best evidence for this has been provided by Hewett,
who found that trading with Comecon resulted in a loss for the
Soviet Union.[22] As is evident from other contexts and from the
manifestation of the free-rider problem in alliances (that is, that
expenditures per capita on a "public good"—defense—decrease as
the size of the state member of alliance diminishes) in the WTO[23]
and in NATO, the great and the powerful can be exploited by the
weak.[24]

The fact that the terms of trade affected the Soviet Union ad-
versely in those years might tempt one to conclude that the advantages that redound to states which manufacture processed goods,
rather than primary products, are truly extraordinary. It might be
argued that even the Soviet Union, with all its noneconomic resources, cannot avoid the exploitative consequences of the terms
of trade. If the strongest power of the second world is in an asymmetrical relationship vis-à-vis the weaker socialist states, consider
the lot of the weaker third world states in their trading relationship
with the behemoth of the first world. Indeed, both Janos Horvath and
Marer have <u>verged</u> on such an argument.[25] Marer observed that the
findings that "Soviet export and import decisions . . . result in a
large net transfer of resources" to the East European members of
Comecon

> bear at least a superficial analogy to the controversial
> Prebisch-Singer thesis . . . Prebisch and Singer argue
> that trade between rich and poor countries tends to re-
> distribute income from the exporters of primary prod-
> ucts to the exporters of manufactures via deteriorating
> terms of trade for the producers of primary products.
> The findings here are consistent with the Prebisch-
> Singer hypothesis, although, we hasten to add, they
> should not be invoked in support of it because the terms
> of trade between the Soviet Union and East Europe are

the outcome of a combination of factors, only one of
which is the relationship between the prices of primary
products and manufactures on the world market. [26]

After the 1973 OPEC oil price increase and the ensuing rise
in virtually all commodity prices, however, it suddenly became
difficult to feel sorry for the unfortunate countries whose major
export products were such primary goods as oil, coal, chromium,
vanadium (not to mention wheat) so desperately needed by the "exploitative" exporters of manufactured goods. Since 1973, in Soviet-
East European trading patterns, as in trading patterns globally,
there has been a dramatic reversal in the terms of trade, to the
benefit of the exporters of primary goods, which, in the Soviet-
East European context, primarily means to the advantage of the
Soviet Union. Given Eastern Europe's (except Rumania's) dependence on the USSR for oil imports (as summarized in Table 6.6),
it is possible that in the next few years we will conclude that the
USSR has taken advantage of its position as an exporter of primary
goods to exploit its developed East European allies. Such an occurrence—exploitation by a primary goods exporting, socialist
state—would challenge the explanatory capacities of the most nimble
of dependency theorists. Central in this regard will be our interpretation of the role of East European investment in the USSR: for
the 1976-80 Five-Year plans, this investment will amount to approximately nine billion rubles; it became a substantial factor only
after the global jump in commodity prices. In return for their
investment, the East European states have generally gotten a rather
good deal, thus making the term "exploitation" premature at the
least. Nevertheless, the challenge to dependency theory posed by
burgeoning East European investment in the USSR lies in its suggestion of a difference between interstate relations in capitalist and
socialist hierarchical regional systems, given the global shift in
the terms of trade: under capitalism, the multinational corporations of the industrial goods exporting regional hegemon invest in
the peripheral states; under socialism, the manufactured goods
exporting peripheral states invest in the primary goods exporting
hegemon.
It is not the dependence of the manufactured goods producing
states on the primary goods exporting states that has exercised
dependency theorists; rather, dependency theorists have presumed
that exporters of primary goods were dependent on states which
exported manufactured goods. A second dimension of the concern
with trade dependence relates to the concentration of trade. It is
assumed that dependent states have high partner concentration and
high commodity concentration, while the dominant developed states

are more diversified in their trading patterns. In a regional system, one might use several straightforward measures to obtain a sense of foreign trade dependence. For example, trade as a proportion of GNP could provide a guide to a state's overall vulnerability to the international market. Similarly, the proportion of Ruritania's trade with the metropole as a fraction of Ruritania's GNP could provide an approximation of Ruritania's dependence on that single country. The dominant power's reciprocal dependence on Ruritania could likewise be computed. Table 6.7 summarizes the total trade as a proportion of GNP for the six largest Latin American countries, the United States, the six East European states, and the USSR. Even allowing for differences in distance, it appears that the East European states are more dependent on trade than are the large Latin American countries; the East European countries are certainly more dependent on trade with the Soviet Union than are the large Latin American states on trade with the United States.

TABLE 6.6

East European Oil Imports from the Soviet Union, 1971
(percent)

Country	Oil Imports
Bulgaria	76
Czechoslovakia	92
GDR	89
Hungary	89
Poland	100
Rumania	0

Source: John M. Kramer, "The Energy Gap in Eastern Europe," Survey 21, no. 1-2 (Winter-Spring 1975): 69.

It might be objected, of course, that this finding is not surprising, since, in general, trade/GNP ratios increase as does GNP per capita, and these data, therefore, may merely reflect the greater development of the East European states. That objection proves less troublesome when one compares the trade/GNP ratios of the East European states with those of representative developed NATO states (see Table 6.8). The incubus of Stalinist autarkic economic policies notwithstanding, the East European states engage in almost as much trade as a fraction of GNP as do the large NATO countries (other than the United States) though nowhere nearly as proportionately as do the Benelux states.

TABLE 6.7

East European and Latin American
Trade Dependencies, 1973
(percent)

Country	Total Trade/GNP	Trade with Regional Hegemon/GNP
United States	9.0	
Argentina	14.1	2.1
Brazil	17.5	4.5
Chile	22.4	3.1
Colombia	20.9	7.8
Mexico	11.8	7.6
Venezuela	31.0	15.1
USSR	5.1	
Bulgaria	37.6	20.3
Czechoslovakia	23.5	7.9
GDR	28.0	10.6
Hungary	33.4	11.8
Poland	18.9	6.3
Rumania	15.9	3.9

Sources: Total trade and trade with regional hegemon are
derived from United Nations, Yearbook of Trade Statistics, 1974;
GNP from U.S. Arms Control and Disarmament Agency, World
Military Expenditures and Arms Trade.

Another almost equally straightforward measure could be derived to compute the extent to which a state's trade is concentrated
on a few states (see Table 6.9). (Space considerations preclude an
evaluation of commodity concentration. Usually, as Hirschman
argued a generation ago, commodity and geographic concentration
co-vary substantially.[27]) My calculations were for the East European states, the largest Latin American states, and for the largest
members of NATO; Canada and Mexico have the highest trade con-
centrations of any of the listed states, including Bulgaria.

The East European states all have higher coefficients of state
trade concentration than do Argentina, Brazil, and Chile. All the
East European states, except Rumania, have higher coefficients of
concentration than do the largest West European states. Although
Colombia, Mexico, and Venezuela have relatively high coefficients,

the image of trade-concentrating Latin America needs to be tempered somewhat, since Argentina, Brazil, and Chile have coefficients of state concentration which are essentially similar to the diversified manufacturing states of the first world. By this index, Argentina actually has a concentration of trade equal to or lower than the FRG, the United States, Great Britain, and France. (With two exceptions, the source for all trade concentration figures in the text is the 1974 U.N. Yearbook of Trade Statistics. The 1957 Cuban index is derived from data in the 1958 Yearbook; the Mongolian index was derived by using the proportions of trade reported by Comecon and equating the figures the U.N. derives for imports to, for example, the USSR from Mongolia as Mongolia's exports to the Soviet Union.)

TABLE 6.8

Trade/GNP Ratios, WTO and NATO Countries, 1973

Country	Total Trade/GNP
WTO	
Bulgaria	37.6
Czechoslovakia	23.5
GDR	28.0
Hungary	33.4
Poland	18.9
Rumania	15.9
NATO	
Belgium and Luxembourg	88.0
Canada	37.6
FRG	26.3
Italy	32.0
Netherlands	73.0
United Kingdom	33.9

Sources: Total trade and trade with regional hegemon are derived from United Nations, Yearbook of Trade Statistics, 1974; GNP from U.S. Arms Control and Disarmament Agency, World Military Expenditures and Arms Trade.

TABLE 6.9

Trade Concentration of Selected Countries

Country	Concentration
WTO	
Soviet Union	.209
Bulgaria	.519
Czechoslovakia	.369
GDR	.441
Hungary	.383
Poland	.368
Rumania	.320
OAS	
United States	.258
Argentina	.234
Brazil	.260
Chile	.290
Colombia	.408
Mexico	.693
Venezuela	.463
NATO	
United States	
Canada	.672
Belgium and Luxembourg	.354
France	.270
FRG	.234
Italy	.260
Netherlands	.232
United Kingdom	.240

Note: The formula used for this table and all other trade concentration figures in the text is a modified Gini index

$$SC = \sqrt{\sum_{j=1}^{n} \cdot \left\{ \frac{E_{ij}}{TE_i} \right\}^2} , \qquad (6.2)$$

where SC = state concentration of trade, E_{ij} = the exports of i to j, and TE_i = the total exports of i. I have called this state concentration, rather than geographic concentration (as Caporaso does), in order to avoid the impression that the measure taps the regional concentration of a state's trade, since it does not. The main trading partners of most East European states are other East Europeans states (including the USSR), but this is not the case for Rumania, where a more politically and geographically diversified pattern is noted.

Source: United Nations, Yearbook of Trade Statistics, 1974.

To add to the picture, I have examined the trade concentration of two non-East European members of Comecon—Cuba and Mongolia. Using the same measure of trade concentration, a more precise statement can now be made about the consequences for Cuba of replacing a proximate capitalist superpower as its dominant trading partner with a distant socialist superpower: whereas in 1958 Cuba had a trade concentration coefficient (.675) essentially the same as that of Canada and Mexico, one effect of the reorientation in trade has been to bring the Cuban trade coefficient more in line with that associated with the Soviet Union's East European allies—.387. This, ironically, is roughly similar to the concentration coefficients for its neighboring "banana republic" Central American states, Costa Rica (.377) and Guatemala (.372), whose main trading partner is the United States. Mongolia, it turns out, has a trade concentration (.743) far in excess of even Mexico or Canada. All told, the results are somewhat mixed. With the relatively developed states of Eastern Europe in mind, however, it would appear that, at the least, the linkages between capitalist-dominated regional system, underdevelopment, and high trade concentration predicted by dependency theory are rather tenuous.

An examination of Soviet-East European relations and a comparison of Soviet-East European relations with United States-Latin American relations, against a backdrop of the four concepts central to dependency theory, do not lend credence to dependency theorists' focus on the causal role of capitalism. To the extent that conditions which dependency theorists have ascribed to relationships between developed and less-developed capitalist states are actually observed, this preliminary inquiry suggests that they are to be found as often, or to an even greater degree, in the Soviet-East European regional system as in asymmetrically configured systems of capitalist states. This in turn provides fuel for the fires of those who are disposed to seek international systemic explanations for the phenomena which dependency theory would explain by reference to domestic political or socioeconomic structure.

There is, however, one way in which variables internal to the states participating in asymmetrically configured systems have played a major role. This is in the attempt to explain which small states will decrease their dependency on the regional hegemon and which will tend to acquiesce in, or even attempt to increase, the existing dependency relationships. In the past, within the U.S.-Latin American and Soviet-East European hierarchical regional systems,[28] the countries that show characteristics typically associated with the internal structures of either the USSR or the United States have been the ones that are least likely to pursue policies which harmonize with the policies of the regional hegemon. Within the Soviet-East European hierarchical system, such states have pursued several strategies designed to increase independence from the Soviet Union, and the Soviet Union has, with varying intensity, resisted these efforts. What needs to be monitored with great care over the next several years is whether the relationship between domestic structure and foreign policy continues to hold in Soviet-East European relations. Reasons for caution in prediction include the new global economic order, the aftermath of Helsinki, and uncertainty as to whether changes in foreign policy—which in the past have had significant portent—will have the same implications in the 1980s.

If the implications are similar, we may have witnessed some changes in Polish foreign policy during the Gierek era which have not been fully appreciated. By previous standards there has been a stunning rearrangement in Polish trade patterns in the 1970s, the only precedent for which was the Rumanian reorientation in the 1960s, which was part of Rumania's efforts gradually to reduce its dependence on the USSR. "Comecon accounted for 63.3 percent of Poland's total trade in 1970; by 1974, that figure had dropped to 47 percent. The percentage representing the developed capitalist countries in 1970 trade figures was 27 percent; in 1974, their share was 44.3 percent . . . whereas Poland's 1970 import figures were divided between Comecon (65.9 percent) and the Western countries (25.8 percent), the Western countries were the leaders in 1974, with 50.8 percent, as opposed to 42.3 percent for Comecon."[29] Beyond that, in 1975 Poland allowed "the full examination of its records and the resources of its copper industry by American specialists"[30] in order to obtain a 240 million dollar loan from the Chase Manhattan Bank to further the development of its copper industry. This step was consistent with a policy of pluralizing the penetration of the system in order to increase freedom of maneuver. A third example concerns Polish efforts to render ambiguous the doctrinal boundaries setting off Soviet-East European relations from those of relations with other Communist parties. Malcolm Browne reports an interview with a member of the Polish Central Committee, who declared, in words faintly echoing the 1968 Czechoslovak Action Program, that "we Polish Communists have an ambition to play an important role in Europe, creating a model of socialism acceptable to everyone, including comrades in both directions."[31]

The reason for caution in interpreting these events is that the energy crisis has altered some of the rules of the game for Soviet-East European relations. In the 1970s, the USSR encouraged the East European states to become less dependent on it as a source of raw materials, urging them instead to seek other additional sources of supply. Undoubtedly, there are individuals in

Moscow who prefer to reduce still further the energy dependence of the East European states on the Soviet Union even if it results in greater independence in other domains, either because the gas or oil can be used domestically or because it can be exported to Western Europe for hard currency. Others, by contrast, would opt for the other alternative—for political solidarity, alliance cohesion, and sales in inconvertible currency rather than for hard currency and possible upheaval in Eastern Europe. Each Soviet faction can find allies within East European elites. We may witness the kind of transnational coalition formation of which Kent N. Brown has written. [32] There are reasons why elites in relatively small states may not seek to lessen dependence on the regional hegemon: changes in dependency relations may weaken the power base of key domestic groups; economic dependence can be considered a form of subsidy for a political alliance; it can mean security of market or security of supplies, or it can constitute a form of protectionism. There are worse things for some elites, a fact dependency theorists have often ignored. What dependency theory has grasped, in a rather primitive way however, is that considerations such as these have generally not prevailed among elites seeking to achieve a basic legitimacy among the citizens of a state.

It remains to be seen whether the past will be prologue in Eastern Europe or whether we will increasingly witness countries which, in the past, have been noted for their interest in acquiring a relatively autonomous status vis-à-vis the USSR, seeking to become more dependent on the USSR only to be rebuffed by Moscow, or, at a minimum, being granted access to guaranteed Soviet markets only after hard bargaining. Thus far the evidence does not suggest a reversal in the previously observed generalization linking internal elite-mass relations with a propensity to enhance autonomy from the Soviet Union. [33] Ironically, the resolution of the issue will depend in large measure on the willingness of Western states to allow East European states, especially Poland, to become increasingly dependent on the West. This, in turn, will be linked intimately with the rate of economic recovery among capitalist industrialized states.

NOTES

1. James R. Kurth, "Testing Theories of Economic Imperialism," in Theories of Economic Imperialism, ed. Steven J. Rosen and James R. Kurth (Lexington, Mass.: D. C. Heath, 1974), p. 3.

2. For recent surveys of the literature, see the essays by Karl Deutsch, Andrew Mack, and James Caporaso, in Rosen and Kurth, op. cit.

3. Kenneth Waltz, Man, the State and War (New York: Columbia University Press, 1959).

4. Robert R. Kaufman, Harry I. Chernotsky, and Daniel S. Geller, "A Preliminary Test of the Theory of Dependency," Comparative Politics 7, no. 3 (April 1975): 303.

5. There is, of course, a sense in which this form of comparison does not allow us to rule out the notion that capitalism, for example, fosters dependent relations. Were one to find that patterns of interaction that were believed to characterize relations among capitalist states are also found, or found in greater measure, to characterize relations among noncapitalist states, a limited construction of that finding would be that there are multiple causes for the occurrence of these relations, rather than that capitalism does not foster these relations. That having been said, it remains the case that, under the conditions specified, the predictive role of socioeconomic structure would be much diminished. David Abernathy, the Stanford African scholar, has given the following example: Suppose we begin with the hypothesis that "Everyone dies under capitalism." When it turns out, as of course it does, that on examination everyone dies under feudalism and socialism as well, there might still be a sense in which capitalism is a cause of death but I rather suspect we would find more interesting the search for other, more proximate, causes.

6. I refer here specifically to the USSR, Bulgaria, Czechoslovakia, the German Democratic Republic, Hungary, Poland, Rumania, and, prior to 1961, Albania. For most practical purposes the system is defined organizationally by the Warsaw Treaty Organization and the Council for Mutual Economic Assistance, though Mongolia, Cuba, and, as of June 1978, Vietnam, are now full members of Comecon.

7. To avoid reiteration of excessively cumbersome phraseology (to wit, "states, the socioeconomic systems of which are capitalist or socialist") I shall speak of "capitalist" or "socialist" states or international systems.

8. "Everybody" knows that area studies are always a couple of years behind trends in a discipline. In fact, however, some specialists in Communist studies have been consciously working in the area of dependency theory for some time. With respect to relations between states, see Kenneth Jowitt, "The Romanian Communist Party and the World Socialist System: A Redefinition of Unity," World Politics 23, no. 1 (October 1970): 38-60; an excellent

study of internal Soviet relations framed against the backdrop of dependency theory is Grey Hodnett's seminal essay, "Technology and Social Change in Soviet Central Asia: The Politics of Cotton Growing," in Henry W. Morton and Rudolf Tökés, Soviet Politics and Society in the 1970's (New York: Free Press, 1974).

9. See especially James Caporaso, "Methodological Issues in the Measurement of Inequality, Dependence, Exploitation," in Rosen and Kurth, op. cit., pp. 91-93. I have borrowed heavily from Caporaso's essay though I have not adopted his position that imperialism is a multiplicative relationship involving inequality, dependence, and exploitation.

10. William Zimmerman, "Hierarchical Regional Systems and the Politics of System Boundaries," International Organization 26, no. 1 (Winter 1972): 18-36. The material in the next two paragraphs borrows heavily from this article.

11. See Radio Free Europe, Romanian Situation Report, February 10, 1976, p. 7, citing Scinteia, September 24, 1975; and RFE, Romanian Situation Report, August 29, 1975, p. 2, for the second statement by Ceausescu, also reported in Scinteia, July 25, 1976.

12. Caporaso, op. cit., p. 100. Caporaso draws in turn on James Lee Ray and J. David Singer, "Measuring the Concentration of Power in the International System," Sociological Methods and Research 1, no. 4 (May 1973): 404. For a similar approach, see James Lee Ray and Charles Gochman, "Capability Disparities in Latin America and Eastern Europe" (Paper delivered at the 1976 International Political Science Association meeting, August 15-21, 1976, in Edinburgh, Great Britain).

13. James Rosenau, "Pre-theories and Theories of Foreign Policy," in Approaches to Comparative and International Politics, ed. R. Barry Farrell (Evanston, Ill.: Northwestern University Press, 1966).

14. Zbigniew Brzezinski, The Soviet Bloc (Cambridge, Mass.: Harvard University Press, 1960).

15. This argument is most fully developed in my study on national-international linkages and Yugoslav political development now nearing completion and, with respect to Thailand, by Samuel P. Huntington, "Trans-national Organizations in World Politics," World Politics 25, no. 3 (April 1973): 364-65.

16. The extent to which this section, in particular, is exploratory should be emphasized. Other measures might well be employed. In a larger study other media data could be employed to advantage. For television, see Jeremy Turnstall, The Media Are American (New York: Columbia University Press, 1977); and Tapio Varis, "Global Traffic in Television," Journal of Communication 24, no. 1 (Winter 1974): 102-9.

17. Radio Free Europe, Polish Situation Report, January 30, 1976, p. 5.

18. Ibid., p. 6; see also RFE, Polish Situation Report, February 20, 1976.

19. Valerie Bunce and John Echols, "Aggregate Data in the Study of Policy Change in Communist Systems" (Paper presented at AAASS annual meeting, October 8-11, 1975, in Atlanta, Georgia).

20. Caporaso, op. cit., p. 100.

21. Paul Marer, "Soviet Economic Policy in Eastern Europe," in Reorientation and Commercial Relations of the Economies of Eastern Europe, Joint Economic Committee, Congress of the United States, 93rd Congress, 2nd Session (Washington, D.C.: Government Printing Office, 1974), p. 144.

22. Edward Hewett, Foreign Trade Prices in the Council for Mutual Economic Assistance (London: Cambridge University Press, 1974).

23. Harvey Starr, "A Collective Goods Analysis of the Warsaw Pact After Czechoslovakia," International Organization 28, no. 5 (Summer 1974): 521-32.

24. On the exploitation of the powerful in the Comecon and OAS contexts, see Zimmerman, op. cit.

25. Janos Horvath, "The Cost of Soviet Aid," Problems of Communism 21, no. 3 (May-June 1972): 76-77; and Marer, op. cit.

26. Marer, op. cit., p. 150. In the version of Marer's paper which appears in the Rosen and Kurth volume, this passage does not appear.

27. For such a study, see Donna Bahry and Cal Clark, "A Dependence Theory of Soviet-East European Relations: Theory and Empirical Testing" (Paper presented at the Conference on Integration in Eastern Europe and East-West Trade, October 28-31, 1976, in Bloomington, Indiana).

28. Zimmerman, op. cit.

29. Thomas E. Heneghan, "Polish Trade and Polish Trends, Economic and Political Considerations," Radio Free Europe Research, November 13, 1975, p. 18.

30. Ibid., p. 13.

31. New York Times, August 10, 1976.

32. Kent N. Brown, "Coalition Politics and Soviet Influence in Eastern Europe" (Paper presented at AAASS annual meeting, October 6-8, 1976, in St. Louis, Missouri).

33. William Zimmerman, "The Energy Crisis, Western 'Stagflation' and the Evolution of Soviet-East European Relations" (Paper presented at the Conference on the Impact of International Economic Disturbances on the Soviet Union and Eastern Europe, Kennan Institute for Advanced Russian Studies, the Wilson Center, Washington, D.C., September 24-26, 1978).

7

THE IMPLICATIONS OF
INTERDEPENDENCE FOR
SOVIET-EAST EUROPEAN RELATIONS:
A PRELIMINARY ANALYSIS OF
THE POLISH CASE

Sarah Meiklejohn Terry

For the better part of the 30–odd years since the end of World
War II, the dominant feature of the relationship between the East
European states[1] and the Soviet Union has been dependence, political and economic as well as strategic. One consequence (and purpose) of that dependence has been to preclude the emergence of interdependent relationships between East Europe and the outside
world. Since the early 1970s, however, developments in the international economic and political environments raise the possibility,
if not the probability, of a fundamental change in relations between
the Soviet Union and her client states. These developments include:
detente and the attendant increases in East-West trade; raw material
shortages, especially in fuels and basic foods, resulting in worldwide
dislocations and inflation; an increasing awareness of the continental
or global scope of mankind's most pressing social and economic
problems (for example, population, food, energy, pollution); and
expanding opportunities for cooperation outside the bloc, in part as
a result of the Conference on Security and Cooperation in Europe.
    These trends have both positive and negative implications for
Soviet interests in East Europe. On the one hand, recent economic

The main body of this essay is a slightly revised and abridged
version of a paper completed in August 1977, under contract with
the Office of External Research, U.S. Department of State. The
postscript was written in January 1980. The author wishes to express her appreciation to the International Research and Exchanges
Board for making possible part of the research on which this study
is based.

trends have transformed the region from a net asset into a net liability, draining off resources (especially oil) which Moscow might
otherwise exchange for badly needed Western technology and foodstuffs, instead of low-quality East European manufactures. Thus,
to the extent that growing East European interdependence with the
West and with alternative sources of raw materials makes these
countries more productive and self-sustaining, it will ease the burden on the Soviet economy. Similarly, Moscow can hope to benefit
directly from technological progress among its allies in the form of
higher quality imports from them. On the other hand, what is beneficial to Soviet economic interests may pose a threat to Soviet political interests in the region, particularly should economic ties with
the non-Communist world develop at the expense of bloc integration
or spill over into closer cooperation in noneconomic relations.
Moreover, while the inevitable connection which some observers
perceive or predict between economic and technological cooperation,
on the one hand, and systemic change in Communist states, on the
other, has yet to be demonstrated conclusively, the possibility of
such a connection is clearly a matter of active concern in the Kremlin.

With these considerations in mind, the purpose of this essay
will be to explore in a preliminary way:

(1) the dimensions of East Europe's interdependence with non-bloc
    countries, particularly in those areas of greatest importance
    to the development of the East European economies, namely,
    technology, food, and energy-related items;
(2) the implications of growing East European interdependence out-
    side the bloc for intrabloc relations, particularly for bilateral
    trade with the Soviet Union and economic integration under the
    Council for Mutual Economic Assistance (CMEA);
(3) the extent to which interdependence might alter East Europe's
    perceptions of international problems or promote, whether
    directly or indirectly, political and economic change within the
    region;
(4) Moscow's likely reaction to such trends, both in its direct re-
    lations with East Europe and in its attitude toward interdepen-
    dence in general; and
(5) the usefulness of the concept of interdependence in the East
    European context, as well as the usefulness of the East Euro-
    pean experience in refining the concept itself.

In view of the complexity of the topic as well as the tentative
and incomplete nature of much of the pertinent evidence, this can at
best be a preliminary and exploratory effort. Therefore, and in

order to give the paper a somewhat clearer focus, I propose to concentrate primarily on the Polish case, giving only limited attention to the other East European states. In so doing, I am fully aware that it is no more accurate to speak of Poland as typical of the region than it is to speak of East Europe as a homogeneous whole; indeed, there is no "typical" East European state. Nonetheless, Poland has been the most aggressive (some would say incautious) member of the bloc in her pursuit of trade ties with the West and today exemplifies, at least in broad outline, the benefits and pitfalls that await others who may opt for her course.

Before turning to the first of the above tasks, it might be useful to reflect briefly on the possible meanings of "interdependence" and, while not to prejudge the utility of the concept here, at least to call attention to several potential problems in its application to East Europe. Neither the idea nor the reality of interdependence is new. Witness, for instance, the scene in Kipling's "The Man Who Would Be King" in which each primitive tribe complains in turn that its enemies upstream "piss in the river and foul our drinking water."[2] What is new is the degree or intensity of the relationships: strategic advances have made possible the annihilation rather than merely the conquest of one's adversary; modern technology has dramatically increased both the volume and speed of global communications; environmental pollution may threaten the well-being of others instead of merely inconvenience them; and more countries are less self-sufficient in basic resources.

If interdependence is not new, neither is it uniformly understood, the diversity of definitions arising in large measure from the fact that many are specific to particular groups of countries or set of relationships and are not meant to reflect the more general phenomenon. As a basic minimum, interdependence is differentiated from mere interaction between countries in that the former is generally understood to imply the mutual dependence of each side on the other, extending beyond any particular transaction, while the latter may occur in the absence of any further liabilities or reduction in autonomy. To this minimal definition, Joseph Nye adds the following criteria for his concept of "complex interdependence" (a concept from which he specifically excludes both East-West and North-South relations): multiple channels of contact between the governments and societies in question; relations involving multiple issues, not arranged in any fixed order of priority and not prejudiced by the threat or use of force; and a blurring of the distinction between foreign and domestic policies (linkage). In addition, Nye acknowledges the asymmetry of many interdependent relationships in his distinction between the "sensitivity" and "vulnerability" of countries to the actions of others, "sensitivity" meaning "liability to costly effects imposed from outside before policies are altered to try and change the situation," and "vulnerability" indicating continued liability "even after policies have been altered."[3] By contrast, in a discussion of East-West relations, Franklyn Holzman and Robert Legvold define interdependence simply as "a level of mutual dependence in which both or all parties view cooperation as a useful but not decisive means for pursuing some or all of their essential goals."[4]

In attempting to fit East Europe into the interdependence framework, several points suggest themselves for further scrutiny. The first concerns the tendency to define interdependence primarily or exclusively in terms of the character, diversity, and intensity of the transactions between the states in question, while the objective or situational factors that give rise to and condition those transactions are excluded from the interdependent relationship itself. "Interdependence" thus becomes a matter essentially of choice, a policy alternative rather than, let us say, an involuntary situation which a country must cope with willy-nilly. One might ask whether by broadening the concept to include the conditioning factors in the political and economic environments the term might better reflect the diversity and asymmetry of the real world and make the analyst more sensitive to the influence of such objective factors as size, geographical location, and resource endowment on the responses of different states to the challenges of a shrinking world. Similarly, it would also allow us to examine under the rubric of interdependence more complex "third party" situations, that is, those in which transactions between "A" and "B" wittingly or unwittingly increase "C's" vulnerability to external pressures and events. On the face of it, these considerations would appear to have particular relevance in analyzing the behavior of the East European states, as opposed to that of the Soviet Union. By virtue of the fact that they are small, geographically exposed, and relatively resource poor, these states have long comprised a political, economic, and strategic buffer zone, rarely able to influence others directly but often affected by policies in which they have little or no say.

Other potential problems in dealing with relatively small and exposed states such as those of East Europe concern: the distinction between interdependence and dependence; and the exclusion, as by Nye, of East-West relations from the definition of complex interdependence due to the presence or threat of force. With regard to the former, the distinction is theoretically desirable but, I think, very difficult to apply in practice, especially as most writers on the subject admit the asymmetry of many interdependent relationships.[5] Indeed, the fact that in relationships with the West, the East European states are far more likely than the Soviet Union to find themselves in a position of relative dependence may mean that those

relationships will conform more closely to the other criteria of
Nye's complex interdependence (multiple channels, multiple issues,
and linkage between foreign and domestic policies) than to the simp-
ler Holzman-Legvold definition, according to which cooperation is
"a useful but not decisive means for pursuing . . . essential goals."
Moreover, this difference may be reinforced by a comparable difference in the role of force in East European-Western as opposed to
Soviet-Western relations. That is, while the strategic balance between East and West tends to limit the freedom of action of the superpowers, it increases the maneuverability of lesser powers such as
those of East Europe by reducing their relative exposure as a buffer
area between the blocs. The threat of force is, in fact, a more
palpable ingredient of relations between the Soviet Union and its
client states than it is between the latter and the West.

What all of this points to is the danger of oversimplifying the
nature of interdependence in East-West relations, particularly the
danger of assuming that, by virtue of their political loyalties, all
members of the bloc will respond to the challenge in the same way.
What seems to be in order is a more flexible, differentiated concept
of interdependence, one that does not merely see existing political
divisions as defining the types of interdependent relationships that
can exist but that takes account of the potential impact of interdependence on those political divisions. We shall return to these and
other questions in the final section of the chapter.

THE DIMENSIONS OF ECONOMIC
INTERDEPENDENCE

By now it is hardly news that East Europe's trade outside the
Socialist bloc, and particularly with the industrialized West, has
risen substantially since 1970—in absolute terms by more than 200
percent between 1970 and 1975, and in several cases as a percentage
of total trade as well. At the same time, the region's hard currency
debt soared from less than $5 billion in 1970, to $19.1 billion at the
end of 1975. The additional debt for 1976 was a record $6.3 billion
(or 36 percent of all imports from the West in that year), bringing
the total figure to an estimated $25.6 billion. (See Table 7.1.)

As significant as these figures may seem, they are not in
themselves a sufficient basis for concluding that the relationship between East Europe and the West now falls under the rubric of "interdependence." Before arriving at that conclusion, we need to know
much more about the nature and intensity of the mutual sensitivities
and vulnerabilities that have arisen as a result of the increased level
of economic transactions—in particular, the symmetry or asymmetry

of such sensitivities and vulnerabilities and the degree of commitment on each side to maintaining, deepening, and balancing the relationship.

TABLE 7.1

East Europe: Estimated Net Hard Currency Debt
at Year-End, 1970-76
(billion U.S. dollars)

Country	1970	1973	1974	1975	1976
Bulgaria	0.7	0.8	1.2	1.8	2.3
Czechoslovakia	0.3	0.8	1.1	1.5	2.1
East Germany	1.0	2.1	2.8	3.8	4.9
Hungary	0.6	0.9	1.5	2.1	2.8
Poland	0.8	1.9	3.9	6.9	10.2
Romania	1.2	2.0	2.6	3.0	3.3
Total East Europe	4.6	8.5	13.1	19.1	25.6

Source: Joan Parpart Zoeter, "Eastern Europe: The Growing Hard Currency Debt," in East European Economies Post Helsinki. A Compendium of Papers Submitted to the Joint Economic
Committee, Congress of the United States, ed. John P. Hardt
(Washington, D.C.: Government Printing Office, 1977), Table 2,
p. 1352. For data concerning the growth of East Europe's trade
with the West between 1970 and 1976, see ibid., Table 1.

Although Poland provides an extreme example of trade reorientation and is therefore atypical of the region, for precisely
this reason the Polish case is useful in illustrating the nature of, as
well as the limits to, interdependent relationships between East
Europe and the West. After a brief overview of recent trends in
Poland's foreign trade, we shall look more closely at the pattern of
that country's transactions with the West in three areas central to
her economic development strategy: energy, food, and industrial
technology.

As Table 7.2 shows, between 1970 and 1975 Poland's total
trade turnover rose by 165 percent, but with exports growing at a
markedly slower pace than imports (by 141 percent and 187 percent,
respectively). The result has been a steadily mounting trade deficit,
which jumped from a mere 240 million devisa złoty (złd) in 1970

TABLE 7.2

Poland's Foreign Trade, by Trading Groups, 1970-76
(million <u>devisa</u> złotys, in current prices)[a]

Trading Group	1970	1971	Percent Increase	1972	Percent Increase	1973	Percent Increase
All countries							
Total	28,621	31,640	10.5	37,745	19.3	47,458	25.7
Exports	14,191	15,489	9.1	18,133	17.1	21,355	17.8
Imports	14,430	16,151	11.9	19,612	21.4	26,103	33.1
Balance	−239	−662		−1,479		−4,748	
CMEA							
Total	18,103	19,613	8.3	22,410	14.3	25,320	13.0
Exports	8,600	9,206	7.0	10,991	19.4	12,418	13.0
Imports	9,503	10,407	9.5	11,419	9.7	12,902	13.0
Balance	−903	−1,201		−428		−484	
Industrial West[c]							
Total	7,749	9,029	16.5	12,194	35.1	18,900	55.0
Exports	4,028	4,622	14.7	5,515	19.3	7,303	32.4
Imports	3,721	4,407	18.4	6,679	51.6	11,597	73.6
Balance	+307	+215		−1,164		−4,294	
Others[d]							
Balance	+357	+324		+113		+30	

[a]Conversion rates for the <u>devisa</u> złoty are as follows: through 1971, \$1 = 4 złd; in 1972, \$1 = 3.68 złd; from 1973, \$1 = 3.32 złd. In constant prices, Poland's trade increased by 85.7 percent between 1970 and 1975, exports by 66.4 percent, imports by 104.3 percent. In 1976, again in constant prices, total trade turnover was 8.1 percent higher than in 1975, exports 5.4 percent higher, imports 10.3 percent higher. <u>RSHZ 1977</u>, Table 3, p. 5.

[b]In constant prices, the corresponding increases were: for total trade turnover, 85.7 percent; for exports, 66.4 percent; and for imports, 104.3 percent; <u>RSHZ 1976</u>, Table 3, p. 5.

1974	Percent Increase	1975	Percent Increase	Percent Increase 1970-75[b]	1976	Percent Increase
62,448	31.6	75,812	21.4	164.9	82,671	9.1
27,625	29.4	34,161	23.7	140.7	36,600	7.1
34,823	33.4	41,651	19.6	188.6	46,071	10.6
-7,198		-7,490			-9,471	
29,355	15.9	37,711	28.5	108.3	41,533	10.1
14,638	17.9	19,453	33.0	126.2	20,846	7.2
14,717	14.1	18,258	24.1	92.1	20,688	13.3
-79		+1,195			+158	
27,695	46.5	31,307	13.0	304.0	34,240	9.5
10,013	37.1	10,768	7.5	167.3	11,711	8.8
17,682	52.5	20,539	16.2	452.0	22,529	9.7
-7,669		-9,771			-10,818	
+550		+1,086			+1,189	

[c]This category includes Japan, Australia, New Zealand, and South Africa, in addition to West Europe and North America.

[d]This category includes those Communist states which are not members of CMEA and the developing countries.

Sources: Rocznik Statystyczny Handlu Zagranicznego [RSHZ] 1976 (Warsaw: GUS, 1976), Table 12, p. 20; RSHZ 1977 (Warsaw: GUS, 1977), Table 9, p. 15.

(equal to 1.7 percent of Poland's imports for that year) to a staggering 7.5 billion złd (or 18 percent of imports) in 1975. While the
gross figures reflect Poland's most visible trade problem—namely,
foreign debt—they mask the sharply divergent patterns that have
emerged in her economic relations with the two dominant groups of
trading partners: CMEA and the industrial West. On the one hand,
compared with the global picture, Polish trade within the CMEA during the 1970-75 period shows both a slower growth rate and an improving balance between exports and imports. (It is worth noting
that by far the sharpest increases in CMEA trade came in 1975, and
were a result less of increased trade volume than of the revised
CMEA pricing formula, reflecting the delayed onset of the energy-
related inflationary spiral that had hit the non-Communist world two
years earlier.)

By contrast, Poland's trade with the industrialized Western
countries grew nearly three times as fast overall, but with an escalating imbalance of imports over exports. Thus, despite the low
initial base, by 1974 trade with this group had almost pulled even
with CMEA trade, and imports from the former actually exceeded
imports from CMEA in both 1974 and 1975. At the same time, exports to the West grew at less than half the rate of imports, with
the result that Poland's balance of payments with Western trading
partners deteriorated from a surplus of just over 300 million złd in
1970, to a deficit of nearly 9.8 billion złd in 1975. By the end of
that year, reliable estimates placed her cumulative hard currency
debt at 6.9 billion <u>dollars</u> (up from $0.8 billion in 1970), with almost
half of the difference attributable to 1975 alone (see Table 7.1). The
peak growth years in this segment of Polish trade were 1972-74,
followed by a marked slackening in the rate of increase of both imports and exports in 1975. The fact that this was the first year
since 1970 in which Poland's trade with CMEA increased at a faster
clip than her trade with the West may be partially explained as a
correction of the distortions caused by the lag in CMEA price increases compared with world levels. However, it may also presage
a reversal of—or at least a partial retreat from—the reorientation
of Polish trade between 1970 and 1974. Indeed, the data for 1976,
although inconclusive, appear to show a marginal extension of trends
begun in 1975, in terms of both a continued slackening of overall increases in trade turnover as well as a slight additional shift back
toward CMEA, but without an improvement in the overall balance.
That is, imports continued to rise faster than exports (and imports
from the West continued to outpace those from CMEA), with the result that the Poles once again accumulated a record-breaking hard
currency deficit of 10.8 billion złd, raising their cumulative debt to
about $10.2 billion, or 40 percent of the East European total.[6] The

marked shift toward the West after 1970, as well as the correction in favor of CMEA that began in 1975, are perhaps most readily apparent from the changes in the percentage distribution of Polish exports and imports displayed in Table 7.3. [7]

One interesting sidelight on these figures is the apparent re-emergence of the Third World as a significant factor in Poland's exports after a slump in 1972-73 (8.6 percent in 1975, up from 5.1 percent in 1973). The data suggest that as much as half of the labored expansion of exports to the West in the early 1970s occurred at the expense of this group, which like CMEA is now recovering as the West's share retreats. Poland's imports from the developing countries have remained substantially lower than her exports; nonetheless, in view of the increasingly tight energy market, as well as the fact that some exports to this group bring in hard currency earnings, this aspect of Poland's "interdependence equation" will warrant further comment.

With this overview in mind, let us now examine more carefully the three sectors of trade relations that are likely to be the most important in defining the degree of Poland's economic interdependence with the West: energy, food, and industrial technology.

Energy

Poland is exceptional among the East European states in that she is the only member of the group that still boasts a favorable energy balance, Romania, the only other member with significant domestic resources, having slipped into the minus column in the early 1970s. Indeed, despite rapid increases in energy use, Poland's generous coal deposits (some only now in the process of exploration and development) have afforded her a fairly steady net fuel surplus, expressed in standard fuel equivalents, of 10-12 percent over consumption. [8] The advantages of this situation are self-evident. Not only has Poland been able to cover most of her energy needs from domestic production (in 1970 coal accounted for 83 percent of energy use and domestic natural gas for another 5 percent), [9] but coal exports have also served as her single most important source of hard currency earnings on the world market—in effect, as fuel for her ambitious modernization strategy of the 1970s.

Yet these benefits should not be overstated, especially as we look to Poland's needs in 1980 and beyond. The favorable energy balance that the Poles continue to enjoy has been based in large measure on significantly lower levels of energy use than pertain in the advanced industrial states or even among several of their CMEA neighbors. Despite a ten-fold increase in electrical power produc-

TABLE 7.3

Poland's Foreign Trade, by Trading Groups, 1970–75
(percent of total trade turnover, exports and imports)

Trading Group	1970	1971	1972	1973	1974[a]	1975	1976
Total turnover	100.0	100.0	100.0	100.0	100.0	100.0	100.0
Socialist	66.2	65.3	62.3	55.7	49.4	52.2	52.2
CMEA	63.2	62.0	59.4	53.4	47.0	49.7	50.2
Other[b]	3.0	3.3	2.9	2.3	2.4	2.5	2.0
Non–Socialist	33.8	34.7	37.7	44.3	50.6	47.8	47.5
Developed capitalist	27.1	28.5	32.3	39.8	44.4	41.3	41.4
Developing	6.7	6.2	5.4	4.5	6.2	6.5	6.1
Exports	100.0	100.0	100.0	100.0	100.0	100.0	100.0
Socialist	63.9	63.1	63.6	60.7	55.7	59.9	59.7
CMEA	60.6	59.4	60.6	58.2	53.0	56.9	57.0
Other	3.3	3.7	3.0	2.5	2.7	3.0	2.7
Non–Socialist	36.1	36.9	36.4	39.3	44.3	40.1	40.3
Developed capitalist	28.4	29.8	30.4	34.2	36.3	31.5	32.0
Developing	7.7	7.1	6.0	5.1	8.0	8.6	8.3
Imports	100.0	100.0	100.0	100.0	100.0	100.0	100.0
Socialist	68.6	67.4	61.2	51.7	44.4	45.8	46.9
CMEA	65.9	64.4	58.2	49.4	42.3	43.8	44.9
Other	2.7	3.0	3.0	2.3	2.1	2.0	2.0
Non–Socialist	31.4	32.6	38.8	48.3	55.6	54.2	53.1
Developed capitalist	25.8	27.3	34.1	44.4	50.8	49.3	48.9
Developing	5.6	5.3	4.7	3.9	4.8	4.9	4.2

[a]The marked decline in the CMEA share of Poland's trade in 1974 reflects the fact that most intra–CMEA prices remained fixed at levels set for the whole 1971–75 plan period, while world prices rose sharply. The CMEA pricing formula was changed in 1975 to allow for annual increases, based first on a three–year and, starting in 1976, on a five–year running average of world prices. Thus, the 1974 data tend to distort the real distribution of Polish trade.

[b]The category of "other Socialist countries" includes the People's Republic of China, the People's Democratic Republic of Korea, the Democratic Republic of Vietnam, and Yugoslavia.

Sources: Rocznik Statystyczny Handlu Zagranicznego [RSHZ] 1976 (Warsaw: GUS, 1976), p. 21; and RSHZ 1977 (Warsaw: GUS, 1977), p. 15.

tion since 1950, for example, Poland's per capita production in 1975 was still more than 70 percent below that of Sweden or the United States and lagged 30-40 percent behind levels in the Soviet Union, East Germany, and Czechoslovakia.[10] In addition, there is suffi- cient evidence of continuing power shortages—a particularly acute problem in rural areas where the lack of capacity is a major ob- stacle to modernization of the agricultural sector—to conclude that the rate of increase in Poland's energy consumption is unlikely to slacken significantly in coming decades. Finally, there simply are limits to the uses of coal, energy needs which in any modern indus- trial economy can only be met with alternative fuels—primarily oil. Thus, Poland will become progressively more dependent on foreign, and, for reasons that will shortly become apparent, non-Communist supplies.

Until recently, the pattern of Poland's energy trade was re- markably stable, uncomplicated, and lucrative: rising imports of crude oil, petroleum products, and natural gas were covered almost exclusively by Soviet deliveries; while rising exports, primarily of hard coal, were divided about 55:45 between Communist and non- Communist customers. From at least 1960 on, earnings from the latter consistently exceeded costs of the former by a factor of 2 or more.[11] As Table 7.4 indicates, as late as 1972 Poland's CMEA partners accounted for 94 percent of her total energy imports—the Soviet Union alone for 82 percent—but absorbed only 57 percent of her energy-related exports, while 42 percent went to the West and 1 percent to the Third World. Since the onset of the worldwide en- ergy squeeze in late 1973, however, Poland's energy trade has be- come both more dispersed and more complex, although initially no less lucrative. In the three years between 1972 (the last full year of pre-embargo prices) and 1975 (the peak year for energy export earnings), the value of Poland's energy exports jumped from 2.5 to 6.9 billion złd (or by 178 percent); during the same period, the cost of energy imports rose from 1.2 to 3.9 billion złd (229 percent). Thus, although imports rose somewhat faster than exports in this critical sector, Poland's overall energy balance at the end of 1975 was still decidedly favorable, with energy sources still accounting for only 9.4 percent of imports but for 20.1 percent of exports (and 34.8 percent of exports to the West).[12] However, the long-term prognosis may not be nearly so rosy as this overview would seem to suggest. Already the data for 1976 show a 33 percent drop in the surplus of exports over imports. Moreover, trends are emerging both in the geographical distribution of Poland's energy transactions and in their commodity structure which may signal the eventual dis- appearance of this sector of Polish foreign trade as a net hard cur- rency earner.

TABLE 7.4

Poland's Exports and Imports of Fuels and Energy,
by Trading Groups, 1970-76
(million devisa złotys)

Trading Group	1970	Percent of Total	1971	1972	1973
Total exports	1,771.8	100.0	2,171.2	2,461.6	2,701.1
Socialist	996.7	56.3	1,167.4	1,409.5	1,543.1
CMEA	984.1	55.5	1,153.5	1,394.8	1,516.3
Non-Socialist	775.1	43.7	1,003.8	1,052.1	1,158.0
Developed capitalist	747.2	42.2	964.1	1,023.3	1,119.1
Developing	27.9	1.5	39.7	28.8	38.9
Total imports	960.2	100.0	1,039.9	1,193.7	1,499.0
Socialist	911.0	94.9	968.4	1,118.0	1,159.5
CMEA	910.7	94.8	968.2	1,117.9	1,159.0
Non-Socialist	49.2	5.1	71.5	75.7	339.5
Developed capitalist	49.2	5.1	71.5	75.7	337.3
Developing	0.0	0.0	0.0	0.0	2.2
Overall Balance (+/-)	+811.6		+1,131.3	+1,267.9	+1,202.1
Balance with CMEA	+73.4		+185.3	+276.9	+357.3
Balance with developed capitalist countries	+698.0		+892.6	+947.6	+781.8
Exports as percent of imports	186.5		209.8	206.2	180.2

Note: The category of fuels and energy includes hard coal, anthracite, brown coal, coke, crude oil, natural gas, petroleum products and synthetic liquid fuels, peat and peat products, and electrical energy.

1974*	1975	Percent of Total	Percent Increase 1970-75	1976	Percent of Total	Percent Increase 1975-76
4,393.4	6,849.6	100.0	286.6	6,614.7	100.0	-3.4
1,572.5	2,835.1	41.4	184.4	2,784.3	42.1	-1.8
1,502.3	2,724.4	39.8	176.8	2,748.2	41.5	0.9
2,820.9	4,014.5	58.6	417.9	3,830.4	57.9	-4.6
2,670.1	3,741.5	54.6	400.7	3,463.2	52.4	-7.4
150.8	273.0	4.0	878.9	367.2	5.5	34.5
1,908.4	3,921.4	100.0	308.4	4,652.3	100.0	18.6
1,160.0	2,698.2	68.8	196.2	3,127.2	67.2	15.9
1,157.6	2,696.2	68.8	196.1	3,123.2	67.1	15.8
748.4	1,223.2	31.2	2,386.2	1,525.1	32.8	24.7
642.8	1,041.1	26.5	2,016.1	1,385.3	29.8	33.1
105.6	182.1	4.6	—	139.8	3.0	-23.2
+2,485.0	+2,928.2			+1,962.4		
+344.7	+28.2			-375.0		
+2,027.3	+2,700.4			+2,077.9		
230.2	175.7			142.2		

*Note the disproportionate share of the non-Socialist markets in 1974 export earnings (64.2 percent) and import costs (39.2 percent) as a result of the lag in CMEA energy price increases.

Sources: Rocznik Statystyczny Handlu Zagranicznego [RSHZ] 1976 (Warsaw: GUS, 1976), pp. 6-9; and RSHZ 1977 (Warsaw: GUS, 1977), pp. 6-9.

Looking first at geographical distribution (again as displayed in Table 7.4), the share of the non-Communist world in Poland's energy export earnings increased from 43 percent in 1972, to 59 percent in 1975, and then dipped fractionally to 58 percent in 1976; for the West alone, the figures were 42 percent, 55 percent, and 52 percent, respectively. The shift was even more startling on the import side, where the non-Communist share jumped from a mere 6 percent in 1972, to 31 percent in 1975, and 33 percent in 1976 (for the West, from 6 percent to 27 percent and 30 percent). The sharp increase in non-CMEA imports is accounted for entirely by oil purchases, necessitated by Moscow's refusal to continue to cover Poland's (indeed, all of East Europe's) rising needs at a time when oil could suddenly command premium prices on the world market.[13] Between 1973 (the first year of substantial purchases outside the bloc) and 1976, such imports of crude oil and petroleum products rose from 1.8 to 4.7 million tons, or from 13 percent to 26 percent of Poland's total imports of these items (see Table 7.6).

The shift away from CMEA in the distribution of Poland's energy exports requires a slightly more complicated explanation. In part, of course, this shift was due to the earlier and sharper price increases for all energy products on the world market, reflected especially in the data in Table 7.4 for 1974 (a year of stable prices in CMEA). But, as a comparison of Tables 7.4 and 7.5 will show, shifts in the volume of exports to different markets also played a role. For instance, the most likely explanation of the dramatic shift in the distribution of export earnings between 1973 and 1974— combined with the more modest shift in distribution by volume and an overall increase in the volume of exports—is that Warsaw sought to cash in on the West's energy crisis, even at the expense of domestic supplies and other East European members of CMEA. (For example, the volume of hard coal exports to non-CMEA customers increased by 28 percent and to the Soviet Union by 5 percent but declined by 22 percent to the rest of CMEA.) On the other hand, the partial recovery of the CMEA's share in export earnings in 1975 and 1976 (reflecting price adjustments within the bloc) plus the overall increase in the value of Poland's energy exports tend to mask the overall decline in export volume since 1974, most ominously in hard coal exports, by far Poland's premier export commodity and dollar earner. Indeed, while the volume of all petroleum imports was 52 percent higher in 1976 than three years earlier and still climbing, shipments of all types of coal increased in the same period by only 15 percent and were showing definite signs of faltering.

How seriously should these figures be viewed? Are they the beginning of a fundamental shift in Poland's energy balance, or do they merely reflect temporary dislocations? Although still inconclusive, the data permit the following observations and projections:

TABLE 7.5

Distribution of Poland's Energy Exports, 1973-76
(thousand metric tons or million kilowatt hours)

Energy Source	1973	Percent	1974	Percent	1975	Percent	1976	Percent
Hard coal	35,857	100.0	40,093	100.0	38,479	100.0	38,944	100.0
to CMEA (total)	16,338	45.6	15,172	37.8	14,699	38.2	14,396	37.0
Soviet Union	9,126	25.5	9,556	23.8	9,818	25.5	9,375	24.1
East Europe	7,212	20.1	5,616	14.0	4,881	12.7	5,021	12.9
to non-CMEA	19,519	54.4	24,921	62.2	23,780	61.8	24,548	63.0
percent energy export earnings	77.8		79.1		80.0		77.2	
Brown coal	4,968	100.0	5,199	100.0	3,442	100.0	3,084	100.0
to CMEA (GDR only)	4,968	100.0	5,198	100.0	3,434	99.8	3,078	99.8
percent energy export earnings	2.4		1.6		1.5		1.4	
Coke	2,780	100.0	2,992	100.0	3,137	100.0	3,110	100.0
to CMEA (total)	2,148	77.3	2,117	70.8	2,286	72.9	2,235	71.9
Soviet Union	664	23.9	683	22.8	900	28.7	888	28.6
East Europe	1,484	53.4	1,434	48.0	1,386	44.2	1,347	43.3
to non-CMEA	632	22.7	875	29.2	851	27.1	875	28.1
percent energy export earnings	11.2		8.6		10.3		10.0	
Petroleum products	1,332	100.0	1,177	100.0	1,601	100.0	2,676	100.0
to CMEA (total)	451	33.9	161	13.7	32	2.0	46	1.7
Soviet Union	443	33.3	113	9.6	13	0.8	11	0.4
East Europe	8	0.6	48	4.1	19	1.2	35	1.3
to non-CMEA	881	66.1	1,016	86.3	1,569	98.0	2,630	98.3
percent energy export earnings	4.6		6.0		5.3		10.8	
Electric power	1,836	100.0	3,279	100.0	918	100.0	436	100.0
to CMEA (East Europe only)	1,699	92.5	2,937	89.6	744	81.1	435	99.9
percent energy export earnings	3.4		3.9		0.8		0.5	

Sources: Rocznik Statystyczny Handlu Zagranicznego [RSHZ] 1975 (Warsaw: GUS, 1975), pp. 18-19, 36-37, 91-92; RSHZ 1976 (Warsaw: GUS, 1976), pp. 92-93; and RSHZ 1977 (Warsaw: GUS, 1977), pp. 18-19, 34-35, 92-93.

TABLE 7.6

Poland's Petroleum Imports, 1970-80
(thousands of metric tons)

Import	1970	1971	1972	1973	1974	1975	1976[a]	1980E[b]	Percent Increase 1970-75	Percent Increase 1975-80E
Crude oil	7,011	7,987	9,703	11,140	10,582	13,306	15,095	—	89.8	—
Soviet Union	7,011	7,987	9,703	10,570	9,755	10,882	11,645	—	55.2	—
Non-CMEA				570	827	2,424	3,450	—	—	—
Petroleum products	2,424	2,267	2,332	3,079	3,019	3,133	3,216	—	29.2	—
Soviet Union	1,573	1,304	1,286	1,334	1,316	1,266	1,635	—	-19.5	—
Other CMEA	718	668	725	470	522	463	327	—	-35.5	—
Non-CMEA	133	295	321	1,275	1,181	1,404	1,254	—	955.6	—
Crude and petroleum products	9,435	10,254	12,035	14,219	13,601	16,439	18,311	27,500	74.2	67.3
Soviet Union	8,584	9,291	10,989	11,904	11,071	12,148	13,280	16,300	41.5	34.2
CMEA total	9,302	9,959	11,714	12,374	11,593	12,611	13,607	c	35.7	—
Non-CMEA	133	295	321	1,845	2,008	3,828	4,704	11,200	2,778.2	192.4
Percent share of Poland's total petroleum imports (by volume)										
Soviet Union	91.0	90.6	91.3	83.7	81.4	73.9	72.5	59.0		
CMEA total	98.6	97.1	97.3	87.0	85.2	76.7	74.3	—		
Non-CMEA	1.4	2.9	2.7	13.0	14.8	23.8	25.7	41.0		

Note: Official Polish figures for petroleum imports from the Soviet Union are consistently lower than official Soviet figures for similar exports to Poland (as cited by Haberstroh in Table 7) for the years 1971–75, the discrepancies ranging from less than 0.1 to more than 1.1 million tons.

[a]Soviet deliveries of crude oil in 1976 appear to have been in line with the plan, which called for the Soviet Union to provide 77 percent of Poland's crude imports in that year; see, for example, Trybuna Ludu, December 11, 1975. However, total Soviet deliveries of crude and petroleum products fell more than 800,000 tons short of Haberstroh's estimate of 14.1 million tons for 1976.

[b]The 1980 estimates for total demand and anticipated imports from the Soviet Union are taken respectively from the Radio Liberty report and Haberstroh article cited below. It is not clear in the sources whether these figures represent planned imports of crude only or of all petroleum products. I have assumed the latter in order not to exaggerate Poland's import needs and in view of the fact that her increased refining capacity should reduce her need for imports of petroleum products. The figure of 16.3 million tons from the Soviet Union represents a sharp drop from an early estimate of 24.5 million tons by Radio Liberty but a significant increase from the figures initially announced by the Poles, according to which the Soviet Union would deliver only 50 million tons during the 1976–80 plan period, or an average of 10 million tons per year. See: Radio Free Europe Research, RAD Background Report/146 (Poland), October 23, 1975: "Hard Currency Loans and Credits to Poland, 1971–1975," p. 16; also Trybuna Ludu, September 29, 1975.

[c]No estimates exist for Polish imports of petroleum products from the other CMEA countries for the 1976–80 period. In view of their declining and relatively insignificant share in Poland's overall petroleum imports as well as the growing strain on petroleum supplies in all of the East European countries, it seems likely that the non-Soviet CMEA share will continue to decrease.

Sources: Rocznik Statystyczny Handlu Zagranicznego [RSHZ] 1971 (Warsaw: GUS, 1971), p. 143; RSHZ 1973 (Warsaw: GUS, 1973), pp. 46, 112; RSHZ 1975 (Warsaw: GUS, 1975), pp. 91–92; RSHZ 1976 (Warsaw: GUS, 1976), pp. 92–93; and RSHZ 1977 (Warsaw: GUS, 1977), pp. 76–77. Jochen Bethkenhagen, "Soviet Gas and Oil Exports to the West: Past Development and Future Potential," Radio Liberty Supplement to the Research Bulletin, April 25, 1975, Table 13, p. 32. John Haberstroh, "Eastern Europe: Growing Energy Problems," in East European Economies Post Helsinki. A Compendium of Papers Submitted to the Joint Economic Committee, Congress of the United States, ed. John P. Hardt (Washington, D.C.: Government Printing Office, 1977), Table 8, p. 386.

With respect to oil imports, Polish demand for crude and petroleum products in 1980 has been estimated at 27.5 million tons—an unofficial but not unreasonable figure in view of increases in demand since 1970 (see Table 7.6 and Notes). Based on the latest available information, it would appear that Soviet deliveries will cover up to 75 percent of this amount, or a maximum of 75 million tons over the five-year period, but as a declining percentage of overall demand. (This represents a 50 percent increase over original plan guidelines, which called for Moscow to cover only 50 percent of Poland's needs, or 50 million tons.[14]) By 1980, Soviet deliveries are projected to run at 16.3 million tons, or 59 percent of anticipated imports, leaving the other 41 percent, or 11.2 million tons, to come from the world market. Thus, even using conservative price projections, Poland's 1980 bill for oil imports could easily reach 9.5 billion złd—4 billion (or $1.2 billion) for imports from outside the bloc.[15] This represents an increase of 86 percent over Poland's earnings from hard coal exports in 1976, and 44 percent over all energy sales in that year. In these circumstances, simply to maintain a positive energy balance, Poland would have to increase both the volume and price of coal exports by close to 40 percent—or else make up the difference with increases in other energy exports.

Is this a realistic expectation? And, more importantly, are the Poles likely to be able to maintain the surplus in energy trade that has helped them finance imports of other badly needed items, particularly Western industrial technology? The answer to the first question is a cautious "maybe"; to the second, "very doubtful." Apart from the 1975 decline in export volume and the apparent softness in 1976 world market prices, there are a number of indications of severe and mounting strains on Poland's domestic coal supplies: numerous reports of electric power shortages and brown-outs; the introduction of coal rationing in the fall of 1976; and a report that, for the first ten months of that year, exports fell 1.9 million tons short of plan.[16] Moreover, the situation seems unlikely to improve during the current plan period. Domestic demand for electricity is expected to grow by 8-9 percent per annum at least through 1980, against planned increases in capacity of only 5-6 percent per annum. Already the generation of power is consuming almost one-fourth of total coal production, and the percentage rises yearly.[17] While it is true that the Poles are currently developing two new and very large deposits—the Bełchatów and Lublin basins—neither will begin producing until 1980, and it is a virtual certainty that initial production will be absorbed by domestic energy needs. Even estimates of exportable surpluses from these new deposits after the mid-1980s are dependent on excessively optimistic projections for the development of nuclear power, which it is hoped will account for 13 percent of electric power generation by 1990, and 40 percent by 2000.[18]

It is possible, of course, that economic pressures will force Poland to become more efficient in energy consumption and thereby cut the rate of increase in demand. On the other hand, such vital development goals as the mechanization of agriculture are heavily dependent on rapid increases in energy use, a fact which severely limits the regime's ability to lower future demand. Moreover, as Table 7.7 indicates, Polish exports of coal, both in absolute terms and as a percentage of production, peaked in 1974, and for the near-to-medium term at least are likely to show only marginal increases in volume. The degree to which this relatively stable volume of exports will continue to cover a rising volume of energy imports will depend on several factors about which we can only speculate—most importantly, price and distribution. With respect to the former, now that the post-embargo surge is over, and especially now that the CMEA formula allows for annual adjustments, prices for all forms of energy are likely to rise in tandem with a minimal time lag. Thus, it is improbable that the Poles will again have the opportunity to profit disproportionately as they clearly did in 1974.

With respect to the geographic distribution, Poland's current surplus in energy trade now derives exclusively from the world market share. Indeed, energy sales to non-CMEA customers in 1976 came to almost 4 billion złd, or within striking distance of the amount needed to cover my "alarmist" projections of her non-CMEA energy bill in 1980. On the other hand, until 1976 the Poles had consistently maintained a slight surplus in their CMEA energy trade. In view of the limitations on export volume, as well as anticipated increases in the cost of energy imports from the Soviet Union, they cannot restore the balance without diverting substantial quantities of coal from Western markets. Yet, it is equally improbable that Moscow agreed to a 50 percent increase in petroleum deliveries to Poland during the current five-year plan period without exacting comparable promises of an increased Polish contribution to the overall CMEA energy balance. In fact, in view of the very recent report that Soviet deliveries of oil to East Europe as a whole actually declined slightly in 1976 from the 1975 level,[19] the figure of 16.3 million tons to Poland in 1980 and 75 million tons over the 1976–80 period must be regarded as highly tentative. Any reduction in that amount will aggravate the Poles' energy balance problems by forcing them either to increase imports from outside the bloc or to rely more heavily on domestic coal, thereby reducing the amount available for export still further.

To attempt to refine these projections any further would be to place too much weight on essentially rough data. What should be clear by now is, first, that in all probability the most the Poles can hope for is that by 1980 energy export earnings will still be sufficient

TABLE 7.7

Poland's Coal Exports in Relation to Production, 1965–76
(million tons)

Year	Hard Coal			Brown Coal		
	Production	Export	Export as Percent of Production	Production	Export	Export as Percent of Production
1965	119	21.0	17.6	22.6	5.2	23.0
1970	140	28.8	20.6	32.8	4.0	12.1
1971	145	30.3	20.8	34.4	3.5	10.3
1972	151	32.7	21.7	38.2	4.1	10.7
1973	157	35.9	22.9	39.2	5.0	12.7
1974	162	40.1	24.7	39.8	5.2	13.0
1975	172	38.5	22.4	39.9	3.4	8.6
1976	179	38.9	21.7	39.5	3.1	7.8
Annual Rates of Increase (percent)						
1965–70	3.5	7.4		9.0	-4.6	
1970–74	3.9	9.8		5.3	7.5	
1970–75	4.6	6.7		4.3	-3.0	
1974–75	6.0	-4.0		0.3	-34.6	
1975–76	4.1	1.0		-0.1	-10.4	

Note: Excluding exports of coke.

Sources: Rocznik Statystyczny Handlu Zagranicznego [RSHZ] 1976 (Warsaw: GUS, 1976), pp. 44, 92–93; and RSHZ 1977 (Warsaw: GUS, 1977), pp. 42, 76.

to cover the costs of energy imports and, second, that at least in this area import substitution is no solution but merely cuts down on exportable surpluses.

Food

Although less complicated than the case of energy, the changing balance of Poland's trade in processed foods and agricultural commodities poses a no less serious problem, for the immediate future at least. Indeed, there is a striking similarity in the roles these two categories of goods play in that country's foreign trade: due to a combination of global and domestic dislocations in supply and demand, food exports, too, can no longer be considered a reliable source of hard currency earnings with which to finance imports of Western industrial products and technology. The major difference between the two categories is that, while the balance in energy trade remains favorable if declining, the food balance has deteriorated much more rapidly.

The data in Table 7.8 tell the story all too clearly. Between 1970 and 1976 Poland's exports of agricultural produce and processed foods increased by 83 percent, while imports rose two and one-half times as fast, or by 221 percent, resulting in an overall deficit in food trade of 2.1 billion z/d in the later year compared with a surplus of 242 million in 1970. Moreover, the distribution of Poland's food trade between Communist and non-Communist (especially Western) trading partners has changed markedly in this period. On the one hand, while exports to other CMEA countries have risen considerably faster than imports from that group (bringing that portion of Poland's food trade roughly into balance), the level of both exports and imports fell in 1976; as a result, CMEA accounted for barely 24 percent of Polish food exports and 13 percent of similar imports. On the other hand, imports from the industrialized Western countries, the group that traditionally accounts for the bulk of Poland's food transactions, soared by 429 percent, while exports to these countries crept up by a mere 57 percent, leaving the Poles with a deficit of 1.8 billion z/d in 1976, compared with a surplus of 700 million in 1970. In addition, it is worth noting that the 1976 export figure, although an improvement over 1975, represents a 6 percent drop from peak sales of 2.5 billion z/d to the West in 1973, and that 1976 food exports accounted for 20 percent of total sales to the West, down from 37 percent in 1970. [20]

To be sure, part of this growing food deficit with the West is due to external (and possibly transient) causes, such as the disastrous Soviet grain harvest of 1975, which caused Moscow to default

TABLE 7.8

Poland's Exports and Imports of Processed Foods and Agricultural Products,
by Trading Groups, 1970-76
(million devisa złotys)

Trading Group	1970	Percent of Total	1971	1972	1973	1974	1975	1976	Percent of Total	Percent Increase 1970-76
Total exports	2,055.7	100.0	1,964.4	2,676.3	3,210.5	3,490.2	3,347.6	3,727.5	100.0	82.8
Socialist	434.2	21.1	392.9	727.7	592.1	983.0	1,089.9	965.2	25.9	122.3
CMEA	415.4	20.2	375.1	711.7	558.4	947.5	1,062.7	891.2	23.9	114.5
Non-Socialist	1,621.5	78.9	1,571.5	1,948.6	2,618.4	2,507.2	2,257.7	2,762.3	74.1	70.4
Developed capitalist	1,488.5	72.4	1,505.2	1,858.2	2,488.4	2,314.5	2,004.9	2,342.7	62.8	57.4
Developing	133.0	6.5	66.3	90.4	130.0	192.7	252.8	419.6	11.3	215.5
Total imports	1,813.9	100.0	2,429.5	2,392.5	3,386.7	4,324.6	4,677.7	5,817.9	100.0	220.7
Socialist	692.8	38.2	1,128.8	863.8	756.0	1,159.4	1,218.1	864.9	14.9	24.8
CMEA	624.4	34.4	1,029.7	757.2	667.3	1,035.1	1,077.5	770.4	13.2	23.4
Non-Socialist	1,120.8	61.8	1,300.7	1,528.7	2,630.7	3,165.2	3,459.6	4,953.0	85.1	341.9
Developed capitalist	789.5	43.5	906.3	1,134.4	2,191.9	2,770.5	2,878.1	4,176.7	71.8	429.0
Developing	331.3	18.3	394.4	394.3	438.8	394.7	581.5	776.3	13.3	134.3
Overall balance (+/-)	+242.1		-465.1	+283.8	-176.2	-834.4	-1,330.1	-2,090.4		
Balance with CMEA	-209.0		-654.6	-45.5	-108.9	-87.6	-14.8	+120.8		
Balance with developed capitalist countries	+699.0		+598.9	+723.8	+296.5	-456.0	-873.2	-1,834.0		

Sources: Rocznik Statystyczny Handlu Zagranicznego [RSHZ] 1976 (Warsaw: GUS, 1976), pp. 6-9; and RSHZ 1977 (Warsaw: GUS, 1977), pp. 6-9.

on deliveries to East Europe; increased grain prices brought on by
a run on world reserves; and new Common Market quotas on agricultural imports from nonmembers. [21] It seems likely, however,
that the main reasons are related to structural problems in Poland's
domestic agricultural economy. Chief among these factors has been
the steep rise in the demand for meat, outstripping harvests of grain
and fodder to produce it and leading to costly imports of grain from
the West. This, combined with low government prices for meat,
has discouraged livestock production by an aging and undermecha-
nized peasant population. During 1976 alone, the numbers of pigs
on private farms dropped by almost 30 percent, and cattle and sheep
by about 10 percent and 23 percent, respectively. [22] The net result
was that Poland had to import 5-6 million tons of grain in both 1975
and 1976 (up from 2.1 million in 1970) at an approximate cost of
$700-800 million per year [23]—a sum equivalent to nearly one-fourth
of her additional hard currency debt for those two years.

There is ample reason to believe that the gap between food imports and exports will continue to widen in the next few years. On
the one hand, exports to the West are likely to soften in the wake of
the sharp declines in livestock breeding noted above. [24] (Meat, poul-
try, and dairy products—the latter also in short supply—accounted
for close to half of Poland's total food exports to the West in both
1975 and 1976.) On the other hand, First Secretary Gierek himself
admitted that Poland would have to import some 8 million tons of
grain and fodder during 1977 in order to cover the shortfall in domestic production and provide for the recovery of livestock herds.
Of this amount, apparently only one million tons were to come from
the Soviet Union (despite the record harvest there in 1976). The
cost of the other 7 million tons, together with essential imports of
meat and other animal products to make up for the decline in domestic production, was estimated by Gierek at close to $1.5 million. [25]

Over the longer term, however, Poland's food imbalance may
be more amenable to correction than the energy problem. As one
commentator argued recently, while the Poles have to import oil
there is no excuse for them not to be self-sufficient in grain and
fodder, given rational policies of specialization and mechanization. [26]
The solutions, however, will come neither quickly nor easily. In the
meantime, the irony of the situation is that Poland is likely to become even more dependent on the West, since both the technology
necessary to achieve self-sufficiency and food supplies to tide her
over will have to come predominantly from that quarter.

Industrial Technology

The pattern of Poland's trade in industrial technology differs
radically from that seen in energy and food. Indeed, the most salient

feature of her economic development and foreign trade strategy since 1971 has been the importation of Western industrial products and technology as the catalyst in a transition to the stage of intensive growth, or the so-called scientific-technological revolution. This strategy envisioned that imports of Western technology, to be financed initially by a combination of credits and exports of basic goods (for example, coal and foodstuffs), would eventually pay for themselves through higher quality products that could be sold readily on world markets. In the process, Poland would be propelled into a more advantageous position in the international division of labor.

How has this strategy worked in practice? On the import side of the ledger it would have to be pronounced a spectacular success; if anything, too much of a good thing. Since figures for "technology" as such are not generally broken out of the broader trading categories, it is no simple matter to come up with precise data.[27] Nonetheless, there are several sets of figures that provide a rough idea of the magnitude of the purchases involved. Of the broad industrial groupings, the two most important categories among Poland's industrial imports from the West in recent years have been the electrical engineering and metallurgical industries. Looking at electrical engineering alone, Table 7.9 shows that between 1970 and 1975 imports from the West surged ahead nearly three and one-half times as fast as all imports in this category. Thus, the Western share of this most important sector of the Polish market rose from 19 percent to 48.8 percent, just fractionally below the CMEA share, which fell in the same period from 79 percent to 49.2 percent. If one combines import figures for both electrical engineering and metallurgy, purchases from the West in 1975 were actually slightly higher (51 percent, up from 21 percent in 1970) than those from within the bloc (47 percent, down from 76 percent). As the data show clearly, however, 1976 saw a marked shift back toward CMEA suppliers, while imports from the West actually declined slightly.

Perhaps a more accurate indication of the role Western technology has played in Poland's "strategy of the 1970s" are the data concerning purchases of capital equipment for complete installations in all branches of industry. Although a relatively small proportion of the engineering industry's total imports—2.3 percent in 1971 and still only 13 percent in 1976—it is a critical segment in that it represents increased capacity to produce technologically superior goods, rather than merely the importation of them.[28] Here both the magnitude of the import increases and the shift in their distribution are little short of staggering. Overall, equipment imports for new industrial installations in 1976 were 18 times higher than in 1971 (see Table 7.10). But where purchases from the CMEA countries rose

TABLE 7.9

Poland's Trade in Engineering and Metallurgical Products, by Trading Groups, 1970-76
(million devisa złotys)

Trading Group	Electrical Engineering							Electrical Engineering and Metallurgical						
	1970	Percent	1975	Percent	1976	Percent	Percent Increase 1970-76	1970	Percent	1975	Percent	1976	Percent	Percent Increase 1970-76
Imports	5,552	100.0	16,928	100.0	19,456	100.0	250.5	8,104	100.0	24,220	100.0	26,356	100.0	225.2
CMEA	4,368	78.7	8,327	49.2	10,521	54.1	140.9	6,177	76.2	11,327	46.8	13,390	50.8	116.8
Developed capitalist	1,047	18.9	8,268	48.8	8,509	43.7	712.9	1,675	20.7	12,269	50.7	12,261	46.5	631.9
Developing	29	0.5	13	0.1	41	0.2	38.6	77	0.9	187	0.8	207	0.8	169.9
Exports	5,915	100.0	14,149	100.0	16,074	100.0	171.8	7,243	100.0	16,469	100.0	18,370	100.0	153.6
CMEA	4,840	81.8	10,504	74.2	11,809	73.5	144.0	5,243	74.8	11,614	70.5	12,883	70.1	137.7
Developed capitalist	316	5.3	1,787	12.6	2,143	13.3	578.4	803	11.1	2,666	16.2	3,114	17.0	288.0
Developing	483	8.2	1,420	10.0	1,534	9.5	217.2	658	9.1	1,534	9.3	1,685	9.2	156.3
Percent total imports														
CMEA	46.0		45.6		50.8			65.0		61.0		64.7		
Developed capitalist	28.1		40.2		37.8			45.0		59.7		54.5		
Percent total exports														
CMEA	56.3		54.0		56.6			63.1		59.7		61.8		
Developed capitalist	7.8		16.6		18.3			19.9		24.7		26.6		
Developing	44.0		48.6		55.6			59.9		52.5		55.6		

Sources: Rocznik Statystyczny Handlu Zagranicznego [RSHZ] 1976 (Warsaw: GUS, 1976), pp. 6-9, 14-15; and RSHZ 1977 (Warsaw: GUS, 1977), pp. 6-9, 13-14.

TABLE 7.10

Poland's Imports of Capital Equipment for Complete
Industrial Installations, by Industry, 1971-76
(thousand devisa złotys)

Industry	1971	Percent	1975	Percent	1976	Percent
Fuel/Energy	0	0.0	2,111	100.0	2,232	100.0
CMEA	0	0.0	na	na	na	na
West	0	0.0	1,859	88.1	2,153	96.5
Metallurgical	0	0.0	135,118	100.0	67,303	100.0
CMEA	0	0.0	16,739	12.4	3,860	5.7
West	0	0.0	116,767	86.4	63,304	94.1
Electrical engineering	0	0.0	216,953	100.0	564,999	100.0
CMEA	0	0.0	6,373	2.9	1,842	0.3
West	0	0.0	204,716	94.4	560,696	99.2
Chemical	67,951	100.0	497,641	100.0	1,055,546	100.0
CMEA	14,504	21.3	25,544	5.1	80,288	7.6
West	53,446	78.7	463,051	93.0	973,411	92.2
Mineral	55,851	100.0	313,694	100.0	216,432	100.0
CMEA	45,549	81.6	67,184	21.4	67,674	31.3
West	9,854	17.6	245,200	78.2	146,451	67.7
Lumber/Paper	4,640	100.0	59,312	100.0	252,754	100.0
CMEA	na	na	na	na	na	na
West	na	na	57,618	97.1	252,717	99.9
Light/Consumer	0	0.0	70,418	100.0	55,869	100.0
CMEA	0	0.0	43,724	62.1	35,828	64.1
West	0	0.0	25,088	35.6	19,156	34.3
Food processing	3,103	100.0	366,223	100.0	74,584	100.0
CMEA	na	na	15,143	4.1	15,790	21.2
West	3,023	97.4	348,404	95.1	58,024	77.8
Construction projects	7,618	100.0	161,982	100.0	238,771	100.0
CMEA	7,151	93.9	11,217	6.9	17,543	7.3
West	na	na	145,681	89.9	217,816	91.2
Totals	139,163	100.0	1,823,452	100.0	2,528,490	100.0
CMEA	67,204	48.3	185,924	10.2	222,825	8.8
West	66,323	47.7	1,608,384	88.2	2,293,728	90.7
Unspecified*	5,636	4.0	29,144	1.6	11,937	0.5

*"Unspecified" refers to imports in these categories not identified by country of origin.
  Sources: Rocznik Statystyczny Handlu Zagranicznego [RSHZ] 1973 (Warsaw: GUS, 1973), pp. 151-53; RSHZ 1976 (Warsaw: GUS, 1976), pp. 131-33; and RSHZ 1977 (Warsaw: GUS, 1977), pp. 116-18. Due to changes in the classification of some imports, comparable figures for 1970 are not available.

only 232 percent, imports from the West increased nearly 35-fold. In essence this means that, where in 1971 Poland's market for complete factories was more or less evenly divided between East and West (roughly 48:52), by 1976 the West held more than 90 percent of a vastly larger market. In fact, the only sector in which this pattern did not hold true was light industry, for which East Germany still supplied more than 60 percent. Thus, if it is true as the Poles boast that approximately 50 percent of the industrial machinery in use in 1976 had been installed since 1971, it is in large part due to these imports of Western technology and equipment. [29]

But what of the second part of their strategy, the assumption that these imports would begin to pay for themselves within a few years through increased exports of manufactured goods to hard currency markets? One need only recall Poland's $10.2 billion debt to conclude that this part of her development strategy has not gone according to script. Despite an increase of close to 300 percent between 1970 and 1976, exports to the West from the engineering and metallurgical industries for the latter year covered only slightly more than one-fourth of the cost of comparable imports. This imbalance was partially offset by the additional 10 percent of engineering exports that went to Third World countries, including some dollar sales to the Arab oil states. But the Poles have made no attempt to conceal their disappointment with this performance. While for several years blame was placed chiefly on the "current crisis of capitalism," the "post-June" reflections have produced a number of admissions that problems of product quality and managerial efficiency cannot be cured solely through massive infusions of Western technology. [30]

What then is the near-term prognosis for Poland's technology trade with the West? On the one hand, it seems clear that imports will have to be cut, not merely as a percentage of the total but in absolute terms as well. This is a reflection, first, of plans to hold 1977 imports from the West to the 1976 level (despite rising demand for fuel and grain from that quarter) and, second, of a reduced rate of investment in basic industries for the duration of the 1976-80 plan period, the latter as a result of revised plan priorities in the wake of the June 1976 food price riots. [31] On the other hand, Western technology is still likely to play a major role in such important goals as the modernization of agriculture and lowering the ratio of raw material consumption to production.

Summary

This review of three important areas in Poland's trade with the industrialized West allows us to draw some preliminary conclusions concerning the nature of the relationship and of the respective sensitivities and vulnerabilities of each side. The first and most obvious conclusion is that Poland has been sustaining a substantial portion of her imports of Western technology through trade surpluses in two commodity groups—food and energy—in which her favorable balance has either turned into a deficit or shows signs of deteriorating under the strains of increasing domestic demand and import needs. Indeed, Table 7.11 shows that, where in 1971 the surplus from food and energy exports exceeded the deficit from machinery and equipment imports by 80 percent, by 1976 the balance had deteriorated to the point where the surplus from energy trade had been virtually wiped out by mounting food deficits, leaving industrial imports to be financed entirely through comparable exports and credits.[32]

Second, the relationship between Poland and the West is highly asymmetrical. With few exceptions, Poland's share in the trade of each of her Western trading partners generally runs between one-third and one-half of the second country's share in Poland's trade; in several cases, the ratios run as much as 10:1 in Poland's disfavor. Moreover, the impact on her imports is almost invariably greater than on exports.[33] Thus, Poland is substantially more vulnerable to changes in market conditions or policy in almost any one of her Western trading partners than vice versa, and this vulnerability is heightened by the fact that her imports from the West are generally far more critical to her economic well-being than her exports are to theirs.

This is not to say that the liabilities are entirely one-sided. The existence of a sizable debt itself creates an element of dependence in the form of a presumed interest on the part of her creditors in the economic stability of the debtor. In addition, some argue that Poland and the other CMEA countries have provided a much needed and apparently insatiable market for a recession-prone West.[34] There can be little doubt that it could be quite painful for several Western countries if any of the more heavily indebted CMEA countries were to default or if these markets were suddenly closed to them. Yet, one can scarcely argue that either (or both) of these eventualities would impose anything like the economic penalties that Poland would suffer if the flow of critical commodities and technology from the West were cut off. In other words, while undoubtedly the West is (in Nye's terminology) "sensitive" to events in Poland and would have to take measures to defray the "costly effects" of those events, Poland is "vulnerable" to events in the West in the sense that she would continue to suffer "costly effects" despite efforts to mitigate them.[35]

This leads to still a third conclusion. In economic relations with the West or with the world market in general the element of

TABLE 7.11

Poland's Trade Balance with the Industrial West in Foods, Fuels, and Technology, 1971–76
(million devisa złotys)

Year	1 Foods	2 Fuels	3 1 + 2	4 Technology[a]	5 Net Balance	Ratio 3:4
1971	+598.9	+892.6	+1,491.5	−824.1	+667.4	1.810
1972	+723.8	+947.6	+1,671.4	−1,870.2	−198.8	0.894
1973	+296.5	+781.8	+1,078.3	−3,310.5	−2,232.7	0.326
1974	−456.0	+2,027.3	+1,571.3	−5,023.3	−3,452.0	0.313
1975[b]	−873.2	+2,700.4	+1,827.2	−6,540.5	−4,713.3	0.279
1976[b]	−1,834.0	+2,077.9	+243.9	−6,367.5	−6,123.6	0.038

[a]The figures for imports and exports of "technology" are taken from the category "machinery and equip–ment" on pages 46–47 (1976) and 44–45 (1977).

[b]If one includes exports of machinery and equipment to the developing countries, some of which were sales for hard currency, this would reduce the deficit in technology trade for 1975 to 5,197.9 million zld, and would mean that the net food/fuel surplus covered 35.2 percent of the technology deficit in that year instead of 27.9 percent. Applying the same method to the 1976 data, the technology deficit would be reduced to 4,914.3 million zld; however, the much reduced food/fuel surplus would have covered only 5.0 percent of that amount.

Sources: Rocznik Statystyczny Handlu Zagranicznego [RSHZ] 1976 (Warsaw: GUS, 1976), pp. 6–9, 46–47; and RSHZ 1977 (Warsaw: GUS, 1977), pp. 44–45.

choice for the Poles—that is, the ability to reduce their vulnerability to external events—has been severely circumscribed. It is sometimes suggested that the Poles are now merely reaping the rewards of their own folly and excessive ambitions. Whether excessively ambitious or not, what began in 1971 as a deliberate policy choice has become progressively a matter of economic, even political viability. The reasons are several, partly of their own making, to be sure, but increasingly beyond their power to control. First, the sheer magnitude of Poland's debt to the West and consequently of her debt service (estimated at between 30 and 50 percent of hard currency earnings)[36] effectively precludes any slackening of efforts to export to hard currency markets. But it may prove just as difficult to cut back on imports. Not only are some of her more important manufacturing exports themselves "import sensitive,"[37] but the proportion of nondiscretionary purchases (fuels, grain, and so on) that Poland must make on world markets is, as we have seen, growing rather than shrinking. A less obvious but no less important pressure derives from burgeoning Soviet trade with the West, which is forcing the Poles (along with the rest of their East European neighbors) to compete with superior Western products for what had always been their most secure as well as their largest market— which they can do only if they can raise the quality of their own products and which has the effect of locking them into the pursuit of Western technology.

A brief look at the other East European countries confirms that Poland's predicament is not merely a consequence of her own incaution. Indeed, although visibly the most overextended (with nearly 40 percent of the total East European debt), her position does not necessarily compare unfavorably with those of her neighbors. For instance, Poland's terms of trade with the West have not suffered nearly as much in the recent inflationary spiral as those of countries more dependent on exports of manufactured goods,[38] a fact which may help account for the continued willingness of Western governments and bankers to lend to the Poles. Moreover, it is not Poland but Bulgaria which sports the highest ratio of debt to hard currency exports (3.4), and with little prospect of being able to increase her exports to the West. Poland ranks second with a debt ratio of 2.7, but the GDR and Hungary are not far behind, at 2.3 and 2.0, respectively; only Romania and Czechoslovakia are substantially lower, at 1.2 and 1.0 at the end of 1976.[39] A slightly different ranking, based on estimated debt service ratios at the end of 1976, again places Bulgaria at the top of the list, with debt service absorbing a whopping 75 percent of her hard currency exports. Poland is again in second place at 50 percent, followed by Romania at 42 percent and Hungary at 40 percent. The debt service ratios of the GDR and Czechoslovakia are estimated at 35 percent and 30 percent, respectively. [40] Finally, as we shall see in the sections that follow, the greater conservatism of some of Poland's neighbors in the end has not shielded them from the pressures of increased competitiveness both within and outside the bloc and may, in fact, have left them less prepared to meet the challenge.

THE IMPACT OF EAST-WEST INTERDEPENDENCE ON CMEA

Whatever the dimensions of economic interdependence with the West, it is intra-CMEA relations, and especially bilateral trade with the Soviet Union, which continue to exercise the dominant influence on Poland as well as on the other East European states. (As Table 7.12 shows, with the exceptions of Poland and Romania, roughly two-thirds of East Europe's trade takes place within the bloc, about one-third with the Soviet Union alone.) This does not mean, however, that we must accept the conventional wisdom which holds that the development of trade and economic ties with the West, on the one hand, and of intra-CMEA trade and integration, on the other, are mutually exclusive trends. [41] In reality, it would appear that the relationship between these trends is more complex and that cooperation with the West sets in motion both centrifugal and, potentially, centripetal forces within CMEA.

With respect to centrifugal forces, the Poles are by no means the only ones who have diverted, whether routinely or sporadically, their scarce "hard goods" to the world market at the expense of their CMEA partners. As Walter Clemens points out, all have at one time or another bolted the bloc with their most marketable commodities in search of their own advantage. [42] While such diversions were most likely to occur in the past when CMEA prices deviated widely from world price levels, [43] the switch to annual price adjustments within the bloc cannot be expected to reduce the temptation significantly as long as all bloc members are faced with the necessity of repaying mounting hard currency debts. Moreover, the evidence suggests an even more fundamental shift, that is, a tendency on the part of several of the East European countries to orient some of their leading economic sectors toward the source(s) of essential inputs for those sectors. This reorientation is due in part to the fact that the industries in question may already produce a country's most marketable exports but increasingly also to a recognition that the technological development or modernization of these industries will to a large extent determine that economy's future competitiveness. This trend has been further stimulated by the growing use of

TABLE 7.12

East Europe and the Soviet Union: Structure of Exports and Imports,
by Trading Groups, 1975
(percent)

Country	Total Trade (million rubles)	Socialist Countries			Non-Socialist Countries		
		Total	CMEA	Soviet Union	Total	Developed	Developing
Bulgaria							
Exports	3,436.0	80.2%	77.5%	55.2%	19.8%	9.4%	10.4%
Imports	3,965.2	72.8	71.3	53.0	27.2	23.1	4.1
Czechoslovakia							
Exports	5,831.3	71.6	66.5	31.7	28.4	19.8	8.6
Imports	6,339.4	69.8	65.6	32.1	30.2	24.6	5.6
East Germany							
Exports	7,517.1	73.2	69.3	36.1	26.8	22.4	4.4
Imports	8,413.0	66.6	63.5	36.0	33.4	29.0	4.4
Hungary							
Exports	3,999.5	72.2	68.5	38.9	27.8	21.4	6.4
Imports	4,645.8	66.2	64.0	34.9	33.8	27.0	6.8
Poland							
Exports	7,686.2	59.9	56.9	31.5	40.1	31.5	8.6
Imports	9,371.4	45.8	43.8	25.3	54.2	49.3	4.9
Romania							
Exports	3,980.0	46.0	38.8	21.4	54.0	34.7	19.3
Imports	3,980.3	43.6	37.2	16.8	56.4	43.4	13.0
Soviet Union							
Exports	24,029.0	60.7	55.6	—	39.3	25.5	13.8
Imports	26,669.5	52.4	48.3	—	47.6	36.4	11.2

Sources: Rocznik Statystyczny Handlu Zagranicznego 1976 (Warsaw: GUS, 1976), pp. 64-65; for percentage of trade with the Soviet Union alone: U.S. Department of Commerce, Bureau of East-West Trade, Selected Trade and Economic Data of the Centrally Planned Economies (Washington, D.C., September 1976), pp. 19, 26, 34, 40, 47, 54.

cooperative ventures and tied loans in which the East European country pays back the Western investment out of production generated by
that investment. Indeed, the East European states have begun to insist on such "buy back" agreements as a means of guaranteeing the
exports necessary to pay off Western loans. Among the more important industries involved are coal and copper mining, meat processing, textiles, clothing, and shoe manufacturing in Poland, a
broad range of agricultural technologies in Hungary, and energy-
related industries in Romania.[44]

Cooperation with the West also generates centrifugal forces
within CMEA insofar as such cooperation remains uncoordinated
and at times in direct competition with CMEA specialization plans.
In other words, members have bolted the bloc with their purchase
orders as well as with their more desirable exports; and, since they
generally do so in order to obtain more advanced technologies than
are available within the bloc, such moves are apt to be at the expense of the more industrialized CMEA countries. For example,
the Czech computer industry (as the designated producer of large-
scale computers for the bloc) was one of the early victims of detente,
which afforded the Soviet Union access to Western computer technology.[45] A less well-known example was the demise of plans for
a CMEA "dream car" as bloc members went their separate ways in
upgrading their respective automotive industries.[46] Ironically, this
understandable preference for Western technology is abetted not only
by the routine overpricing of capital goods in intra-CMEA trade,[47]
but by the fact that from a purely mechanical or administrative point
of view—reliability of deliveries, lack of bureaucratic red tape, frequency of contact between operational levels of the cooperating firms,
and so on—cooperation with Western firms is often easier than with
counterparts within the bloc. As a recent article on polish-Czech
cooperation observed:

> To be sure, contacts at the level of heads of ministries
> or associations have increased considerably of late;
> but so far as specialists from the branches or factories
> are concerned, whether Polish or Czech, they travel
> more often to Tokyo or New York than to each other.
> Moreover, such contacts [as exist] are limited to the
> directors and a narrow group of specialists.[48]

Finally, it is worth noting that the increase in CMEA's share
in the trade of all East European countries in 1975 was almost entirely absorbed by rising exchanges with the Soviet Union (reflecting price changes for oil and other raw materials) and was in no
way indicative of an upsurge in trade, much less integration, on a
bloc-wide scale. Indeed, for several of the countries, trade with

the rest of East Europe as a percentage of total trade continued to decline, reflecting the pressure to increase exports both to the Soviet Union and the West.[49]

On the other hand, centripetal forces are also at work. While the initial impact of increased trade and industrial cooperation with the West may run counter to the interests of bloc cooperation and specialization, the consequent improvement in the structure and quality of East Europe's output provides, at least potentially, a more rational and favorable basis for such cooperation and specialization within CMEA in the longer term. In addition, some observers see the magnitude of East Europe's debt itself as a centripetal force requiring members to cut their imports from the West to a minimum and enforcing greater reliance on each other.[50]

Looking for the moment solely at the Polish case, it is quite apparent that, whatever difficulties she may encounter in expanding exports to the West, Western investments in that country have markedly improved her relative position within CMEA. To be sure, the smaller deterioration in Poland's terms of trade both within and outside the bloc has been due in large part to her raw material exports, especially of coal.[51] But the structure of Poland's trade with her CMEA partners has also improved, due both to sharply increased capacity in certain sectors (providing import substitutes as well as exports) and to the greater comparative attractiveness of some products. Moreover, it is certain that the full impact of Western investments on her trade balance has yet to be felt, since many projects are still under construction or have yet to reach full capacity. For instance, the impact of the mammoth new Katowice foundry on imports and exports of metallurgical products (long a bottleneck in Polish industry) will begin to appear only in the 1977 trade statistics.[52]

Polish-Czech trade figures provide a striking example of this shift, particularly in view of the role that the Czechs have traditionally played as a major source of industrial technology for Poland and the fact that Czechoslovakia has been the bloc laggard in developing economic ties with the West. As Table 7.13 shows, between 1970 and 1975 Poland's exports to Czechoslovakia increased nearly twice as fast as imports from that country (159 percent as opposed to 81 percent), giving her an export/import ratio in the later year of 1.22, as opposed to 0.85 in 1970. While she bettered her relative position in every category but one, the most notable improvements came in the three branches of industry which provide a rough guide to a country's technological development and which, incidentally, represent 90 percent of Czechoslovakia's exports to Poland: the metallurgical, electrical engineering, and chemical industries. In the latter two categories, Poland actually exported more than she

TABLE 7.13

Poland's Trade with Czechoslovakia, 1970 and 1975

(million devisa złotys)

Economic Sector	Imports from Czechoslovakia					Exports to Czechoslovakia					Ratio of Exports to Imports	
	1970	Percent of Total	1975	Percent of Total	Percent Increase 1970-75	1970	Percent of Total	1975	Percent of Total	Percent Increase 1970-75	1970	1975
Total trade turnover	1,241.5	100.0	2,248.8	100.0	81.3	1,059.0	100.0	2,741.6	100.0	158.9	0.85	1.22
Fuels and energy	9.5	0.8	8.2	0.4	-13.9	115.3	10.9	362.5	13.2	214.4	12.12	43.98
All industry	1,231.7	99.2	2,239.7	99.6	81.8	901.5	85.1	2,334.0	85.1	158.9	0.73	1.04
Metallurgy	153.1	12.3	391.1	17.4	155.5	59.8	5.7	254.3	9.3	325.2	0.39	0.65
Electrical engineering	879.5	70.8	1,549.6	68.9	76.2	688.1	65.0	1,655.3	60.4	140.6	0.78	1.07
Chemical	99.9	8.1	97.2	4.3	-2.8	61.4	5.8	197.5	7.2	221.7	0.61	2.03
Mineral	43.3	3.5	71.3	3.2	64.8	13.6	1.3	23.4	0.9	72.2	0.31	0.33
Lumber/Paper	3.9	0.3	10.7	0.5	176.5	10.1	1.0	27.6	1.0	173.6	2.60	2.57
Light/Consumer	30.8	2.5	63.2	2.8	105.0	31.1	2.9	92.2	3.4	196.5	1.01	1.46
Processed food	4.0	0.3	8.6	0.4	117.5	27.6	2.6	67.8	2.5	145.9	6.95	7.86
Other industry	17.2	1.4	48.0	2.1	178.5	9.8	0.9	16.0	0.6	62.3	0.57	0.33
Agriculture and forestry	0.0	0.0	0.4	0.0	—	41.5	3.9	44.2	1.6	6.5	—	106.35
Other	0.4	0.0	0.5	0.0	25.0	0.7	0.0	0.9	0.0	28.6		

Note: Fractional discrepancies in columns are due to rounding.

Source: Rocznik Statystyczny Handlu Zagranicznego 1976 (Warsaw: GUS, 1976), p. 199.

imported in 1975. (Table 7.14 shows a similar improvement in the structure of Poland's trade with East Europe as a whole and, to a lesser extent, with the Soviet Union.)

This does not by any stretch of the imagination mean that the Poles have "solved" their quality problems (see further discussion below), and no doubt part of the Polish surplus can be attributed to the repayment of earlier deficits.[53] Nonetheless, there is enough evidence to suggest that they are also beginning to reap the benefits of technology transfer from the West in their exports of machinery and equipment, consumer goods, and other products—and, by contrast, that the Czechs are reaping the disadvantages of their tardiness in seeking advanced Western technology. One telling index is their mutual trade in automobiles: in 1965, Poland exported a mere 256 cars to Czechoslovakia, while importing in return nearly ten times that number (2,222); by 1975, the Poles sold nearly 13,000 to the land of the (aging) Škoda works, while importing only 3,000.[54] In another case, the Poles turned to the West for the machinery to upgrade and expand their leather and shoemaking industries when the Czechs (ironically once renowned for their shoes and hitherto the sole source of such machinery for Poland) were unable to supply either the quantity or quality of machines sought by the Poles.[55]

A second intriguing example is the planned upsurge in Polish-Romanian trade. Although Romania has not traditionally been among Poland's more important trading partners, the projected level of exchanges between the two for the 1976–80 plan period was 300 percent higher than for the years 1971–75, and much of the increase in trade and cooperation was to be concentrated in areas in which one or both partners have benefited from Western technological assistance: copper, aluminum, oil drilling and refining, metallurgy and machine tools, and the automobile and agricultural machine industries, as well as consumer products.[56] While it is far too early to discern the full significance of these developments, the renewed interest the Poles and Romanians are showing in each other seems to suggest that those countries that have taken greatest advantage of East-West cooperation may now find each other more attractive trading partners within the bloc and may become the most likely sources of substitutes for Western products should the debt burden or political factors force a curtailment of direct imports from the West. However, if the Polish-Romanian example is indeed a harbinger of things to come, it seems likely that the trend will gather momentum slowly, since the output of many Western-assisted projects will be absorbed initially by buy-back provisions as well as the often insatiable demand in domestic markets.

On a region-wide basis, economic and technological cooperation with the West could in the long term improve the overall quality

TABLE 7.14

Structure of Poland's Trade with East Europe and the
Soviet Union, by Sector, 1970 and 1975
(million devisa złotys)

	1970			1975		
Sector	1 Exports	2 Imports	Ratio 1:2	3 Exports	4 Imports	Ratio 3:4
Fuel/Energy	979.0	895.4	1.09	2,721.2	2,674.9	1.02
East Europe	473.5	140.1	3.38	1,111.6	180.2	6.17
Soviet Union	505.5	755.3	0.67	1,609.6	2,494.7	0.65
All industry	7,310.5	8,137.3	0.90	16,152.5	14,738.8	1.10
East Europe	2,855.0	3,822.4	0.75	7,310.3	7,194.5	1.02
Soviet Union	4,455.7	4,314.9	1.03	8,842.3	7,544.5	1.17
Metallurgical	570.8	1,796.6	0.32	1,077.7	2,979.5	0.36
East Europe	316.7	444.1	0.71	791.9	1,018.9	0.78
Soviet Union	254.1	1,352.5	0.19	285.8	1,960.6	0.15
Electrical engineering	4,807.0	4,365.9	1.10	10,450.1	8,323.7	1.26
East Europe	2,075.5	2,317.5	0.90	5,113.3	4,629.3	1.11
Soviet Union	2,731.5	2,048.5	1.33	5,336.9	3,694.4	1.44
Chemical	696.2	731.8	0.95	1,576.9	1,489.6	1.06
East Europe	184.6	437.3	0.42	583.1	780.2	0.75
Soviet Union	511.6	294.5	1.74	993.8	709.5	1.40
Mineral	36.6	171.5	0.21	64.1	273.6	0.23
East Europe	30.7	131.7	0.23	50.6	130.7	0.39
Soviet Union	5.9	39.8	0.15	13.5	142.9	0.09
Lumber/Paper	149.5	222.4	0.67	245.3	444.2	0.55
East Europe	37.8	68.8	0.55	59.0	88.1	0.67
Soviet Union	111.7	153.6	0.73	186.3	356.1	0.52
Light/Consumer	812.5	535.2	1.52	2,053.7	718.9	2.85
East Europe	74.2	211.9	0.35	325.2	262.4	1.24
Soviet Union	738.4	323.2	2.28	1,728.5	456.5	3.79
Food processing	175.7	195.9	0.90	596.2	315.3	1.89
East Europe	109.3	121.8	0.90	330.6	148.7	2.22
Soviet Union	66.5	74.1	0.90	265.6	166.6	1.59
Agriculture	234.3	405.1	0.59	458.6	665.0	0.69
East Europe	193.7	56.2	3.45	136.4	171.2	0.80
Soviet Union	40.7	348.9	0.12	322.2	493.7	0.65
Total trade	8,530.6	9,443.4	0.90	19,336.5	18,104.8	1.07
East Europe	3,527.3	3,998.4	0.88	8,560.2	7,548.0	1.13
Soviet Union	5,003.3	5,445.1	0.92	10,776.3	10,556.8	1.02

Source: Rocznik Statystyczny Handlu Zagranicznego 1976 (Warsaw: GUS, 1976),
pp. 198-206.

of CMEA trade and possibly even promote integration, but only to the extent that such cooperation aids those countries in solving the problems that have served as the major obstacles to true specialization and integration in the past, that is, low productivity, poor quality and marketability of manufactures, unreliability of deliveries and service, and the absence of any means to measure real costs or comparative advantage—all of which combine to keep CMEA trade locked into a barter system so rigid that it continually undermines the professed bloc goal of rational specialization.[57] Elimination of any, or even all, of these problems is no guarantee that economic integration will become a reality; that eventuality will depend in the first instance on political and economic forces within the bloc. In any event, it is a matter of increasing speculation whether Moscow is any longer interested in genuine integration. But it is a virtual certainty that integration—or simply a rationalization of economic relations within the bloc—will not materialize until and unless CMEA trade becomes more than an "exchange of inefficiencies."

Whether or not East-West cooperation will in the end contribute to such a rationalization will depend on a number of factors: whether, for instance, growing intrabloc trade in goods produced from Western technology increases the pressure for a fundamental reform of the CMEA pricing system (an estimated 10-15 percent of CMEA trade is already cleared in convertible currencies);[58] also whether the effect of East-West cooperation is to make the CMEA economies more or less competitive, more or less compatible. So far that cooperation has been largely uncoordinated—likely due less to Western influence than to East Europe's fear of Soviet domination of their economic relations with the West.[59] The absence of coordination does not necessarily lessen the prospects for cooperation within the bloc, witness the Polish-Romanian example just cited. Much will depend on the extent to which Western assistance is used to enhance the natural strengths of the individual economies or whether their development strategies remain locked in the pattern of "structural bilateralism" that has dominated intra-CMEA relations to date.

In the meantime, from the point of view of defining and assessing "interdependence" in the East European context, we are faced with the interesting phenomenon alluded to at the end of the last section: to wit, that the growth of East-West trade has given rise to demands for higher quality products within the bloc, thereby forcing even the more conservative and hesitant members into East-West trade and credit markets. Once again, Soviet behavior has been the critical factor; that is, it is the Soviet opening to the West which has placed the smaller East European members of CMEA in the unenviable position of having to compete for their largest and hitherto most secure market. [60] The consequences for any country that fails to keep pace in its technological development are readily evident from Czechoslovakia's current predicament. Once the premier producers of industrial technology for the bloc, the Czechs now appear to be in danger of losing their privileged position—if, indeed, they have not already lost it. [61] Moscow's abrupt shift to Western computer technology at the expense of the Czechs has already been mentioned, as has Warsaw's turn to the West for modern shoemaking machinery. An even more serious indication of Prague's difficulties is a recent report that the Škoda—Czechoslovakia's highly popular automobile, which has long been an important export item both within and outside the bloc, and the production of which accounts for about one-fourth of her total industrial output—is suffering from lagging sales at home and abroad and is in serious need of modernization. [62] In addition, Czech officials have admitted that the main reason for underfulfillment of the export plan for 1976 was the failure of Czech industry to produce enough marketable goods or to adapt "to the more demanding attitudes adopted by foreign customers to product quality"—almost certainly a reference to other CMEA customers rather than to the West, where demands for quality have always been high. Hardest hit, according to the Czechs themselves, have been exports of machine tools, textile machinery, refrigerators, and electronic products. [63]

The Czechs, of course, are not the only ones who are losing or in danger of losing what were once regarded as captive markets. The Hungarians, too, have hinted that the Soviets have begun rejecting some of their goods on grounds of poor quality. [64] And, since the Hungarians are often simply more candid than others about such delicate matters, it is a safe bet that the same thing has happened elsewhere. One lesson of these experiences would seem to be that, as long as some CMEA countries (and particularly the Soviet Union) pursue a strategy of economic modernization through cooperation with the West, it becomes a matter of economic survival for the others to follow suit. Whatever the risks of exposure and indebtedness to the West, they are less onerous in the long run than the risks of obsolescence. Even the loyal Bulgarians have gotten the message and, as an increasingly important producer of minicomputers and computer components for CMEA, are trying to avoid the earlier fate of the Czech computer industry by purchasing the most advanced computer technology that U.S. export controls will allow. [65]

INTERDEPENDENCE AND POLITICAL CHANGE

One reason for studying changes in the nature of international relations—including the emergence of "interdependent" relationships—

is to determine the impact of such changes on the policies and behavior, both foreign and domestic, of the states involved. This is
at best an inexact art, particularly when one is attempting to gauge
the influence of external factors on domestic change or to extrapolate
the probable influences of international trends that are only in the
process of unfolding.[66] Short of establishing clear cause-and-effect
relationships, we may nevertheless be able to suggest the ways in
which East European perceptions of key international and domestic
issues have changed as the "interdependent" relationships in question have been maturing.

Thoughtful East Europeans have long understood that, regardless of ideological affinities, their problems and interests as relatively small nations differ from those of a continental power such
as the Soviet Union—that size, the lack of a balanced resource base,
and greater geographical exposure automatically make them more
vulnerable to external pressures.[67] The fact that these situational
factors were somewhat muted in East Europe's initial response to
the food and energy crises of the 1970s was in all probability due to
two circumstances. First, the CMEA market, and primarily the
Soviet Union, temporarily shielded the region's economies from the
full impact of these crises. Second, other things being equal, the
East European regimes tend to follow Moscow's lead on global issues. On the other hand, as the protective shield of CMEA isolation disintegrates, it is evident not only that shortages and dislocations on world markets are intensifying East Europe's sense of exposure and vulnerability but that they are gradually altering perceptions of key problems of development both at home and abroad.
Once again the Polish case is instructive.

Perceptions of Global Issues

The impact appears to have been greatest on attitudes toward
global food and population problems, no doubt reflecting the seriousness of Poland's own food crisis. And, while the range of published
opinion is wide, a critical view of the Third World has become increasingly evident.

The first rash of articles appeared at the time of the U.N.
Population and Food Conferences held in Bucharest and Rome in
1974. Official coverage of the conferences generally conformed to
the main points of Kremlin policy, that is, that the world population
explosion and attendant food shortages would be solved only by social
and economic development under Socialist systems and not, as the
imperialists argue, by limiting fertility—although one finds little of
the strident tone or demagogic claims (for example, that the earth

can support 30-40 billion people) that marked Soviet coverage. [68]
On the other hand, feature articles, not only in Trybuna Ludu but in
the important weeklies, offered a much broader spectrum of opinion.
At one end were those who ground out the standard line embellished
by florid praise for the "rational" agricultural policies and high agricultural growth rates of the Socialist countries. [69] A series of three
articles by a leading commentator on agricultural matters for the
economic weekly Życie Gospodarcze presented a much more balanced view. Although the author did not challenge the official line,
his tone was factual and nonideological, and his focus as much on
the technical and economic problems of raising production in the
poor countries as on the conference hall polemics. In the end, he
seemed implicitly to place greatest responsibility on the developing
countries themselves to carry out the structural reforms that must
accompany increased investments and technology if the latter are to
be effective. However, the author did not relate world food problems to Poland's own situation. [70]

By far the most candid and pessimistic of the articles to appear in this period was Andrzej Lubowski's "The Spectre of Over-
population Hovers Over the World." Here, possibly for the first
time and accompanied by a wealth of data, was a stark admission
that the food problems of the poor are not caused merely by a mal-
distribution of the world's resources or by the failures of capitalism
but by the effects of geometric population growth on economic development, that the critical problem is not the absence of development
but the fact that increases in production are more than offset by
rising population, making it impossible to break the cycle of mal-
nutrition, low life expectancy, low productivity, and so forth.
Lubowski, too, avoided relating the global problem directly to
Poland's food situation but neither did he make preposterous claims
about bloc agriculture. And he concludes with a plea for a new ethic:
man in harmony with nature, not man over nature, questioning
whether the history of the human race is not akin to a Greek tragedy
in which the hero proceeds toward a fate which he has unwittingly
created for himself. [71]

Perhaps the most politically significant commentary on food
and population issues at this stage was made by the head of the
Polish delegation to the Bucharest Conference and vice chairman of
Poland's Planning Commission, Józef Pajestka, whose formal interviews at the time of his return from Bucharest stuck close to the
official line. [72] On the eve of the Rome Conference a few months
later, however, another article by Pajestka showed considerably
greater sophistication and concern in several respects. This time,
for instance, he connected the resource, food, and population crises,
noting more than once that while the ensuing strains and dislocations

would primarily affect relations between the developed capitalist
states and the Third World, the Socialist countries could not escape
the impact entirely. In addition, Pajestka addressed the question
of "dependencies" [zależności], noting: "The rapid economic development of the world is increasing the demand for resources and, as
a result, also the economic interdependence [or mutual dependence]
of countries on a worldwide scale." While large states such as the
United States, Soviet Union, and People's Republic of China had until
recently been virtually self-sufficient in resources, this was no
longer the case (although the Soviet Union remained in the best relative position). However, he continued,

> An incomparably greater growth of resource dependency
> is observable among the other economically developed
> countries of the world, which do not possess such ex-
> tensive territories and natural endowments. In particu-
> lar, this affects Western Europe, Japan, and the Social-
> ist countries of Eastern Europe (excluding the USSR),
> [which are consequently] . . . especially sensitive to
> the global situation and policies. [73]

Implicit in the article was the assumption that, irrespective of political or economic systems, the larger, more self-sufficient units
do not share the problems of the small and medium-sized states.
Pajestka did not go beyond this recognition to spell out policy implications; but the assumption itself, and sporadic attempts to act
upon it, have been a recurrent theme in East European politics
throughout the postwar period. [74]

More recently, press commentary has run increasingly along
the gloomy lines expressed in the Lubowski article, and some writers have begun openly to make the connection between Poland's food
problems and the general global situation. This trend has been particularly evident since the beginning of 1976, following several bad
harvests in Poland and a second disastrous harvest in the Soviet
Union, the latter event causing Moscow to suspend grain deliveries
to Poland and other East European states. Under headlines such as
"The World Food Market and Our Needs" or "Does Hunger Threaten
the World?," writers have betrayed a deep pessimism about world
food prospects over the next several decades, suggesting that the
general tendency for rising incomes to be spent on higher quality
foods will upset the delicate balance between Poland's grain imports and meat exports and that the only salvation is to become
more self-sufficient in grain production. [75]

One striking feature of the recent spate of articles not evident
at the time of the 1974 conferences has been the distinct lack of

sympathy shown for the more radical elements in the developing countries. A number of Polish commentators seem especially piqued that these countries should lump the Socialist bloc together with the developed capitalist world as a target of their demands. Among other things, they suggest that for many Third World leaders anti-imperialism is little more than a convenient tactic; that economic aid, while essential in theory, may be counterproductive in practice; that it is not enough simply to divide the loaf of human bread more equitably; and that Third World governments are unwilling to face the realities of development, including the need to tighten their own belts and carry out essential structural reforms. [76] To be sure, such views are at most only dimly reflected in more official forums. [77] Still, the fact that such outspoken articles have been published, as well as the appearance of occasional reports on the forecasts of such groups as the International Federation of Institutes of Advanced Studies or the Club of Rome, [78] bespeak a genuine concern on the part of the leadership over the impact that global resource problems will have on Poland.

On the whole, discussion of the implications for Poland of the world energy crisis has been less candid. The reasons are several: the fact that East Europe has continued to enjoy the partial protection of the CMEA energy market; Poland's own highly favorable energy balance, especially in 1974 and 1975; and the extreme sensitivity of questions related to energy trade and development within CMEA. Hence the stock assertion, endlessly repeated, that Poland's future energy security is guaranteed through joint development of Soviet resources; hence also the very scanty treatment of oil purchases outside CMEA.

This circumspection has not meant complacency, however; nor has it obscured growing signs of concern as Poland's deteriorating energy balance and shrinking CMEA protection have exposed her increasingly to the world petroleum market. As early as the beginning of 1974, shortly after the onset of the Arab oil embargo, there were warnings that, while they might temporarily escape the "negative effects" of the crisis due to domestic resources and CMEA ties, in the longer run the Poles would have to adapt to world trends and the new conditions might demand a reevaluation of development concepts. Moreover, some suggested, they could take little comfort from this temporary respite inasmuch as it was at best a "benefit" of backwardness and, the apparent contradiction notwithstanding, would now have to curb their tendency to "throw fuel around." On the other hand, the consensus of expert opinion seemed to be that the crisis should not be viewed as an obstacle to development or as an excuse for returning to autarkic policies. Rather, it should be seen as the occasion for accelerating modernization (especially the incorporation of energy-saving technologies) and for even greater involvement with the rest of the world, including the oil-producing countries of the Third World.[79]

While energy problems have remained in the headlines continually since the time of the embargo, the press began to betray a new sense of urgency toward the end of 1976, reflecting no doubt the passing of that temporary respite from the "negative effects" of the world crisis. Subjects of special concern are the continued "energy-intensiveness" of the Polish economy and the fact that the rate of increase in the demand for virtually all forms of energy is rising instead of falling. Indeed, the Poles themselves admit that they consume more than twice as much energy to produce a given unit of national income as either France or West Germany.[80] Even cautious admissions that Poland may become a net importer of energy—once an unspoken taboo—have begun to appear.[81]

Perhaps more than her food deficit, which, though clearly more serious now than in the past, has been a recurring feature of Polish economic life, the energy crunch is altering the Poles' perception of their place in the international economic order in subtle and sometimes contradictory ways. On the one hand, during the past several years they have made a genuine effort to cultivate markets among the oil producers of the Middle East. The immediate purpose was not so much to pay for direct oil imports from OPEC—CMEA oil still being substantially cheaper[82]—but rather to establish Poland as an alternative and reliable source of modern technology and services against the day (apparently now at hand) when Soviet oil would no longer cover her needs.[83] In fact, Polish exports to several OPEC countries, although still a small fraction of total exports, have risen as much as ten-fold since 1970.[84]

On the other hand, this image of Poland as a bearer of modernization to the oil-rich but economically underdeveloped, often in direct competition with the major industrial states of the West, contrasts sharply with the emerging view of her place in the world energy pecking order. For instance, a 1977 article, aptly titled "The Energy Order and the Economic Order,"[85] divides the countries of the world into three groups: first, the energy-surplus countries, which are clearly in the best relative position; second, the highly developed countries which, though net importers of energy, can absorb more easily its higher cost than can the third group, the underdeveloped or only moderately developed net importers of energy whose relative position continues to worsen. The author implies that Poland falls or is in imminent danger of falling into the third category—"if Poland becomes a net importer of energy," he writes without any disclaimers or arguments to the contrary. Such an eventuality would perforce impose "changes in our economic structure in the direction of energy- and material-saving modes of production and consumption." It would also intensify the competition for markets in the highly developed countries, not only because these countries must themselves cover their rising energy import costs but also because the "upper stratum" of developing countries (for example, Brazil, Mexico, South Korea) must likewise step up their efforts to penetrate these markets. Moreover, warns the author, this latter group will provide "extraordinarily stiff competition" for Poland's consumer and engineering exports.[86]

The Polish response to this complex situation is only now beginning to emerge, and no clear pattern is yet discernible. One alternative would be to focus export efforts more narrowly in areas where she has a clear advantage. The idea of such specialization is far from new, and its practice by others has been the source of admiring comment in the Polish press.[87] Yet, as one writer complains, it is an idea with a "rich history" which has so far produced only "meagre results."[88] However, specialization may now be getting a much needed boost from a second strategy, namely, joint undertakings with foreign firms in third countries. To date, the Poles are involved in at least a half-dozen major projects, all with Western firms and primarily for the construction of petrochemical or fertilizer plants in developing countries.[89] The advantages of such joint undertakings would seem to be twofold: first, they allow Poland to participate in projects that would otherwise be beyond her resources and expertise; second, they partially offset the otherwise competitive relationship between Polish and Western firms in third markets, a situation often not favorable to Polish exports.

While none of the above in any way diminishes the importance of the CMEA market for Poland—on the contrary, mounting external pressures make it imperative to satisfy as many needs as possible within the bloc—these changes in the perception of her place in the international economic order cannot help but alter also perceptions of relations with the Soviet Union. In terms of energy, for example, the critical point is no longer that the Soviet Union is a fraternal Socialist country but that it is among the energy giants of the world and, however that energy is disposed of, likely to benefit accordingly.[90] In addition, the Soviet Union (along with several of the smaller CMEA members) is now explicitly seen as a competitor in third markets, particularly among the OPEC countries.[91] Both of these factors seem likely to accentuate the differences between Moscow's and Warsaw's perceptions of certain international situations. For instance, the Poles clearly have a greater stake in oil price stability and uninterrupted trade relations with the Middle East—and therefore also in overall stability in that region. Likewise, they are far less likely to benefit from the promotion of revolutions in the Third World, especially to the extent that these would threaten access to developing markets gained independently or through cooperative ventures with the West. Finally, they have an unequivocal interest in the prosperity of Western economies, both as export markets and now as potential partners.

Impact on Domestic Change

In 1970 Gregory Grossman observed that, in "striking" contrast to Soviet literature on economic reform which "almost never mentions foreign trade, . . . one will rarely read more than half a page [of the vast East European literature on reforms] before running into the imperatives of foreign trade as a major reason for economic reform." By way of explanation, he cited "the great difference in the relative importance of foreign trade" in the Soviet Union (where the ratio of exports to national income is about 5 percent) compared with East Europe (where comparable ratios run between 15 and 40 percent, or even higher). "One of the most important consequences of a very high dependence of any economy on foreign trade," Grossman continued:

> is that it exercises a very harsh and immediate disciplining effect on the country's planners and leaders. A country that is highly dependent on foreign trade typically has to pay an immediate and heavy economic price in the form of a balance-of-payments deficit for overly ambitious or imprudent policies. A country such as the Soviet Union or China that indulges in adventures of the same kind very often has political dimensions through which to absorb these effects . . . [such as] political repression of the population. . . . A smaller country may also use political repression to compensate for economic mistakes, but this may not be enough to absorb the effects. . . . So, dependence on foreign trade may force economists, planners, and political leaders to rethink their ways of doing things and to search for more rational solutions. [92]

In the years since Grossman made these observations, East Europe's trade with the West has mushroomed, as has its debt and degree of dependence on that trade. Yet the relationship between foreign trade dependency, on the one hand, and systemic change in these countries, on the other, remains hazy and controversial. Nor need one look far for the reasons. In the first place, we still lack access to the kind of information on decision-making processes essential to tracing such influence effects. Second, the East European regimes, although clearly enjoying greater autonomy than in the past, still remain in the shadow of the Soviet Union. That is, it is still Moscow which ultimately determines the limits of domestic reform, a fact that imposes its own "harsh discipline" on the East European leaderships. Finally, domestic change is almost invariably the product of many factors, of which "interdependence" or increased vulnerability to outside forces and events may only be one. In other words, even with adequate insight into decision making, and even without the distortions of Moscow's watchful eye, it is highly unlikely that we could discover a predictable pattern of linkages between external influences and internal effects.

Nonetheless, such linkages, however indirect or unpredictable, can at times exert a critical influence on domestic decisions: possibly by tipping the balance of power among contending domestic forces; influencing the timing of a decision; or, in a more general sense, placing the system under such stress that it can no longer absorb added strains without itself undergoing change. It is especially in this latter sense, it seems to me, that "interdependence" should be regarded as a potential influence for systemic change in East Europe. That is, several of these systems (most visibly but not only Poland) now operate in an environment so taut, so inflexible or unamenable to amelioration through their own actions that they are being forced, as Grossman suggested, "to rethink their ways of doing things and to search for more rational solutions."

The irony of the situation, at least for the Poles, is that many of the problems which they are now being forced to rethink are the very same ones for which they initially sought solutions through trade and cooperation with the West: low productivity and product quality, lack of innovation, inability to adapt to changing market conditions, and so on. In other words, where the opening to the West was pursued originally as a means of overcoming the bottlenecks and inadequacies of their domestic economy, it is now in large part the urgency of coping with the strains produced by expanded external ties which is increasing the pressures for domestic change. To be sure, these strains have been magnified by such unanticipated events as the oil crisis, worldwide inflation, and recession in the West. But these "extraneous" factors have at most merely brought a speedier realization of the limits of technological transfusions as a cure-all for Poland's economic malaise and of the need for a more comprehensive systemic approach. Moreover, the Poles are coming to recognize that it is not simply a question of how to prevent the technology gap from widening again in the future but of being able to derive the full benefits of the technology already imported.

The discussions and arguments over economic strategy and organization currently taking place in the Polish press are anything but new; indeed, the litany of complaints and problems is depressingly familiar: managers and workers alike prefer the less demanding life of producing for the domestic and (at least until recently) CMEA markets, even when that production is based on imported Western technology; production for export, to East or West, is still largely a byproduct of production for internal consumption—a matter of disposing of whatever is left over—with little if any concern for the needs or preferences of potential foreign customers; there are too few incentives to make use of material- or energy-saving techniques, not to hoard unneeded capital equipment, and so on; and innovations, too few to begin with, more often than not remain on the drawing boards. What is new, or at least what is being admitted with greater candor and authority, is that, just as Poland's export problems cannot be blamed solely or even primarily on recession or discrimination in the West, neither can the solution to her problems be purchased abroad. Having already gone the route of massive imports of Western technology, the Poles have begun to recognize that they must now focus in on their fundamental organizational and motivational problems if the advantages of that huge investment are not to be dissipated. [93]

The results to date have been meager and seem to point in the direction of more rather than less central control, especially over investment and import decisions;[94] nor is there any clear consensus among the experts as to the proper remedies. Still, the discussions are beginning to take some intriguing turns. Since late 1976, there has been an upsurge of interest in Hungary's New Economic Mechanism, particularly in monetary policy as a tool for economic control—an interest evidenced by the recent translation into Polish of one of the earliest and most important theoretical works on the NEM and by the appearance of several other major articles. [95] In the agricultural sector, also, the intense pressure on the Poles to boost domestic production in the face of intolerable import costs has brought about a shift of investment priorities in favor of agriculture and is now forcing the regime to grapple with the complex and politically volatile issues of land ownership and utilization posed by the improper cultivation or outright abandonment of more than two million hectares of land, mostly by worker-peasants with marginal or fragmented holdings and by aging peasants with no one to take over their farms. Although the ultimate disposition of this land is still being decided, it is already apparent that the corrective measures will include the sale of additional land to efficient private farmers, stepped-up technical assistance to the private sector, and possibly the encouragement of new and less threatening forms of private

cooperation to permit mechanization and specialization on hitherto
fragmented and inefficient parcels—all policies resisted in the past
as inconsistent with progress toward socialism in the countryside. [96]

Perhaps the most interesting area for speculation concerns the
actual or potential impact of mounting external pressures on domestic
political processes and institutions, in particular on the vision of the
emerging "developed socialist society." Although the real issues in
the debate over "developed socialism" are often obscured by the
numbing uniformity of bloc rhetoric and obligatory tributes to the
example of Soviet Socialism, one can find signs of fundamental differences of opinion between those who envision the future as an extension and perfection of the present via scientific management and
cybernetics and those who see a greater sense of social responsibility, initiative, and productivity arising only through the development
of a more open and genuinely participatory political system. [97]

It is this latter approach that has flourished in Poland under
the impact of the current economic crisis and especially during the
months of tension and reassessment that have followed the food price
riots of June 1976. Contributors to the discussion include prominent
scholars, journalists, and political figures, and their views have
been aired in the pages of Nowe Drogi, the theoretical monthly of
the Central Committee, as well as in the more liberal Polityka or
Życie Warszawy. The particular targets of their attention vary:
local self-government, enterprise management and trade union organization, representative organs, administrative behavior, or the
total relationship between society and governing organs. But the
underlying theme of their arguments is the same: the imperative of
what Polityka editor-in-chief Rakowski calls "co-responsibility" and
the futility of demanding greater initiative, discipline, or understanding from the citizenry without giving them a greater voice in the
fundamental decisions of society. As a leading legal scholar wrote
in the September 1976 issue of Nowe Drogi:

> It is to be expected that in conditions of a developed so-
> cialist society a reciprocal linkage characterized not
> only by the influence of economic development on the
> emergence of new premises for the development of so-
> cialist democracy, but likewise by the increasing influ-
> ence of socialist democracy on the tempo of economic
> progress, will emerge with still greater intensity. The
> failure to fully understand the connection between the
> strategy of socioeconomic development and the develop-
> ment of socialist democracy and self-management can
> become increasingly troublesome. . . .

The dynamization of social forces, the creation of conditions for ever broader mobilization of social energy, depends on the improvement of structural forms which will awaken a creative attitude and activity in man. Toward this end socialist democracy must be developed and improved in accordance with existing needs and possibilities, [and must be] considered not as a congealed state, but as a constantly ascending process. [98]

This is not to suggest that notions of political reform have been smuggled into Poland in the baggage of "interdependence." Although the immediate political context and details of reform proposals vary, the basic ideals of socialist democracy have enjoyed considerable currency since the heady days of the Polish October. Nor is there any guarantee that today's reformers will be any more successful in bringing their proposals to fruition than others have been in the past. The influence of external pressures in the reform process is at best partial and indirect, and the systemic obstacles remain formidable. [99] What makes these pressures a potentially more powerful influence for systemic change in today's context is that they have brought old issues to the fore with a new sense of urgency, that they have narrowed the options open to the regime in dealing with these issues and have increased the penalties of inaction. That the Gierek regime appreciates the urgency of the moment is suggested by the fact that articles such as the one quoted above are cleared at the very highest level of the Central Committee (some very likely by Gierek himself), and by the appointment of its author, an articulate if cautious spokesman for moderate reform, to a select panel of experts to advise the first secretary on socioeconomic problems. [100]

There are a number of indications that, while tensions currently run higher in Poland than in the other countries of the region, the Poles are not alone in their difficulties—or in the discovery that increasing vulnerability to external influences may force their political leaders "to rethink their ways of doing things." In Hungary, for instance, the Kadar regime has recently begun experimenting with "direct democracy" in 50 test enterprises in an attempt to combat quality and productivity problems and to instill "a new spirit of responsibility" and discipline on the job. Similarly, in the agricultural sector, the Hungarians are introducing several programs aimed at raising the productivity of small-scale private farming, which are as unorthodox as they are innovative in that they amount to subsidies by the state and cooperative sector. [101] The remaining regimes are inclined to neither the candor nor the innovativeness of the Hungarians; but we can get some idea of the magnitude of the problems they face from the fact that all of them are counting on increased labor productivity to produce 85-90 percent (or more) of the increases in industrial output during the 1976-80 plan period, a goal which is clearly unattainable without genuine efforts to counter widespread alienation and indifference among the workers and general populations.[102]

INTERDEPENDENCE AND SOVIET-EAST EUROPEAN RELATIONS[103]

No aspect of East Europe's growing interdependence with the non-Communist world poses greater uncertainties for the analyst than the question of Moscow's likely response—uncertainties due not only to the opaqueness of Soviet commentary on such sensitive matters but also to the contradictions, or at least ambiguities, in their behavior. The prevailing assumption has long been that the Kremlin leadership would pursue detente and tolerate a significant degree of East European involvement with the outside world only as long as these policies did not result in East Europe's dependence on the West or threaten Moscow's vital interests in that region.[104] Yet, defining those interests and the nature and degree of the threat to them is no simple matter. Certainly, in the ultimate test of a threat to Communist control in one of these countries (as in Hungary and Czechoslovakia), the conventional wisdom has been borne out by events, although, ironically, few foresaw either invasion. Short of this extreme challenge, however, Soviet interests in East Europe are characterized more by ambivalence than by the single-minded concern for control often attributed to them. For every indication of Kremlin concern over the dimensions and possible consequences of East Europe's dealings outside of the CMEA, and particularly with the West, there are contraindications of a fair degree of tolerance over the years for limited diversity and reform at home and activism abroad, a tolerance implying awareness of the advantages as well as the risks of recent trends.[105]

Looking first at the risks or disadvantages, both actual and potential, of East Europe's emerging interdependence,[106] the Soviets cannot but be concerned over the tendency of East-West trade to preempt many of the region's most marketable resources and manufactures. Indeed, as we saw earlier, they have begun showing their displeasure by rejecting some shipments of low-quality goods. Given the trends already noted toward Western insistence on tied loans and East European insistence on buy-back agreements, this source of tension is not likely to disappear in the near future. A second source of considerable disquiet in the Kremlin must be the very real risk of ideological and political erosion as a result of extensive exposure to and interaction with the West—if not necessarily among the East European elites themselves, at least within their restless and sophisticated populations. Likewise, the increasing insistence of Western creditors on more detailed financial and technical data as a condition for loans opens up unwelcome opportunities for close scrutiny of, and possibly influence over, the economies of the region. In this connection, the Poles have recently made unprecedented concessions in exchange for two large loans, setting an example that the Soviets may well not appreciate. In one instance, they allowed full disclosure of information on their copper industry in order to obtain a $240 million development loan; in the second, they agreed to permit the emigration of 120,000 ethnic Germans as part of an agreement which included a credit of DM 1 billion from the West German government.[107]

The lack of coordination among the CMEA countries in their pursuit of Western technology has also come in for guarded warnings, to the effect such behavior "can weaken the effectiveness of economic integration among the fraternal countries and can introduce a disorganizing element, for instance in plans to establish uniform types for machinery and equipment, for setting industrial standards and for the purchase of licenses."[108] Finally, the very magnitude of East Europe's trade with the West and now of its hard currency debts carries with it the continual risk that Moscow will have to bail one or more of them out, either with loans and stepped-up deliveries of critical goods, as in the case of Poland in 1976-77, or by easing the burden of their obligations to CMEA's joint investment program, as may now be happening in connection with the Orenburg pipeline project.

On the other hand, the Soviet Union does derive some very tangible benefits from East Europe's opening to the West and to the world market in general. To the extent, for instance, that these countries can find alternative sources of oil and other scarce resources, the drain that they represent on the Soviet economy will be reduced, while the Soviets will be able to market more of their natural wealth to the West in exchange for the technology they themselves need. At the same time, the prospect of having to make substantial and burdensome purchases of energy from the world market has apparently made several East European countries more willing to participate in the joint development of Soviet resources as the price for assured access to those resources in later years. Moreover, as the largest market by far for East Europe's manufacturing exports, the Soviet Union eventually reaps substantial if indirect benefits from the incorporation of Western technology in those manufactures, without incurring either the hard currency costs or the risks of unwanted scrutiny of (or influence on) its own economy. In fact, the region served as the main "conduit" for goods between the West and the Soviet Union for several years before the latter was willing to open its economy directly to substantial Western imports. [109]

Even the asymmetry of the East European-Western economic relationship has hidden advantages from the Soviet point of view, in the form of leverage which increases as a country approaches the limits of its credibility and creditability (a point that both Poland and Bulgaria may fast be nearing). At this point, the Kremlin is in a position to impose conditions for its aid or even to decide not to aid its client, forcing the latter to cut back drastically on its trade with the West or even to default on its debts. And, while it was long thought that Moscow could not afford either the embarrassment or the adverse effect on its own credit rating of letting one of its smaller CMEA partners go into default, it has been suggested lately that default (or the threat of default) could prove to be a handy device both for chastening the more independent-minded among the East Europeans and for warning the West against excessive meddling. [110]

One may also question whether the feared "disorganizing" impact of East-West trade and cooperation on CMEA specialization and integration is of such overriding concern to the Soviet Union as is assumed. Two astute observers of the CMEA scene, Andrzej Korbonski and Paul Marer, suggest that despite the continual barrage of pro-integration pronouncements the Soviets may not want "to push economic integration much further than it now stands."[111] The probable reasons for their loss of interest are several. As Marer points out, such momentum as exists for integration has been maintained only by "Soviet willingness to supply a growing volume of energy and raw materials" to East Europe, a pattern they are now reluctant to perpetuate. In addition, genuine integration would eventually entail the assumption of greater responsibility for the other economic (and political) liabilities of their smaller partners and could be expected to generate increased pressure for genuine currency convertibility within the bloc with all of the disagreeable implications of that move for planning and price reform. [112] By contrast, the present emphasis on bilateral cooperation agreements with the individual countries, as opposed to multilateral coordination, affords Moscow selective control while minimizing the risks of contamination by unorthodox ideas. In addition, it has the advantage of not arousing the apprehensions of the smaller countries over the prospects for a supranational planning organization. [113]

Not surprisingly, Soviet sources provide only the most minimal clues as to how these risks and benefits balance out in the

mental scales of the Kremlin leadership.[114] Do they comprehend
the full extent of East Europe's growing vulnerability to outside
economic forces—the tautness of these systems and the shrinking
margin separating foreign and domestic policies? Or are they still
"blinded" by the relatively small impact which the external environment has on the vastly larger, more insulated Soviet system? Even
if the former, are they aware of the role that Soviet policy itself has
played in promoting this vulnerability, first by insisting that the
East Europeans buy more of their basic resources from the world
market and second by opening their own vast market to Western
competition? To be sure, in moments of acute crisis, Moscow has
responded with substantial credits and other economic concessions
(such as the promises of increased oil and grain deliveries to Poland
for 1977). But, in essence, they are treating the symptoms while
seeming to ignore the underlying disease—a practice which could
soon become prohibitively expensive.[115]

Perhaps the most accurate description of Soviet policies toward East Europe today is that they are "drifting" and "defensive,"
that the Kremlin is "responding, defensively and uncertainly, to
events and trends in [the region] rather than trying to shape them."[116]
Indeed, there is little evidence that the Soviet leaders have carefully
considered the consequences for their political interests in East
Europe of policies being pursued for broader strategic and economic
gain. Nor, in view of recent attacks on "Eurocommunism" and other
comments on the limits of "diversity in socialism," is it likely they
will soon give the East European regimes greater latitude in solving
their own systemic problems.[117] Given the age of the present leadership, any basic change in approach will have to wait for the post-
Brezhnev era, if then. For, while past succession periods have
witnessed ferment and experimentation in East Europe, they generally have not favored successful reform. All of this suggests that
the problems and tensions of the region will loom large in the coming transition period.

THE MEANING OF INTERDEPENDENCE
IN THE EAST EUROPEAN CONTEXT

In the course of the foregoing discussion, I have used the
term "interdependence" rather liberally without, apart from a few
introductory comments, directly questioning its applicability to the
relationships under examination. At this point, therefore, it seems
appropriate to reexamine the concept in the light of the evidence
presented with an eye, first, to its utility in the East European context and, second, to the possible usefulness of the East European
experience in refining the concept of interdependence itself.

Do East Europe's relations with the West today constitute interdependence? There is no simple "yes" or "no" answer. Certainly, in the Polish case, the relationship defies easy categorization. On the one hand, in view of the asymmetry of the relationship, it is somewhat misleading to speak of interdependence, or mutual dependence, when in fact the dependencies are very much one-sided. On the other hand, if one uses as a yardstick the several definitions of interdependence cited earlier, it quickly becomes clear that Poland's relations with the West conform more closely to Nye's criteria—multiple channels of contact, multiple issues, the absence of force, and linkage between foreign and domestic policies—than to the Holzman-Legvold definition, according to which East-West interdependence signifies merely "a level of mutual dependence in which both or all parties view cooperation as a useful but not decisive means for pursuing some or all of their essential goals" (emphasis added). It is perfectly true that Nye's criteria do not apply with the same force in this instance as in relations among Western states, but this should not be allowed to obscure the qualitative change in Polish-Western relations in the last decade or the fact that cooperation with the West has become not merely a useful but also a decisive means of pursuing some of their essential goals.

The conclusions that one can draw from this observation are several. First, it points up the very substantial difference in the perspectives from which the Poles (and by inference the other East Europeans) and the Soviets must approach their relations with the West. In the latter case, it is the Holzman-Legvold definition which would seem most appropriate, while Nye's criteria have little relevance. Indeed, as is argued persuasively by others, the Kremlin can reasonably conclude that the present level of East-West trade and cooperation can be maintained without exerting an intrusive influence on its policies, that the "economic well-being" of the Soviet Union will not "become seriously vulnerable to zigs and zags in Western economic behavior," or even that "Western economic life will become more dependent" on that trade than Soviet.[118] Moreover, Moscow is in a much better position than its East European allies to control the scope and intensity of its involvement with the outside world—to draw back from that involvement without crippling its economy should the political costs become too high, and to avoid being pushed into a greater degree of involvement than it prefers (as the East Europeans are being pushed by the actions of the Soviet Union itself).

These differences underscore the advantages of a more flexible, differentiated concept of interdependence, one that encompasses not only the transactions involved in an interdependent relationship but also the objective or situational factors that give rise to and condition those transactions. In opting out of the more finite approach, the alternative is not inevitably to settle for some amorphous lowest common denominator. We might attempt to see interdependent relationships along a spectrum, ranging from those generated by objective situational factors through several stages which are increasingly the result of deliberate policy decisions. Among the categories of interdependencies I would view as at least partially situational are: strategic, environmental, demographic, and economic (especially with respect to resources). This is not to suggest that these areas of interdependence do not involve "transactions," merely that such transactions are not necessary to create a condition of interdependence.

Unquestionably such conditions are conducive to a further development of interdependent relationships, that is, transactions consciously aimed at taking advantage of situational factors or at ameliorating their negative consequences. But a state may also attempt to reduce the impact of interdependence by increasing its self-sufficiency, as in instances where the potential spillover from an increased level of transactions is viewed as undesirable. In either case, a degree of "interdependence" is present; it is other political and economic variables which will determine the response, whether toward accepting (or exploiting) the challenges presented by interdependence or retreating from them. Those variables may be both objective and subjective in nature. Among the objective factors are the size, geographic location, resources, and level of economic development of a state, all of which affect its exposure or vulnerability to external pressures. Subjective factors include predisposing experiences or attitudes within a society, or the immediate political situations, which may bias the overall picture either by reinforcing the objective factors or by counterbalancing them.

Given this multiplicity of variables, it is obviously difficult in many instances to arrive at a simple cause-and-effect explanation of country X's response to situation Y. But, by disaggregating the notion of interdependence in this way, we may emerge with a concept which, though admittedly less tidy, better reflects the diversity of the real world and which is, therefore, more useful as a tool for analyzing the responses of various states to specific situations, whether actual or potential.

From this perspective, East Europe is further advanced along the spectrum of interdependent relationships than is the Soviet Union in at least two respects. First, these countries are objectively more interdependent simply in terms of these situational exposures; second, they are more interdependent by virtue of the level, nature, and potential impact of the transactions that have arisen from a combination of these situational pressures and conscious policy choice. Moreover, at least some of the East Europeans (most notably the

Poles, Hungarians, and Romanians) have come to acknowledge increasingly their interdependence and, rather than draw back from greater involvement, are responding by attempting to find more effective ways of meeting the challenge. Their success in so doing will depend not only on their own resourcefulness and discipline or on the reception they find in the West and elsewhere, but ultimately on whether Moscow is prepared to acknowledge their special circumstances and needs by allowing them greater latitude in solving their own problems—or, alternatively, to pay the economic price of not doing so.

A POSTSCRIPT ON POLAND: JANUARY 1980

In the two and one-half years since this study was first completed, the overall slowdown in the growth of Poland's trade and the push to bring exports and imports into balance, both barely discernible in the 1976 data, have continued and even accelerated. Despite unrelenting inflationary pressures, total trade turnover (in current prices) rose by only 8 percent and 7.1 percent in 1977 and 1978, respectively, and was scheduled to increase by a mere 3.5 percent in 1979. At the same time, imports have increased at less than half the pace of exports, while planned imports for 1979 were set at 51.5 billion złd, or scarcely more than 1 percent above the 1978 level, against planned exports of 47.5 billion złd, or 6.2 percent over 1978. As a result, Poland's overall trade deficit has been cut from 9.5 billion złd in 1976 to 6.2 billion in 1978, and to an estimated 4 billion in 1979. In addition, the data continue to show a shift in the geographic distribution of Polish trade in favor of the Socialist countries, a shift most obvious in the case of imports, where the Socialist share has risen from 47 percent in 1976, to 54 percent in 1978, and to a projected 58 percent in 1979. In the meantime, imports from the West have dropped not only as a percentage of total imports but in absolute terms as well, from a high of 22.5 billion złd in 1976 to 20.6 billion in 1978, and almost certainly to less than 20 billion in 1979. Thus, by 1978, imports from CMEA were running 28 percent above those from the West, and in 1979 possibly as much as 40 percent. [119]

Unquestionably, both the slowdown in trade growth and the retreat into the CMEA market reflect concerted efforts on the part of the Gierek regime to bring Poland's trade into balance by the early 1980s and to gain control over the escalating debt. Yet this strategy clearly has not worked as well as had been hoped in that exports, while rising faster than imports, have fallen significantly short of plan. In 1978, for instance, less than half the planned increase was achieved, and projected 1979 exports were still below the 1978 plan level. Thus improvements in the deficit (also significantly smaller than hoped) have been achieved only through sharp cuts in planned imports, including those of non-CMEA oil as well as of Western machinery and other industrial supplies. Moreover, an improving deficit picture does not mean a decline in total debt, estimated at year-end 1978 at $15 billion. With $4.1 billion (or close to 75 percent of planned hard currency exports) due to mature in 1979, it was a foregone conclusion that Poland's cumulative debt would rise by considerably more than the 1979 trade deficit and may well have reached (or passed) the $18 billion mark. [120]

Just how painfully these figures impinge on the Polish economy becomes clear when we survey recent trends in the three product areas examined earlier: energy, food, and industrial technology. Looking first at the energy area, it is readily apparent that my original prognosis—that the best the Poles could hope for by 1980 was that energy export earnings would still cover the cost of energy imports—was too optimistic. True, Poland's total petroleum imports in 1980 will not come close to the earlier estimate of 27.5 million tons. (They reached 20 million tons in 1978 and were expected to drop slightly in 1979; with Soviet deliveries close to plan, this means that imports from the world market will fall far below the projected 11.2 million tons.) [121] In the meantime, world market prices for oil have escalated beyond all expectations, pulling CMEA prices up in their wake, while Poland's exports of coal, far more stable in price, have barely managed to recover the 1974 level of 40 million tons. As a result, Poland's net energy surplus dropped from a peak of 2.9 billion złd in 1975 to 0.4 billion in 1978; during 1979 it is almost certain that Poland became a net energy importer. [122]

Moreover, the Gierek regime's ability both to hold down oil imports and to maintain the volume of coal exports cannot be viewed as a sign that a domestic energy balance has been achieved or that the Poles have made significant progress toward a rationalization of energy use. On the contrary, although the drop in the investment rate since 1976 has eased the upward pressure on energy consumption somewhat, there is ample evidence that a mounting energy deficit is having disruptive and costly effects throughout the economy, and even that the Polish economy has become more rather than less energy-intensive in the last three years. For example, where in 1974 a 1 percent increase in GNP required only a 0.5 percent increase in energy use, the corresponding increase in 1978 was more than 1.5 percent. The reasons for this phenomenon are complex and offer little hope for quick or easy solutions: a development strategy heavily biased toward raw material production and energy-intensive industries (including development of new energy sources); urgent and long-neglected investments in housing and social infrastructure, which can be further deferred only at great social cost; the drive to modernize the agricultural sector; and continued use of obsolete industrial technologies, as well as the "enormous wastefulness" of the communal economy.[123]

Even in the longer term, prospects for a turnaround in Poland's energy trade are slim. Production of hard coal is expected to rise, but at a slower pace than in the 1970s (at most by 3 percent per year to 1985, and probably by an average of only 2 percent per year to 2000). Brown coal production, after several years of stagnation, should also begin to show steady increases; but, in view of domestic needs, it is unlikely that the rate of increase (probably about 4 percent per year) will be high enough to release much additional hard coal for export.[124] At the same time, despite repeated cuts in estimates of crude requirements and despite the low level of imports from the world market through 1979, such imports are still expected to rise sharply, possibly to a level of 13 to 14 million tons by the mid-1980s—an amount that by then could easily cost in excess of $3.5 billion.[125] Nor will alternative energy sources provide significant relief in the coming decade; Poland's first nuclear power reactor, originally scheduled for completion in 1981, is at least five years behind plan, and a joint coal gasification project with West Germany has apparently been delayed indefinitely.[126]

Recent trade performance in agricultural and processed food products presents an even more dismal picture. A series of poor to middling harvests has forced a continuation of grain and feed imports (almost exclusively from the West) at a rate of 8 to 9 million tons per year, while declining meat exports have had to be partially offset by imports of meat to cover the domestic shortfall. The net of these trends was a food trade deficit in 1978 of 2.65 billion złd ($800 million), or double the 1975 figure. Especially hard hit were food exports to the West, which fell to their lowest level since 1972 (1.88 billion złd) and accounted for a mere 13.4 percent of total exports to the West (vs. 34 percent in 1973 and 20 percent as late as 1976), causing one analyst to suggest that "this category [of exports] is losing its significance."[127] That 1979 saw any improvements in this area is most improbable. By mid-year it was already apparent that the harvest would be a poor one, and Gierek himself admitted that this would mean additional cuts in food exports together with the continuation of grain imports in excess of 8 million tons for at least another year.[128] For the near term, it would appear that the Poles have abandoned the goal of self-sufficiency in grains and would be satisfied if they could bring imports down to a more manageable level.[129]

Interestingly enough, the one bright spot in Poland's trade picture as the 1970s drew to a close was the area of technology and industrial manufactures. By 1978, engineering exports to the West had increased 85 percent over the 1976 level (to nearly 4 billion złd) and for the first time comprised the largest single category of exports to these countries (28.3 percent, compared with 18.3 percent in 1976, and 7.8 percent in 1971). Indeed, including sales to the developing countries (many of which are hard currency sales), engineering products likely accounted for 35 percent of all exports to non-Socialist countries in 1978.[130] Moreover, since imports of Western technology peaked in 1976 and have since been on the decline, it is apparent that the Poles have been able to trim the deficit in their technology trade with the West very substantially.[131] Yet every silver lining also has its cloud. In this case, it is the fact that the reduction in Western technology imports has been less a matter of choice than a measure forced on them by their present financial straits and that it has not been without disruptive effects both on current production and on long-term modernization goals— most importantly, the goal of reducing the energy intensiveness of Polish industry.[132]

How, then, have these growing economic difficulties affected Polish policies and perceptions, whether foreign or domestic? For example, have the prospects for systemic reform at home been enhanced or reduced? Can one detect changes in Poland's attitude toward CMEA integration? Toward OPEC and the Third World? Or toward East-West interdependence in general?

Looking first at the domestic side, one can hardly point to major policy innovations in the last few years; nor does fundamental reform appear more likely in 1980 than it did in 1976-77. Indeed, the Gierek leadership seems to be paralyzed by its multiple dilemmas. Nonetheless, there has been a discernible shift in the tone of discussions and a crystallization of issues. With the exception of the top leadership which persists (perhaps only for public consumption?) in blaming Poland's woes on the deteriorating international economic situation and adverse weather conditions, one finds among Polish commentators today an overwhelming concern with the internal causes of their predicament. As one of Poland's foremost economists has remarked, at a time when world export levels are rising "considerably faster than ours . . . looking for the sources of our failures mainly in external constraints is a gross exaggeration."[133] The litany of complaints about the inadequacies of the "economic mechanism" is not new: the failure of efforts to instill in the Polish economy a pro-export orientation, to motivate industry through economic incentives to produce for export or to cooperate with other industries producing for export; the failure to reflect the true

cost of energy and other scarce resources in the domestic price
structure, thereby undermining conservation efforts; the lack of
responsibility and initiative at the enterprise level; and the inability
of the system to adapt, or simply a lack of interest in adapting, to
changes in external market conditions. These and other complaints
have appeared repeatedly in the press for several years.[134]

What is new is a growing sense of urgency over the way in
which domestic economic dislocations are beginning to feed on and
compound one another, threatening to drag the whole economy into
a downward spiral. To cite only one example, transportation bottlenecks have apparently resulted in frequent delays in the shipment of
coal (both for domestic use and for export), leading to improper
storage and a deterioration in the quality of significant amounts of
this vital resource and thus exacerbating both Poland's energy and
export problems.[135] New also, at least in degree, is a genuine
sense of alarm, both within and outside of the Party, over the deepening social and political malaise afflicting Polish society and consequently a greater willingness to subject all aspects of the current
situation to searching reexamination. To the cautiously worded
warnings of a few years ago—about the need for a sense of "co-
responsibility" or the danger of allowing the development of the
superstructure to lag behind the socioeconomic base[136]—have been
added stark admissions (not in the official press to be sure) of a
near total collapse of public confidence in the entire system of government, based on the popular conviction that "a radical change in
[its] operation . . . is both absolutely necessary and completely impossible."[137] That in the face of a crisis of such proportions literally no one expects the regime to mount a serious reform effort
merely bears out Janusz Zielinski's observation that the economic
conditions that give rise to pressures for systemic reforms seldom
coincide with the political conditions essential to their successful
implementation.[138]

Amidst this general state of <u>immobilisme</u>, the one area in
which policy concessions or adjustments seem likely is agriculture.
Spurred on by the twin energy and grain crises, the press has become remarkably candid about the causes of Poland's agricultural
plight: that by a variety of indexes (net product per hectare, energy-
and material-intensiveness and therefore import-intensiveness of
production) the private peasant farms are more efficient and productive than the large state farms; and that, within the private sector,
the highest rate of production with the least burden on Poland's
trade balance occurs on farms of three hectares or less. Yet, it
is precisely in this category of small farms (and garden plots) that
an irrational price structure and discriminatory policies toward the
private sector have led to a sharp drop in meat and dairy produc-

tion.[139] One should not conclude from this that the Polish leadership is about to abandon its long-term goal of socializing the countryside; in view of negative demographic trends it cannot. What does seem probable, however, is that the regime will take a more pragmatic approach toward the private sector, that it will defer its ideological aspirations in the interests of maximizing production in the near-to-medium term. This would entail not only measures to stimulate small-scale farming and livestock production based primarily on local supplies but also stepped-up support for larger specialized private farms in bringing idle or underutilized land back into full production.[140]

In the area of foreign policy and, in particular, foreign economic relations, the impact of recent developments has been more diffuse. On the one hand, in view of the growing energy squeeze and the need to cut industrial and technology imports from the West, it is not surprising that one finds an increased emphasis on the importance of the Soviet Union as Poland's major supplier of oil and other raw materials—or, in general, of the CMEA market and long-term intrabloc specialization and integration. Yet one should not read into this a full-scale retreat from the world market, on which the Poles will be increasingly dependent for increments in petroleum requirements, for grains, industrial components and energy-efficient technologies, as well as for markets for their exports. Equally important are subtle signs of pressure for change within CMEA itself, especially for a modification of those price and trade mechanisms which tend to reinforce the inflexible and uncompetitive nature of the domestic economic system and which therefore pose a serious obstacle to meeting the competitive requirements of the world market.[141]

Particularly in a year that began with revolution in Iran and ended with the Soviet invasion of Afghanistan, Poland's interdependence with world markets and need for stability in those markets has been made graphically and painfully evident. Along with several other East European countries, the Poles were looking largely to Iran to fill the gap between their oil needs and Soviet deliveries; and the search for alternative sources in the volatile conditions of 1979 has given rise to a more skeptical and occasionally critical view of OPEC[142] as well as to sober appraisals of the prospects for Poland's trade in this part of the world.[143] It is still too soon to draw any conclusions about the impact of Afghanistan; yet it takes little prescience to surmise that it will be the East Europeans, perhaps most especially the Poles, who will pay the heaviest price for the collapse of detente.[144]

NOTES

1. For the purposes of this paper, "East Europe" refers to the six Communist states of that region which are currently active members of the Council for Mutual Economic Assistance (CMEA): Bulgaria, Czechoslovakia, East Germany, Hungary, Poland, and Romania. Yugoslavia, an associate member, is not included, nor is Albania which, while formally a member, has not been active since 1961.

2. In a more serious vein, Karl Marx used the term "interdependence," as did the historian E. H. Carr several decades ago. See Walter C. Clemens, Jr., "Interdependence and/or Security: A Soviet Dilemma," p. 1, and Angela Stent Yergin, "Soviet-West European Interdependence and Its Implications for U.S. Policy," pp. 3-4, papers prepared under contract with the Office of External Research, U.S. Department of State, 1977; also Walter C. Clemens, Jr., The U.S.S.R. and Global Interdependence: Alternative Futures (Washington, D.C.: American Enterprise Institute, 1978), pp. 1-3.

3. Joseph S. Nye, Jr., "Independence and Interdependence," Foreign Policy, no. 22 (Spring 1976): 129-61; and Robert O. Keohane and Joseph S. Nye, Power and Interdependence (Boston: Little, Brown, 1977), esp. pp. 8-17.

4. Franklyn Holzman and Robert Legvold, "The Economics and Politics of East-West Relations," in World Politics and International Economics, ed. C. Fred Bergsten and Lawrence B. Krause (Washington, D.C.: Brookings Institution, 1975), p. 275.

5. In contrast to Nye and others, Lincoln Bloomfield seems more inclined to include situational factors in his definition of interdependence and, at least implicitly, to recognize the impossibility of segregating dependent from interdependent relationships. See his "Toward a Strategy of Interdependence," Special Report of the Department of State, no. 17 (July 1975).

6. Paweł Bozyk, "Handel zagraniczny 1971-1980," Zycie Gospodarcze, April 3, 1977; also Bozyk's comments on the disappointing 1976 results in his "Handel zagraniczny 1977: jaki bedzie ten rok?" Polityka, Export-Import Supplement, January 22, 1977. See also Table 7.1.

7. In an effort to play down the significance of the increase in the West's share of their trade, the Poles frequently argue that this increase is overstated by trade data in current prices due to the faster rate of inflation in the West than in CMEA. In a sense they are right; however, they neglect to mention the equally important fact that manufactured goods have been consistently overpriced in intra-CMEA trade since the 1950s. For estimates of the extent

of this overpricing, see Paul Marer, Postwar Pricing and Price Patterns in Socialist Foreign Trade (1946-1972), International Development Research Center Report, no. 1 (Bloomington: Indiana University, 1972), esp. pp. 53-65. In view of both forms of distortion, although they tend to offset each other, it is impossible to regard official trade statistics as anything more than a rough indicator of trade shares.

8. For a comparison of the overall energy balances in the six East European members of CMEA plus Yugoslavia, see "Selected Demographic and Economic Data on Eastern Europe," comp. William F. Robinson, Radio Free Europe Research [RFER[, RAD Background Report/90 (Eastern Europe), April 29, 1977, p. 27.

9. J. Richard Lee, "Petroleum Supply Problems in Eastern Europe," in Reorientation and Commercial Relations of the Economies of Eastern Europe, ed. John P. Hardt (Washington, D.C.: Joint Economic Committee, U.S. Congress, 1974), pp. 417-19. The comparable figure for coal in 1960 was 94 percent.

10. RFER, Polish Situation Report/8, March 5, 1976, pp. 3-6; Rocznik Statystyczny 1961 (Warsaw: Głowny Urząd Statystyczny [GUS], 1961), p. 467; and Rocznik Statystyczny 1976 (Warsaw: GUS, 1976), pp. 569, 584.

11. Rocznik Statystyczny Handlu Zagranicznego [RSHZ] 1970 (Warsaw: GUS, 1970), pp. 16-19, 33-34, 40-41; and RSHZ 1976 (Warsaw: GUS, 1976), pp. 16-19.

12. RSHZ 1976, pp. 14-15.

13. For detailed discussions of Moscow's oil trade, see Herbert Sawyer, "Soviet Energy Policy in Eastern Europe: Economic, Technological and Political Implications" (Paper presented to the annual meeting of the American Association for the Advancement of Slavic Studies, St. Louis, Mo., October 6-9, 1976); and Jochen Bethkenhagen, "Soviet Gas and Oil Exports to the West: Past Development and Future Potential," Radio Liberty, Supplement to the Research Bulletin, April 25, 1975.

14. Trybuna Ludu, September 29, 1975; I am assuming that both the original figure of 50 million tons and the upward revision to 75 million refer to crude oil and petroleum products. If the 1980 estimate of Poland's needs (27.5 million tons) includes only crude requirements, then her situation is even more serious than this analysis suggests, although increased refining capacity should reduce imports of petroleum products.

15. These calculations are based on the assumption that the price for Soviet oil within CMEA will have reached the 75 ruble/ton level by 1980, and that the world price will be at least $110/ton (or $15/barrel). Note: 1 devisa złoty equals .225 rubles; 3.32 złd equals $1. (See postscript for updated data.)

16. The Economist (London), December 18, 1976. Even the relative candor of the press can be taken as an index of the seriousness of the situation. See, for example, Jerzy Redlich, "Zaopatrzenie rynku w węgiel," Trybuna Ludu, March 16, 1977.

17. RFER, Polish Situation Report/8, March 5, 1976, p. 2; Redlich, op. cit., notes that the percentage of coal production used for power production in 1976 was 24.3 percent, up from 17.7 percent in 1971, and 23.0 percent in 1975. For a discussion of the continual increases in the demand for heat in both the residential and industrial sectors (now accounting for approximately one-fourth of all fuel consumed), see Lech Froelich, "Energia staje się złotem świata," Życie Gospodarcze, May 29, 1977.

18. RFER, Polish Situation Report/44, December 19, 1975, pp. 4-6; and RFER, Polish Situation Report/8, March 5, 1976, pp. 3-6.

19. New York Times, June 11, 1977. Based on the figures in this report, which were taken from the May 1977 issue of the Soviet foreign trade journal—and assuming that approximately 18 percent of Soviet oil deliveries to Communist countries continued to go to non-East European states (Sawyer, op. cit., p. 28)—it would appear that 1976 deliveries of crude and petroleum products to East Europe amounted to about 60 million tons. This compares with deliveries of 63 million tons in 1975 and projected 1976 deliveries of 68 million tons. See John Haberstroh, "Eastern Europe: Growing Energy Problems," in East European Economies Post Helsinki, ed. John P. Hardt (Washinton, D.C.: Joint Economic Committee, U.S. Congress, 1977), p. 386.

20. RSHZ 1977 (Warsaw: GUS, 1977), pp. 8-9, 14.

21. The percentage of Poland's food exports going to Common Market countries dropped from 50 percent in 1971, to 32 percent in 1975, rising slightly to 35 percent in 1976. Ibid., pp. 8-9.

22. Życie Gospodarcze, March 20, 1977; the May 8 issue also reported that marketed supplies of veal for the first quarter of 1977 were more than 20 percent below the first quarter of 1976.

23. Andrzej Lubowski, "Pasze do wzięcia," Życie Gospodarcze, September 12, 1976.

24. Redlich, "Zaopatrzenie rynku," and Bozek, "Handel zagraniczny 1977."

25. Trybuna Ludu, December 2, 1976.

26. Lubowski, op. cit. Concerning the capital intensiveness of modern agricultural production, see also "Koszty wzrostu produkcji rolnej," interview with Professor Augustyn Woś, Director of the Institute of Agricultural Economics, in Życie Gospodarcze, September 15, 1976.

27. The London Economist (December 18, 1976): 119, gives a figure of $17 billion worth of machinery and equipment imported between 1971 and 1975, of which more than $7 billion came from the West. On the basis of official Polish trade statistics and using the official conversion rates, imports from the West in the two branches of industry to be analyzed below came to just short of $10 billion, or some 56 percent of Poland's total trade with those countries, in those same years. Using a slightly different breakdown, which affords data for imports of machinery and equipment alone (RSHZ 1976, p. 46), the comparable figure is around $6.6 billion.

28. These figures do not by any means represent the total additions to productive capacity, which include also partial installations and modernization; however, it is extremely difficult if not impossible to extract these latter figures from available data. The overall figures for imports of "machinery and equipment" (see preceding note) are nearly as high as those for all engineering imports and clearly include far more than capital equipment.

29. Trybuna Ludu, March 29, 1977.

30. RFER, Polish Situation Report/8, March 16, 1977, pp. 1-3; and Bozek, "Handel zagraniczny 1977."

31. Ibid.; and Bożek, "Handel Zagraniczny 1971-1980."

32. See, for example, Wiesław Szyndler-Głowacki, "Handel zagraniczny a gospodarka żywnościowa," Życie Gospodarcze, June 27, 1976. Comparing the costs of grain imports only with earnings from exports of hard coal, the author notes that in 1970 the former absorbed only 57 percent of the latter (or 780 million złd), but that by 1975 the percentage was 70 percent (or 2.3 billion złd). Polityka, June 11, 1977, p. 2, allowed as how agricultural and energy items were the fastest growing sectors of Poland's imports in 1976, with increases over 1975 of 34 percent and 18 percent, respectively.

33. See Tables 13 and 32, RSHZ 1976, pp. 22-27, 58.

34. For a comprehensive discussion of these and other aspects of East-West interdependence, see Richard Portes, "East Europe's Debt to the West: Interdependence is a Two-Way Street," Foreign Affairs 55 (1977): 751-82.

35. See Note 3, above.

36. Portes, op. cit., p. 761, suggests 30 percent as a "conservative" estimate. The figure of 50 percent as of the end of 1976 is given by Joan Parpart Zoeter, "Eastern Europe: The Growing Hard Currency Debt," in East European Economies Post Helsinki, ed. John P. Hardt (Washington, D.C.: Joint Economic Committee, U.S. Congress, 1977), p. 1367.

37. Portes, op. cit., p. 768.

38. For calculations of changes in the terms of trade of the East European members of CMEA, see Paul Marer, "Economic

Performance, Strategy, and Prospects in Eastern Europe," in East European Economies Post Helsinki, ed. John P. Hardt (Washington, D.C.: Joint Economic Committee, U.S. Congress, 1977), p. 549.

39. Portes, op. cit., pp. 761-68; Portes points out that these ratios are not excessively high by comparison with those of many developing countries, for example, 2.6 for Argentina, 2.1 for Brazil, 3.1 for Chile, 2.6 for Peru, and 3.2 for Turkey, all as of year-end 1975.

40. Zoeter, op. cit., p. 1367.

41. For a rebuttal of this view, see, for example, Paul Marer, "Prospects for Integration in Eastern Europe: The Council for Mutual Economic Assistance," in Political Development in Eastern Europe, ed. Jan F. Triska and Paul M. Cocks (New York: Praeger, 1977), pp. 256-74.

42. Clemens, op. cit., p. 44.

43. Harry Trend, "Comecon at the Beginning of 1977," RFER, RAD Background Report/65 (Eastern Europe), March 25, 1977, p. 11.

44. One of the better sources of information on current and prospective purchases of Western technology by CMEA countries is the weekly rundown of contracts and bids, "What's New in Your Industry," at the back of each issue of Eastern Europe Report, the weekly review of East-West trade published by Business International. The Romanian case is especially interesting in view of the sale of a Canadian nuclear power plant to the Romanians (Boston Globe, May 22, 1977), and the latters' intention to invest in American coal through Occidental Petroleum (New York Times, May 31, 1977). Both developments indicate a continuing determination on Bucharest's part to remain independent of the Soviet Union for the bulk of their energy resources.

45. Connie M. Friesen, The Political Economy of East-West Trade (New York: Praeger, 1976), pp. 66, 70, 137-43.

46. Andrzej Krzysztof Wróblewski, "Samochód RWPG: fantazja na kółkach," Polityka, Export-Import Supplement, February 19, 1977.

47. See note 7, above.

48. Andrzej Lubowski, "Polska-Czechosłowacja: współpraca przez miedze," Zycie Gospodarcze, July 10, 1977. For a comment on the preference of Hungarian enterprises for Western machinery, see Eastern Europe Report, January 30, 1976, p. 26. Among the reasons mentioned are faster deliveries, sales and advertising skills, and reliable supplies of spare parts.

49. Only Czechoslovakia's trade figures for 1975 show increases in East Europe's share of both exports and imports, and fractional increases at that; for all of the other countries, the East European share of exports or imports (or both) declined. Most of

these figures are available in U.S., Department of Commerce, Bureau of East-West Trade, Selected Trade and Economic Data of the Centrally Planned Economies (September 1976): 19, 26, 34, 40, 47, 54; the missing figures can be estimated by using the data on the distribution of CMEA trade in RSHZ 1976, pp. 64-65. Particularly striking is the decline in East Europe's share of Poland's energy trade, on both the export and import sides: where in 1970 the other five countries took 26.9 percent of her fuel and energy exports and provided 14.6 percent of comparable imports, by 1975 these shares had dropped to 16.2 percent and 4.6 percent, respectively. RSHZ 1975, pp. 76, 195-202; and RSHZ 1976, pp. 78, 198-205.

50. See, for example, Portes, op. cit., p. 777.

51. However, Poland's terms of trade may not fare as well in the next few years as they did in 1974-75, since it appears that the price of coal is not keeping pace with oil; see Daniel Passent, "Mapa pogody," Polityka, Export-Import Supplement, June 18, 1977.

52. In fact, the 1977 data do show a slight improvement in the area of metallurgy, in the form both of reduced imports and increased exports; see RSHZ 1978 (Warsaw: GUS, 1978), pp. 6-9, 78-80.

53. Lubowski, "Polska-Czechosłowacja."

54. RSHZ 1970, p. 133; and RSHZ 1976, pp. 121-22.

55. Eastern Europe Report (April 23, 1976): 128; also Zygmunt Chabowski, "W polskich butach," Polityka, Export-Import Supplement, June 18, 1977.

56. Życie Gospodarcze, May 29, 1977; and RFER, Polish Situation Report/14, May 27, 1977, p. 5. The projected threefold increase in Polish-Romanian trade during the current plan period compares with a planned increase of just over 50 percent in Polish-Czech exchanges (Życie Gospodarcze, July 11, 1977).

57. For a discussion of the CMEA barter system, see Lawrence J. Brainard, "The CMEA Financial System and Integration" (Paper presented to the Conference on Integration in Eastern Europe and East-West Trade, Indiana University, October 31, 1976). A good example of how the "structural bilateralism" of intra-CMEA trade may lead to irrational and uneconomic investments is the requirement that petrochemical products can be traded only in exchange for other petrochemical products, thus forcing all countries to develop a substantial petrochemical industry regardless of their resource base. See Robert Mosóczy, "Development of Hungary's Economic Cooperation with the Comecon Countries," translated from Közgazdaságí Szemle, no. 7/8 (1975), in Soviet and Eastern European Foreign Trade 12, no. 4 (Winter 1976-77): 13-14.

58. Brainard, op. cit., pp. 2, 7, 20. For reports of Hungarian and, to a lesser extent, Polish views on price reform, see

Sandor Ausch, Theory and Practice of CMEA Cooperation (Budapest: Akademiai Kiado, 1972), reviewed with several related books by Roger E. Kanet, "Hungarian Views of CMEA Integration," Problems of Communism 29, no. 1 (January–February 1977): 67–69; Trend, op. cit., pp. 12–13; and Jerzy Kleer's interview with Soviet CMEA official, Yurii S. Shiraev, in Polityka, Export-Import Supplement, April 16, 1977.

59. Angela Stent Yergin, now Assistant Professor of Political Science at Georgetown University, reported to me, on the basis of interviews in Europe and the Soviet Union in late 1975, that West European specialists on East-West trade were keenly aware of apprehensions on the part of the East Europeans that any bloc-to-bloc agreement between CMEA and the EEC would be dominated on their side by Moscow.

60. Such a sensitive matter is obviously not discussed openly within the bloc, but it is not hard to find references to the growing share of the capitalist world in Soviet trade or the increasing competitiveness of the Soviet market. See, for example, Jerzy Kleer, "ABC handlu radzieckiego," Polityka, Export-Import Supplement, May 21, 1977; and Andrzej Krzysztof Wróblewski, "Konkurencja pod reke ze współpraca," Polityka, Export-Import Supplement, June 18, 1977.

61. For reports of Czech concern over their relative position, particularly over the competition their machinery exports are meeting not only from the West but from their erstwhile customers within CMEA, see "Czechoslovakia: Slow Start for 1976" and "Czechoslovak Party Congress Stresses Trade Problems," Eastern Europe Report (April 9, 1976): 107–8, and (April 23, 1976): 123–25; also RFER, Czechoslovak Situation Report/15, April 14, 1976; and "Survey of East European Developments in 1976," December 23, 1976, pp. 33–34.

62. As reported in the New York Times, January 29, 1977.

63. "Unsatisfactory Foreign Trade Balance in 1976," RFER, Czechoslovak Situation Report/18, May 18, 1977, pp. 4–13. Ironically, as Richard Portes points out (op. cit., p. 767), the Czechs recognized the need to begin replacing their aging industrial machines fully a decade ago; however, the 1968 suggestion that they seek a $500 million loan for the purchase of Western machinery was viewed as a provocation by Moscow. This amount was almost precisely the magnitude of their additional hard currency debt in 1975, but by then most of it had to be used for imports of raw materials and fuels.

64. RFER, "Survey of East European Developments in 1976," p. 41.

65. U.S., Departments of State and Commerce, "Foreign Economic Trends and Their Implications for the United States: Bulgaria" (Washington, D.C.: Government Printing Office, April 1975), p. 8.

66. As James Rosenau, a pioneer in the development of cross-system analysis, has remarked: "Recent years have witnessed substantial clarification of the dynamics that underlie political behavior at the individual, local, national, and international levels, but the capacity to move predictively back and forth among two or more of these levels is presently lacking." James N. Rosenau, "Theorizing Across Systems: Linkage Politics Revisited," in Conflict Behavior and Linkage Politics, ed. Jonathan Wilkenfeld (New York: David McKay, 1973), p. 25. For a general discussion of external influences on political change in East Europe, see my paper under that title in Political Development in Eastern Europe, ed. Jan F. Triska and Paul M. Cocks (New York: Praeger, 1977), pp. 277-314.

67. See, for example, Eugen Loebl's account of the early postwar period in Czechoslovakia in his Stalinism in Prague: The Loebl Story (New York: Grove Press, 1969).

68. Polish coverage of these conferences was quite extensive, especially by comparison with the Soviet press—although, needless to say, one finds no mention of the Soviet role in precipitating the 1972 run on world grain supplies. See especially Trybuna Ludu for the last week of August and the first two weeks of November 1974; for a review of Soviet coverage of the conferences, see Radio Liberty Report/53, 1975.

69. For example, Maciej Łukasiewicz, "Wyżywienie a polityka," and Stanisław Albinowski, "Żywność i polityka," in Trybuna Ludu, November 3 and 17, 1974, respectively. Along the same lines, though less obtuse, is the report from the Rome conference in Polityka by Andrzej Zalewski, "Droga do władzy nad głodem" (November 30, 1974).

70. Marcin Makowiecki, "Wyzywić świat," September 15, 1964); "Nadzieje świata głodujacych" (December 1, 1974); and "Kosztowne technologii" (December 8, 1974).

71. "Widmo przeludnienia krąży nad światem," Życie Gospodarcze, November 3, 1974.

72. Trybuna Ludu, August 31, 1974; also "Czy bedzie miejsce dla wszystkich?" Polityka, September 14, 1974.

73. "Rozdroże świata," Polityka, November 2, 1974. At the very end of the article, Pajestka made an interesting comment to the effect that, while Western Europe and Japan have been hard hit by the oil squeeze, "on the other hand, thanks to their potential political and economic dynamism, they are able to find new solutions

of interest likewise to the socialist countries." He was apparently referring here to the possible linkage of internal deflationary measures in those countries to an expansion of cooperation with socialist countries.

74. Among the more interesting though little known manifestations of this tendency have been the several efforts at establishing a kind of Polish-Czechoslovak economic condominium. The first such effort, in 1947-48, just after both countries had been prevented from joining the Marshall Plan, envisioned a broad range of cooperative undertakings. While in no sense anti-Soviet, the Polish-Czech program was explicitly based on a recognition of the complementarity of the two economies and of their special needs and interests as relatively small states. This effort succumbed to CMEA in 1949, but the concept was revived (again unsuccessfully) in 1956-57.

75. See, for example, Henryk Wojciechowski, "Światowy rynek żywności a nasze potrzeby," and Jerzy Gdynia, "Czy świat grozi głód?" both in Zycie Gospodarcze, May 2 and June 27, 1976, respectively.

76. See, for example, Wiesław Gornicki, "Gorycz," Kultura, February 29, 1976; Wojciech Giełzyński, "Riksza i odrzutowiec," Polityka, May 8, 1976; Jerzy Kleer, "Rozterki Trzeciego Świata," Polityka, February 21, 1976; Włodzimierz Wowczuk, "Konfrontacje biednych i bogatych," Polityka, January 1, 1976; and D. F., Świat łaknie żywności," Polityka, June 5, 1976.

77. See, for example, Kazimierz Olszewski, "Socialist Economic Integration and International Relations," World Marxist Review (May 1977): esp. 71-72, where he also complained about the tendency of some in the Third World to make the same demands of the Socialist countries as of the "imperialists."

78. See Augusto Forti, "Stan naszej planety," with an introduction by Jerzy Jaruzelski, and the full-page interview with American biologist and ecologist Paul Ehrlich, under the headline "Potrzebna nam jest druga arka," in Kultura (Warsaw), July 11 and November 21, 1976, respectively. Also noteworthy is the inclusion of Jan Szczepański, the doyen of Polish sociology, on the advisory committee of the Club of Rome's "Alternatives to Growth" program; Poland is the only Soviet bloc country so represented.

79. Waldemar Frackowiak, Longin Skalec, and Hubert Witczak, "Kryzys przyspiesza zmiany," Zycie Gospodarcze, February 3, 1974; "Co z kryzysem surowcowym?" and "Kryzys surowcowy i my," a two-part roundtable discussion summarized by Wiesław Szyndler-Głowacki, Zycie Gospodarcze, February 10, 17, 1974.

80. Lech Froelich, "Energia staje sie złotem świata," and "Racjonalnie gospodarować energie," Zycie Gospodarcze, May 29,

1977, and November 21, 1976, respectively; also Maria Wesołowska, "Sprawa osobista," Polityka, December 4, 1976; and Redlich, op. cit. (see note 16 above).

81. Marian Ostrowski, "Ład energetyczny i ład ekonomiczny," Życie Gospodarcze, July 3, 1977.

82. According to official trade data for 1975, only 17 percent of crude imports from non-Soviet sources came directly from OPEC countries (all of it from Algeria) and, if petroleum products are included, the figure drops to 11 percent; this represents a mere 2.5 percent of Poland's total crude and petroleum product imports in that year, and the comparable figures for 1976 were even lower: 10 percent of non-Soviet crude, 7.7 percent of crude and products, and less than 2 percent of total oil imports. RSHZ 1976, pp. 92-93; and RSHZ 1977, pp. 76-77.

83. Concerning Poland's efforts to expand trade with Iran, see Karol Małcużyński, "Polska-Iran na nowym etapie," Trybuna Ludu, November 17, 1974; and Witold Michałowski, "Na perskim rynku," Polityka, Export-Import Supplement, March 19, 1977. In Libya: RFER, Polish Situation Report/6, February 15, 1974, pp. 1-4; and Józef Stefczyk, "Polska na rynku libijskim," Życie Gospodarcze, October 31, 1976. In Iraq: Wiesław Gumola, "Polska-Irak," Życie Gospodarcze, October 26, 1975; Wiesław Szyndler-Głowacki, "Irackie przyspieszenie," and "Polacy nad Tygrysem," Życie Gospodarcze, November 2, 16, 1975. Of all of these articles, only the most recent one on Iran (March 1977) stated that Poland had begun buying Iranian crude, although the 1974 RFER report on trade with Libya claimed that the latter had agreed to supply Poland with oil in increasing amounts through 1980, something which was apparently not reported in the Polish media.

84. Between 1970 and 1975, Poland's exports to Libya rose tenfold, to Iran more than twelvefold, to Iraq (with which the Poles already had a higher level of trade in 1970) twofold, to Algeria (the only OPEC country from which Poland imported crude oil in 1974-76) twentyfold, and to Saudi Arabia (from which the Poles now import small quantities of petroleum products) nearly fourfold. RSHZ 1977, pp. 23-25.

85. Ostrowski, op. cit.

86. On this point, see also Tadeusz Burzykowski, "Przemysł lekki: wysokie wymagania," Polityka, Export-Import Supplement, June 18, 1977.

87. See, for example, Wiesław Szyndler-Głowacki, "Szwecja bez cudów: czego możemy nauczyć się od sąsiadów zza Bałtyku," and "Konstruktywne współdziałanie: po wizycie Edwarda Gierka w Szwecji," Życie Gospodarcze, June 1, 15, 1975; also Marcin Makowiecki, "Specjalizacja Duńczyków," Życie Gospodarcze, October 31, 1976.

88. Andrzej Konieczny, "W poszukiwaniu polskich specjalności: śladem bogactw naturalnych," Trybuna Ludu, March 29, 1977. See also Aleksander Paszyński, "Premia za poradę," Polityka, Export-Import Supplement, April 17, 1976; and "Nasze specjalności," interview with the director of "Bumar," Życie Gospodarcze, July 31, 1977.

89. Aleksander Paszyński, "Jak wyjść na swoje," Polityka, Export-Import Supplement, June 18, 1977; also his "Spółka dobra na wszystko," Polityka, Export-Import Supplement, March 19, 1977.

90. The Poles cannot, of course, say this directly; but they can and occasionally do reprint Soviet articles which convey, sometimes inadvertently, essentially the same message. See, for example, Aleksiej Oborotow, "ZSRR: kompleks paliwo-energetyczny," which appeared in Życie Gospodarcze on October 31, 1976, shortly before Gierek's last trip to Moscow, during which he asked for and got a substantial increase in Soviet oil deliveries to Poland through 1980.

91. See, for example, Michałowski's article on trade with Iran and the three articles on Iraq cited in note 83, above. One particularly interesting comment in this regard concerns the advantage Yugoslavia apparently derives in competition for contracts on third markets as a result of the highly trained Gastarbeiters who come back from West Germany. See Paszyński, "Jak wyjść na swoje."

92. Gregory Grossman, "Foreign Trade, Economic Reform, and Technology," in East-West Trade and the Technology Gap: A Political and Economic Appraisal, ed. Stanislaw Wasowski (New York: Praeger, 1970), pp. 151-52.

93. See, for example, Jerzy Kleer, "Koniunktura a handel," Polityka, April 3, 1976; Bożek, "Handel zagraniczny 1977"; Aleksander Jung, "Zgrzyty w mechanizmach," Polityka, Export-Import Supplement, May 21, 1977; Pawel Bożek, "Mit produkcji antyimportowej," Polityka, Export-Import Supplement, December 18, 1976; and RFER, Polish Situation Reports/8 (March 16, 1977, pp. 1-3), and 18 (July 11, 1977, pp. 1-4).

94. RFER, Polish Situation Report/12, May 11, 1977, pp. 6-10 ("Another Management Reorganization").

95. The book is Béla Ciskós-Nagy's Socialist Economic Policy, first published in Hungarian in 1969 and translated into English in 1973; the Polish edition appeared in the fall of 1976. See also Szymon Jakubowicz, "Reforma po wegiersku," Polityka, January 1, 1977; Lajos Faluvégi, "Wegry: rozwój instrumentów finansowych," Życie Gospodarcze, July 10, 1977 (a slightly condensed translation of "Development of the Financial Regulators and the New Hungarian Five-Year Plan," Acta Oeconomica 16 (1976); and Lech Szyszko,

"Pieniądz i instrumenty pieniężne w sterowaniu procesami inwestycyjnymi," Życie Gospodarcze, July 24, 1977.

96. Augustyn Woś, "Możliwości wzrostu produkcji rolnej i przebudowa rolnictwa," Życie Gospodarcze, June 26, 1977; RFER, Polish Situation Report/13, May 20, 1977 ("Agriculture Reviewed Again"); and the following articles from Polish Perspectives: Kazimierz Barcikowski, "The Tasks of Agriculture" (September 1976): 3-12; "The Press in Review: Agriculture" (February 1977): 55-60; and Wiktor Zujewicz, "Modernization of Agriculture" (May 1977): 11-14.

97. World Marxist Review frequently carries materials on "developed socialism"; especially interesting for comparative purposes are summaries of bloc-wide conferences. See, for example, "The Present-Day Problems of Socialist Democracy and Its Perspectives" (March 1975): 100-22.

98. Sylwester Zawadzki, "Z zagadnień demokracji socjalistycznej," Nowe Drogi (September 1976): 40-53; for an interview with Zawadzki, who is a deputy to the Sejm, or parliament, and editor-in-chief of Poland's leading legal journal as well as a professor of law at the University of Warsaw, see "Demokracja: z prądem czy pod prąd?" Polityka, July 23, 1977. For Mieczysław Rakowski's views, see his series "Nasze polskie sprawy" in the following issues of Polityka: December 25, 1976, January 8 and January 22, 1977; see also Thomas E. Heneghan and Ewa Celt, "Polityka and Polish Politics," RFER, RAD Background Report/151 (Poland), July 26, 1977. Other items of interest include: Jerzy Bafia, "Prawo i praworządność w kształtowaniu świadomości socjalistycznej," Nowe Drogi (May 1977): 55-62; Jerzy J. Wiatr, "Demokracja i samorządność," Życie Warszawy, December 9, 1976; Jan Puchalski, "Dylematy," Polityka, February 19, 1977; and Jacek Maziarski, "Korzenie demokracji," Polityka, March 26, 1977.

99. A good example of the cyclical nature of political reform in Poland is the functioning of the Sejm, or parliament, which has been upgraded following every crisis since 1956, only to be eased from the limelight once the regime has regained its confidence. See Sarah M. Terry, "The Sejm as Symbol: Recent Polish Attitudes Toward Political Participation," in Policy and Politics in Gierek's Poland, ed. Roger E. Kanet and Maurice D. Simon (Boulder, Colo.: Westview, forthcoming 1980).

100. Concerning Zawadzki's appointment, see Trybuna Ludu, May 31, 1977; and RFER, Polish Situation Report/15, June 7, 1977, pp. 7-9. The matter of clearance was related to me in late 1976 by a well-placed Party member and scholar.

101. Concerning the experiment in enterprise democracy, see RFER, "Survey of East European Developments in 1976," p. 41. Concerning developments in agriculture, see RFER, Hungarian Situation Report/20, June 7, 1977; also Situation Reports/8 (March 1, 1977), and 18-19 (May 20 and 31, 1977). For a Hungarian comment on the impact of external inflation on the domestic economy, see István Hagelmayer, "Internal Effects of External Inflation and of Deterioration in the Terms of Trade," in Soviet and East European Trade 12, no. 4 (Winter 1976-77): 19-39.

102. Eastern Europe Report (April 9, 1976): 106. The reported figure for Czechoslovakia is 90 percent (RFER, "Survey of East European Developments in 1976," p. 33); yet a U.S. Foreign Service officer, who returned from that country in 1976, told me that morale and discipline among the Czechs are so low and absenteeism so rampant that it is a common assumption among Western diplomats that the economy of the country is being held together only with the help of hidden Soviet subsidies.

103. A slightly revised and abridged version of this section appears in Sarah M. Terry and Andrzej Korbonski, "The Impact of External Economic Disturbances on the Internal Politics of Eastern Europe: The Polish and Hungarian Cases," in Transmission and Response: Impact of International Economic Disturbances on the Soviet Union and Eastern Europe, ed. Egon Neuberger and Laura D'Andrea Tyson (New York: Pergamon Press, forthcoming 1980).

104. See, for example, Clemens, op. cit., pp. 18-20, 43.

105. Andrzej Korbonski, "Detente, East-West Trade, and the Future of Economic Integration in Eastern Europe," World Politics 28 (1976): 580-81.

106. In the following discussion, and apart from other sources cited, I am indebted to Marer, "Economic Performance, Strategy, and Prospects in Eastern Europe," op. cit.

107. Thomas E. Heneghan, "Polish Trade and Polish Trends: Economic and Political Considerations," RFER, RAD Background Report/158 (Poland), November 13, 1975, pp. 11, 13, 20.

108. Yu. Korminov and I. Petrov, "Razriadka napriazhennosti i khoziaistvennoe sotrudnichestvo," Voprosy Ekonomiki (February 1976): 57-67; see also Eastern Europe Report (April 16, 1976): 113-14.

109. Korbonski, op. cit., p. 582.

110. See, for example, Portes, op. cit., p. 770; and Business Week (May 3, 1976): 118-19. This view is shared by some Poles, one of whom (an economist) told me in the fall of 1976 that at least some members of the Soviet leadership probably viewed the Polish crisis as a blessing in disguise, allowing Moscow to exercise more control over the Gierek regime.

111. The point was first made by Korbonski, op. cit., pp. 582-83, then picked up by Marer, "Prospects for Integration," pp. 257-70. Marer's reference to the central role of Soviet resources is borne out by the more recent literature, in which the subject of integration has become virtually inseparable from that of the joint investment projects being carried out in the Soviet Union. In this connection, the assertion by a former official in the Polish planning apparatus that, in the early 1970s, CMEA turned down a proposal for joint development of newly discovered brown coal deposits in central Poland, is especially interesting. See Andrzej Korbonski, "Poland and the Council for Mutual Economic Assistance," in Economic Integration in Eastern Europe and East-West Trade, ed. Paul Marer and J. Michael Montias (Bloomington: Indiana University Press, forthcoming).

112. See, for example, Kleer's interview with Shiraev (Note 58, above); also A. Marszalek, "Joint Planning Is a New Form of Cooperation Among CMEA Member Countries," Planovoye Khoziaistvo (August 1976); and L. Meyerovich and G. Linenburg, "Questions of Economic Accountability of International Economic Associations," Planovoye Khoziaistvo (June 1976), both excerpted in the Current Digest of the Soviet Press (November 3, 1976): 5-6, 27-28.

113. Concerning the current emphasis on bilateralism, see the London Economist's Quarterly Economic Review of Poland and East Germany, no. 2 (1977): 20-22.

114. Clemens' observation (op. cit., p. 20) that Soviet literature does not reflect these concerns was borne out by the frustrating efforts of two research assistants who scanned much recent Soviet literature for clues to their views.

115. Portes, op. cit., p. 770.

116. This description appeared in a draft of Marer, "Economic Performance, Strategy and Prospects in Eastern Europe," but was not repeated in the published version.

117. See, for example, G. Shakhnazarov, "The Socialist Future of Mankind," Pravda, July 23, 1976, excerpted in Current Digest of the Soviet Press (August 18, 1976): 9.

118. See esp. Clemens, op. cit., p. 18; also Yergin, op. cit.

119. RSHZ 1978, p. 15; Jerzy Borowski, "Handlu zagraniczny 1979: zdecyduje eksport," Życie Gospodarcze, February 25, 1979; Eugeniusz Możejko, "Handel zagraniczny: w perspektywie lat osiemdziesiątych" (2 parts), Życie Gospodarcze, August 12, 19, 1979; Daniel Passent, "Nie ma dynamiki—nie ma pieniędzy," interview with Foreign Trade Minister Jerzy Olszewski, Polityka, Export-Import Supplement, January 20, 1979; Roman Stefanowski, "Poland's Hard Currency Debt: Only a Relative Improvement," RFER, RAD Background Report/230 (Poland), October 23, 1979.

120. As late as December 1978, officials claimed the deficit for 1979 would be held to 1,200 billion złd ($400 million at the new rate of 3.1 złd to the dollar). This was clearly an unrealistic figure even then and did not correspond to the overall trade plan, according to which the expected trade deficit was 4 billion złd ($1.3 billion), almost all in non-CMEA trade. In a preliminary report in late December 1979, First Deputy Finance Minister Krzak admitted that new debt for the year would be close to $2 billion, raising Poland's total debt to between $17 and 18 billion (although one should keep in mind that the Poles tend to understate their debt). Repayments of principal and interest in 1980 will amount to some $5 billion. Stefanowski, op. cit.; and RFER, Polish Situation Report/1, January 9, 1980, pp. 6-8.

121. RSHZ 1978, pp. 76-77; Krzysztof Krauss, "Program osadzony w realiach: rozmowa z Eugeniuszem Szyrem, Ministrem Gospodarki Materiałowej," Życie Gospodarcze, November 11, 1979; RFER, Polish Situation Report/25, November 27, 1979, pp. 5-9; see also Table 7.6. Non-CMEA imports of crude and petroleum products, 4.7 million tons in both 1976 and 1977, probably remained below the 5 million ton mark in 1978 and 1979 as well. However, of the 13.8 million tons of crude expected from the Soviet Union in 1979, 800,000 tons were reportedly above plan and therefore sold at world prices and in hard currency.

122. For the first six months of 1979, the Poles had a deficit of 103 million złd in their energy trade; Stefanowski, op. cit. Earnings from energy exports to the West in 1978 were actually 16 percent lower than in 1975, and accounted for only 22.4 percent of total exports to the West, compared to 34.8 percent in the earlier year; Borowski, op. cit.; and Możejko, "Handel zagraniczny (2)."

123. Concerning the mounting energy bottlenecks and dislocations, see esp. Lech Stefański, "Węgiel," Polityka, December 1, 1979; Wiktor Herer and Władysław Sadowski, "Kierunki myślenia o przyszłości," Polityka, December 15, 1979; and RFER, Polish Situation Reports/16 and 27, July 19 and December 20, 1979, respectively. According to the last mentioned, Poland's electrical energy shortfall during peak demand hours in September 1979 was estimated at 39 percent of total capacity. Concerning the energy intensiveness of the Polish economy, see Andrzej Gdula, "Kierunki zwiększania efektywności w gospodarce energetyczny," Nowe Drogi, no. 10 (1979): 120-34; Tadeusz Podwysocki, "Węgiel," Życie Gospodarcze, November 12, 1978; Lech Froelich, "Ciężkie nie znaczy lepsze," Życie Gospodarcze, January 21, 1979; and RFER, Polish Situation Report/10, May 9, 1979, pp. 1-4.

124. Lech Froelich, "Węgiel," Życie Gospodarcze, December 2, 1979; and Podwysocki, op. cit. A prediction of a sixfold

increase in brown coal production by 2000 reported by RFER (Polish Situation Report/10, May 9, 1979) would seem to be totally unrealistic and is wholly out of line with other estimates. Podwysocki suggests that Polish exports of hard coal could reach 50 million tons (about 25 percent above the 1978-79 level) by 1985, but adds that 30 million tons would go to CMEA countries; this would mean a substantial decline in the volume of deliveries to non-CMEA customers. On the other hand, an OECD report concludes that Poland will not be able to increase coal exports significantly at least to 1990; J. P., "Węgiel w roku 2000: prognoza OECD," Polityka, Export-Import Supplement, March 17, 1979.

125. Krauss, op. cit.; RFER, Polish Situation Report/25, November 27, 1979, pp. 5-7. The estimate of 13-14 million tons from the world market assumes a stabilization of Soviet deliveries at approximately the 1979 level (see note 121); the cost estimate is based on a 10 percent per annum increase from the January 1980 price for Saudi crude ($24/barrel or $170/ton).

126. Concerning prospects for nuclear power, see RFER, Polish Situation Report/27, December 20, 1979, pp. 10-11; and Andrzej Lubowski, "Echo Harrisburga," Życie Gospodarcze, April 22, 1979. On the delay of the coal gasification project, see Business Week (May 14, 1979): 48.

127. Możejko, op. cit.; Stefanowski, op. cit., p. 10; and Zdzisław Grochowski, "Co dalej z importen zbóż," Polityka, Export-Import Supplement, October 20, 1979.

128. Gierek made this admission in his report to the fifteenth plenum of the Party's Central Committee in June 1979; however, this part of his report was not carried in Trybuna Ludu (June 13th), apparently due to the sensitivity of the debt question; see RFER, Polish Situation Report/13, June 19, 1979, p. 1.

129. Grochowski (op. cit.) suggests that even a reduction to 5 million tons per year will require a major effort. This conclusion is supported by the June 1979 livestock census, which showed a continuing decline in the numbers of hogs, cattle, and sheep; see Życie Gospodarcze, August 12, 1979.

130. Możejko, Handel Zagranicrny (2)"; Borowski, op. cit. The data through 1977 suggest that engineering exports to the developing countries add about 7 points to the share of that category in all exports to world markets; see RSHZ 1978, pp. 8, 14. The change in the composition of Polish exports to the West is evident in trade with West Germany, where engineering products accounted for 23 percent of Poland's sales in 1978, and metallurgy for an additional 19 percent; RFER, Polish Situation Report/19, August 31, 1979, p. 4.

131. In 1976 Poland's engineering exports to the West covered only 25 percent of comparable imports from the West, and in 1977

34 percent; RSHZ 1978, pp. 6-9. Although the precise data for 1978 are not yet available, it seems likely that the figure for that year was in excess of 50 percent.

132. See, for example, Passent, op. cit.; Gdula, op. cit.; and Władysław Baka, "Orientacja proeksportowa," Życie Gospodarcze, February 3, 1980.

133. This view, expressed by Paweł Bożyk, represented the consensus of a recent forum on Poland's export problems; "Eksport: być albo nie być," Polityka, Export-Import Supplement, June 16, 1979.

134. See the forum cited in preceding note, and the following articles from Polityka's Export-Import Supplement: A. P., "Diagnozy i propozycje" (September 22, 1979); Stanisław Grużewski, "Priorytet dla eksportu" (October 20, 1979); Andrzej K. Wroblewski, "Albo sprawiedliwość, albo eksport" (November 17, 1979); and Stanisław Grużewski, "Specjalizacyjne niekonsekwencje" (December 15, 1979). Also Zygmunt Szeliga, "Otwarcie: przed VIII Zjazdem PZPR," Polityka, October 27, 1979; Andrzej Lubowski, "Polubić eksport," Życie Gospodarcze, December 16, 1979; and Baka, op. cit.

135. Stefański, op. cit.; see also Szeliga, op. cit.; and Herer and Sadowski, op. cit.

136. See note 98 above.

137. See especially J. B. de Weydenthal, "The Unofficial Report on Polish Politics and Society," RFER, RAD Background Report/239 (Poland), November 2, 1979; also Szeliga, op. cit.; and Jerzy J. Wiatr, "Z socjologii władzy," Polityka, January 20, 1979. Especially in private conversations, one senses a mood of despair and resignation; a word not uncommonly heard to describe the present state of affairs is "gnicie" ("rot" or "decay").

138. Janusz Zieliński, "On System Remodelling in Poland: A Pragmatic Approach," Soviet Studies (January 1978): 34; see also discussion in Terry and Korbonski, op. cit.

139. Grochowski, op. cit.; Herer and Sadowski, op. cit.; Alicja Bulak, "Dlaczego nie chcą hodować?" Życie Gospodarcze, March 18, 1979; Ludwik Staszyński, "Chów zwierząt w drobnych gospodarstwach," Życie Gospodarcze, April 8, 1979.

140. Marcin Makowiecki, "Struktury efektywne: rozmowa z prof. dr. Augustynem Wosiem," Życie Gospodarcze, December 9, 1979; Stefan Zawodziński, "Specjalizacja produkcji w indywidualnych gospodarstwach rolnych," Nowe Drogi (October 1979): 46-53; Franciszek Kolbusz, "Kontynuacja polityki rolnej podstawa rozwoju rolnictwa," Nowe Drogi (December 1979): 49-58.

141. For reports of "stormy discussions" within CMEA over such questions as the system of economic planning and administration,

currency convertibility, and the desirability of adapting to world prices, see Jacek Poprzeczko, "Uczeni o RWPG," Polityka, Export-Import Supplement, May 18, 1979; Andrzej Lubowski, "Teoria i praktyka integracji," Życie Gospodarcze, April 29, 1979; also RFER, Polish Situation Report/11, May 25, 1979, pp. 7-9.

142. See, for example, RFER, Polish Situation Report/25, November 27, 1979 ("Poland, Short of Oil, Attacks OPEC"); and Jerzy Mostowy, "OPEC: perspektywy produkcji," Życie Gospodarcze, January 13, 1980. Algeria, Iraq, and possibly Libya also sell some oil to Poland; but relations with the last two, at least, have not been trouble-free; see, for example, RFER, Polish Situation Report/4, February 27, 1979, pp. 3-4.

143. Concerning Poland's "limited possibilities" in trade with Persian Gulf states, see Daniel Passent, "Z czym do Kuwejtu?" Polityka, Export-Import Supplement, March 17, 1979; also Aleksander Paszyński, "Nasz przyczółek w Algerii," Polityka, June 16, 1979.

144. For early indications of Polish concern, see John Darnton's dispatch from Warsaw in the New York Times, February 1, 1980.

8

THE COMMUNIST BALKANS AT
THE UNITED NATIONS

Robert Weiner

With the exception of Yugoslavia, the East European states,
along with the Soviet Union, have in the past been considered the
most cohesive voting bloc in the United Nations. It has caucused as
a group and displayed the greatest degree of intrabloc consistency
in the voting behavior of its members. Thomas Hovet, Jr., in his
classic study of bloc politics in the United Nations, could not find
any significant instances of voting differences between the Soviet
Union and its East European allies.[1]

However, since 1948, with the defection of Yugoslavia and
the later deviance by Albania and Romania, the monolithic facade of
Soviet bloc unity has in fact been broken. For example, in 1949, the
Soviet Union objected to the election of Yugoslavia to the nonpermanent seat "reserved" for East Europe on the Security Council,
though the latter was nevertheless elected. By 1963, both Albania
and Romania demonstrated voting behavior which diverged from
that of the Soviet Union.

With the intensification of polycentrism in the Communist
world, and especially following the emergence of the Sino-Soviet
schism, the U.N. environment offered unique and unparalleled opportunities for foreign policy deviance on a wide variety of issues.
During a session of the General Assembly, states can, depending on
their foreign policy style, express their differences from the Soviet
Union openly in debate and underscore their differences in the roll
call and recorded votes taken in the main committees and plenary
sessions. Such votes allow the opportunity for expressing various
nuances of independence. Roll call and recorded votes, which are
usually taken on controversial issues, tend to bring intrabloc differences out into the open. When a vote is taken, a state has five
options available: vote yes, vote no, abstain, be absent, or be
present and not vote at all.

The purpose of this chapter is to examine the foreign policies of the four Balkan communist members of the United Nations— Albania, Bulgaria, Romania, and Yugoslavia. The framework for the comparison[2] is based upon the typology devised by Cal Clark and Robert Farlow.[3] Clark and Farlow categorize Albania's foreign policy as realignment, Bulgaria's as subalignment, Romania's as partial alignment, and Yugoslavia's as nonalignment.[4]

By realignment, Clark and Farlow mean that Albania's foreign policy has been marked by shifting of protectors when necessary to ensure its national interest: in 1948, to Yugoslavia; in the 1950s to the Soviet Union; and in the 1960s up to 1977, to the People's Republic of China.[5] The Bulgarian policy of subalignment is characterized as basically a mirror image of the foreign policy of the Soviet Union; thus Bulgarian policy will tend to be "highly correlated" with Soviet foreign policy. The Romanian policy of partial alignment is characterized by convergence with the Soviet Union on a number of key issue areas but also by innovation and independence in several major areas. As Clark and Farlow note, "Partial alignment signifies a voluntary grouping of party-states seeking to cooperate on the basis of reciprocal advantage."[6] The Yugoslav policy of nonalignment is marked by vigorous objection to a division of the world into Eastern and Western alliances and a championing of the causes of the Third World in various international forums.[7]

This work will also address itself to the question of whether any of the other East European states—Czechoslovakia, the German Democratic Republic, Hungary, and Poland—can be accurately characterized, at least in their behavior at the United Nations, as realigned, subaligned, partially aligned, or nonaligned.[8]

Investigation of the four models of foreign policy will draw on an analysis of votes taken at the U.N. General Assembly, especially, but not exclusively, during four sessions (thirtieth through thirty-third, 1975-78), a total of 386 recorded votes. An analysis of voting behavior should identify not only issue areas that produced differences between the Soviet Union and the Balkan states—but also issue areas that result in a convergence of positions.

Some Chinese and East European voting behavior will also be compared in order to determine whether or not deviance has resulted in a closer identification by East Europe with the Chinese voting position at the United Nations. One would expect, for example, a closer identification between Albania and China than between Bulgaria and China.

In addition, the analysis of voting behavior at the United Nations can shed some light on the extent to which Yugoslavian foreign policy may be functioning as a model for the other three Balkan states. Here the expectation is that Yugoslavia's foreign policy may be functioning as a model for Romania's foreign policy at the United Nations.

Finally, a comparison of the foreign policies of the four Balkan states will also focus on the question of innovation and adaptation. [9] An effort will be made to determine which deviant states are more innovative in presenting new proposals at the United Nations, and we may also see which of the foreign policies of the Balkan states are more adaptive in the sense of adapting to the will of the majority of the United Nations and voting with the majority on most issues.

FOREIGN POLICY AS AN ISSUE AREA

The approach used in investigating the foreign policies of the Communist Balkan states will utilize James Rosenau's concept of foreign policy as an issue area. [10] The General Assembly of the United Nations considers clusters of issues, which can be grouped into issue areas. For the purposes of this analysis, the following issue areas have been distinguished: support for the United Nations; the Middle East; decolonization; arms control and disarmament; and the new international economic order. As Rosenau points out, issue areas can also be categorized on the basis of values. Under "support for the United Nations," the concern is whether or not the foreign policy of each communist Balkan state has resulted in more or less support for the world organization. The boundaries of this critical issue area are delineated by four issues: U.N. peacekeeping; U.N. Charter reform; the U.N. budget; and U.N. peacemaking. For example, if an East European state votes for the U.N. budget, the effect of that vote is to support the activities of the United Nations.

U.N. REPRESENTATION OF EAST EUROPE

East European representation at the United Nations began with three original members—Czechoslovakia, Poland, and Yugoslavia. In 1955, after a number of unsuccessful bids, Albania, Bulgaria, Hungary, and Romania were admitted as part of a "package deal." [11] In 1973, at the twenty-eighth session, the GDR was admitted as part of yet another "package deal" which resulted in West German membership. Still, East Europe has found it difficult to secure a proportionate share of offices in the U.N. system. It was not until 1967 that an East European was elected to the presidency of the General Assembly. [12] The election of Corneliu Manescu, the foreign minister of Romania, to the presidency of the Twenty-Second General Assembly was followed by the election of Stanislaw Trepczynski of

Poland (1972) and Lazar Mojsov of Yugoslavia at the thirty-second session (1977).

By the thirty-third session, 17 vice presidents were also being elected each year based on "equitable geographical distribution."[13] East Europe is allocated one vice president. Thus, from the First through the Thirty-Fourth General Assembly, only Albania has not been elected to the office of vice president of the General Assembly.[14]

At the thirty-third session of the General Assembly, a rather interesting situation arose when many Third World states, especially the African Group,[15] lobbied for the passage of a resolution (33/138) to increase the number of vice presidents from 17 to 21. The purpose of the resolution was to increase the number of vice presidents allocated to Africa and Asia; it kept the number of vice presidencies allocated to East Europe at one. As a nonaligned state, Yugoslavia supported the resolution, but Romania, an East European state but also a member of the Group of 77, abstained. (Romania was one of three states to abstain, the other two being Afghanistan and Israel.) Bulgaria and the Soviet Union voted against the resolution, while Albania did not participate in the vote at all. The resolution was adopted by a vote of 105 in favor, 29 against, and three abstentions.

The Economic and Social Council, a separate organ of the U.N. system which reports to the General Assembly, has also had East European representation since its beginning, again with the sole exception of Albania.

A breakdown of East European representation in the U.N. Secretariat as of June 1978[16] indicates Albania's deviant status: there were no Albanians whatsoever in the Secretariat as of that date. By comparison, Romania had eight of her nationals in the Secretariat, a number somewhat less than the maximum of her "desirable range" of six to eleven staff members.[17] Bulgaria had a total of ten staff members, while Yugoslavia enjoyed the largest representation with 18 members.

An important representational position in the U.N. system is that of nonpermanent member of the Security Council. Originally six members and expanded to ten in 1965, East Europe as a region is allotted one of these seats under a "gentleman's agreement readied in 1946."[18] All of the states under consideration—again, save for Albania—have been elected nonpermanent members of the Security Council and have served as council president on a rotating basis.

SUPPORT FOR THE UNITED NATIONS

One of the several indicators for "support for the United Nations" is support for U.N. peacekeeping operations.[19] Yugoslavia, for example, has not only supported U.N. peacekeeping operations but has played a key role in the formation of peacekeeping forces.[20] During the Middle East crisis of 1956, Yugoslavia introduced a resolution in the Security Council which declared, according to the Uniting for Peace Resolution of 1950, that the council should convene an emergency special session of the General Assembly. This led to the creation of the first United Nations Emergency Force (UNEF-I). Yugoslavia also contributed a national contingent to UNEF-I, as well as to other U.N. peacekeeping operations. In the United Nation's Special Committee on Peacekeeping Operations, Yugoslavia has pointed out that its policy as a nonaligned country was based upon the assumption that peacekeeping activities are part of a general tendency to strengthen the effectiveness of the United Nations in maintaining international peace and security.[21]

Romania, which followed the Soviet position in opposing UNEF-I in 1956, and the United Nations' peacekeeping operations in the Congo in 1960, recently has been more supportive of U.N. peacekeeping than have the Soviets. For example, Romania supported the creation and continuation of the Second United Nations Emergency Force (UNEF-II), which was formed in 1973, and, more importantly, did not oppose—as did the Soviets and Bulgarians—the use of this force in the Sinai after the second Egyptian-Israeli disengagement agreement in 1975. Moscow declared in 1976 that it would not pay for those portions of UNEF-II stemming from this agreement, since it had been negotiated outside the U.N. framework.

At the thirty-second session of the General Assembly, voting differences also emerged on several resolutions dealing with the financing of U.N. peacekeeping operations in the Middle East. For example, while the Soviet Union and Bulgaria abstained, Romania voted for General Assembly Resolutions 32/4B and 32/4C, which set forth the guidelines for the system of financing UNEF-II and UNDOF (United Nations Disengagement Observer Force, established in 1974 between Israeli and Syrian forces in the Golan Heights). Yugoslavia voted for these resolutions, while Albania cast a negative vote. At the thirty-third session of the General Assembly, Romania either voted for or abstained on a series of resolutions dealing with the financing of UNEF-II and UNDOF. For example, Romania abstained, while the Soviet Union voted against two resolutions (33/13E and 33/13F) designed to suspend U.N. financial regulations so as to reimburse countries that had contributed to UNEF and UNDOF.[22] Bulgaria voted against 33/13E and 33/13F. There is no record of an Albanian vote on 33/13E and 33/13F. Albania voted against, Romania and Yugoslavia for, and Bulgaria and the Soviet Union abstained on Resolution 33/13A, which empowered the Secretary General to enter into additional financial commitments for UNEF-II and UNDOF during the period October 25 to November 30,

1978. This pattern (Albania—no, Bulgaria and the Soviet Union—abstain, Romania and Yugoslavia—yes) repeated itself on all four parts of the resolution (33/13) dealing with the financing of these forces. In connection with Resolution 33/14, which concerned the financing of the UNIFIL (the United Nations Interim Force in Lebanon, established in 1978), Albania, Bulgaria, and the Soviet Union voted no, while Romania and Yugoslavia voted yes.

Albania consistently voted against the creation, financing, and extension of the mandates of all peacekeeping forces.[23] Albania stated that it opposes U.N. peacekeeping operations as a matter of principle, since it believes that such operations are designed to advance the interests of the two superpowers, which are competing with each other to divide the world into spheres of influence.[24] Though derived from different motives, Albania's voting behavior has thus occasionally converged with that of Bulgaria and the Soviet Union. In the spring of 1978, at the Eighth Special Session of the General Assembly, which met to consider the financing of the operations of UNIFIL,[25] Albania voted along with Bulgaria and the Soviet Union against a resolution (S-8/2) authorizing the expenditure. UNIFIL had been created by Security Council Resolution 425 (1978) following the Israeli invasion of southern Lebanon in March 1978 after an increasing number of raids into Israel by the Palestine Liberation Organization. The Soviet Union not only voted against Resolution S-8/2 but also announced that it would not consider itself financially obligated to support UNIFIL.[26] The Soviet Union believed that Israel should be responsible for the expenses involved.[27] On the other hand, both Romania and Yugoslavia voted for the provision of funds for UNIFIL. Support for U.N. peacekeeping operations by two medium-sized states like Romania and Yugoslavia can also be seen as a reflection of the stated foreign policy objective of small and medium-sized states to support decisions they perceive as strengthening their national security.

One issue related to peacekeeping on which three of four of the Balkan communist states have agreed involves Cyprus. Bulgaria, Romania, and Yugoslavia all voted for Resolution 33/15, which urged the parties involved in the conflict in Cyprus to cooperate with the peacemaking efforts of the Secretary General and the UNFICYP (United Nations Force in Cyprus).

On the issue of charter reform, these states have also differed in the nature of their "support for the United Nations." States supporting charter reform claim they want to strengthen the organization and increase its effectiveness, while those opposing reform, not surprisingly, take similar positions.[28] Albania has not shown any particular interest in the issue of charter reform, while Bulgaria's policy reflects the Soviet position, that is, that there is no necessity to change the existing system.[29] Yugoslavia and Romania have both adopted a more enthusiastic approach to charter innovation. Romania, in particular, has taken a special interest in the reform of the U.N. Charter, voting, for example, for the establishment of a U.N. Ad Hoc Committee on Charter Review in 1974, which the Soviet Union opposed. At the thirtieth session of the General Assembly in 1975, Romania submitted a comprehensive document, containing many suggestions for reform of the charter.[30] Some of the specific recommendations Romania offered to deal with "inadequacies" in the charter were: (1) the creation of a standing commission of the General Assembly for the peaceful settlement of disputes; (2) an increase in the number of nonpermanent members of the Security Council on the basis of regional geographical representation; and (3) modification of the veto power in the Security Council (in a working paper submitted in 1976 to the Special Committee on the Charter of the United Nations and on the Strengthening of the Role of the Organization, which replaced the Ad Hoc Committee, Romania did not go so far as to suggest the abolition of the veto but rather proposed that the veto be extended to new members representing geographical regions in an expanded Security Council); (4) deletion of references to "enemy" states of World War II in the charter;[31] and (5) greater emphasis on decision making by consensus in the General Assembly rather than by voting.

Both Romania and Yugoslavia have joined with the Third World in lobbying for charter reform, contending that the structure of the United Nations should be updated to reflect the changes that have occurred in the world during the past 30 years. However, the Soviets have vigorously defended the existing provisions of the charter, particularly the veto. In 1974, in the Legal Committee, the Soviets cosponsored an unsuccessful draft resolution that would have stressed the inadvisability of taking any action at present on charter review.[32]

Romania and Yugoslavia have also supported improvement in the codification of international law. For example, in 1949, Yugoslavia proposed U.N. adoption of a code of behavior governing relations between states, and in 1975 Romania suggested that a Universal Code of Interstate Behavior be formulated at the United Nations.

Another item on the agenda on which countries can indicate support for the United Nations is the organization's budget. At the thirty-third session, on two key resolutions (33/180A and 33/180C) dealing with the budget, Albania did not participate in either vote, Bulgaria voted against both, and both Romania and Yugoslavia voted for the resolutions and approval of the budget. Resolutions 33/180A and 33/180C dealt with the revised budget appropriations for the Biennium 1978-79.

THE MIDDLE EAST

The Middle East has emerged as another major issue area, with the adoption of more and more resolutions focusing on the problem of the Palestinians. All four Balkan states have generally supported the Palestinians' call for national self-determination; demanded Israeli withdrawal from the Arab territories occupied following the war in 1967; underscored the PLO's right to participate in any peace negotiations; and affirmed the right of every state in the region to enjoy an independent existence, free from threats or use of force.

However, differences among these states emerge in this issue area as well. Romania and Yugoslavia support Israeli-Egyptian negotiation as a step toward the resolution of the Arab-Israeli conflict in the Middle East, but with Yugoslavia more critical of the Israelis.[33] Yugoslavia[34] has also emphasized the role of the PLO in Middle East negotiations, while Albania views all Soviet and U.S. involvement in the Middle East as a policy designed to divide and weaken the Arabs so that U.S. "imperialism" and Soviet "social-imperialism" can perpetuate their respective spheres of influence.[35] At the thirty-third session, Albania added a warning to the Arab states not to be influenced by the Chinese policy of reaching an accommodation with the United States.[36]

Bulgaria, which maintains that it has a special interest in the problem because of its geographical proximity to the area, has mirrored the Soviet attitude toward the region and in 1978 specifically criticized separate Egyptian-Israeli peace negotiations.[37]

Romanian policy toward the Middle East at the United Nations has been characterized by some flexibility. For example, in 1967, at the Fifth Emergency Special Session, Romania deviated from the Soviet Union by abstaining on the preamble and three out of four operating paragraphs of a Soviet draft resolution condemning Israel.[38] Nor did the Romanians indicate early support for the Palestinians at the United Nations. At the twenty-second session of the General Assembly in 1967, Romania abstained on a resolution requesting the Secretary General appoint a custodian to protect and administer Arab property and assets in Israel. The Soviet Union voted for the resolution, which was not adopted. At the twenty-third session of the General Assembly, Romania abstained on a similar resolution, which also was not adopted.

But, during the twenty-ninth session of the General Assembly, in 1974, Romania voted for Resolution 3236, which recognized "the right of the Palestinian people to regain its rights by all means in accordance with the purpose and principles of the Charter of the United Nations." Furthermore, the resolution recognized that the

Palestinians should be viewed as a principal party in ensuring peace in the Middle East. In explaining its vote, Romania pointed out that it was necessary to recognize the PLO as an active participant in all negotiations.[39] Romania also was a cosponsor of Resolution 3237, which extended observer status to the PLO. In Security Council debate, Romania supported the inclusion of the PLO in council deliberations. Romania is also a member of the Committee on the Exercise of the Inalienable Rights of the Palestinian People and has voted for resolutions condemning Israeli treatment of Palestinians in the occupied territories and condemning Israeli settlements on the West Bank.

On the other hand, Romania has been reluctant to participate in the vote for some of the more extreme resolutions. At the Conference on the International Woman's Year, which met in Mexico in the summer of 1975, Romania consistently did not participate in the vote for resolutions linking Zionism to colonialism and apartheid. During the acrimonious debate at the thirtieth session of the General Assembly that year on Resolution 3375, which equated Zionism with racism, the Soviet Union and all the other East European states voted for the resolution, while Romania did not participate in the vote at all. In addition, at a U.N. Conference on Desertification in 1977, the Soviet Union and Yugoslavia supported, while Romania abstained, on a resolution criticizing an Israeli study of the Negev Desert as historically inaccurate.[40]

DECOLONIZATION

The issue area of decolonization is one in which there would be a reasonable expectation of convergence of communist Balkan foreign policies. Indeed, Romania has converged with the Soviet Union and the other Balkan Communist states in voting for resolutions condemning all manifestations of colonialism and neocolonialism. Yet some differences have emerged between Romania and the Soviet Union on resolutions dealing with East Timor and the Western Sahara. These residues of colonialism have created problems for Indonesia in East Timor and for Morocco, Mauritania, and Algeria in the Western Sahara. At the thirty-third session of the General Assembly, rather than commit itself and risk offending Indonesia and those Arab states supporting it or risk offending Algeria, Morocco, and Mauritania, Romania did not participate in the vote on resolutions dealing with these issues. While Yugoslavia abstained, Albania, Bulgaria, and the Soviet Union voted for Resolution 33/39, which reaffirmed "the inalienable right of the people of East Timor to self-determination and independence." Two resolutions were adopted in connection with the question of Western Sahara. Albania did not participate in the votes either on Resolution 33/31A. which reaffirmed the right of the people of Western Sahara to self-determination, or Resolution 33/31B, supporting the work of an ad hoc committee of the Organization of African Unity attempting to negotiate a settlement to the dispute. On the other hand, Bulgaria, the Soviet Union, and Yugoslavia voted for Resolution 33/31A, but Bulgaria and the Soviet Union abstained, while Yugoslavia voted against Resolution 33/31B.

A large number of resolutions adopted by the General Assembly focus on Namibia, Zimbabwe, and South Africa itself. Issues relating to the southern part of Africa usually result in the greatest convergence between the policies of the Soviet Union, Albania, Bulgaria, Romania, and Yugoslavia. For example, at the Ninth Special Session of the General Assembly, which dealt with Namibia, all these states voted for Resolution S-9/2, the Declaration on Namibia and Programme of Action in Support of Self-Determination and National Independence for Namibia. This resolution reaffirmed that Namibia was the direct responsibility of the United Nations, recognized SWAPO (the Southwest African People's Organization) as the sole legitimate representative of the Namibian people, deplored nuclear aid to South Africa, and urged the Security Council to institute sanctions against South Africa, according to the terms of Chapter VII of the U.N. Charter (threats to international peace and security). During the debate, Romania underscored the responsibility of the Security Council for implementing the resolution the assembly was to adopt. [41] Bulgaria emphasized the necessity of instituting a total embargo against South Africa. [42] On the other hand, Albania's position emphasized the dangers posed to the national liberation movements in South Africa by U.S. "imperialism" and Soviet "social-imperialism." [43]

ARMS CONTROL AND DISARMAMENT

Recently, the United Nations has been devoting considerable attention to arms control and disarmament. In 1978, the Tenth Special Session focused on the issue area of arms control and disarmament, dealing with a myriad number of issues ranging from SALT (Strategic Arms Limitation Treaty) to the regulation of conventional weapons.

Albania's position was that the Tenth Special Session did not go far enough in implementing genuine disarmament because it failed to get at the "real roots" of the arms race. According to its view of the world, both superpowers continued to arm themselves with stockpiles of nuclear weaponry while the SALT and conventional arms reduction negotiations between East and West in Vienna were insignificant. [44] Bulgaria, on the other hand, supported both the SALT negotiations and the session's final document. [45]

Moreover, in comparison to Romania and Yugoslavia, Albania was distinctly less enthusiastic about some of the organizational changes that took place in the U.N. system's arms control and disarmament machinery. For example, the special session decided to expand the existing Conference of the Committee on Disarmament to include more nonnuclear states, plus the five nuclear powers, into a new Committee on Disarmament (CD). Albania viewed this as merely a symbolic change, [46] while Romania welcomed the expansion. Yugoslavia also approved of the expansion but expressed the view that the new committee should include only the five existing nuclear powers.

Albania also has rejected the notion that the creation of nuclear free zones and zones of peace could contribute to arms control and disarmament. Albania's position on nuclear free zones stands in contrast to the support for the concept of regional denuclearization registered by the other Balkan states. For example, at the nineteenth session of the General Assembly in 1964, Bulgaria presented an elaborate proposal for the transformation of the Balkans into a nuclear free zone. [47]

In 1957 Romania lobbied without much success for the denuclearization of the Balkans, [48] and, in 1959, Romania repeated her call for a treaty among Balkan states to create a nuclear free zone, in which the Balkan states would not allow the storage of atomic or nuclear weapons on their territory. In 1963, Romania expressed support for the concept of a series of nuclear free zones in Europe stretching from the Nordic countries to the Adriatic. Bucharest also welcomed the denuclearization of Latin America, established by the Treaty of Tlatelolco (1967). [49] Previously, at the eighteenth session of the General Assembly in 1960, Romania had voted in favor of this zone, while the Soviet Union had abstained.

For its part, Yugoslavia has taken a special interest in the transformation of the Mediterranean into a nuclear free zone. [50]

At the thirty-third session, Albania did not participate in votes on resolutions calling for the implementation of a declaration on the denuclearization of Africa, the establishment of a nuclear free zone in the region of the Middle East, the establishment of a nuclear weapon free zone in South Asia, and the declaration of the Indian Ocean as a zone of peace. In contrast, on Resolution 33/65, which called for a nuclear weapon free zone in South Asia, Bulgaria and the Soviet Union abstained, as did Yugoslavia, while Romania voted yes.

At the thirty-third session, Albania (as well as China) did not participate in the vote on a resolution calling upon states to reduce their military budgets. Although the issue of the reduction of military budgets was originally raised by the Soviet Union, Bulgaria and the Soviet Union abstained, while Romania and Yugoslavia voted in favor of the resolution (33/67). The Soviets abstained because they objected to the language in the resolution, which called for the development of an "instrument for standardized reporting on the military expenditure of member states."

Romania and Yugoslavia have generally been more critical than Bulgaria of the failure of the two superpowers to provide technological aid to the developing countries for the peaceful uses of nuclear energy. For example, at the Review Conference for the Nuclear Nonproliferation Treaty, which met in May 1975, both Romania and Yugoslavia submitted reservations to the final conference declaration, which had been adopted by consensus. The reservations criticized the failure of the conference to make progress on the question of the peaceful application of nuclear explosions.[51]

In 1975, the innovative nature of Romanian foreign policy was underscored when it submitted a wide-ranging group of proposals on arms control and disarmament, suggesting, among other things, that the United Nations set up a development fund for poor nations financed from savings generated by disarmament.

THE NEW INTERNATIONAL ECONOMIC ORDER

Since 1974 the majority of Third World countries in the United Nations have lobbied for a global redistribution of the world's capacity to produce wealth from North to South, that is, the establishment of a "New International Economic Order" (NIEO). The United Nations has held several special and extra sessions, adopted numerous resolutions, and created a number of committees to stimulate the movement toward this new order.[52]

Until recently, Albania had not shown much interest in the subject. At the thirty-third session of the General Assembly, Albania did not participate in a number of votes dealing with the NIEO and did not participate in a vote on a resolution concerning the establishment of a Special Fund for Land-Locked Countries. Similarly, Tirana did not participate in a vote on a Plan of Action to Combat Desertification.

Bulgaria's position on the NIEO has closely followed that of the Soviet Union, that is, the present inequitable distribution of global wealth is considered the responsibility of the capitalist nations.[53] Bulgaria agrees with the Soviet Union that it is the phenomenon of neocolonialism which results in the perpetuation of the developing countries' predicament on the periphery of the world economy, and contributes to the widening of the economic gap between industrialized and non-industrialized states. According to this line of reasoning, the Socialist countries are therefore under no obligation to contribute to the NIEO.[54]

Both Romania and Yugoslavia have been more supportive of the creation of a NIEO than Albania, Bulgaria, or the Soviet Union. Both Romania and Yugoslavia are members of the Group of 77, a negotiating group of developing countries (now numbering over 100) which emerged at the First United Nations Conference on Trade and Development (UNCTAD I) in 1964. Yugoslavia is a member of the Asian subgroup, and Romania was admitted as a member of the Latin American subgroup in 1976.[55]

The Balkan states and the Soviet Union have voted together on some of the substantive issues of the NIEO, such as the adoption of a Charter on the Economic Rights and Duties of States, adopted at the twenty-ninth session of the General Assembly (1974). The Soviets and the East Europeans also voted cohesively with the Third World against attempts by the United States and other Western industrialized states to amend this charter.[56]

A major difference between Romania and Yugoslavia on the one hand, and Bulgaria and the Soviet Union on the other, occurs over the allocation of the United Nation's organizational resources for the NIEO. Bulgaria and the Soviet Union have been less supportive of the creation of new bodies and allocations of financial resources for the NIEO than have Romania and Yugoslavia. For example, in 1977 Bulgaria and the Soviet Union opposed, while Romania and Yugoslavia supported, the creation of the post of Director General for Development and International Economic Cooperation (Resolution 32/197, adopted without a vote).[57] Bulgaria and the Soviet Union have been much more conservative fiscally and critical of attempts to include the financing of new U.N. units or actions for the NIEO within the regular U.N. budget.

At the thirty-third session, Romania not only expressed its support for the convening of a U.N. special session in 1980 to focus on development but also presented the rather intriguing proposal that negotiations in the General Assembly should result in specific commitments by states to contribute to the NIEO in the form of a Code of International Economic Relations.[58]

Romania and Yugoslavia have also attached more importance than Bulgaria and the Soviet Union to a U.N. Conference on Science and Technology for Development; support for the creation of the International Fund for Agricultural Development as a specialized agency; the conversion of the United Nations Industrial Development Organization into a specialized agency; the role of the Economic Commission for Europe in contributing to the economic development of poor, southern European states; and support for a Common Fund for the Integrated Programme for Commodities.

OTHER EAST EUROPEAN STATES

It may be useful to consider briefly whether any of the other East European members of the United Nations—the German Democratic Republic, Czechoslovakia, Hungary, and Poland—have shown any evidence of deviation from the Soviet Union and if such deviance takes the form of subalignment, realignment, partial alignment, or nonalignment.

In the last few sessions of the General Assembly, the GDR has placed more emphasis on African problems than it has in the past.[59] For example, at the thirty-second session of the General Assembly, the GDR stated:

The upsurge of the national liberation struggle, assisted by the strength of steadily mounting international solidarity, makes us confident that the cause of the peoples of Zimbabwe, Namibia and South Africa will be victorious. The German Democratic Republic pledges to continue supporting that struggle to the best of its ability.[60]

Czechoslovakia recently seems to be more subaligned than Bulgaria on such issues as representation of Cambodia at the United Nations, being one of the most critical of all the East European states of the ousted Pol-Pot regime, during the general debate of the thirty-fourth session of the General Assembly.[61]

Poland has deviated somewhat from the Soviet Union on the issue of peacekeeping. In 1973, Poland contributed troops to the Second United Nations Emergency Force (UNEF-II) and in 1974 to the United Nations Disengagement Observer Force (UNDOF). Poland was the first Warsaw Pact state to participate in U.N. peacekeeping operations, and its participation took place against a background of Soviet acquiescence in the creation of UNEF-II and UNDOF. Bulgaria also offered to contribute troops in 1973 to the U.N. peacekeeping operations in the Middle East. In discussing participation in U.N. peacekeeping operations, Poland stressed that UNEF-II and UNDOF should be viewed as an emergency measure and not a substitute for a comprehensive settlement. Poland also explained its participation in U.N. peacekeeping operations by stating that it was upholding the principles of the charter and contributing to the maintenance of international peace and security.[62]

By the thirtieth session of the General Assembly (1975), however, Soviet support for UNEF-II and UNDOF had eroded. The Soviets objected to paying for the financial upkeep of UNEF-II as well as UNDOF.[63]

Still, at the thirtieth session of the General Assembly, Poland voted along with Romania and Yugoslavia for a resolution providing for the financing of UNEF-II, while Bulgaria and the Soviet Union abstained. Poland stayed in UNEF-II, despite Soviet objections to its new duties incurred as a result of the separate Egyptian-Israeli disengagement agreement. At the thirty-third session (1978), Poland voted for resolutions (33/13B, 33/13C, and 33/13D) financing UNEF-II and UNDOF, while the Soviets abstained; and Poland abstained while the Soviet Union voted against Resolution 33/13E, which also focused on financing those two forces.

Poland has thus followed a somewhat ambivalent policy toward peacekeeping. For instance, Poland along with the Soviet Union voted against a resolution (33/14) at the thirty-third session dealing with the financing of UNIFIL. On the other hand, at the same session, Poland abstained while the Soviets voted against a resolution dealing with the work of the U.N. Special Committee on Peacekeeping Operations, which urged members to strengthen U.N. peacekeeping capabilities. Poland has been a member of the committee since it was set up in 1965.

Poland has also deviated from the Soviet Union on votes dealing with regional arms control and the scale of assessments for the United Nation's regular budget. Consequently, Poland's current foreign policy at the United Nations could be evolving into one of partial alignment.

VOTING ALIGNMENT

In order to measure Albania's realignment, Bulgaria's subalignment, Romania's partial alignment, and Yugoslavia's nonalignment, an index of voting agreement was calculated for the four Balkan states and the Soviet Union.[64] The index is based on an analysis of 131 votes in the plenary of the thirty-third session.

Because Albania missed 83 of the 131 votes, it was not included in the calculations. At the least this indicates uneven interest in a number of issue areas. For example, on the issue area of the "Middle East," Albania did not participate in a number of votes, such as the right of return of Palestinians, the Report of the Committee on the Exercise of the Inalienable Rights of the Palestinian people, and a resolution dealing with the work in the Secretariat of a Special Unit on Palestinian Rights. On the other hand, Albania did vote for other resolutions dealing with the Middle East, ranging from concern for the living conditions of Palestinians to condemnation of the use of cluster bombs by Israel in southern Lebanon. Albania also did not participate in any votes dealing with the regular budget of the United Nations. Moreover, Albania did participate in votes on resolutions dealing with decolonization and peacekeeping. In at least one instance, Albania was the only nation to vote against a resolution (33/91C) criticizing the lack of progress made by the superpowers in the SALT negotiations.

The index of voting agreement with the Soviet Union during the thirty-third session for the three Balkan states is shown in Table 8.1.

TABLE 8.1

Index of Agreement with the Soviet Union,
Thirty-Third Session

Bulgaria/Soviet Union	99.8
Yugoslavia/Soviet Union	74.4
Romania/Soviet Union	74.0

Source: United Nations, Resolutions and Decisions Adopted by the General Assembly during its Thirty-Third Session (New York: Department of Public Information, February 5, 1979).

The Bulgarian policy of subalignment, with an IA (Index of Agreement) of 99.8, is the highest of all the Balkan communist states. The Romanian and Yugoslavian IAs are almost identical, perhaps indicating that Romanian foreign policy may be undergoing even a further transformation from partial alignment to nonalignment, especially since 1976, when Romania joined the Group of 77. Further, there is an IA of 86.5 between Romania and Yugoslavia, higher than that of Yugoslavia/Bulgaria (72.5) or Yugoslavia/Soviet Union (74.4).

Finally, an effort was made to determine whether the foreign policies of Romania and Yugoslavia were more adaptive in the sense that there was greater voting agreement between these two deviants and the majority in the General Assembly than between Bulgaria and the majority. The expectation was that Romania's policy of partial alignment and Yugoslavia's policy of nonalignment would result in a greater IA with the majority than would Bulgaria's policy of subalignment. The findings were as illustrated in Table 8.2.

TABLE 8.2

Index of Agreement with General Assembly Majority
Thirty-Third Session

Yugoslavia/Majority	97.3
Romania/Majority	86.1
Soviet Union/Majority	74.4
Bulgaria/Majority	74.0

Source: United Nations, Resolutions and Decisions Adopted by the General Assembly during its Thirty-Third Session (New York: Department of Public Information, February 5, 1979).

Thus, Yugoslavia's policy of nonalignment has resulted in the highest IA, 97.3, with Romania second, and the Soviet Union and Bulgaria voting with the majority with about the same frequency. Clearly, partial alignment and nonalignment are more adaptive to the U.N. majority than is subalignment.

CONCLUSION

Albania's foreign policy at the United Nations is that of an outsider, a state which has not adapted its policies or actions to the political process of the U.N. system. Albania's policy of realignment is marked by an unwillingness to participate in any decisions reached by consensus in the General Assembly. Albanian disassociation from consensual politics in the General Assembly differs from Romanian emphasis on decision making by consensus as a key element in the "democratization" of the United Nations. Albania has not been elected to any significant U.N. offices since its admission in 1955; it misses a large number of U.N. votes; and its voting behavior follows a pattern which is not supportive of the United Nations.[65]

Romania and Yugoslavia have used the United Nations as a foreign policy forum. They have pursued more innovative foreign policies than either Albania or Bulgaria. For example, Romania and Yugoslavia were the only East European states to attend the 1972 U.N. Conference on the Human Environment. Romania and Yugoslavia have been more supportive of the United Nations on such issues as peacekeeping and the U.N. budget as well as on arms control and disarmament and the New International Economic Order. Romania has also played a key role at the United Nations in studying the economic and social consequences of disarmament. The highest degree of convergence in the foreign policies of the four Balkan states and the Soviet Union seems to occur on the issue area of decolonization, especially with respect to southern Africa. There is also a great deal of convergence on the Middle East issue area but with some Romanian reluctance to support more extreme resolutions.

At the same time, no significant deviance from the Soviet Union in the foreign policies of Czechoslovakia, the GDR, and Hungary can be discerned. However, recent Polish foreign policy has shown some tendencies for transformation into partial alignment.

NOTES

1. See Thomas Hovet, Jr., Bloc Politics in the United Nations (Cambridge, Mass.: Harvard University Press, 1960).
2. For an interesting approach to comparative foreign policy, see Edward L. Morse, A Comparative Approach to the Study of Foreign Policy: Notes on Theorizing (Princeton, N.J.: Princeton University Press, 1971).
3. See Cal Clark and Robert Farlow, Patterns of Foreign Policy and Trade: The Communist Balkans in International Politics (Bloomington: International Development Research Center, Indiana University, 1976).
4. Ibid., p. 6.
5. Peter Prifti dates Albania's alliance with Yugoslavia from 1944-48, with the Soviet Union from 1948-61, and with China from 1961-77. See Peter R. Prifti, Socialist Albania Since 1944: Domestic and Foreign Developments (Cambridge, Mass.: MIT Press, 1978). Also see Michael Kaser, "Albania's Self-Chosen Predicament," The World Today (June 1979): 259-68.
6. Clark and Farlow, op. cit., p. 9.
7. See Rudolf L. Tökés, "Eastern Europe in the 1970s: Detente, Dissent, and Eurocommunism," in Eurocommunism and Detente, ed. Rudolf L. Tokés (New York: New York University Press, 1978), p. 493. Also see Alvin Z. Rubinstein, Yugoslavia and the Nonaligned World (Princeton, N.J.: Princeton University Press, 1970), p. 77.

8. The Ukraine and Byelorussia, although members of the United Nations, are not included.

9. For a discussion of political innovation in the foreign policy of socialist states, see Zvi Gitelman, "Toward a Comparative Foreign Policy of Eastern Europe," in From the Cold War to Detente, ed. Peter J. Potichnyj and Jane P. Shapiro (New York: Praeger, 1976), p. 159.

10. See especially "Foreign Policy as an Issue-Area," in James N. Rosenau, The Scientific Study of Foreign Policy (New York: Free Press, 1971), p. 404. On the comparative study of foreign policy, see James N. Rosenau, "Comparative Foreign Policy: One-Time Fad, Realized Fantasy, and Normal Field," pp. 3-38, in International Events and the Comparative Analysis of Foreign Policy, ed. Charles W. Kegley et al. (Columbia: University of South Carolina Press, 1975). Also see Ronald Haly Linden, Bear and Foxes: The International Relations of the East European States, 1965-1969 (New York: Columbia University Press, 1979); James N. Rosenau, "Comparing Foreign Policies: Why, What, How," in Comparing Foreign Policies: Theories, Findings, and Methods, ed. James N. Rosenau (New York: John Wiley and Sons, 1974), pp. 3-22.

11. See John G. Stoessinger, The United Nations and the Superpowers (New York: Random House, 1965), p. 22.

12. For earlier East European efforts to elect a president of the General Assembly, see Sydney D. Bailey, The General Assembly of the United Nations (New York: Praeger, 1964), pp. 50-55.

13. U.N. Resolution 1990 (XVIII) contained the guidelines for the election of vice presidents of the General Assembly. In Resolution 1990 (XVIII), East Europe was only allocated one vice presidents in contrast to "Western Europe and others," which were allocated two vice presidents.

14. It would seem that Albania was not elected because its "turn" did not come until after 1961, and thus too late to be elected with Soviet support. I am indebted to Ronald Haly Linden for bringing this point to my attention.

15. The African Group is one of several caucusing groups in the General Assembly which attempts to coordinate its position on various issues. See Harold K. Jacobson, Networks of Interdependence (New York: Knopf, 1979), p. 119.

16. See U.N. Document, A/33/176, September 21, 1978, Annex, p. 8.

17. The number of staff allocated to each member of the Secretariat is computed by a formula weighing the three factors of membership, size of population, and assessment for the regular U.N. budget.

18. Bailey, op. cit., p. 161.

19. For an interesting analysis of support for the United Nations, see Thomas J. Volgy and Jon E. Quistgaard, "Learning About the Value of Global Cooperation: Role-Taking in the United Nations as a Predictor of World-Mindedness," Journal of Conflict Resolution (June 1975): 349. Also see John F. Clark, Michael K. O'Leary, and Eugene R. Wittkopf, "National Attributes Associated with Dimensions of Support for the United Nations," International Organization (Winter 1971): 11-25.

20. See Rubinstein, op. cit., p. 143.

21. U.N. Document, A/AC.121/28, August 15, 1978, p. 24.

22. U.N. Document, A/33/PV.84, January 5, 1979, pp. 27-29.

23. For the Albanian position on U.N. peacekeeping, see U.N. Document, A/33/PV.87, January 17, 1979, p. 89.

24. U.N. Document, A/33/PV.68, December 1, 1978, p. 7.

25. The special session was necessary under a procedure established by the Thirty-Second General Assembly requiring the Secretary General to put before the assembly any new budgetary outlays of $10 million or more relating to the maintenance of peace and security (Resolution 32/214; compare U.N. Document, A/32/490, December 20, 1977, p. 134).

26. U.N. Document, A/S-8/PV.2, April 22, 1978, p. 56.

27. U.N. Document, A/S-8/PV.1, April 20, 1978, p. 56.

28. For example, for the Soviet position that charter reform would weaken the effectiveness of the United Nations, see U.N. Document, A/10102, June 2, 1975.

29. See U.N. Document, A/C.6/33/SR.60, December 12, 1978, pp. 8-9.

30. U.N. Document, A/C.6/437, November 3, 1975.

31. Article 107 of the charter says, "Nothing in the present Charter shall invalidate or preclude action, in relation to any state which during the Second World War has been an enemy of any signator, to the present Charter, taken or authorized as a result of that war by the Government having responsibility for such action." This could be viewed as justifying Soviet intervention in Romania, since Romania was an ally of Germany during World War II. Romania has taken the position that such obsolete clauses of the charter should be dropped so that all U.N. members would fall into a single category.

32. See U.N. Document, A/C.6/33/SR.60, December 12, 1978, pp. 8-9.

33. See U.N. Document, A/33/PV.70, December 5, 1978, p. 7.

34. U.N. Document, A/33/PV.65, November 30, 1978, p. 47.

35. See the Albanian statement in U.N. Document, A/33/PV.61, November 28, 1978, p. 32; also see U.N. Document, A/33/PV.70, December 5, 1978, p. 86.

36. U.N. Document, A/33/PV.20, October 4, 1978, p. 31.

37. U.N. Document, A/33/PV.64, November 29, 1978, pp. 88-90.

38. U.N. Monthly Chronicle (July 1967): 78-79.

39. U.N. Monthly Chronicle (December 1974): 42.

40. Albania and Bulgaria did not attend the conference.

41. U.N. Document, A/S-9/PV.4, April 25, 1978, p. 31.

42. U.N. Document, A/33/PV.59,. November 21, 1978, p. 32.

43. U.N. Document, A/S-9/PV.6, April 26, 1978, p. 81.

44. U.N. Document, A/S-10/PV.27, July 6, 1978, p. 163.

45. U.N. Document, A/S-10/PV.27, July 6, 1978, p. 182.

46. U.N. Document, A/C.1/33/PV.12, October 24, 1978, p. 49.

47. See Robert R. King, "Bulgaria," in Communism in Eastern Europe, ed. Teresa Rakowska-Harmstone and Andrew Gyorgy (Bloomington: Indiana University Press, 1979), p. 184.

48. U.N. Document, A/12/PV.689, September 26, 1957, p. 161.

49. For example, Resolution 2286 welcomed the treaty as "an event of historic significance in the efforts to prevent the proliferation of nuclear weapons." For a summary of the Treaty of Tlatelolco, see William L. Tung, International Organization under the United Nations System (New York: Thomas Y. Crowell, 1969), pp. 123-24.

50. U.N. Document, A/S-10/PV.27, July 6, 1978, p. 92.

51. U.N. Document, A/10215, September 6, 1975, Annex, p. 4.

52. See Robert W. Cox, "Ideologies and the New International Economic Order: Reflections on Some Recent Literature," International Organization (Spring 1979): 257-302. Also see Robert W. Tucker, The Inequality of Nations (New York: Basic Books, 1977).

53. U.N. Document, TD/211, May 28, 1976, p. 3.

54. See U.N. Document, A/C.2/31/21, October 4, 1976.

55. As Alvin Rubinstein points out, Yugoslavia's inclusion in the Asian subgroup at UNCTAD I in 1964 can also be explained by the personal relationship between Tito on the one hand and Nehru and Nasser on the other. See Rubinstein, op. cit., p. 174. Romania was admitted to the Group of 77 at its Third Ministerial Meeting in Manila in 1976.

56. See U.N. Document, A/C.2/SR.1648, December 6, 1974, p. 438.

57. U.N. Document, A/32/PV.109, December 20, 1977, p. 6.

58. At the twelfth session of the General Assembly (1957) Romania had also suggested that an agreement on international economic relations among states be drawn up. See U.N. Document, A/C.2/SR.465, October 17, 1957, p. 71.

59. Also see William F. Robinson, "Eastern Europe's Presence in Black Africa," Radio Free Europe Research, RAD Background Report/142, June 21, 1979, p. 9.

60. U.N. Document, A/32/PV.13, September 29, 1977, p. 36.

61. See U.N. Document, A/34/PV.10, September 26, 1979, p. 88.

62. U.N. Document, A/C.5/SR.1750, November 26, 1975, p. 331.

63. As pointed out at the thirty-third session, the Soviets took the position that they could not be held responsible for additional expenses for UNEF-II stemming from the Egyptian-Israeli agreements of September 4, 1975. See U.N. Monthly Chronicle (January 1979): 73. In the case of UNDOF, the Soviets said that they would not pay because of inefficiency in operations. See U.N. Monthly Chronicle (January 1979): 74.

64. For a discussion of the method used in the calculations, see Arend Lijphart, "The Analysis of Bloc Voting in the General Assembly," The American Political Science Review (December 1963): 902-17.

65. Robert C. Angell has ranked, in order, Yugoslavia, Romania, Bulgaria, and Albania in terms of national "support for world order," which can be linked to support for the United Nations. See Robert C. Angell, "National Support for World Order," Journal of Conflict Resolution (September 1973): 438.

9

EAST EUROPE:
SOVIET ASSET OR BURDEN?
THE POLITICAL DIMENSION

Andrzej Korbonski

In recent years there has been some discussion among Western scholars as to whether East Europe would continue to be viewed by the leaders of the Soviet Union—still the hegemonial power in the region—as a major asset, or whether its value, especially in the economic and military realms, had declined to such an extent that at the end of the 1970s the Kremlin might perceive East Europe more as a burden than as an asset. The purpose of this essay is to examine some of the issues connected with this question with special emphasis on its political dimension.

A BIT OF CONCEPTUALIZING

The task of conceptualizing the various issues involved in this question was made immeasurably easier by Vernon Aspaturian who addressed this and other related problems in a pioneering article on whether East Europe has indeed become a political–ideological liability to the Soviet Union.[1] While Aspaturian managed to solve some of the definitional ambiguities, there are still several conceptual loose ends to be tied.

Research for this paper was aided by a grant from the UCLA Center for International and Strategic Affairs, the assistance of which is hereby gratefully acknowledged. An early version of the paper was presented at the annual meeting of the American Political Science Association in Washington, D.C., in August 1979. The author wishes to thank Alex Alexiev, Ronald Linden, William Potter, and Sarah Terry for their penetrating criticism which helped to clarify many of his thoughts.

To begin with, there is the problem of defining East Europe. Over the years this has become more and more difficult. In fact, we may be approaching the point when the use of the term "East Europe" is becoming less and less precise and analytically useful.[2] Nevertheless, the present task is to investigate the cost-benefit relationship between East Europe and the Soviet Union; thus it is imperative to come up with an acceptable working definition of this particular region. The six countries—Bulgaria, Czechoslovakia, East Germany, Hungary, Poland, and Romania—are not only located in a well-defined geographical area of Europe but also have several essential features in common, including political and economic structures and institutions, patterns of rapid socioeconomic changes, membership in at least two important regional organizations, and, to a great extent, a common historical—especially post-World War II—heritage.

The differences among the individual states are less easily observable. On the one hand, they relate to the problem of nation and state building, participation and welfare, and the way the particular regimes managed to deal with and solve the various developmental and systemic crises.[3] They stem also from many deeply rooted cultural and socioeconomic phenomena that add up to national political cultures which, despite at least three decades of Communist efforts to eradicate or weaken them, continue to influence the respective countries' foreign and domestic policies.

Still, as a baseline, all these states share, although not to the same degree or along the same dimensions, a substantial economic dependence upon the Soviet Union, a profound political dependence characterized by the need to keep international and especially domestic policies within parameters established by Moscow, and a direct military vulnerability based on geography and recent history. While, on balance, systemic similarities seem to outweigh the differences, it is the presence of persisting and often growing differences among the individual states that makes East Europe a fascinating yet frustrating focus of research.

The next concepts to be defined are asset and burden. The dictionary definitions of asset refer to something valuable, or to an advantage. This can also be read as an antonym of burden or liability, which in turn denote the existence of a disadvantage, a drawback, or vulnerability.[4] While all these concepts are clearly valid at a given point in time, their main weakness is their static character, and my own preference would be for a more dynamic concept that could be analyzed and dissected over time. Therefore I propose to use the term "asset" as a source of income which, in turn, may be defined as a stream of recurrent benefits or gains—tangible and/or psychic—accruing to the owner of the asset, which is likely to continue for more than just a brief period of time. One may view benefit either as an added concrete, positive value that improves the position of the holder of the asset relative to his former position or with respect to his adversaries or as the ability of the asset's owner to deny the income or benefit accruing to his opponent. In line with this it may be argued that the Soviet hegemony over East Europe represents not only a source of concrete benefits or losses to the Soviet Union but also that the Kremlin's mastery over the region benefits the Soviet Union by denying the control over the area to Moscow's adversaries, be it the West or the People's Republic of China.

In the same vein, the notion of burden would imply a source of recurrent losses which, however, in contrast to income, the holder of the burden hopes will not last for a long time since, were they to do so, they might eventually destroy the value of the asset. In other words, there is a certain degree of asymmetry between these two concepts: while the stream of income may (preferably) continue indefinitely, the economists tell us that no owner of an asset behaving rationally would be willing to sustain indefinite losses. Instead he would liquidate the asset and transfer his capital elsewhere to more profitable uses. Obviously, over time an asset can be transformed into a burden, and Aspaturian is right again in suggesting that assets and liabilities may be viewed as extreme ends of a continuum.[5]

It is beyond the scope of this chapter to examine the process of a possible transformation of East Europe and/or its component parts from a Soviet political asset into a burden; that most fascinating process deserves separate treatment. What I am doing here is engaging in a bit of comparative statics by comparing balance sheets for four successive periods of time without, however, examining the process of change within and between periods. On the other hand, an attempt will be made to summarize briefly the criteria used by the Soviet leadership in arriving at their respective perceptions and judgments in each period. These criteria do change, of course, in accordance with such factors as the changes in the international situation resulting from the emergence of the Soviet Union as a global power, which may conceivably reduce the value of East Europe to Moscow, or changes in Soviet priorities in the region as between conformity and viability.

The investigation will cover the period of the past two decades, 1960-80. The choice of this particular period was largely arbitrary. On the one hand, 20 years seems long enough to observe some significant indigenous systemic and policy changes in East Europe and the Soviet Union. In addition, the past two decades have witnessed major changes in the environment external to the Soviet Union and East Europe which inevitably shaped and influenced the process of changes in the region. One can mention in this regard the defection of Albania, the emergence of the Sino-Soviet conflict, the Vietnam War, the Ostpolitik and its consequences, the intervention in Czechoslovakia, U.S.-Soviet detente, the energy and raw materials dislocations, and, most recently, the escalating conflicts in the Third World, notably in Africa, the Middle East, and Southeast Asia. As will be shown, both internal and external factors have influenced the changing Soviet-East European relationship since the late 1950s.

The next methodological question to be addressed is the measurement of assets and liabilities and the stream of benefits or losses they generate. While the question of finding a proper yardstick to measure socioeconomic concepts is never easy, it is particularly difficult in the case of political phenomena. In comparison, for example, estimating the value of East Europe as an economic or military asset or burden can be accomplished more readily, and for reasons that are obvious, with standard empirical methods: in each case we deal with magnitudes that are quantifiable and hence measurable and comparable, albeit imperfectly. Not so in the political realm, where measurement remains fuzzy across systems. Rather than engage in definitional hairsplitting, I propose to consider the political value to Moscow of each East European country as an aggregate sum of its economic, strategic-military, "proxy," and ideological "values." Given that the boundaries between these arenas have become largely obliterated, especially in these systems, where virtually all socioeconomic activities tend to be heavily politicized, the problem becomes one of how to estimate the political "value" to the Soviet Union of each individual country. A "value," whether positive or negative, is inherently a subjective judgment, and, thus, to answer the question posed, we must try to look at East Europe and its individual components through the eyes of the Soviet leaders. This appears to be a legitimate enterprise since the purpose of this chapter is to arrive at a judgment regarding East Europe's value to Moscow, even though our knowledge of the perceptions, beliefs, and images held by the Kremlin oligarchy tends to be scant.[6]

It may be taken for granted that the Soviet perception of East Europe was not uniform and that Moscow viewed each country in the region differently, the ultimate image being influenced by a mix of Marxism-Leninism and past history. Thus, there is little doubt, for example, that at the time of the Communist takeover, Moscow seemed to view many of the countries in the traditional fashion, showing implicitly or explicitly its greater affinity with Bulgaria, Czechoslovakia, and Yugoslavia than with Hungary, Poland, and Romania. The seizure of power and subsequent imposition of the Stalinist model did not essentially change the existing stereotypes except, of course, for Yugoslavia and the Soviet Union, whose respective images of each other have not been quite the same since June 1948. It would also appear that over the years the Kremlin has learned some lessons from the events of the first 25 years of Communist rule in the area and that, above all, it became much better informed about the situation in the individual East European countries, as a result of which its perception of the various changes and processes in the region has acquired greater depth and sophistication. [7]

ASSET OR BURDEN ?

The answer to the question of whether in the past 20 years East Europe represented an asset or a burden to the Soviet Union is displayed in Table 9.1. The 20-year period 1960-80 is divided into four separate sub-periods in order to facilitate an unambiguous judgment about a given country's relationship with respect to the Soviet Union. In addition, I wanted to show the changes that occurred in that relationship during the past two decades, and this could be illustrated more clearly by tracing the process of changes from one sub-period to another.

The first period, 1960-65, covers the last few years of Khrushchev's rule, prior to his ouster in 1964. The period witnessed a number of important events and developments that affected Moscow's perception of East Europe, among them the open acknowledgment of the Sino-Soviet conflict, the defection of Albania from the Soviet to the Chinese orbit, Khrushchev's failure to establish a CMEA-wide planning agency, and Romania's declaration of economic independence from the rest of the region.

The next period, 1965-70, represented the first five years of the Brezhnev rule. Here the most important single event, obviously, was the Soviet intervention in Czechoslovakia and the proclamation of the "Brezhnev Doctrine." Nevertheless, this apparent return to greater ideological conformity with and subservience to Moscow, was largely offset by the rapid rapprochement with West Germany that culminated in the Bonn-Moscow and Bonn-Warsaw treaties signed in 1970.

The processes of detente got into high gear during the next period, 1970-75. Here the critical mileposts were the treaty between the two German states, the four-power agreement on the status of Berlin, SALT I, the initiation of the Mutual and Balanced Force Reduction (MBFR) talks in Vienna, and the signing of the Final Act of the Conference on Security and Cooperation in Europe in Helsinki, in August 1975.

The final period, 1975-80, was characterized by a gradual decline in the level of East-West detente, which had culminated at Helsinki. This was partly due to the emergence of the Soviet Union as a key and dynamic global actor capable of influencing the state of affairs in such remote areas as Angola and Ethiopia, and most recently in Afghanistan; partly to the changes in the international economic order characterized by the growing energy and raw materials crisis, recession and increasing difficulties associated with East-West trade; and

TABLE 9.1

East Europe: Soviet Asset or Burden, 1960–80

	1960–65					1965–70					1970–75					1975–80					1960–80				
	E	M-S	P	I	POL	E	M-S	P	I	POL	E	M-S	P	I	POL	E	M-S	P	I	POL	E	M-S	P	I	POL
Bulgaria	0	+	0	++	+	0	+	0	++	+	+	+	+	++	++	+	+	+	++	++	+	+	+	++	++
Czechoslovakia	+	+	+	+	+	+	+	0	–	0	+	+	0	–	0	0	+	+	–	+	0	+	+	–	+
East Germany	++	++	+	+	++	++	++	+	+	++	++	++	++	+	++	+	++	++	+	++	++	++	++	+	++
Hungary	0	+	0	–	0	0	+	0	0	0	0	+	0	+	0	0	+	0	+	0	0	+	0	+	+
Poland	0	+	0	0	0	–	+	0	0	0	–	+	0	–	–	–	+	0	–	–	–	+	0	–	–
Romania	0	0	0	+	0	–	–	0	0	–	–	–	–	0	–	–	–	–	–	–	–	–	0	–

Note: E = economic; M-S = military-strategic; P = proxy; I = ideological; and POL = political. Asset = +; burden = –; and neither asset nor burden = 0.

Source: Author's judgments.

partly to the growth of domestic political opposition in several East European countries, related undoubtedly, at least in part, to the Helsinki and Belgrade conferences.

To sum up, the four sub-periods may be viewed as representing a 20-year cycle that began with a period of relative relaxation but also uncertainty in Soviet-East European relations during Khrushchev's final years, followed by a drive for greater conformity in the early Brezhnev period and another relatively relaxed stretch during the early 1970s, and ending in what appears to be another period of uncertainty and potential instability in the relationship between the Kremlin and the rest of the Warsaw alliance, somewhat reminiscent of the last few years of Khruschev's rule. Clearly, Moscow's perception of the role and weight of East Europe in its own calculus of profits and losses was bound to be influenced greatly by the changes and shifts from one period to another.

As suggested earlier, the judgment as to whether an individual country represented a political asset or liability to the Soviet Union was based on the total of judgments in four subcategories: economic, military-strategic, "proxy," and ideological. Obviously, to calculate the value, be it positive or negative, of East Europe and the individual states to Moscow from the above points of view is not simple. More often than not each country in the region represented a mix of assets and liabilities which might or might not offset each other; the task at hand was to arrive at a sort of a balance sheet between them, for each country and period. Needless to say, this also involved the implicit weighting of each subcategory, which complicated the final result still further.

As a rough approximation, a country's status as a Soviet economic asset or burden depended on such factors as its ability to supply the Soviet Union with scarce ("hard") goods and with factors of production—both capital and labor—or, in contrast, to the given state's strong dependence on the Soviet Union for the delivery of badly needed commodities, mostly raw materials and foodstuffs.[8]

The military-strategic relationship was shaped by a number of variables which determined whether the country played a major role in the Soviet national security system. They included such tangible and measurable indicators as the sheer size of the country's armed forces, the quantity and quality of its military hardware, and the country's geographical location relative to both the Soviet Union and the West, as well as such intangible factors as the degree of reliability of the national armed forces and their presumed willingness to obey Soviet commands in times of emergency.[9]

The "proxy" designation was intended to indicate the value of each country to Moscow as its proxy, or alter ego, in different international environments: communist camp, the Third World, dealing with the West, and different international organizations and gatherings, both formal and informal. For example, this included acting on behalf of the Soviet Union at various international conferences and forums, such as the United Nations and its agencies, as measured by votes and expressions of support for Soviet positions; dealing with perceived threats to the unity of the Moscow-led communist camp, be it Eurocommunism, Titoism, or Maoism, again measured by the volume and degree of support for Moscow; and making human and material resources available to the Kremlin to be used at its discretion in such different international environments as Angola, Ethiopia, Ghana, Vietnam, or Zambia.

Finally, the rubric "ideological" refers to the success or failure of a communist polity to become firmly embedded in a given society, thus validating if not legitimizing the Soviet-type brand of Marxism-Leninism as the potentially universalistic model. It does not necessarily mean total adoption of all Soviet institutions and policies but rather the basic adherence to such essential principles as the Leninist conception of the role of the party, nationalization and control of key sectors of the economy, media censorship, and belief in proletarian internationalism. Like the previous variables, the ideological factor is difficult if not impossible to measure, and the ultimate judgment on that score was highly impressionistic.

The aggregate judgment regarding each country being a political asset or burden was simply based on the addition of individual rankings in each category. The question that may be legitimately raised concerns the additivity of the judgments. The implicit assumption is, of course, that the total, positive or negative, was equal to the sum of its parts, each of which had equal weight. Yet, it may be argued that some of the variables have been more crucial than others and that they should have carried greater weight. While both assumptions are arbitrary, treating all variables equally rather than differentially had an advantage of simplicity. It may be argued that assigning different weights to individual categories would magnify potential distortion without making the estimate any more sophisticated or "scientific."

One final comment is in order here. As indicated earlier, each country in the region was assumed to be viewed through the eyes of the Kremlin leaders who then made a judgment as to whether the country represented an asset or a burden to the Soviet Union. That judgment was, most likely, influenced by two major factors: first, Moscow's perception of the performance of every country under each of the four rubrics and in each of the four periods; and, second, the criteria applied by the Soviet leaders in evaluating that performance. These criteria were bound to change over time, reflecting a variety of things: changes in the international situation and in the "correlation of forces," changes in the priorities of the Soviet ruling elite, and many others.

For example, there is little doubt that East-West detente after 1972 accompanied by arms control measures and expansion of East-West commercial relations has affected Soviet perceptions of East Europe. Similarly, the perennial tension and occasional sharp clashes between Soviet interests in the region—especially economic and ideological—inevitably influenced the image of the area and of the individual countries held by the Kremlin.

The most basic conflict has been that between viability and cohesion, or between, on the one hand, the desire to see in East Europe viable, stable, and efficient economies that would not require periodic support and would supply the Soviet Union with needed goods and, on the other hand, the requirement that the same countries must approximate in some fashion the Soviet model. [10]

It is clear that there is a sort of ebb and flow to these conflicts. Thus, throughout part of Khrushchev's rule the Kremlin valued economic viability more than conformity. Under Brezhnev the emphasis seemed to have shifted toward greater control and conformity, culminating in the invasion of Czechoslovakia and the suppression of the "Prague Spring." Since then, one may argue, Moscow again has become somewhat more tolerant of deviations from the norm, as witnessed by its policy of apparently benign neglect with regard to the events in Poland. Whether the recent intervention in Afghanistan augurs another shift in policy toward East Europe remains to be seen.

THE INDIVIDUAL COUNTRIES

Bulgaria has traditionally been viewed as Moscow's most faithful ally in East Europe ever since the Communist takeover of the region some 35 years ago. However, this conventional wisdom did not fit reality, and there is considerable evidence of Bulgarian deviation from the straight and narrow path and close alliance with the Soviet Union. [11] Economically, Bulgaria seems to have been neither an asset nor a burden, except for the most recent period when the growing economic cooperation between the two countries, which included transfer of Bulgarian labor to the Soviet Union, might be viewed as making Bulgaria more valuable economically to Moscow than in the past. From the military-strategic point of view, Bulgaria appeared as a moderately important asset to the Kremlin: its geographical location with borders on two NATO countries, Greece and Turkey, and with Yugoslavia had to be of some interest to the Soviet military planners, even though Bulgaria's military potential has been on the modest side and no Soviet troops have been stationed there for more than 20 years.

Sofia's behavior on the international scene has been characterized, by and large, by an adherence to the Soviet line, although there have been some interesting departures from it.[12] The 1970s witnessed growing Bulgarian involvement in the Third World, mostly Africa, where its activities complemented to some extent the Soviet and East German efforts. Bulgaria was also used as a Soviet proxy in at least two international forums: as Moscow's mouthpiece against Eurocommunism and as the Kremlin's agent against Yugoslavia, using the Macedonian question as its excuse. Finally, ideologically Bulgaria continued essentially to emulate the Soviet model and, except for the still largely unexplained attempt at a military coup in 1965, there has been no evidence of any serious departure from the traditional norm. On balance, then, Bulgaria has to receive fairly high marks throughout the period as a Soviet political asset.

The case of Czechoslovakia is, needless to say, more complicated. Whereas in general it was a major economic asset to Moscow in the later 1950s and early 1960s, it may be hypothesized that the past 15 years or so have manifested a change in this respect: Czechoslovakia's economic performance and its ability to fulfill Moscow's demands has been overshadowed by that of East Germany and probably also of Hungary, and today Czechoslovakia appears to be neither an economic asset nor a liability to the Kremlin.

It may be assumed that even before 1968 the Soviet leadership viewed Czechoslovakia as a military-strategic asset, partly because of its location facing West Germany, its important armament industry, and its contribution to the military strength of the Warsaw Pact.[13] After the 1968 Soviet intervention, the military value of the country probably remained essentially unchanged. The presence of Soviet troops added to its importance despite the rapprochement with the Federal Republic of Germany, yet this was clearly offset in the aftermath of the invasion by the demise of traditional Soviet-Czechoslovak friendship and the negative impact on the reliability of the Czechoslovak armed forces. As in the case of Bulgaria, Czechoslovakia has become more active in the Third World in the 1970s, mostly as a purveyor of arms, thus reinforcing Soviet initiatives in various parts of the globe. Also, like Bulgaria, Czechoslovakia has been used by the Kremlin as its mouthpiece against Eurocommunism. This role was likely to be of considerable value to Moscow since, after all, it was the Soviet intervention in Czechoslovakia that contributed signally to the emergence of Eurocommunism.

The most interesting changes, of course, occurred in the ideological arena. Until the mid-1960s Czechoslovakia might be described as a generally faithful follower and successful imitator of the Soviet model. The second half of the decade, however, witnessed a rapid transformation and liberalization of the Czechoslovak political and economic systems, followed by a reimposition of what may be called a neo- or pseudo-Stalinist system which, it may be speculated, has gone so far as to become an embarrassment to the Soviet Union, especially in the post-Helsinki period. Thus, ideologically, at least, Czechoslovakia has become a liability which, however, could not fully offset the country's positive performance and achievements on other counts, making it on balance a Soviet political asset, albeit less clear-cut an asset than Bulgaria or East Germany.

There is little doubt that it was East Germany which throughout the entire period remained by far the Kremlin's most valuable asset. Before the Soviet entry into the arena of East-West trade, East Germany was the major if not the sole supplier of technologically advanced goods to the Soviet Union, and, even though its importance may have declined somewhat as a result of Western competition for the Soviet markets, today it is still an economic asset for Moscow. Militarily, not only has East Germany served as a crucial Soviet offensive springboard and defensive bastion, but its military has enjoyed the reputation of being probably the most reliable component of the Warsaw Pact.[14] East Germany may be viewed as acting as a Soviet proxy throughout the early part of the period with respect to Berlin and West Germany, and one of the most interesting recent developments has been the rapid rise of the German Democratic Republic as a Soviet proxy in the Third World, especially in Africa, where it has aided and abetted Soviet and Cuban efforts in Angola, Ethiopia, and other parts of the continent.[15] Ideologically, East Germany managed to tow the line successfully, despite being the prime target of West German Ostpolitik and of some dissident activities following the Helsinki Conference in 1975. On the whole, then, despite some serious policy disagreements, particularly with respect to the rapprochement with West Germany, the GDR might well be seen as the Kremlin's most valuable asset in East Europe over the past 20 years.

This has clearly not been the case with Hungary. A good argument can be made to show that from the economic standpoint Hungary has neither contributed greatly to Soviet welfare nor derived any great benefits from being a Soviet ally.[16] Since the armed intervention of November 1956 and the permanent stationing of Soviet forces in Hungary since then, the country may be considered a Soviet military asset. Its proximity to Austria and Yugoslavia (not to mention other potentially deviant allies, such as Romania) is certainly an advantage to Soviet military planners, even though the Hungarian military is not likely to be among the most reliable and trustworthy components of the Warsaw Treaty. For reasons that are not easily ascertained, Hungary has not been

very active as a Soviet proxy throughout the world, and its performance at various international forums has tended to be rather lack-
luster, testifying to its principal preoccupation with domestic politics
and economics. The significant exception was Hungary's hostile
attitude toward Romania, which has been utilized occasionally by the
Kremlin, eager to isolate Romania from the rest of the East European alliance.

In the ideological realm Hungary has undergone a rather interesting metamorphosis from being close to an ideological liability in
the late 1950s to becoming somewhat of an asset in the late 1970s.
During the earlier period, due to the strong influence of the events
of October–November 1956, and despite Kadar's valiant efforts to
stabilize the political situation and establish a modus vivendi between the resurrected party and the society at large, the country
could hardly qualify as a Soviet asset. In the late 1960s, Kadarism
appeared to have taken hold and was eventually accompanied by
innovative economic reforms which made Hungary a rather unique
member of the East European camp.

My judgment is that during that period Hungary ceased to be a
liability but has not yet become an asset for the Kremlin. It may be
argued, however, that this did happen in the most recent period
(1975-80). Hungary's systemic experiment showed little change as
compared with the previous period, yet, apparently, it became
accepted and made almost legitimate by Moscow, which could point
to Hungary with some pride as an example of a reformed Communist
system that stayed within the pale, demonstrating thereby Soviet
willingness to tolerate a considerable degree of diversity. Indeed,
the last few years have witnessed a definite Hungarian-Soviet
rapprochement, implying that the Soviet leadership has begun to
view Hungary as a valuable ally.[17] On balance, it may be hypothesized that in the past 20 years Hungary's assets have offset its
liabilities.

Poland, not unexpectedly, could not be easily placed in either
the asset or burden column. In the 1960s and early 1970s the country appeared to be neither an economic asset nor a liability to the
Soviet Union. Together with nearly all the other East European
countries it relied on the Soviet Union as a supplier of raw materials
and as a market for its industrial products, the respective values
of which tended largely to offset each other, at least until 1974.[18]
Poland's situation changed in the mid-1970s, when for a variety of
reasons the country was rapidly becoming somewhat of an economic
basket case that had to be bailed out by Moscow and, paradoxically,
the West.[19]

It may be taken for granted that, on balance, despite a host of
problems, the Kremlin has viewed (and still views) Poland as a

military-strategic asset, especially as long as the Soviet forces remain in East Germany. Doing so, however, necessitates maintaining supply routes through Poland, and this paramount consideration is likely to overshadow many others, including the fact that the Polish armed forces, second most powerful in the Warsaw alliance, may not be entirely reliable in the event of an East-West armed confrontation.

Like Hungary, Poland has not been greatly involved in the Third World for reasons that remain largely obscure, and it has not been particularly active in other international environments. Overall, its contribution to Soviet causes in those areas has not been particularly impressive.

The most complex and at the same time most interesting dimension was the Polish-Soviet relationship in the realm of ideology. In the late 1950s, next to Yugoslavia, Poland was the ideological maverick in the Communist camp, but gradually under Gomulka's leadership it began to move back into the fold, only to explode again in December 1970. The last few years have reflected once again the country's ideological decay, manifested in workers' riots, the emergence of a lively dissident movement, and the growth in the power and influence of the Church—all of them surely anathemas in Kremlin's eyes. There is little doubt, then, that Poland has hardly been an ideological asset for the Soviet Union. Quite the opposite, and this fact, combined with the clear-cut economic liability, has made Poland most likely a political burden to Moscow.

Romania has also had a checkered relationship, to put it mildly, with the Soviet Union. In contrast to other CMEA members, Romania's economic relations with the Soviet Union have been rather stormy, starting in the early 1960s when Bucharest openly challenged Moscow's ideas about greater economic integration and specialization.[20] Since Romania managed to remain self-sufficient in food and some basic raw materials, especially energy sources, it has been much less dependent than the other East European countries on Soviet generosity and good will. Beginning in the 1960s, in order to provide the grist for its "multilateral development" it turned toward the West and eventually the Third World for trade and credits. All in all, from the economic point of view Romania was neither an asset nor a liability to Moscow.

Militarily, the Kremlin probably viewed Romania increasingly as a major liability. While the Soviet intervention in Czechoslovakia in 1968 clearly put a damper on Ceausescu's drive to loosen the insitutional constraints imposed by Romania's membership in the Warsaw Treaty Organization (WTO), the last few years have seen the revival of autonomous Romanian tendencies, culminating in a Romanian-Soviet confrontation at the meeting of the Warsaw Pact

Political Consultative Committee in November 1978.[21] In this light one may assume that the Kremlin leaders have been viewing Romania as a military-strategic burden rather than an asset. Additional factors were Romania's attitude toward MBFR, its geographical location, which prevented Soviet access to its ally Bulgaria and its potential adversary, Yugoslavia, and Bucharest's refusal to allocate a large share of its resources to defense.[22]

Insofar as Romania's role on the international scene was concerned, there also its policies could only be perceived as detrimental to Soviet interests. To begin with, Romania's behavior in the Third World, and especially in Africa, was clearly in conflict with that of Moscow and Havana.[23] The same was true for Romania's activities at the various international forums, be it the Conference on Security and Cooperation in Europe or the Eighteen Nation Disarmament Committee. Romania's drive toward expanding its membership in the existing international groupings and thus increasing the number of what Kenneth Jowitt calls the "identity references," flew directly in the face of Soviet policy.[24] Thus, in the category "proxy" Romania clearly has been a major liability to the Kremlin.

The ideological relationship between Bucharest and Moscow has been probably the most complex of the various "connections." Under Gheorghiu-Dej Romania was, by and large, a faithful adherent to the Soviet model and, at least until 1965, the country could be considered as an ideological asset. However, with the arrival of Ceausescu on the scene the situation has changed rather drastically. On the basis of available evidence (and with a hefty dose of conventional wisdom) it appears that for the past 15 years or so the performance of the Romanian domestic political system has given Moscow relatively little cause for complaint.[25] It remains the most tightly controlled polity in East Europe. On the other hand, Romania's behavior on the international arena could hardly have pleased the Kremlin. It may be assumed that this came close to being a typical case of a zero-sum game for the Soviet Union which, on balance, derived neither benefits nor losses under this rubric and which thus far refrained from interfering with the status quo. The overall judgment is that, together with Poland, Romania was seen, most likely, as a serious burden for the Soviet Union.

THE REGION

Thus far the attempt to calculate the Soviet-East European cost-benefit ratio has been confined to individual countries. However interesting, this still leaves unanswered the question of whether East Europe as a whole could be considered a political asset or liability to the Soviet Union. A thorough answer would require a separate treatment, and at this stage all that has been done is to indicate a possible approach to solving the question.

The main difficulty was clearly that of finding an appropriate weighting system that would allow us to aggregate the individual country rankings and arrive at a composite judgment for the region as a whole. Whatever weights were to be chosen ultimately, whether those based on respective populations, gross national product figures, sizes of military establishments, or combinations of these and other variables, the final judgment was bound to be highly arbitrary. Still, regardless of the bias involved in the choice, one might argue that at least the relative rankings, the order of magnitude of the various influences, and the general direction of changes in the respective variables did not violate basic rationality and pointed to the fact that on the eve of the 1980s East Europe continued, on balance, to be perceived by Moscow as a Soviet political asset.

This judgment confirms to a large extent the view expressed some time ago by Zvi Gitelman, who stated:

> Politically, Eastern Europe has been a mixed blessing to the USSR. The existence of socialist systems in the area has increased its size, and hence the prestige and quantitative power, of the socialist camp led by the Soviet Union, but the political instability of the area, which results partially from the consequences of its modernization, has imposed on the USSR the role of policeman. . . . But even if the costs of association with Eastern Europe along present lines become very high in economic and political terms, the costs of dissociation might well be higher. [26]

WHAT ABOUT THE FUTURE ?

The conclusion that Kremlin leaders today still probably view East Europe as a major asset is not exactly earth-shattering. In fact, one may argue that it is so common-sensical that one wonders whether the whole exercise was worth the effort. Still, the conclusion that the value of East Europe as a Soviet asset has declined in the course of the past two decades may be seen as not utterly devoid of interest. Moreover, the periodic testing of what over the years has become a deeply entrenched conventional wisdom, is not only useful but also frequently interesting, if only because of the impact of rapid changes in both the international and East European regional environments. For much too long East Europe has been treated, to use Charles Gati's apt phrase, as a "forgotten region."[27] The fact that for a variety of reasons a number of East European states has become active international actors is only one aspect of the process of change that has been taking place in the region throughout the 1970s and which is likely to continue into the 1980s.

It was stated at the outset that in the final analysis the judgment as to whether East Europe constituted an asset or a burden lay in the eyes of the beholder, in this case those of the Soviet leadership. It is also, undoubtedly, a function of Soviet national interests, as interpreted at a given time by the current occupants of the Kremlin. As was suggested earlier, as some of these interests change, so does the perception of whether any East European country or the region as a whole serves or hurts Moscow's goals and objectives.

On another occasion I hypothesized that with one or, possibly, two exceptions the original major Soviet objectives in aiding and abetting the communist takeover of East Europe after World War II have not changed greatly in the past 35 years. I also stated that "despite a number of significant political, economic and social changes in Eastern Europe, the Soviet hegemony over the region . . . remained essentially unimpaired although threatened by several crises and challenges."[28]

Does this mean, though, that the most important Soviet interest in East Europe remains security? Since it is clear that in the missile age geography appears to be much less important as a strategic factor, may it still be presumed that Moscow continues to view the region as a valuable piece of real estate to be protected against hostile foreign influences so that it can be considered a reliable first line of defense in the event of a conventional attack against the Soviet Union from the West?

The evidence appears somewhat mixed and confusing. On the one hand, it is obvious that Moscow will resist serious attempts by external powers to undermine its hegemony in the region in both the short and the long run. On the other hand, a sharp Soviet reaction against such attempts was focused on those East European countries which either did not belong to the Warsaw Pact (Yugoslavia) or whose military-strategic value was not exorbitant (Romania). The shrill Soviet attacks on the summer 1978 visit of Chinese Party Chairman Hua Kuo-feng to those two countries was a good testimony to Soviet paranoia and Moscow's determination to tolerate no competition in the area. Incidentally, these attacks were much stronger than the Soviet reaction to past visits to strategically more important Poland by Presidents Nixon, Ford, and Carter, and, most recently, Pope John Paul II. Similarly, I am not aware of any

unusual Soviet sensitivity about the risk of contamination to East
Germany, another strategically important country, stemming from
that state's growing involvement in international politics. In the
same vein, it may be speculated that the major reason behind the
Soviet invasion of Czechoslovakia in 1968 was not so much security
as the perceived political-ideological threat presented by the
Dubcek regime.[29]

Whether all this means a decline in the importance of security
considerations relative to the economic and political ones remains
to be seen. The same applies to the question of which of the East
European countries will continue to be Soviet assets and which will
turn into liabilities, and vice versa. An important element in this
matrix is time. It may be argued that in the short run the Soviet
Union can easily afford to carry a burden, even a heavy one, just
as a conglomerate can afford to maintain a losing branch or a department store an unprofitable line of goods. In the longer run, however,
neither is capable of sustaining heavy losses indefinitely. In such
situations, either the burden is jettisoned or the liability is transformed into an asset.

The former is not likely to happen with respect to East Europe.
The only defections from the Soviet camp have been voluntary and, although resented by Moscow, could not have been prevented at a toler-
able cost. The latter prospect (transforming a liability into an asset)
is more probable, although clearly not without risk. Changing a
burden into an asset is not likely to be achieved peacefully and may
require the use of violence, including Soviet-armed intervention,
as was the case in Hungary in 1956. In the era of detente and the
spirit of Helsinki, such an intervention was bound to be a costly
enterprise, especially as the two countries that were most likely
being perceived as liabilities, Poland and Romania, were generally
assumed to be willing to resist any Soviet encroachment on their
sovereignty. This may well have meant that rather than intervene
the Kremlin was willing to extend the time period for carrying the
burden, especially since transforming a liability into an asset
through the use of armed force comes close to throwing the baby out
with the bath water.[30] With the apparent demise of the U.S.-Soviet
detente caused by the Soviet intervention in Afghanistan the odds
against the use of violence in East Europe obviously have dropped
rather sharply.

What about the possibility of an asset turning into a burden in
the 1980s? This has happened in the past, and it may be hypothesized that it may occur again. Which of the three countries that are
presently viewed as assets—Bulgaria, Czechoslovakia, and East
Germany, and possibly also Hungary—are likely to create difficulties
for the Soviet Union in the foreseeable future? My feeling is that

none of the four is a plausible candidate. There is not much evidence in Bulgaria's postwar history to indicate a serious potential for a drastic change. Both Czechoslovakia and Hungary have had their respective moments of glory and having paid for them may have second thoughts about going through the same process again. Paradoxically, it is East Germany that may well be the prime target. Except for the brief explosion of June 1953, the German Democratic Republic has seemingly been the model of consistency and stability, yet one may speculate that, as demonstrated by the flurry of excitement generated by the Helsinki Final Act, the facade of tranquility may hide considerable dissatisfaction with the existing state of affairs.[31] Whether it will surface is anybody's guess, and the same is true for the Soviet reaction, which may well be swift in the light of East Germany's special status within the Warsaw Pact.

In the meantime, however, I am prepared to argue that over the years Moscow has learned some lessons from the events that took place in East Europe in the past 20 years and that at some point the Kremlin began to see itself more as a leader of a conventional politico-military-economic alliance than a vozhd of an ideological camp engaged in a sharp struggle with the capitalist world.[32] This new self-image may have meant that the Kremlin realized that the leadership of an alliance represented an obligation to provide aid and support for its members instead of exploiting them. Hence the Soviet willingness to supply CMEA members with oil and raw materials at favorable prices—at least until recently—and to ship grain to East Europe, even when a poor Soviet harvest made such shipments highly burdensome.

To put it somewhat differently, it may be said that in the past few years the Soviet Union has become much better informed about the situation in the individual East European countries, and as a result its perception of the various changes and processes in the region has acquired greater depth and sophistication. For example, Moscow has been aware for some time of the potential linkage between economic well-being and the system's legitimacy and has provided economic aid to regimes such as the Polish one which face a serious legitimacy crisis due to economic difficulties with which they could not cope. There is also some evidence pointing to a somewhat greater tolerance by the Kremlin of the various dissident movements, if not at home then at least in some of the East European countries. Altogether it seems that Moscow has learned some important lessons from the many crises, and it is doing its best to avoid their repetition.

Whether the above interpretation is valid or not remains to be seen. Right now, however, Soviet interests in East Europe are said to be characterized more by ambivalence than by the single-minded concern for control often attributed to them. For every indication of the Kremlin's concern over the dimensions and possible consequences of Eastern Europe's dealings . . . with the West, there are contra-indications of a fair degree of tolerance over the years for limited diversity and reform and activism abroad—a tolerance implying awareness of the advantages as well as the risks of recent trends.[33]

Indeed, one may hazard a guess that the Soviet leaders have not really carefully considered the consequences for their political interests in East Europe of their own global policies pursued for broader strategic and economic gains.

In light of these ambiguities all that can be done is to engage in some more or less informed guessing and speculating, of which this essay can serve as an example.

NOTES

1. Vernon V. Aspaturian, "Has Eastern Europe Become a Liability to the Soviet Union? I. The Political-Ideological Aspects," in The International Politics of Eastern Europe, ed. Charles Gati (New York: Praeger, 1976), pp. 17-36.

2. Andrzej Korbonski, "The Prospects for Change in Eastern Europe," Slavic Review 33, no. 2 (June 1974): 219. See also Vernon V. Aspaturian, "Eastern Europe in World Perspective," in Communism in Eastern Europe, ed. Teresa Rakowska-Harmstone and Andrew Gyorgy (Bloomington: Indiana University Press, 1979), pp. 20-21.

3. Among the studies focusing on the process of development and modernization in East Europe, are Charles Gati, ed., The Politics of Modernization in Eastern Europe (New York: Praeger, 1974); Carl Beck and Carmelo Mesa-Lago, eds., Comparative Socialist Systems (Pittsburgh: University of Pittsburgh Center for International Studies, 1975); and Jan F. Triska and Paul M. Cocks, eds., Political Development in Eastern Europe (New York: Praeger, 1977).

4. Aspaturian, "Has Eastern Europe Become a Liability," p. 17.

5. Ibid.

6. For an excellent brief discussion of the problem of perception in international relations, see Robert Jervis, "Hypotheses on Misperception," World Politics 20, no. 3 (April 1968): 454-79.

7. Some of these ideas are developed further in Andrzej Korbonski, "The Case of Eastern Europe: Images and Realities" (Paper presented at a conference on "Images and Realities in International Relations," The Hebrew University of Jerusalem, June 1978).

8. For an extensive discussion of the cost-benefit calculus of the Soviet-East European economic relations, see Paul Marer, "Is Eastern Europe a Soviet Asset or Burden? The Economic Dimension" (Paper presented at the annual meeting of the American Political Science Association, Washington, D.C., August 1979).

9. For an interesting discussion, see Dale R. Herspring and Ivan Volgyes, "Political Reliability in the Eastern European Warsaw Pact Armies," Armed Forces and Society 6, no. 2 (Winter 1980): 270-96; and A. Ross Johnson, "Has Eastern Europe Become a Liability to the Soviet Union? II. The Military Aspect," in Gati, The International Politics of Eastern Europe, op. cit., pp. 37-58. For a different approach to this question, see Lawrence T. Caldwell, "Eastern Europe: Soviet Asset or Burden? The Military Dimension" (Paper presented at the annual meeting of the American Political Science Association, Washington, D.C., August 1979).

10. For an excellent analysis of this conflict, see J. F. Brown, "Soviet Relations with Eastern Europe" (Paper presented at the Annual Meeting of the American Political Science Association, Washington, D.C., August 1979).

11. Thus, Ronald Linden notes, after examining East European international interactions during the 1965-69 period, "Especially interesting is the negative deviant position of Bulgaria. While the overall magnitude of this deviance is not great, general views of Bulgaria's position in the bloc would lead one to expect a positive, even greatly positive, deviance if any. Instead it is Czechoslovakia and Hungary that back up East Germany as the alliance's most loyal member in terms of international interactions." Ronald H. Linden, Bear and Foxes (Boulder, Colo.: East European Quarterly, 1979), p. 49. See also William C. Potter, "External Demands and East Europe's Westpolitik" (Paper presented at the meeting of the Western Slavic Association, Reno, Nevada, February 1978), pp. 31-35. On the other hand, between 1960 and 1965 Bulgaria received almost as much Soviet aid as the other five East European countries combined, suggesting that economic aid has been a reward for political loyalty. In 1970, Bulgaria, received credits totaling $575 million, which might be interpreted in a similar light. Paul Marer, "The Economies of Eastern Europe and Soviet Foreign Policy," mimeographed, fn. 8.

12. Linden, op. cit., pp. 45-46, 171-72.

13. Czechoslovakia had no navy, but in the late 1960s her army and air force strength was closely behind that of Poland, the strongest military power in the Warsaw Pact, outside of the Soviet Union.

Thomas W. Wolfe, Soviet Power and Europe 1945-1970 (Baltimore, Md.: Johns Hopkins University Press, 1970), p. 484.

14. It has been said that "the East Germans are the most likely to be actively engaged in combat operations against the West." Herspring and Volgyes, op. cit., p. 289.

15. For an interesting, up-to-date account, see Melvin Croan, "East Germany and Africa" (Paper presented at a conference on "The Communist States and Africa," Naval Postgraduate School, Monterey, California, July 1979).

16. Soviet-Hungarian trade was practically balanced in the period 1969-76, and it only turned against Hungary in 1977. Martin J. Kohn, "Soviet-Eastern European Economic Relations, 1975-78," in Soviet Economy in a Time of Change, A Compendium of Papers Submitted to the Joint Economic Committee, 96th Congress, 1st Session, vol. 1 (Washington, D.C.: Government Printing Office, 1979), p. 261.

17. This was clearly apparent during Brezhnev's June 1979 visit to Hungary, which was viewed as much more successful than similar encounters in the past. Radio Free Europe Research, Situation Report, Hungary/12, June 15, 1979.

18. Kohn, op. cit., p. 261. Poland currently supplies 90 percent of Soviet freight car imports, 44 percent of diesel engines imports, and 30 percent of electrical engineering imports, while the Soviet Union supplies Poland with 100 percent of its natural gas imports, 70 percent of all oil imports, 65 percent of iron ore, and 60 percent of cotton. Radio Free Europe Research, Situation Report Poland/11, May 25, 1979.

19. For a concise account, see CIA, National Foreign Assessment Center, "The Scope of Poland's Economic Dilemma," Research Paper ER78-10340U, July 1978.

20. For details, see John M. Montias, "Background and Origins of the Romanian Dispute with Comecon," Soviet Studies 16, no. 2 (October 1964): 125-52; and Economic Development in Communist Romania (Cambridge, Mass.: MIT Press, 1967), pp. 187-205.

21. At the meeting, attended by all top Warsaw Pact leaders, Romania sharply rejected a Soviet demand to increase defense spending supposedly to counter the increase in the NATO defense budget. Charles Andras, "A Summit with Consequences," Radio Free Europe Research, RAD Background Report/271 (Eastern Europe), December 14, 1978.

22. Alex Alexiev, "Romania and the Warsaw Pact: The Defense Policy of a Reluctant Ally," RAND Paper P-6270, January 1979, passim.

23. For a recent and interesting account, see Trond Gilberg, "Romania, Yugoslavia, and Africa: 'Nonalignment and Progressivism'" (Paper presented at a conference on "The Communist States

in Africa," Naval Postgraduate School, Monterey, California, July 1979).

24. Sylva Sinanian, Istvan Deak, and Peter C. Ludz, eds., Eastern Europe in the 1970s (New York: Praeger, 1972), pp. 181-82.

25. For some indicators of Romania's standing in the Warsaw alliance, see Jan F. Triska and Paul M. Johnson, "Political Development and Political Change," in Beck and Mesa-Lago, op. cit., pp. 251-55.

26. Zvi Gitelman, "The Impact on the Soviet Union of the East European Experience in Modernization," in Gati, The Politics of Modernization in Eastern Europe, op. cit., pp. 270-271.

27. Charles Gati, "The Forgotten Region," Foreign Policy, no. 19 (Summer 1975): 135-45.

28. Andrzej Korbonski, "Soviet Interests in Eastern Europe," in U.S. Senate, Committee on Foreign Relations, Perceptions: Relations Between the United States and the Soviet Union (Washington, D.C.: Government Printing Office, 1979), pp. 159-60.

29. Jiri Valenta, Soviet Intervention in Czechoslovakia 1968 (Baltimore, Md.: Johns Hopkins University Press, 1979), pp. 21-25. See also, Grey Hodnett and Peter J. Potichnyj, The Ukraine and the Czechoslovak Crisis (Canberra: Australian National University, 1970), passim.

30. It has also been suggested that "rather than run the risks of a difficult military campaign, a political crisis in the USSR, and the destruction of the domestic political base for an East European Communist regime, Moscow will refrain from military intervention against an East European Communist leader who promises to lead his nation to war in defense of its sovereignty." Christopher D. Jones, "Soviet Hegemony in Eastern Europe: The Dynamics of Political Autonomy and Military Intervention," World Politics 29, no. 2 (January 1977): 239.

31. For a recent account, see Melvin Croan, "New Country, Old Nationality," Foreign Policy, no. 37 (Winter 1979-80): 148-50; and "Regime, Society and Nation: The GDR after Thirty Years," East Central Europe 6, pt. 2 (1979): 148-50.

32. For an opposing view, see R. Judson Mitchell, "A New Brezhnev Doctrine," World Politics 30, no. 3 (April 1978): 375-77, who postulates the emergence of a new, much closer, "organic" relationship between the Soviet Union and its junior allies in East Europe.

33. Sarah M. Terry and Andrzej Korbonski, "The Impact of External Economic Disturbances on the Internal Politics of Eastern Europe: The Polish and Hungarian Cases," Kennan Institute for Advanced Russian Studies Occasional Paper, no. 42, September 1978, p. 33.

10

RESEARCH ON EAST EUROPEAN FOREIGN POLICY: OTHER NEEDS, OTHER AREAS, NEW DIRECTIONS

Roger E. Kanet

For more than a third of a century the Soviet Union has played a dominant role in East Europe. Initially the Soviet position in the area was maintained almost exclusively through the use of superior military power and coercion, as they established communist regimes modeled on the Stalinist system that had been created in the Soviet Union itself. Since Stalin's death, substantial changes in the Soviet-East European relationship have occurred, although the basic Soviet goal of control has remained constant. The mechanisms of control have become more sophisticated and include efforts to integrate the region economically, politically, and militarily more fully into the Soviet system—even though the ultimate resort to military coercion still looms as a distinct possibility. On the other hand, relations of the East European states with other portions of the world have grown significantly during the past 20 years, and differentiation among the foreign policies of the East European states has become evident. Unfortunately, however, Western scholarship has not always kept pace with developments either within East Europe itself or in the relations of the states of the region with the outside world. East Europe has remained, to a very substantial degree, a "forgotten region," not only for U.S. diplomacy, as Charles Gati has noted,[1] but also for much of U.S. scholarship.

The substantive studies included in this volume provide ample evidence of the degree to which the analysis of communist politics

Portions of the present essay are based on a paper entitled "Soviet-East European Integration: The State of Western Scholarship," presented at the annual meeting of the American Political Science Association, New York, August 30–September 3, 1978.

has evolved during the last decade. Ten years ago a comparable collection of articles would most probably have included discussion of the weaknesses of the "traditional" descriptive approach to the study of communist politics and the benefits to be gained by the application of contemporary social scientific concepts and models to communist studies.[2] Rather than engaging in the type of advocacy that characterized virtually all theoretically or quantitatively based analyses in the past, the present authors assume the appropriateness of their various approaches and proceed with the analysis of the questions at hand. Concepts such as "linkage," "perception," "dependency," and others taken from the social sciences are now familiar to the student of East Europe.

Unfortunately, however, the development of the social scientific approach to the study of Communist systems has meant neither that Communist studies have been completely integrated into the social sciences nor that our understanding of politics, including foreign policy, in East Europe is complete or even firmly based. For the most part students of general international politics continue to ignore the research of area specialists, even though the latter increasingly pose questions similar to those that concern the generalists, often employ the same concepts and models, and attempt explicitly to fit their analyses into categories that extend beyond East Europe. Among the communist states, those of East Europe continue to be ignored the most by students of general international relations. The end result has been a partial integration of communist studies into the field of general social science and international politics, that is, an infusion of systematic social science methods into the corpus of communist studies without, however, a corollary influence of the results of those studies on the development of the social sciences. On the other hand, the increasing focus on "behavioral" methods in the analysis of the domestic and foreign policy of the East European states has not led necessarily to a more complete understanding of the foreign policies of the East European states. Even though recent research has succeeded in demonstrating that politics, including foreign policy, in East Europe is not sui generis, it has tended to ignore the historical roots of contemporary East Europe.[3] On occasion one gets the impression that some of the recent quantitatively based analyses of Eastern European politics were motivated far more by the availability of certain types of data rather than by the desire to explain significant political processes. The primary purpose of the present essay will be to provide a brief assessment of the state of U.S. scholarship on East European foreign policy—excluding that of Yugoslavia—and to point out areas and directions for future research.[4]

A large percentage of recent research on the foreign policies of the East European states either has focused primarily on the issue of deviation from Soviet policy or has provided only very general overviews of policy. Anyone who has attempted to find up-to-date analyses of the foreign policies of individual East European countries is well aware of the fact that such studies are not being published. For example, not a single general volume dealing with postwar Polish foreign policy is listed in the excellent, recently published, bibliography on International Relations of Eastern Europe: A Guide to Information Sources, edited by Robin A. Remington.[5] The numerous articles on Polish foreign policy tend to cover and update the same material. The situation has been similar for Romania. Although numerous articles have appeared on Romania's autonomy with respect to the Soviet Union, not until recently have more general monographic treatments of Romanian foreign policy been published.[6] Overall there is a serious dearth of general monographic studies, whether descriptive or analytic, on the foreign policies of the individual East European states.[7] The substantial number of descriptive articles that deal with various elements of the foreign policies of the individual communist states does not really fill this void, nor do those that treat aspects of East European international relations.[8] There exists, therefore, a serious need for a series of comprehensive studies of the foreign policies of the individual East European countries. Not only are such studies required in their own right, if we are to understand more fully the foreign policy orientations of the communist states, but they are also important in order to provide a basis on which general comparative studies can build.

A second, closely related area in which additional research is needed concerns the relations of East Europe with specific groups of states and policy in specific issue areas. With the exception of the numerous studies of relations among the communist states themselves and of policy—in particular commercial policy—toward the West, there is an almost complete absence of solid research in these areas. For example, in spite of the significant and visible growth of relations between the East European countries and the developing world, virtually no attention has been devoted to this subject.[9] In addition, little interest has been expressed in studying the policies of the East European countries in the United Nations or other international organizations—except as a means of measuring cohesion or deviance in "intrabloc" relations.

In sum, there has been little interest among those who have entered the field of East European studies during the past decade or so, in building on the earlier tradition of historically based political analysis. This has resulted in a dearth of comprehensive descriptive-analytic work on virtually all aspects of the foreign relations of the East European states with the exception of intrabloc relations and East-West commercial ties. For the most part, the focus in the studies that have appeared is on the Soviet Union and the relative position of East European states relative to their giant neighbor to the east.

An area of research in which visible strides have been made during the decade of the 1970s has been the comparison of the foreign policy orientations of the East European states. Ronald Linden's Bear and Foxes: The International Relations of the East European States, 1965-1969 is by far the most ambitious of these attempts to employ quantitative indicators—in this case, events data and attitudinal data derived from content analysis—in order to measure the degree of cohesion and divergence in the foreign policies of the European communist states.[10] What should be evident by now, both from Linden's research and that of a number of other scholars, is that the foreign policies of the East European states are not identical; levels of development, geographical location, domestic political situations, and various other factors have resulted in divergence in the foreign policies of these states, and one cannot treat these states merely as appendages of the Soviet Union and willing tools of Soviet foreign policy interests. What is not as clear, however, is the combination of factors that goes into the making of foreign policy in East Europe. What precisely are the domestic social, cultural, political, and economic considerations that we must take into account in our attempt both to understand the policy of, for example, Poland or Czechoslovakia, and to evaluate the differences among the foreign policies of the members of the Warsaw Treaty Organization? Unfortunately, far too little research has been conducted to date on the relationship between domestic and foreign policy in the European communist states. For the most part this type of research will have to be conducted, initially at least, on an individual country basis. Only then will it be possible to discuss in more broadly comparative terms the relative influence of various factors on the foreign policies of individual countries.

Another aspect of the foreign relations of the European Communist states that has received serious consideration has been the integration process. By far the greatest scholarly effort has been expended on describing and analyzing the economic relationships among the members of the Council for Mutual Economic Assistance (CMEA) and on assessing the prospects for successful integration of their economies. Much of the literature is primarily descriptive in nature and attempts to delineate the various agreements on planning coordination and production specialization and cooperation that have been reached within the context of the CMEA.[11] In addition, efforts have been made to determine the degree to which the agreements that have been reached have actually been implemented, the impact they are having on the economies of the individual countries, and the overall problems that continue to retard effective integration.[12]

In spite of the amount of published research on economic relations among the communist states of Europe and, more specifically, the integration process within the CMEA, important questions remain unanswered. Most important, from my point of view, are those concerning the actual success of the integration process and the implications of the various cooperation and specialization agreements for both the domestic and foreign economic activity of the smaller East European members of the CMEA and the long-term political relationships within the region.

When we turn to the question of forms of integration other than economic we find that the literature is far less complete and enlightening. In fact, few Western authors have ventured into this field.[13] To what extent, for example, does the economic integration and cooperation presently underway spill over into other areas in the relations among the CMEA member countries? Needless to say, the data problems facing the scholar who attempts to deal with questions of this sort are greater than those related to trade and other economic relationships. Although it is possible to obtain some information about political consultation and cooperation in the preparation of ideological materials and textbooks, for example, it is much more difficult to assess the impact of such "cooperative" behavior on the political systems of the individual countries. Nonetheless, the fact that Soviet plans call for the eventual total integration of the CMEA countries[14] makes it important for us to understand both the efforts toward political, military, and cultural integration and the overall prospects for the long-term success of these activities.

Some of the articles included in the present collection speak to the problems or gaps to which I have referred, while others continue the development of cohesion-conformity analysis. First of all, several of the articles add significant factual information to our knowledge of specific aspects of the foreign policies of East Europe. For example, Sarah Terry's examination of the impact of growing economic interdependence with the West on relations among CMEA members provides us with additional information on recent Polish foreign policy. However, she organizes her discussion in such a way as to make her analysis relevant to a broader set of issues than those related exclusively to Poland. Andrzej Korbonski's systematic assessment of the relative political asset for the Soviet Union represented by East Europe builds on several earlier attempts to treat this issue. William C. Potter, Robert Weiner, and Donna Bahry and Cal Clark are all interested in the cohesiveness of the foreign policies of various East European countries. Potter focuses on the question of East European acquiescence to Soviet demands on the issue of policy toward West Germany. He makes especially clear that domestic factors as well as external demands influenced the evolution of foreign policy in East Europe. Weiner, on the other hand, examines the positions taken by the four communist Balkan states in their voting in the United Nations in order to identify those issue areas on which the four countries have differed. Finally, Bahry and Clark examine the relationship between economic dependence and political conformity in Soviet-East European relations and conclude that political conformity is not primarily a function of economic dependence.

The three remaining substantive articles in the present volume are concerned primarily with the application of concepts from general international politics theory to the study of East Europe. Cal Clark's examination of Balkan foreign policies employs James Rosenau's linkage framework. Clark concludes, along with Potter, that variation in the foreign policies of the East European states is, in part, a function of domestic political factors. William Zimmerman is concerned with the possible applicability of dependency theory and concludes, on the basis of his initial tests, that Soviet-East European relations "fit" the four central concepts of dependency theory as well as, if not more closely than, U.S.-Latin American relations—this, in spite of dependency theorists' virtually exclusive focus on capitalism as a causal factor in economic imperialism. Finally, Richard Hermann provides a detailed mapping of politically relevant Weltanschauungen in contemporary Poland within the context of a broader concern with the relevance of perceptual analysis in the study of foreign policy.

In conclusion, I would like to emphasize the fact that, although the study of East European foreign policy is still an "underdeveloped area" in political science, a number of significant books and articles—in addition to those already mentioned—have appeared during the course of the last decade that have made a substantial contribution to our better understanding of the place of East Europe in world affairs and of the foreign policies of the East European states. These include the two volumes edited by Charles Gati on modernization in East Europe and East European foreign policy,[15] as well as the contributions included in Political Development in Eastern Europe, edited by Jan F. Triska and Paul M. Cocks,[16] and Comparative Socialist Systems: Essays on Politics and Economics, edited by Carmelo Mesa-Lago and Carl Beck.[17] These books, plus a number of articles in scholarly journals and in other edited volumes, have helped to bring the study of East European foreign policy into the mainstream of political science. However, much remains to be accomplished—not the least being the development of solid, historically based analyses of the foreign policies of the East European states.

NOTES

1. Charles Gati, "The Forgotten Region," Foreign Policy no. 19 (1975): 135-45.

2. For example, the 1971 meetings of the Northeastern Slavic Conference, held in Montreal, included a panel discussion on "The Comparative Approach to the Study of Communist Foreign Policy," in which the major argument focused on the need for the development of a comparative approach in the study of Communist foreign policy. A revised and expanded version of the discussion was published as "Symposium on the Comparative Study of Communist Foreign Policies," Studies in Comparative Communism 8 (1975): 5-65.

3. For a criticism of this aspect of recent communist studies, see Hannes Adomeit and Robert Boardman, "The Comparative Study of Communist Foreign Policy," in Foreign Policy Making in Communist Countries: A Comparative Approach, ed. Hannes Adomeit and Robert Boardman (New York: Praeger, 1979), pp. 2-3.

4. For an earlier assessment of studies of integration and related processes in East Europe, see Roger E. Kanet, "Integration Theory and the Study of Eastern Europe," International Studies Quarterly 18 (1974): 368-92. For a less critical interpretation, see Cal Clark, "The Study of East European Integration: A 'Political' Perspective," East Central Europe 2, no. 2 (1975): 132-45.

5. (Detroit: Gale Research Company, 1978). The only exceptions are several books dealing with specific aspects of Polish foreign policy, for example, relations with Germany.

6. See, for example, Ion Ratiu, Contemporary Romania: Her Place in World Affairs (Richmond, England: Foreign Affairs, 1975); and Aurel Braun, Romanian Foreign Policy Since 1965: The Political and Military Limits of Autonomy (New York: Praeger, 1978). Both of these books, however, emphasize the Romanian relationship with the Soviet Union, as does Jacques Lévesque's Le Conflit sino-soviétique et l'Europe de l'Est: Ses incidences sur les conflits soviéto-polonais et soviéto-roumain (Montréal: Les Presses de l'Université du Montréal, 1970).

7. This comment does not apply fully to the status of research on Yugoslav foreign policy. Books such as Alvin Z. Rubinstein's Yugoslavia and the Nonaligned World (Princeton, N.J.:

Princeton University Press, 1970); and Lars Nord, Nonalignment and Socialism: Yugoslav Foreign Policy in Theory and Practice (Stockholm: Rabén and Sjögren, 1975), clearly fit into the category of broad treatments of foreign policy.

8. The collections of primarily descriptive treatments of the foreign policies of the Communist states edited over the past 15 years by Adam Bromke and his associates meet only a part of the need for more detailed treatment of East European foreign policies. See Adam Bromke, ed., The Communist States at the Crossroads: Between Moscow and Peking, with an introduction by Phillip E. Mosely (New York: Frederick A. Praeger, 1965); Adam Bromke and Phillip E. Uren, eds., The Communist States and the West (New York: Frederick A. Praeger, 1967); Adam Bromke and Teresa Rakowska-Harmstone, eds., The Communist States in Disarray, 1965-1971 (Minneapolis: University of Minnesota Press, 1972); and Adam Bromke and Derry Novak, eds., The Communist States in the Era of Détente, 1971-1977 (Oakville, Ont.: Mosaic Press, 1979).

9. Robin Remington lists only six items in her bibliography: three (including two books) deal with Yugoslav nonalignment policy and relations with developing countries; two articles treat Romanian-Third World relations only peripherally; and one, now ten years old, concerns East European economic resistance. See Robin Remington, The International Relations of Eastern Europe: A Guide to Information Sources (Detroit: Gale Research Co., 1978), p. 257. The recent series of articles published by Radio Free Europe on the relations of East European states with the countries of sub-Saharan Africa does fill a part of this void. See Radio Free Europe Research, RAD Background Report, nos. 50, 75, 77, 92, 118, and 142 (1979). There exists, in addition, a growing literature in West Germany on East European relations with developing countries. See, for example, Jürgen Nötzold, "Die RGW-Staaten und der Nord-Süd Dialog," Aussenpolitik, XXX, no. 1 (1979), pp. 192-209 and H. Bischof, "Militärbeziehungen zwischen den kommunistischen Staaten und der Dritten Welt," Monatsberichte des Forschungsinstituts der Friedrich-Ebert-Stiftung (June 1977), pp. 403-30.

10. (Boulder, Colo.: East European Quarterly, 1979). Other significant recent attempts to compare the foreign policies of the European Communist states include Jeffrey Simon's Comparative Communist Foreign Policy, 1965-1976 (Santa Monica, Calif.: RAND, 1977), which employs foreign trade and policy statements to map foreign policy orientations; and Cal Clark and Robert L. Farlow, Comparative Patterns of Foreign Policy and Trade: The Communist Balkans in International Politics (Bloomington: International Development Research Center, Indiana University, 1976), which relies primarily on trade data; and several of the articles in Adomeit and Boardman, eds., op. cit.

11. See, for example, Richard Szawlowski, The System of the International Organizations of the Communist Countries (Leyden: A. W. Sijthoff, 1976), and the monumental documentary collection edited by William E. Butler with the title A Source Book on Socialist International Organizations (Alphen aan den Rijn: Sijthoff and Noordhoff, 1978). Both of these volumes emphasize the legal-organizational structure within which CMEA is operating. For descriptive studies of recent developments within the CMEA, see NATO, Directorate of Economic Affairs, COMECON: Progress and Prospects (Brussels: NATO, Directorate of Economic Affairs, [1977]).

12. See, for example, the analyses of the CMEA written by Josef M. van Brabant. These writings include Bilateralism and Structural Bilateralism in Intra-CMEA Trade (Rotterdam: Rotterdam University Press, 1973); Essays on Planning, Trade and Integration in Eastern Europe (Rotterdam: Rotterdam University Press, 1974); and East European Cooperation: The Role of Money and Finance (New York: Praeger, 1977).

13. Important exceptions to this statement include the work of Andrzej Korbonski, especially his "Detente, East-West Trade, and the Future of Economic Integration in Eastern Europe," World Politics 28 (1976): 568-89; Teresa Rakowska-Harmstone, "'Socialist Internationalism' and Eastern Europe—A New Stage," Survey 22, no. 1 (1976): 38-54, and no. 2 (1976): 81-86; and Christopher Jones, "Soviet Hegemony in Eastern Europe: The Dynamics of Political Autonomy and Military Intervention," World Politics 29 (1977): 216-41.

14. See Rakowska-Harmstone, op. cit.

15. The Politics of Modernization in Eastern Europe: Testing the Soviet Model (New York: Praeger, 1974), and The International Politics of Eastern Europe (New York: Praeger, 1976). In addition, there exists a substantial and growing literature in western Europe—especially in West Germany—that provides detailed, descriptive analyses of many aspects of the foreign political and economic relations of the East European states. See, for example, Hans-Adolf Jacobsen, Gert Leptin, Ulrich Scheaner, and Eberhard Schulz, eds., Drei Jahrzehnte Aussenpolitik der DDR (Munich-Vienna: R. Oldenbourg Verlag, 1979).

16. (New York: Praeger, 1977).

17. (Pittsburgh: Center for International Studies, University of Pittsburgh, 1975).

ABOUT THE EDITOR AND CONTRIBUTORS

DONNA BAHRY is Assistant Professor of Political Science at New York University. She has written articles on measurement problems in the analysis of communist policy and on fiscal and regional policies in the Soviet Union.

CAL CLARK received his Ph.D. from the University of Illinois and is presently a Lecturer at New Mexico State University. He is coauthor of Comparative Patterns of Foreign Policy and Trade: The Communist Balkans in International Politics, and has published in such professional journals as American Political Science Review, Comparative Political Studies, East Central Europe, International Studies Quarterly, Journal of Conflict Resolution, Political Methodology, Southeastern Europe, and Western Political Quarterly.

RICHARD K. HERRMANN is a Research Associate at the University Center for International Studies and Visiting Instructor in the Department of Political Science at the University of Pittsburgh. He is completing his dissertation entitled "Competitive Soviet World Views and Soviet Foreign Policy 1967-1979: Soviet Perceptions of the Development of Sino-American Rapprochement."

ROGER E. KANET is Professor of Political Science and a member of the Russian and East European Center of the University of Illinois at Urbana-Champaign. His most recent publications include Politics and Policy in Gierek's Poland (coedited with Maurice D. Simon), and articles on the foreign political and economic relations of the Soviet Union and Poland.

ANDRZEJ KORBONSKI is Professor of Political Science at the University of California, Los Angeles. He is the author of The Politics of Socialist Agriculture in Poland, 1945-1960, and has written on various aspects of East European politics and economics.

RONALD H. LINDEN is Assistant Professor in the Department of Political Science of the University of Pittsburgh. He is the author of Bear and Foxes: The International Relations of the East European States, 1965-1969, and has been Associate Editor and Editor of Issues Before the General Assembly of the United Nations.

WILLIAM POTTER is Assistant Director, Center for International and Strategic Affairs, University of California, Los Angeles. He has contributed to The Journal of Conflict Resolution, Western Political Quarterly, Problems of Communism, and Papers of the Peace Science Society (International). He is the editor of Verification and SALT, coauthor of SALT and Beyond: A Handbook on Strategic Weapons and Means for Their Control, and author of a forthcoming book on Nuclear Power and Nonproliferation: An Interdisciplinary Perspective.

SARAH MEIKLEJOHN TERRY is Assistant Professor of Political Science at Tufts University, and an Associate of the Russian Research Center of Harvard University. She is currently completing a book on the origin of the Oder-Neisse boundary and is editing a volume on Soviet policy in Eastern Europe.

ROBERT WEINER teaches at Boston State College and has published articles in Orbis and East European Quarterly. He is currently working on a book dealing with Romanian foreign policy at the United Nations.

WILLIAM ZIMMERMAN is Professor of Political Science at the University of Michigan. His major publications relate to Soviet foreign policy and Yugoslavia. The work reprinted herein is part of a continuing interest in the political economy of socialism.